WISDOM,

WIT AND WHIMS

OF

Distinguished Ancient Philosophers;

EMBRACING

THE MOST IMPORTANT AND INTERESTING INCIDENTS OF THEIR HISTORY, THEIR PERSONAL MANNERS AND HABITS, AND ANECDOTES OF THEIR INTERCOURSE AMONG THE HIGH AND THE LOW, WITH THEIR MOST REMARKABLE APOTHEGMS, PROVERBS, AND PITHY REPLIES TO DIFFICULT AND CURIOUS QUESTIONS, ALPHABETICALLY ARRANGED.

BY JOSEPH BANVARD, A.M.,

AUTHOR OF "PLYMOUTH AND THE PILGRIMS," "NOVELTIES OF THE NEW WORLD," "ROMANCE OF AMERICAN HISTORY," ETC., ETC.

NEW YORK:
SHELDON, LAMPORT & BLAKEMAN,
115 NASSAU STREET.
1855.

STEREOTYPED BY
THOMAS B. SMITH
216 William St., N. Y.

PRINTED BY
E. O. JENKINS,
114 Nassau St

WISDOM, WIT, AND WHIMS

OF

DISTINGUISHED ANCIENT PHILOSOPHERS.

Preface.

In preparing the present volume, the compiler availed himself of the works of various authors, the principal of which were, "The History of Philosophy from the Earliest Periods, drawn up from Brucker's Historia Critica Philosophiæ, by William Enfield, LL.D;" "The Lives and Opinions of Eminent Philosophers, by Diogenes Laertius, translated by C. D. Yonge, B. A.;" and "Stanley's History of Philosophy and Lives of the Philosophers," neither of which has ever been published in this country.

No attempt is made to develop the various systems of Philosophy which at different ages have prevailed, but simply to present the most interesting and important events in the history of the philosophers themselves. The work contains a great amount of curious and instructive information, which, hitherto, has not been accessible to the general reader. The most of those whose memoirs are here given were authors, and many of them produced numerous works. There were also many philosophers of the same names; but in the following pages, reference has been made only to the most distinguished.

Contents.

WISDOM, WIT, AND WHIMS

OF

DISTINGUISHED ANCIENT PHILOSOPHERS.

ÆDESIUS.

ÆDESIUS was of Cappadocia. He pretended to supernatural communications with the Deity, and practised theurgic arts. Among the wonderful events which are said to have happened to him, one is, that in answer to his prayer, his future fate was revealed to him in hexameter verses, which suddenly appeared upon the palm of his left hand.

ÆSCHINES.

ÆSCHINES was the son of Charinus, the sausage-maker, but, as some writers say, of Lysanias; he was a citizen of Athens, of an industrious disposition from his boyhood upwards, on which account he never quitted Socrates.

And this induced Socrates to say, the only one who knows how to pay us proper respect is the son of the sausage-seller. Idomeneus asserts, that it was he who, in the prison, tried to persuade Socrates to make his escape, and not Crito. But that Plato, as he was rather inclined to favor Aristippus, attributed his advice to Crito.

Æschines discovered an early thirst after knowledge, and, though oppressed by poverty, devoted himself to the pursuit of wisdom under the tuition of Socrates. When he first became his disciple, he told Socrates, that the only thing which it was in his power to present him, in acknowledgment of his kindness in instructing him, was himself. Socrates replied, that he accepted, and valued the present, but that he hoped to render it more valuable by culture. He adhered to his master with unalterable fidelity and perseverance, and enjoyed his particular friendship.

Having spent many years in Athens, without being able to rise above the poverty of his birth, he determined, after the example of Plato, and others, to visit the Court of Dionysius, the tyrant of Sicily, who was at that time, either through vanity or jealousy, a general patron of philosophers. Upon his arrival in Syracuse, though slighted, on account of his poverty, by Plato, he was introduced to the prince by Aristippus, and was liberally rewarded for his Socratic dialogues. He remained in Sicily till the expulsion of the tyrant, and then returned to Athens. Here, not daring to become a pubilc rival of Plato or Aristippus, he taught philosophy in private, and received payment for his instructions. Afterwards, in order to provide himself with a more plentiful subsistence, he appeared as a public orator; and Demosthenes, probably because he was jealous of his abilities (for he excelled in eloquence), became his opponent. Besides orations and epistles, Æschines wrote seven Socratic dialogues in the true spirit of his master, on temperance, moderation, humanity, integrity, and other virtues. Of these only three are extant.

Timon said of him, "The speeches of Æschines which do not convince any one." Aristippus suspected the genuineness of some of his dialogues; accordingly, they say that when he was reciting some of them at Megara, he ridiculed him, and said to him, "O you thief, where did you get that?"

The account as given by Stanley is, that being very poor,

Socrates bade him take some of his dialogues and make money with them, which, Aristippus suspecting when he read them at Megara, derided him, saying, "How came you by these plagiary?"

At another time Aristippus falling out with him, was asked what became of his friendship? He answered, "It is asleep, but I will wake it." He used to define the chief good, as a gentle motion tending to sensation.

ALCMÆON.

Alcmæon of Crotona, was a disciple of Pythagoras. He attained a high degree of reputation for his knowledge of nature and of medicine. He is said to have been the first person who attempted the dissection of a dead body.

He taught that the moon is in the form of a boat, and when the bottom of the boat is turned towards the earth, it is invisible. The brain is the chief seat of the soul. Health consists in preserving a due mean between the extremes of heat and cold, dryness and moisture.

AL-FARABI.

One of the most celebrated philosophers of the school of Bagdat was Al-Farabi, or more properly Abu Nasr, a native of Balch Farab, who flourished in the tenth century. He was born of wealthy parents; but, preferring the pursuits of philosophy to those of riches, he devoted himself to study at Bagdat, where he made such proficiency in learning, that he became one of the most eminent philosophers of his age. He studied mathematics and medicine, but chiefly excelled in logic. His learning and abilities were universally admired, and great men and princes were emulous to load him with honors and rewards. But Al-Farabi refused every offer of this kind; and, either through his love of philosophy, or perhaps through a natural gloominess of temper, gave himself up to solitude and an abstemious life. He constantly slept, even during winter, upon straw; his countenance was always sorrowful, and he found no consolation in anything but philosophy. The cast of his mind led him to dread all intercourse with the world as destructive of innocence, and to lament the imperfection and vanity of human life. He employed his time in study, and read the writings of Aristotle with unwearied attention. He wrote sixty distinct treatises on different parts of the Aristotelian philosophy, which were read and admired, not only among the Arabians but also among the Jews, who began about this time to adopt the Aristotelian mode of philosophising. Many of his books were translated from Arabic into Hebrew.

JACOBUS-AL-KENDI.

Jacobus-Al-Kendi of Bassora, was an Arabian philosopher who flourished about the beginning of the ninth century. He yielded implicit submission to Aristotle, and was chiefly employed in interpreting his writings. He also studied mathematics, astronomy and medicine.

Abulfaragius, speaking of Al-Kendi, relates a memorable instance of his moderation towards a malicious adversary. Whilst this philosopher was visiting the schools of Bagdat, which was at this time the chief resort of the learned, his attempts to promote the study of philosophy, and to reconcile the doctrines of Islamism with the principles of reason, gave great offence to one of the interpreters of the Koran, who, doubtless, began to be afraid lest the increase of knowledge should expose the absurdity of the vulgar superstitions. This bigot publicly expressed the most vehement indignation against Al-Kendi, and accused him of impiety and heresy. Al-Kendi, however, instead of restraining the fury of his persecutor by violence, as through his interest with the Caliph he might easily have done, generously adopted the more gentle method of attempting to subdue his malignity by enlightening his understanding. Having detected the design which this Abu Maashar (that was the zealot's name) had formed upon his life, he employed against him no other weapons than the monitions and precepts of philosophy. Well knowing the power of wisdom to meliorate the temper, he found means to engage a preceptor to instruct him, first in mathematics, and afterwards in philosophy. The consequence was, that the man who had, not long before, inveighed with savage ferocity against Al-Kendi, soon became sensible of his folly, and offered himself as pupil to the philosopher whom he had persecuted. Al-Kendi received him with the most meritorious condescension, and his convert became an ornament to his school. In fine, on account of his virtues no less than his learning, Al-Kendi is entitled to an honorable rank among philosophers.

ANACHARSIS.

Anacharsis, the Scythian, was the son of Gnurus, the brother of Caduides, the king of the Scythians. But his mother was a Greek woman, owing to which circumstance he understood both languages. He preferred the pursuits of wisdom to those of ambition. He visited Athens, and was conducted by Toxaris, his countryman, to the house of Solon, the famous Athenian. Legislator. Having arrived there, he requested one of the attendants to inform his master that Anacharsis a Scythian, was at the door, and requested to be received into the house as his guest and friend. To this message Solon's answer was, that "friendships are best formed at home." To which Anacharsis replied, "Then let Solon, who is at home, make me his friend, and receive me into his house." Solon, struck with the smartness of the reply, admitted him as his guest, and finding him, on account of his good sense and probity, worthy of his confidence, allowed him to share his friendship. Anacharsis, on his part, became such an admirer of Solon, that he constantly associated with him till he made himself master of all the knowledge which that wise man possessed. During his residence in Athens, he was honored with the privilege of citizenship, an honor never before conferred upon a barbarian.

After the death of Solon, Anacharsis travelled through a great part of the world in search of wisdom, and at last returned into his own country, probably with the hope of communicating to his countrymen the wisdom he had acquired in Greece. But they were too much attached to their old opinions and customs, to endure with patience the bold attempts which he made to introduce among them the institutions and manners of the Greeks. As he was one day hunting, an arrow, sent, some say, from the hand of his brother, put an end to his life. He lamented with his last breath the jealousy and folly of his countrymen, who would not suffer one wiser than themselves to live among them.

Anacharsis was famous for a manly and nervous kind of language, which was called, from his country, Scythian eloquence. He is said to have invented the anchor and the potter's wheel; but these instruments were known before his time; perhaps he first introduced the use of them among the Scythians. Among many other ingenious sayings, ascribed by Laertius to Anacharsis, are the following: Being asked by what means a man addicted to intemperance might be taught sobriety, he replied, "by placing before his eyes a drunken man. The vine," he said, "bears three kinds of fruit; the first, pleasure; the second, intoxication; the third, remorse." An Athenian of infamous character upbraiding him with being a Scythian, he said: "My country is indeed a disgrace to me, but you are a disgrace to your country." The epistles which bear his name were probably produced at a later period in the school of the Sophists.

He also said that he marvelled how the Greeks, who make laws against those who behave with insolence, honor Athletæ because of their beating one another. When he had been informed that the sides of a ship were four fingers thick, he said, "That those who sailed in one were removed by just that distance from death." He used to say that oil was a provocative of madness, "because Athletæ, when anointed in the oil, attacked one another with mad fury."

"How is it," he used to say, "that those who forbid men to speak falsely, tell lies openly in their vintners' shops?" It was a saying of his, that he "marvelled why the Greeks, at the beginning of a banquet, drink out of small cups, but when they have drunk a good deal, then they turn to large goblets." And this inscription is on his statues—"Restrain your tongues, your appetites, and your passions." He was once asked if the flute was known among the Scythians: and he said, "No, nor the vine either." At another time, the question was put to him, which was the safest kind of vessel? and he said, "That which is brought into dock." He said, too, that the strangest thing that he had seen among the Greeks was, that "They left the smoke* in the mountains, and carried the wood down to their cities." Once, when he was asked, which were the more numerous, the living or the dead? he said, "Under which head do you class those who are at sea."

* Some propose to read *karpon*, fruit, instead of *kapnon*, smoke, here; others explain this saying as meaning that the Greeks avoided houses on the hills in order not to be annoyed with the smoke from the low cottages, and yet did not use coal, but wood, which made more smoke.

When he was asked what there was among men which was both good and bad, he replied, "The tongue." He used to say "That it was better to have one friend of great value, than many friends who were good for nothing." Another saying of his was, that "The forum was an established place for men to cheat one another, and behave covetously." Being once insulted by a young man at a drinking party, he said, "O, young man, if now that you are young you cannot bear wine, when you are old you will have to bear water."

When beholding the tomb of Mausolus he said, "A sumptuous monument is a petrified fortune." It is said that he was never seen to laugh or smile.

ANAXARCHUS.

Anaxarchus was a native of Abdera, a pupil of Diogenes and an intimate acquaintance of Alexander. He had for an enemy Nicocreon, the tyrant of Cyprus. On one occasion, when Alexander at a banquet asked him what he thought of the entertainment, he is said to have replied, "O king, everything is provided very sumptuously; and the only thing wanted is to have the head of some satrap served up;" hinting at Nicocreon. And Nicocreon did not forget his grudge against him for this; but after the death of the king, when Anaxarchus, who was making a voyage, was driven against his will into Cyprus, he took him and put him in a mortar, and commanded him to be pounded to death with iron pestles. And then they say that he, disregarding this punishment, uttered that celebrated saying, "Beat the bag of Anaxarchus, but you will not beat Anaxarchus himself." And then, when Nicocreon commanded that his tongue should be cut out, it is said that he bit it off, and spit it at him. And we have written an epigram upon him in the following terms:—

> Beat more and more; you're beating but a bag;
> Beat, Anaxarchus is in heav'n with Jove.
> Hereafter Proserpine will rack your bones,
> And say, Thus perish, you accursed beater.

Anaxarchus, on account of the evenness of his temper and the tranquillity of his life, was called the Happy. And he was a man to whom it was very easy to reprove men and bring them to temperance. Accordingly, he produced an alteration in Alexander who thought himself a God, for when he saw the blood flowing from some wound that he had received, he pointed to him with his finger, and said, "This is blood, and not:—

> "Such stream as issues from a wounded God;
> Pure emanation, uncorrupted flood,
> Unlike our gross, diseas'd, terrestrial blood."

But Plutarch says that it was Alexander himself who quoted these lines to his friends.

They also tell a story that Anaxarchus once drank to him, and then showed the goblet, and said:—

> Shall any mortal hand dare wound a God?

ANAXAGORAS.

Anaxagoras of Clazomene, born on the first year of the seventeenth Olympiad, was a disciple of Anaximenes. He inherited from his parents a patrimony, which might have secured him independence and distinction at home; but such was his thirst after knowledge, that about the twentieth year of his age, he left his country, without taking proper precautions concerning his estate, and went to reside at Athens. Here he diligently applied himself to the study of eloquence and poetry, and was particularly conversant with the works of Homer, whom he admired as the best preceptor, not only in writing, but in morals. Engaging afterwards in speculations concerning nature, the fame of the Milesian school induced him to leave Athens, that he might attend upon the public instructions of Anaximenes. Under him he became acquainted with his doctrines, and those of his predecessors, concerning natural bodies and the origin of things. So ardently did he engage in these inquiries, that he said concerning himself that he was born to contemplate the heavens. Visiting his native city, he found that, whilst he had been busy in the pursuit of knowledge, his estate had run to waste; upon which he remarked, that to this ruin he owed his prosperity. One of his fellow-citizens complaining that he, who was so well qualified, both by rank and ability, for public offices, had shown so little regard for his country, he replied, "My first care is for *my* country," pointing to heaven. After remaining for some years at Miletus, he returned to Athens, and there taught philosophy in private. Among his pupils were several eminent men, particularly the tragedian Euripides, and the orator and statesman Pericles; to whom some add Socrates and Themistocles.

The high degree of reputation which he had acquired at length excited the jealousy and envy of his contemporaries, and brought upon him a cruel persecution. It is generally agreed that he was thrown into prison, and condemned to death; and that it was with difficulty that Pericles obtained from his judge the milder sentence of fine and banishment; but the nature of the charge alleged against him is variously represented. The most probable account of the matter is, that his offence was, the propagation of new opinions concerning the gods, and particularly, teaching that the sun is an inanimate fiery substance, and consequently not a proper object of worship. There can be no doubt that Anaxagoras, who was indefatigable in his researches into nature, ventured, on many occasions, to contradict and oppose the vulgar opinions and superstitions. It is related that he ridiculed the Athenian priests for predicting an unfortunate event from the unusual appearance of a ram which had but one horn; and that, to convince the people that there was nothing in the affair which was not perfectly natural, he opened the head of the animal, and showed them that it was so constructed as necessarily to prevent the growth of the other horn. Such offensive freedoms as these were probably the cause of his persecution. Silenus, in the first book of his Histories, says, that in the archonship of Lysanias a large stone fell from heaven; and that in reference to this event Anaxagoras said, that the whole heaven was composed of stones, and that by its rapid revolutions they were all held together; and when those revolutions get slower, they fall down.

When one of his friends expressed regret on account of his banishment from Athens, he said, "It is not I who have lost the Athenians, but the Athenians who have lost me." Being asked just before his death, whether he wished to be carried for interment to Clazomene, his native city, he said, "It is unnecessary; the way to the regions below is everywhere alike open." In reply to a message sent him, at that time, by the senate of Lampsacus, requesting him to inform them in what manner they might most acceptably express their respect for his memory after his decease, he said, "By ordaining that the day of my death be annually kept as a holiday in all the schools of Lampsacus." His request was complied with, and the custom remained for many centuries. He died about the age of seventy-two years. The inhabitants of Lampsacus expressed their high opinion of his wisdom by erecting him a tomb. It is also said that two altars were raised in honor of his memory, one dedicated to Truth, the other to Mind, an appellation which was given him on account of the doctrine which he taught concerning the origin and formation of nature.

Two predictions are ascribed to him which were remarkably fulfilled; one was, that on a certain day a stone would fall from the sun, and on the appointed day a stone did fall from the sun in a part of Thrace, near the river Ægos. Plutarch states that in his time this stone was not only shown but greatly reverenced by the Peloponnesians.

At another time he signified, when the weather was fair, that there would be a heavy rain and storm, by going to the Olympic games in a shaggy skin, or leathern dress, prepared for such a change; and as it did rain according to his prediction, the people honored him as though he possessed supernatural knowledge.

ANAXILAUS.

Anaxilaus of Larissa, who lived in the time of Augustus, professed himself a follower of Pythagoras, but chiefly that he might obtain the greater credit to the pretensions which he made to an intimate acquaintance with the mysteries of nature. Pliny relates several curious arts, by which he raised the wonder and terror of the ignorant multitude, among which was that of giving a livid and ghastly hue to the countenance by means of sulphureous flame. It is probable that he practised his deceptions under the notion of supernatural operations; for he was banished from Italy, by the order of Augustus, for the crime of magic.

ANAXIMANDER.

Anaximander, the son of Praxiadas, was a citizen of Miletus. He first taught philosophy in a public school, and is therefore often spoken of as the founder of the Ionic sect. He was born in the third year of the forty-second Olympiad. Ciecero calls him the friend and companion of Thales; whence it is probable that he was a native of Miletus. That he was employed in instructing youth, may be inferred from an anecdote related concerning him; that, being laughed at for singing (that is, probably, reciting his verses) ill, he said, "We must endeavor to sing better, for the sake of the boys." Anaximander was the first who laid aside the defective method of oral tradition, and committed the principles of natural science to writing. It is related of him, that he predicted an earthquake; but, that he should have been able in the infancy of knowledge to do what is, at this day, beyond the reach of philosophy, is incredible. He lived sixty-four years.

There can be little doubt that mathematics and astronomy were indebted to Anaximander. He framed a connected series of geometrical truths, and wrote a summary of his doctrine. He was the first who undertook to delineate the surface of the earth, and mark the divisions of land and water upon an artificial globe. The invention of the sun-dial is ascribed to him. He also was the first discoverer of the gnomon; and he placed some in Lacedæmon, on the sun-dials there, as Pharorinus says in his Universal History, and they showed the solstices and the equinoxes; he also made clocks. He was the first person, too, who drew a map of the earth and sea, and he also made a globe; and he published a concise statement of whatever opinions he embraced or entertained; and this treatise was met with by Apollodorus, the Athenian.

And Apollodorus, in his Chronicles, states, that in the second year of the fifty-eighth Olympiad, he was sixty four years old. And soon after he died, having flourished much about the same time as Polycrates, the tyrant, of Samos.

ANTISTHENES.

Antisthenes was born at Athens about the nineteenth Olympiad. His father was an Athenian, his mother a Thracian, or, according to Plutarch, a Phrygian.

Being on one occasion reproached because his mother was a Phrygian, he replied, "Cybele, the mother of the gods, was a Phrygian."

He became the founder of a school, the sole object of which was to support a rigid moral discipline.

In his youth he was engaged in military exploits, and acquired fame by the valor which he displayed in the battle of Tanagra. His first studies were under the direction of the sophist Gorgias, who instructed him in the art of rhetoric. Soon growing dissatisfied with the futile labors of this school, he sought for more substantial wisdom from Socrates. Captivated by the doctrine and the manner of his new master, he prevailed upon many young men, who had been his fellow-students under Gorgias, to accompany him. So great was his ardor for moral wisdom, that though he lived at Piræus, which was at the distance of forty *stadia* from the city, he came daily to Athens to attend upon Socrates. This wise man, at the same time that he made morality the only subject of his instructions, powerfully recommended virtuous manners to his disciples by his own example. Despising the pursuits of avarice, vanity, and ambition, he sought the reward of virtue in virtue itself, and declined no labor or suffering which virtue required. This noble consistency of mind was the part of the character of Socrates which Antisthenes chiefly admired; and he resolved to make it the object of his diligent imitation. Whilst he was a disciple of Socrates, he discovered his propensity towards severity of manners by the meanness of his dress. He frequently appeared in a thread-bare and ragged coat. Socratos, who had great penetration in discovering the characters of men, remarking that Antisthenes took pains to expose rather than conceal the tattered state of his dress, said to him, "Why so ostentatious? Through your rags I see your vanity."

After the death of Socrates, whilst all good men were lamenting his fate, and were indignant against his persecutors, Antisthenes, by a seasonable jest, hastened the deserved punishment of Melitus and Anytas. Meeting with certain young men from Pontus, who came to Athens with a design of attending upon Socrates, whose fame had reached their country, he publicly introduced them to Anytas, assuring them that he far exceeded Socrates in wisdom. This sarcastic encomium inflamed the resentment of the Athenians who happened to be present against the author of the disgrace which had been brought upon their city by their putting to death so excellent a man. The consequence was, that Anytas was soon banished, and Melitus sentenced to death.

Whilst Plato and other disciples of Socrates were, after his death forming schools in Athens, Antisthenes chose for his school a public place of exercise without the walls of the city, called the Cynosargum, or the Temple of the White Dog; whence some writers derive the name of the sect of which he was the founder. Others suppose that his followers were called Cynics from the snarling humor of their master. Here he inculcated, both by precept and example, a rigorous discipline. In order to accommodate his own manners to his doctrine, he wore no other garment than a coarse cloak, suffered his beard to grow, and carried a wallet and staff like a wandering beggar. Renouncing all the splendid luxuries of life, he contented himself with the most simple diet, and refrained from every kind of effeminate indulgence. In his discourses he censured the manners of the age with a degree of harshness which produced him the surname of the Dog. He expressed the utmost contempt for pleasure, accounting it the greatest evil, and saying that he would rather be mad than addicted to a voluptuous manner of living. Towards the close of his life the gloomy cast of his mind and the moroseness of his temper increased to such a degree, as to render him troublesome to his friends, and an object of ridicule to his enemies. In his last illness he was fretful and impatient: tired of life, yet loth to die. When Diogenes, at that time, asked him whether he needed a friend, Antisthenes replied, "Where is the friend that can free me from my pain?" Diogenes presented him with a dagger, saying, "Let this free you:" but Antisthenes answered, "I wish to be freed from pain, not from life." Neither his doctrine nor his manners were sufficiently inviting to procure him many followers. He paid little respect to the gods and the religion of his country; but as might be expected from a disciple of Socrates, he thought justly concerning the Supreme Being. In his book which treats on Physics, says Cicero, he observes that "the gods of the people are many, but the God of nature is One." Antisthenes wrote many books, of which none are extant, except two declamations under the names of Ajax and Ulysses.

The sum of the moral doctrine of Antisthenes and the Cynic sect is this:—Virtue alone is a sufficient foundation for a happy life. Virtue consists, not in a vain ostentation of learning, or an idle display of words, but in a steady course of right conduct. Wisdom and virtue are the same. A wise man will always be contented with his condition, and will live rather according to the precepts of virtue, than according to the laws or customs of his country. Wisdom is a secure and impregnable fortress; virtue, armor which cannot be taken away. Whatever is honorable is good; whatever is disgraceful is evil. Virtue is the only bond of friendship. It is better to associate with a few good men against a vicious multitude, than to join the vicious, however numerous, against the good. The love of pleasure is a temporary madness.

He was also the first person who ever gave a definition of discourse; saying, "Discourse is that which shows what anything is or was." And he used continually to say, "I would rather go mad than feel pleasure." And, "One ought to attach one's self to such women as will thank one for it." He said once to a youth from Pontus, who was on the point of coming to him to be his pupil, and was asking him what things he wanted, "You want a new book, and a new pen, and a new tablet;"—meaning a new mind. And to a person who asked him from what country he had better marry a wife, he said, "If you marry a handsome woman, she will be common;* if an ugly woman, she will be a punishment to you." He was told once that Plato spoke ill of him, and he replied, "It is a royal privilege to do well, and to be evil spoken of." When he was being initiated into the mysteries of Orpheus, and the priest said that those who were initiated enjoyed many good things in the shades below, "Why, then," said he, "do not you die?" Being once reproached as not being the son of two free citizens, he said, "And I am not the son of two people skilled in wrestling; nevertheless, I am a skilful wrestler." On one occasion he was asked why he had but few disciples, and said, "Because I drove them away with a silver rod." When he was asked why he reproved his pupils with bitter language, he said, "Physicians, too, use severe remedies for their patients." Once he saw an adulterer running away, and said, "O unhappy man! how much danger could you have avoided for one obol!" He used to say, as Hecaton tells us in his Apophthegms, "That it was better to fall among crows, than among flatterers; for that they only devour the dead, but the others devour the living." When he was asked what was the most happy event that could take place in human life, he said, "To die while prosperous."

On one occasion one of his friends was lamenting to him that he had lost his memoranda, and he said to him, "You ought to have written them on your mind, and not on paper."

* There is a play on the similarity of the two sounds, *koine*, common, and *poine*, punishment.

A favorite saying of his was, "That envious people were devoured by their own disposition, just as iron is by rust." Another was, "That those who wish to be immortal ought to live piously and justly." He used to say, too, "That cities were ruined when they were unable to distinguish worthless citizens from virtuous ones."

On one occasion he was being praised by some wicked men, and said, "I am sadly afraid that I must have done some wicked thing." One of his favorite sayings was, "That the fellowship of brothers of one mind was stronger than any fortified city." He used to say, "That those things were the best for a man to take on a journey, which would float with him if he were shipwrecked." He was once reproached for being intimate with wicked men, and said, "Physicians also live with those who are sick; and yet they do not catch fevers." He used to say, "that it was an absurd thing to clean a cornfield of tares, and in war to get rid of bad soldiers, and yet not to rid one's self in a city of the wicked citizens." When he was asked what advantage he had ever derived from philosophy, he replied, "The advantage of being able to converse with myself." At a drinking party, a man once said to him, "Give us a song," and he replied, "Do you play us a tune on the flute." When Diogenes asked him for a tunic, he bade him fold his cloak. He was asked on one occasion what learning was the most necessary, and he replied, "To unlearn one's bad habits." And he used to exhort those who found themselves ill spoken of, to endure it more than they would any one's throwing stones at them. He used to laugh at Plato as conceited; accordingly, once when there was a fine procession, seeing a horse neighing, he said to Plato, "I think you too would be a very frisky horse:" and he said this all the more, because Plato kept continually praising the horse. At another time, he had gone to see him when he was ill, and when he saw there a dish in which Plato had been sick, he said, "I see your bile there, but I do not see your conceit."

He used to advise the Athenians to pass a vote that asses were horses; and, as they thought that irrational, he said, "Why, those whom you make generals have never learnt to be really generals, they have only been voted such."

A man said to him one day, "Many people praise you." "Why, what evil," said he, "have I done?" When he turned the rent in his cloak outside, Socrates seeing it, said to him, "I see your vanity through the hole in your cloak." On another occasion, the question was put to him by some one, as Phanias relates, in his treatise on the Philosophers of the Socratic school, what a man could do to show himself an honorable and a virtuous man; and he replied, "If you attend to those who understand the subject, and learn from them that you ought to shun the bad habits which you have." Some one was praising luxury in his hearing, and he said, "May the children of my enemies be luxurious." Seeing a young man place himself in a carefully studied attitude before a modeller, he said, "Tell me, if the brass could speak, on what would it pride itself?" And when the young man replied, "On its beauty." "Are you not then," said he, "ashamed to rejoice in the same thing as an inanimate piece of brass?" A young man from Pontus once promised to recollect him, if a vessel of salt fish arrived; and so he took him with him, and also an empty bag, and went to a woman who sold meal, and filled his sack and went away; and when the woman asked him to pay for it, he said, "The young man will pay you, when the vessel of salt fish comes home."

Whenever he saw a woman beautifully adorned, he would go off to her house, and desire her husband to bring forth his horse and his arms; and then if he had such things, he would give him leave to indulge in luxury, for that he had the means of defending himself; but if he had them not, then he would bid him strip his wife of her ornaments.

And the doctrines he adopted were these. He used to insist that virtue was a thing which might be taught; also, that the nobly born and virtuously disposed, were the same people; for that virtue was of itself sufficient for happiness, and was in need of nothing, except the strength of Socrates. He also looked upon virtue as a species of work, not wanting many arguments, or much instruction; and he taught that the wise man was sufficient for himself; for that everything that belonged to any one else belonged to him. He considered obscurity of fame a good thing, and equally good with labor. And he used to say that the wise man would regulate his conduct as a citizen, not according to the established laws of the state, but according to the law of virtue. And that he would marry for the sake of having children, selecting the most beautiful woman for his wife. And that he would love her; for that the wise man alone knew what objects deserved love.

Diocles also attributes the following apophthegms to him. "To the wise man, nothing is strange and nothing remote. The virtuous man is worthy to be loved. Good men are friends. It is right to make the brave and just one's allies. Virtue is a weapon of which a man cannot be deprived. It is better to fight with a few good men against all the wicked, than with many wicked men against a few good men. One should attend to one's enemies, for they are the first persons to detect one's errors. One should consider a just man as of more value than a relation. Virtue is the same in a man as in a woman. What is good is honorable, and what is bad is disgraceful. Think everything that is wicked, foreign. Prudence is the safest fortification; for it can neither fall to pieces nor be betrayed. One must prepare one's self a fortress in one's own impregnable thoughts."

He also said, "As rust consumes iron so doth envy the heart of man."

"The harmony of brethren is a stronger defence than a wall of brass."

"The man who is afraid of another, whatever he may think of himself, is a slave."

"We ought to aim at such pleasures as follow labor, not at those which go before labor."

"A feast is not pleasant without company, nor riches without virtue."

"Him that contradicteth, we must not again contradict, but instruct, for a mad man is not cured by another's becoming mad."

To some who applauded a piper he said, "He is a bad man or else he would never have been so good a piper."

Being asked what a feast was, he said, "The occasion of surfeits."

He used to lecture in the Gymnasium, called Cynosarges, not far from the gates; and some people say that it is from that place that the sect got the name of Cynics. And he himself was called Haplocyon (downright dog.)

He was the first person to set the fashion of doubling his cloak, as Diocles says, and he wore no other garment. And he used to carry a stick and a wallet; but Neanthes says that he was the first person who wore a cloak without folding it. But Sosicrates, in the third book of his Successions, says that Diodorus, of Aspendos, let his beard grow, and used to carry a stick and a wallet.

He is the only one of all the pupils of Socrates, whom Theopompus praises and speaks of as clever, and able to persuade whomsoever he pleased by the sweetness of his conversation. And this is plain, both from his own writings, and from the Banquet of Xenophon. He appears to have been the founder of the more manly Stoic school.

He was the original cause of the apathy of Diogenes, the temperance of Crates and the patience of Zeno, having himself, as it were, lain the foundations of the city which they afterwards built. And Xenophon says that in his conversation and society, he was the most delightful of men, and in every respect the most temperate.

So numerous were the books of Antisthenes, and so various their subjects, that Timon called him a universal chatterer.

APOLLONIUS.

Apollonius Tyaneus was follower of the Pythagoric doctrine and discipline. The principal circumstances of his life, as far as credit can be given to his fabulous biographer, Philostratus, are as follows:

Apollonius, of an ancient and wealthy family in Tyana, a city of Capadocia, was born about the commencement of the Christian era. At fourteen years of age his father took him to Tarsus, to be instructed by Euthydemus, a rhetorician; but he soon became dissatisfied with the luxury and indolence of the citizens, and obtained permission from his father to remove, with his preceptor, to Ægas, a neighboring town, where was a temple of Esculapius. Here he conversed with Platonists, Stoics, Peripatetics, and Epicureans, and became acquainted with their doctrines. But finding the Pythagorean tenets and discipline more consonant to his own views and temper, than those of any other sect, he made choice of Euxenus for his preceptor in philosophy; a man who indeed lodged his master's precepts in his memory, but paid little regard to them in practice. Apollonius, however, was not to be diverted from the strictness of the Pythagorean discipline even by the example of his preceptor. He refrained from animal food, and lived entirely upon fruits and herbs. He wore no article of clothing made of the skins of animals. He went bare-footed and suffered his hair to grow to its full length. He spent his time chiefly in the temple of Esculapius among the priests, by whom he was greatly admired.

After having acquired reputation at Ægas, Apollonius determined to qualify himself for the office of a preceptor in philosophy by passing through the Pythagorean discipline of silence. Accordingly, he remained five years without once exercising the faculty of speech. During this time he chiefly resided in Pamphylia and Cilicia. When his term of silence expired, he visited Antioch, Ephesus, and other cities, declining the society of the rude and illiterate, and conversing chiefly with the priests. At sun-rising he performed certain religious rites, which he disclosed only to those who had passed through the discipline of silence. He spent the morning in instructing his disciples, whom he encouraged to ask whatever questions they pleased. At noon he held a public assembly for popular discourse. His style was neither turgid nor abstruse, but truly Attic. Avoiding all prolixity, and every ironical mode of speech, he issued forth his dogmas with oracular authority, saying, on every occasion, This I know, or, Such is my judgment; herein imitating the manner of Pythagoras. Being asked why, instead of dogmatically asserting his tenets, he did not still continue to inquire; his answer was: "I have sought for truth, when I was young; it becomes me now no longer to seek, but to teach what I have found." Apollonius, that he might still more perfectly resemble Pythagoras, determined to travel through distant nations. He proposed his design to his disciples, who were seven in number, but they refused to accompany him. He therefore entered upon his expedition, attended only by two servants. At Ninus he took as his associate Damis, an inhabitant of that city, to whom he boasted that he was skilled in all languages, though he had never learned them, and that he even understood the language of beasts and birds. The ignorant Assyrian worshipped him as a god; and, resigning himself implicitly to his direction, accompanied him wherever he went.

At Babylon, Apollonius conversed with the Magi, receiving from them much instruction, and communicating to them many things in return; but to these conferences Damis was not admitted. In his visit to India, he was admitted to an interview with the king, Phraortes, and was introduced by him to Iarchus, the eldest of the Indian gymnosophists. Returning to Babylon, he passed from that city to Ionia, where he visited Ephesus, and several other places, teaching the doctrine, and recommending the discipline, of Pythagoras. On his way to Greece, he conversed with the priests of Orpheus at his temple in Lesbos. Arriving at Athens at the time when the sacred mysteries were performing, Apollonius offered himself for initiation; but the priest refused him, saying, that it was not lawful to initiate an enchanter. He discoursed with the Athenians concerning sacrifices, and exhorted them to adopt a more frugal manner of living.

After passing through some other Grecian cities and the island of Crete, Apollonius went into Italy, with the design of visiting Rome. Just before this time, Nero, probably either because he had been deceived by the pretensions of the magicians, or was apprehensive of some danger from their arts, gave orders that all those who practised magic should be banished from the city. The friends of Apollonius apprized him of the hazard which was likely, at this juncture, to attend the purposed visit to Rome; and the alarm was so great, that, out of thirty-four persons who were his stated companions, only eight chose to accompany him thither. He nevertheless persevered in his resolution, and under the protection of the sacred habit obtained admission into the city. The next day he was conducted to the Consul Telesinus, who was inclined to favor philosophers of every class, and obtained from him permission to visit the temples, and converse with the priests.

From Rome Apollonius travelled westward to Spain. Here he made an unsuccessful attempt to incite the procurator of the province of Bætica to a conspiracy against Nero. After the death of that tyrant he returned to Italy, on his way to Greece; whence he proceeded to Egypt, where Vespasian was making use of every expedient to establish his power. That prince easily perceived that nothing would give him greater credit with the Egyptian populace than to have his cause espoused by one who was esteemed a favored minister of the gods, and therefore did not fail to show him every kind of attention and respect. The philosopher, in return, adapted his measures to the views of the new emperor, and used all his influence among the people in support of Vespasian's authority.

Upon the accession of Domitian, Apollonius was no sooner informed of the tyrannical proceedings of that emperor,and particularly of his proscription of philosophers, than he assisted in raising a sedition against him, and in favor of Nerva, among the Egyptians; so that Domitian thought it necessary to issue an order that he should be seized, and brought to Rome. Apollonius, being informed of the order, set out immediately, of his own accord, for that city. Upon his arrival he was brought to trial; but his judge, the pretor Ælian, who had formerly known him in Egypt, was desirous to favor him, and so conducted the process that it terminated in his acquittal.

Apollonius now passed over into Greece, and visited the temple of Jupiter at Olympia, the cave of Trophonius in Arcadia, and other celebrated seats of religion. Wherever he went he gained new followers. At length he settled at Ephesus, and there formed a school in some degree similar to the ancient Pythagorean college; but with this material difference, that in the school of Apollonius the door of wisdom was open to all, and every one was permitted to speak and inquire freely.

Concerning the fate of Apollonius, after he settled at Ephesus, nothing certain is related. The time, the place, and the manner of his death are unknown. It is probable that he lived to an extreme old age, and died in the reign of Nerva. Damis, who attached himself to this philosopher at Babylon, accompanied him in his subsequent travels, and after his death became his memorialist. Philostratus has loaded his account of the life of this extraordinary man with so many marvellous tales, that it is exceedingly difficult to determine what degree of credit is due to his narrative. He relates, for example, that while the mother of Apollonius was pregnant, the Egyptian divinity Proteus appeared to her, and told her that the child she should bring forth was a god; that his birth was attended with a celestial light; that in the Esculapean temple at Ægas he predicted future events; that at the tomb of Achilles he had a conference with the ghost of that hero; and that whilst he was publicly discoursing at Ephesus, he suddenly paused, as if struck with a panic, and then cried out, "Slay the tyrant," at the very instant when Domitian was cut off at Rome. If to these tales we add the accounts which Philostratus gives of the efficacy of the mere presence of Apollonius, without the utterance of a single word, in quelling popular tumults; of the chains of Prometheus, which Apollonius saw upon Mount Caucasus; of speaking trees, of pigmies, phœnixes, satyrs, and dragons, which he met with in his eastern tour; and of other things equally wonderful; it will be impossible to hesitate in ascribing the marvellous parts, at least, of Philostratus's narrative to his ingenuity, or credulity.

Different opinions have been entertained concerning the character of Apollonius. Some have supposed the whole series of extraordinary events related concerning him to have been the mere invention of Philostratus and others for the purpose of obstructing the progress of Christianity, and providing a temporary prop for the falling edifice of paganism. Others, remarking that Apollonius had acquired a high degree of celebrity long before the time of his biographer, refer the origin of these tales to the philosopher himself; but with respect to the manner which this is to be done they are not agreed. Some apprehend that he was intimately acquainted with nature, and deeply skilled in medicinal arts, and that he applied his knowledge and skill to the purposes of imposture, that he might pass among a credulous multitude for something more than human; while others imagine that he accomplished his fraudulent designs by means of a real intercourse with evil spirits. The truth probably is, that Apollonius was one of those impostors who profess to practice magic arts, and perform other wonders, for the sake of acquiring fame, influence, and profit, among the vulgar. In this light, even according to his own biographer, he was regarded by his contemporaries, particularly by the priests of the Eleusinian and Trophonian mysteries, and by Euphrates, an Alexandrian philosopher. Lucian, who lived in the time of Trajan, and Apuleius, who flourished under Antoninus Pius, rank him among the most celebrated magicians. Origen, who had seen a life of Apollonius, now lost, which was written by Maragenes, prior to that of Philostratus, writes thus:—"Concerning magic, we shall only say, that whoever is desirous of knowing whether philosophers are to be imposed upon by this art, let him read the memoirs of Apollonius, written by Maragenes, who, though a philosopher, and not a Christian, says, that philosophers of no mean repute were deceived by the magical arts of Apollonius, and visited him as a person capable of predicting future events." Eusebius, in his answer to Hierocles, who wrote a treatise, in which he drew a comparison between Jesus Christ and Apollonius Tyaneus, speaks of the latter as a man who was eminently skilled in every kind of human wisdom, but who affected powers beyond the reach of philosophy, and assumed the Pythagorean manner of living as a mask for his impostures. The narrative of his life, by Philostratus, though doubtless abounding with fictions, serves at least to confirm this opinion.

How successfully Apollonius practised the arts of imposture, sufficiently appears from the events which followed. The dominion over the minds of men, which he found means to establish during his life, remained and increased after his death, so that he long continued to be ranked among the divinities. The inhabitants of Tyana, proud of the honor of calling him their fellow-citizen, dedicated a temple to his name; and the same privileges were granted to them as had usually been conferred upon those cities where temples were raised, and sacred rites performed, in honor of the emperors. Aurelian, out of respect to his memory, showed the Tyaneans peculiar favor. Adrian took great pains to collect his writings, and preserve them in his library: Caracalla dedicated a temple to him, as to a divinity among men; and Alexander Severus, in his domestic temple, kept the image of Apollonius, with those of Abraham, Orpheus, and Christ, and paid them divine honors. The common people, in the meantime, ranked Apollonius in the number of deified men, and made use of his name in incantations; and even among the philosophers of the Eclectic sect he was regarded as a being of a superior order, who partook of a middle nature between gods and men.

ARCESILAUS.

Arcesilaus was the son of Seuthes or Scythes, and a native of Pitane in Æolia.

He was the original founder of the Middle Academy, and the first man who professed to suspend the declaration of his judgment, because of the contrarieties of the reasons alleged on either side. He was likewise the first who attempted to argue on both sides of a question, and who also made the method of discussion, which had been handed down by Plato, by means of question and answer, more contentious than before.

He became a pupil of Xanthus the musician, and after that attended the lectures of Theophrastus, and subsequently came over to the Academy to Crantor. For Mæreas his brother, urged him to apply himself to rhetoric; but he himself had a preference for philosophy, and when he became much attached to him Crantor asked him, quoting a line out of the Andromeda of Euripides :—

O virgin, if I save you, will you thank me?

And he replied by quoting the next line to it:—

O take me to you, stranger, as your slave,
Or wife, or what you please.

And ever after that they became very intimate, so that they say Theophrastus was much annoyed, and said, "That a most ingenious and well-disposed young man had deserted his school."

For he was not only very impressive in his discourse, and displayed a great deal of learning in it, but he also tried his hand at poetry, and there is extant an epigram which is attributed to him, addressed to Attalus, which is a follows:—

Pergamus is not famed for arms alone,
But often hears its praise resound
For its fine horses, at the holy Pisa.
Yet, if a mortal may declare,
Its fate as hidden in the breast of Jove,
It will be famous for its woes.

There is another addressed to Mendorus the son Eudamus, who was attached to one of his fellow pupils:—

Phrygia is a distant land, and so
Is sacred Thyatire, and Cadanade,
Your country Menodorus. But from all,
As the unvaried song of bards relates,
An equal road lies to Acheron,
That dark unmentioned river; so you lie
Here far from home; and here Eudamus raises
This tomb above your bones, for he did love you,
Though you were poor, with an undying love.

But he admired Homer above all poets, and always used to read a portion of his works before going to sleep; and in the morning he would say that he was going to the object of his love, when he was going to read him. He said, too, that Pindar was a wonderful man for filling the voice, and pouring forth an abundant variety of words and expressions. He also, when he was a young man, wrote a criticism on Ion.

And he was a pupil likewise of Hipponicus, the geometrican, whom he used to ridicule on other points as being lazy and gaping; but he admitted that in his own profession he was clear sighted enough, and said that geometry had flown into his mouth while he was yawning. And when he went out of his mind, he took him to his own house, and took care of him till he recovered his senses.

And when Crates died, he succeeded him in the presidency of his schools, a man of the name of Socrates willingly yielding to him.

And as he suspended his judgment on every point, he never, as it is said, wrote one single book. But others say that he was once detected correcting some passages in a work of his; and some assert that he published it, while others deny it, and affirm that he threw it into the fire.

He was exceedingly fond of employing axioms, very concise in his diction, and when speaking he laid an emphasis on each separate word.

He was also very fond of attacking others, and very free spoken, on which account Timon in another passage speaks of him thus:—

> You'll not escape all notice while you thus
> Attack the young man with your biting sarcasm.

Once, when a young man was arguing against him with more boldness than usual, he said, "Will no one stop his mouth with the knout?"* But to a man who lay under the general imputation of low debauchery, and who argued with him that one thing was not greater than another, he asked him whether a cup holding two pints was not larger than one which held only one. There was a certain Chian named Hemon, exceedingly ugly, but who fancied himself good looking, and always went about in fine clothes: this man asked

* Perhaps there is a pun here; *astragalos* means not only a knout composed of small bones strung together, but also a die.

him one day, "If he thought that a wise man could feel attachment to him;" "Why should he not," said he, "when they love even those who are less handsome than you, and not so well-dressed either?" and when the man, though one of the vilest characters possible, said to Arcesilaus as if he were addressing a very rigid man:—

> O, noble man, may I a question put,
> Or must I hold my tongue?

Arcesilaus replied:—

> O wretched woman, why do you thus roughen
> Your voice, not speaking in your usual manner?

And once, when plagued by a chattering fellow of low extraction, he said:—

> The sons of slaves are always talking vilely.

Another time, when a talkative man was giving utterance to a great deal of nonsense, he said, that "He had not had a nurse who was severe enough." And to some people he never gave any answer at all. On one occasion a usurer who made pretence to some learning, said in his hearing that he did not know something or other, on which he rejoined:—

> For often times the passing winds do fill
> The female bird, except when big with young.*

And the lines come out of the Ænomaus of Sophocles. He once reminded a certain dialetician, a pupil of Aleximes, who was unable to explain correctly some saying of his master, of what had been done by Philoxenus to some brick-makers. For when they were singing some of his songs very badly he came upon them, and trampled their bricks under foot, saying, "As you spoil my works so will I spoil yours."

And he used to be very indignant with those who neglected proper opportunities of applying themselves to learning; and he had a peculiar habit, while conversing, of using the ex-

* There is a pun here whieh is untranslateable. The Greek word meaning usury, and also offspring or delivery.

pression, "I think," and "So and so," naming the per ., "will not agree to this." And this was imitated by several of his pupils, who copied also his style of expression and everything about him. He was a man very ready at inventing new words, and very quick at meeting objections, and at bringing round the conversation to the subject before him, and at adapting it to every occasion, and he was the most convincing speaker that could be found, on which account numbers of people flocked to his school, in spite of being somewhat alarmed at his severity, which however they bore with complacency for he was a very kind man, and one who inspired his hearers with abundant hope, and in his manner of life he was very affable and liberal, always ready to do any one a service without any parade, and shrinking from any expression of gratitude on the part of those whom he had obliged. Accordingly once, when he had gone to visit Ctesibius who was ill, seeing him in great distress from want, he secretly slipped his purse under his pillow; and when Ctesibius found it, "This," said he "is the amusement of Arcesilaus." And at another time he sent him a thousand drachmas. He it was also who introduced Archias the Arcadian to Eumenes, and who procured him many favors from him.

And being a very liberal man and utterly regardless of money, he made the most splendid display of silver plate, and in his exhibition of gold plate he vied with that of Archecrates and Callecrates; and he was constantly assisting and contributing to the wants of others with money; and once, when some one had borrowed from him some articles of silver plate to help him entertain his friends, and did not offer to return them, he never asked for them back or reclaimed them; but some say that he lent them with the purpose that they should be kept, and that when the man returned them, he made him a present of them as he was a poor man. He had also property in Pitana, the revenues from which were transmitted to him by his brother Pylades.

Moreover, Eumenes, the son of Philetærus, supplied him with many things, on which account he was the only king to whom he addressed any of his discourses. And when many philosophers paid court to Antigonus and went out to meet him when he arrived, he himself kept quiet, not wishing to make his acquaintance. But he was a great friend of Hierocles, the governor of the harbors of Munychia and the Piræus; and at festivals he always paid him a visit. And when he constantly endeavored to persuade him to pay his respects to Antigonus, he would not; but though he accompanied him as far as his gates, he turned back himself. And after the sea-fight of Antigonus, when many people went to him and wrote him letters to comfort him for his defeat, he neither went nor wrote; but still in the service of his country, he went to Demetrias as an ambassador to Antigonus, and succeeded in the object of his mission.

And he spent all his time in the Academy, and avoided meddling with public affairs, but at times he would spend some days in the Piræus of Athens, discoursing on philosophical subjects, from his friendship for Hierocles, which conduct of his gave rise to unfavorable reports being raised against him by some people.

Being a man of very expensive habits, for he was in this respect a sort of second Aristippus, he often went to dine with his friends. He also lived openly with Theodote and Philæte, two courtesans of Elis; and to those who reproached him for this conduct, he used to quote the opinions of Aristippus. He was also very fond of the society of young men, and of a very affectionate disposition, on which account Aristi, the Chian, a Stoic philosopher, used to accuse him of being a corrupter of the youth of the city, and a profligate man. He is said also to have been greatly attached to Demetrius, who sailed to Cyrene, and to Cleochares of Mydea, of whom he said to his messmates, that he wished to open the door to him but that he prevented him.

Demochares the son of Laches, and Pythocles the son of Bugelus, were also among his friends, and he said that he humored them in all their wishes because of his great patience. And, on this account, those people to whom I have before alluded, used to attack him and ridicule him as a popularity hunter and vain-glorious man. And they set upon him very violently at an entertainment given by Hieronymus, the Peripatetic, when he invited his friends on the birthday of Alcymeus, the son of Antigonus, on which occasion Antigonus sent him a large sum of money to promote the conviviality. On this occasion, as he avoided all discussion during the continuance of the banquet, when Aridelus proposed to him a question which required some deliberation, and entreated him to discourse upon it, it is said that he replied, "But this is more especially the business of philosophy, to know the proper time for everything." With reference to the charge that was brought against him of being a popularity hunter, Timon speaks, among other matters, mentioning it in the following manner:—

He spoke and glided quick among the crowd,
They gazed on him as finches who behold
An owl among them. You then please the people!
Alas, poor fool, 'tis no great matter that;
Why give yourself such airs for such a trifle?

However, in all other respects he was so free from vanity, that he used to advise his pupils to become the disciples of other men; and once, when a young man from Chios was not satisfied with his school, but preferred that of Hieronymus, whom I have mentioned before, he himself took him and introduced him to that philosopher, recommending him to preserve his regularity of conduct. And there is a very witty saying of his recorded. For when some one asked him once, why people left other schools to go to the Epicureans, but no one left the Epicureans to join the other sects, he replied, "People sometimes make eunuchs of men, but no one can ever make a man of an eunuch."

At last, when he was near his end, he left all his property to his brother Pylades. He never married a wife, and never had any children. He made three copies of his will, and deposited one in Eretria with Amphicritus, and one at Athens with some of his friends, and the third he sent to his own home to Thaumasias, one of his relations, entreating him to keep it.

He died, as Hermippus relates, after having drunk an excessive quantity of wine, and then became delirious, when he was seventy-five years old; and he was more beloved by the Athenians than any one else had ever been. And we have written the following epigram on him;—

O wise Arcesilaus, why didst thou drink
So vast a quantity of unmixed wine,
As to lose all your senses, and then die?
I pity you not so much for your death,
As for the insult that you thus did offer
The Muses, by your sad excess in wine.

ARCHYTAS.

Archytas of Tarentum acquired such celebrity for his knowledge of philosophy that many illustrious names are found amongst his disciples. He prudently withheld all chastisement from his servants and inferiors when in a state of passionate excitement. To one of his dependents who had offended him, he said, "It is well for you that I am angry; otherwise I know not what you might expect." He taught that virtue should be pursued for its own sake in every condition of life: that the mind is more injured by prosperity than by adversity, and that there is no pestilence so destructive to human happiness as pleasure.

He was a Pythagorean; and he it was who saved Plato's life by means of a letter, when he was in danger of being put to death by Dionysius.

He was a man held in very general esteem on account of his universal virtue; and he was seven times appointed general of his countrymen, when no one else had ever held the office for more than one year, as the law forbade it to be held for a longer period.

Aristoxenus says, that this Pythagorean was never once defeated while acting as general. But that as he was attacked by envy, he once gave up his command, and his army was immediately taken prisoner.

He was the first person who applied mathematical principles to mechanics, and reduced them to a system; and the first also who gave a methodical impulse to descriptive geometry in seeking, in the section of a demicylinder for a proportional mean, which should enable him to find the double of a given cube. He was also the first person who ever gave the geometrical measure of a cube, as Plato mentions in his Republic.

He invented cranes and screws, and made a pigeon of wood that flew, but when she once rested could not rise.

He said it is as hard to find a man without deceit, as a fish without bones. Horace states that he perished by shipwreck.

ARISTIPPUS.

Aristippus was by birth a Cyrenean, but he came to Athens, as Æschines says, having been attracted thither by the fame of Socrates.

He, having professed himself a Sophist, as Phanias, of Eresus, the Peripatetic, informs us, was the first of the pupils of Socrates who exacted money from his pupils, and who sent money to his master. And once he sent him twenty drachmas, but had them sent back again, as Socrates said that his dæmon would not allow him to accept them; for, in fact, he was indignant at having them offered to him.

He was a man very quick at adapting himself to every kind of place, and time, and person, and he easily supported every change of fortune.

> Yet Aristippus every dress became,
> In every various state of life the same.

For which reason he was in greater favor with Dionysius than any of the others, as he always made the best of existing circumstances. For he enjoyed what was before him pleasantly, and he did not toil to procure himself the enjoyment of what was not present. On which account Diogenes used to call him the king's dog. And Timon used to snarl at him as too luxurious, speaking somewhat in this fashion:—

> Like the effeminate mind of Aristippus,
> Who, as he said, by touch could judge of falsehood.

They say that he once ordered a partridge to be bought for him at the price of fifty drachmas, and when some one blamed him, "And would not you," said he, "have bought it if it had cost an obol?" And when he said he would, "Well," replied Aristippus, "fifty drachmas are no more to me."

Dionysius once bade him select which he pleased of three beautiful courtesans, and he carried off all three, saying that even Paris did not get any good by preferring one beauty to the rest. However, they say, that when he had carried them as far as the vestibule, he dismissed them; so easily inclined was he to select or to disregard things. On which account Strato, or, as others will have it, Plato, said to him, "You are the only man to whom it is given to wear both a whole cloak and rags." Once when Dionysius spit at him, he put up with it; and when some one found fault with him, he said, "Men endure being wetted by the sea in order to catch a tench, and shall not I endure to be sprinkled with wine to catch a sturgeon?"

Once Diogenes, who was washing vegetables, ridiculed him as he passed by, and said, "If you had learned to eat these vegetables, you would not have been a slave in the palace of a tyrant." But Aristippus replied, "And you, if you had known how to behave among men, would not have been washing vegetables." Being asked once what advantage he had derived from philosophy, he said, "The power of conversing without embarrassment with all classes of men." When he was reproached for living extravagantly, he replied, "If extravagance had been a fault, it would not have had a place in the festivals of the gods." At another time he was asked what advantage philosophers had over other men; and he replied, "If all the laws should be abrogated, we should still live in the same manner as we do now." Once, when Dionysius asked him why the philosophers haunt the doors of the rich, but the rich do not frequent those of the philosophers, he said, "Because the first know what they want, but the second do not."

On one occasion he was reproached by Plato for living in an expensive way; and he replied, "Does not Dionysius seem to you to be a good man?" And as he said that he did; "And yet," said he, "he lives in a more expensive manner than I do, so that there is no impossibility in a person's living both expensively and well at the same time." He was asked once in what educated men are superior to uneducated men; and answered, "Just as broken horses are superior to those that are unbroken." On another occasion he was going into the house of a courtesan, and when one of the young men who were with him blushed, he said, "It is not the going into such a house that is bad, but the not being able to go out." Once a man proposed a riddle to him, and said, "Solve it." "Why, you silly fellow," said Aristippus, "do you wish me to loose what gives us trouble, even while it is in bonds?" A saying of his was, that "it was better to be a beggar than an ignorant person; for that a beggar only wants money, but an ignorant person wants humanity." Once when he was abused, he was going away, and as his adversary pursued him and said, "Why are you going away?" "Because," said he, "you have a license for speaking ill; but I have another for declining to hear ill." When some one said that he always saw the philosophers at the doors of the rich men, he said, "And the physicians also are always seen at the doors of their patients; but still no one would choose for this reason to be an invalid rather than a physician."

Once it happened, that when he was sailing to Corinth, he was overtaken by a violent storm; and when somebody said, "We common individuals are not afraid, but you philosophers are behaving like cowards;" he said, "Very likely, for we have not both of us the same kind of souls at stake." Seeing a man who prided himself on the variety of his learning and accomplishments, he said, "Those who eat most, and who take the most exercise, are not in better health than they who eat just as much as is good for them; and in the same way it is not those who know a great many things, but they who know what is useful, who are valuable men." He gave admirable advice to his daughter Aretes, teaching her to despise superfluity. And being asked by some one in what respect his son would be better if he received a careful education, he replied, "If he gets no other good, at all events, when he is at the theatre, he will not be one stone sitting upon another." Once, when some one brought his son, to introduce him, to be educated, he demanded five hundred drachmas; and when the father said, "Why, for such a price as that I can buy a slave." "Buy him then," he replied, "and you will have a pair."

It was a saying of his that he took money from his acquaintances, not in order to use it himself, but to make them aware in what they ought to spend their money. On one occasion, being reproached for having employed a hired advocate in a cause that he had depending: "Why not," said he; "when

I have a dinner, I hire a cook." Once he was compelled by Dionysius to repeat some philosophical sentiment; "It is an absurdity," said he, "for you to learn of me how to speak, and yet to teach me when I ought to speak;" and as Dionysius was offended at this, he placed him at the lowest end of the table; on which Aristippus said, "You wish to make this place more respectable." A man was one day boasting of his skill as a diver; "Are you not ashamed," said Aristippus, "to value yourself upon that which every dolphin can do better?" On one occasion he was asked in what respect a wise man is superior to one who is not wise; and his answer was, "Send them both naked among strangers, and you will find out."

As a commentary upon this last saying take the following. In his way from Corinth to Asia, he was shipwrecked upon the island of Rhodes. Accidentally observing, as he came on shore, a geometrical diagram upon the sand, he said to his companions, "Take courage, I see the footsteps of men." When they arrived at the principal town of the island, the philosopher soon found means to engage the attention of the inhabitants, and procured an hospitable reception for himself and his fellow-travellers; a fact which confirms one of this philosopher's aphorisms; "If you ask what advantage a man of learning has above one who is illiterate, send them together among strangers, and you will see."

To a man who was boasting of being able to drink a large quantity without getting drunk he said, "A mule can do the same thing."

When a person once blamed him for taking money from his pupils, after having been himself a pupil of Socrates: "To be sure I do," he replied, "for Socrates too, when some friends sent their corn and wine, accepted a little, and sent the rest back; for he had the chief men of the Athenians for his purveyors. But I have only Eutychides, whom I have bought with money." And he used to live with Lais the courtesan, as Sotion tells us in the Second Book of his Successions. Accordingly, when some one reproached him on her account, he made answer, "I possess her, but I am not possessed by her: since the best thing is to possess pleasures without being their slave, not to be devoid of pleasures." When some one blamed him for the expense he was at about his food, he said, "Would you not have bought those things yourself if they had cost three obols?" And when the other admitted that he would, "Then," said he, "it is not that I am fond of pleasure, but that you are fond of money." On one occasion, when Simus, the steward of Dionysius, was showing him a magnificent house, paved with marble (but Simus was a Phrygian, and a great toper), he hawked up a quantity of saliva and spit in his face; and when Simus was indignant at this, he said, "I could not find a more suitable place to spit in."

Charondas, or as some say, Phædon, asked him once, "Who are the people who use perfumes?" "I do," said he, "wretched man that I am, and the king of the Persians is still more wretched than I; but, recollect, that as no animal is the worse for having a pleasant scent, so neither is a man; but plague take those wretches who abuse our beautiful unguents." On another occasion, he was asked how Socrates died; and he made answer, "As I should wish to die myself." When Polyxenus, the Sophist, came to his house and beheld his women, and the costly preparation that was made for dinner, and then blamed him for all this luxury, Aristippus after awhile said, "Can you stay with me to day?" and when Polyxenus consented, "Why then," said he, "did you blame me? it seems that you blame not the luxury, but the expense of it." When his servant was once carrying some money along the road, and was oppressed by the weight of it (as Bion relates in his Dissertations), he said to him, "Drop what is beyond your strength, and only carry what you can." Once he was at sea, and seeing a pirate vessel at a distance, he began to count his money; and then he let it drop into the sea, as if unintentionally, and began to bewail his loss; but others say that he said besides, that it was better for the money to be lost for the sake of Aristippus, than Aristippus for the sake of his money. On one occasion, when Dionysius asked him why he had come, he said, to give others a share of what he had, and to receive a share of what he had not; but some report that his answer was, "When I wanted wisdom, I went to Socrates; but now that I want money, I have come to you." He found fault with men, because when they are at sales, they examine the articles offered very carefully, but yet they approve of men's lives without any examination. Though some attribute this speech to Diogenes. They say that once at a banquet, Dionysius desired all the guests to dance in purple garments; but Plato refused, saying:—

> "I could not wear a woman's robe, when I
> Was born a man, and of a manly race."

But Aristippus took the garment, and when he was about to dance, he said very wittily:—

> "She who is chaste, will not corrupted be
> By Bacchanalian revels."

He was once asking a favor of Dionysius for a friend, and when he could not prevail, he fell at his feet; and when some one reproached him for such conduct, he said, "It is not I who am to blame, but Dionysius who has his ears in his feet." When he was staying in Asia, and was taken prisoner by Artaphernes the Satrap, some one said to him, "Are you still cheerful and sanguine?" "When, you silly fellow," he replied, "can I have more reason to be cheerful than now when I am on the point of conversing with Artaphernes?" It used to be a saying of his, that those who enjoyed the encyclic course of education, but who had omitted philosophy, were like the suitors of Penelope; for that they gained over Melantho and Polydora and the other maid-servants, and found it easier to do that than to marry the mistress. And Ariston said in like manner, that Ulysses when he had gone to the shades below, saw and conversed with nearly all the dead in those regions, but could not get a sight of the Queen herself.

On another occasion, Aristippus being asked what were the most necessary things for well-born boys to learn, said, "Those things which they will put in practice when they become men." And when some one reproached him for having come from Socrates to Dionysius, his reply was, "I went to Socrates because I wanted instruction, and I have come to Dionysius because I want diversion." As he had made money by having pupils, Socrates once said to him, "Where did you get so much?" and he answered, "Where you got a little." One day, when he had received some money from Dionysius, and Plato had received a book, he said to a man who jeered him, "The fact is, money is what I want, and books what Plato wants." One day he asked Dionysius for some money, who said, "But you told me that a wise man would never be in want;" "Give me some," Aristippus rejoined, "and then we will discuss that point;" Dionysius gave him some, "Now then," said he, "you see that I do not want money." When Dionysius said to him:—

> "For he who does frequent a tyrant's court
> Becomes his slave, though free when first he came:"

He took him up, and replied:—

> "That man is but a slave who comes as free."

He once quarrelled with Æschines, and presently afterwards said to him, "Shall we not make it up of our own accord, and cease this folly; but will you wait till some blockhead reconciles us over our cups?" "With all my heart," said Æschines. "Recollect, then," said Aristippus, "that I, who am older than you, have made the first advances." And Æschines answered, "You say well, by Juno, since you are far better than I; for I began the quarrel, but you begin the friendship." And these are anecdotes which are told of him.

ARISTON.

ARISTON the Bald, a native of Chios, surnamed the Scion, said, that the chief good was to live in perfect indifference to all those things which are of an intermediate character between virtue and vice; making not the slightest difference between them, but regarding them all on a footing of equality. For that the wise man resembles a good actor, who, whether he is filling the part of Agamemnon or Thersites, will perform them both equally well.

And he discarded altogether the topic of physics and of logic, saying that the one was above us, and that the other had nothing to do with us; and that the only branch of philosophy with which we had any real concern was ethics.

He also said that dialectic reasonings were like cobwebs, which, although they seem to be put together on principles of art, are utterly useless. And he did not introduce many virtues into his scheme, as Zeno did; nor one virtue under a great many names, as the Megaric philosophers did; but defined virtue as consisting in behaving in a certain manner with reference to a certain thing. And as he philosophized in this manner, and carried on his discussions in the Cynosarges, he got so much influence as to be called a founder of a sect. Accordingly, Miltiades and Diphilus were called Aristoneans.

He was a man of very persuasive eloquence, and one who could adapt himself well to the humors of a multitude. On which account Timon says of him: —

> And one, who from Ariston's wily race
> Traced his descent.

Diocles, the Magnesian, tells us, that Ariston having fallen in with Polemo, passed over to his school, at a time when Zeno was lying ill with a long sickness. The Stoic doctrine to which he was most attached, was the one that the wise man is never guided by opinions. But Persæus argued against this, and caused one of two twin brothers to place a deposit in his hands, and then caused the other to reclaim it; and thus he convicted him, as he was in doubt on this point, and therefore forced to act on opinion. He was a great enemy of Arcesilaus. And once, seeing a bull of a monstrous conformation, having a womb, he said, "Alas! here is an argument for Arcesilaus against the evidence of his senses." On another occasion, when a philosopher of the academy said that he did not comprehend anything, he said to him, "Do not you even see the man who is sitting next to you?" And as he said that he did not, he said:—

> Who then has blinded you, who 's been so harsh,
> As thus to rob you of your beaming eyes?

It is said that he, being bald, got a stroke of the sun, and so died. And we have written a jesting epigram on him in Scazon iambics, in the following terms:—

> Why, O Ariston, being old and bald,
> Did you allow the sun to roast your crown?
> Thus, in an unbecoming search for warmth,
> Against your will, you 've found out chilly Hell.

ARISTOTLE.

Aristotle was a native of Stagira, a town of Thrace, on the borders of the bay of Strymon, which at that time was subject to Philip of Macedon. His father was a physician, named Nicomachus; his mother's name was Estiada. From the place of his birth he is called the Stagyrite. Ancient writers are generally agreed in fixing the time of his birth in the first year of the ninety-ninth Olympiad. He received the first rudiments of learning from Proxenus, of Atarna, in Mysia, of whom he always retained a respectful remembrance.

In gratitude for the care which he had taken of his early education, he afterwards honored his memory with a statue, instructed his son Nicanor in the liberal sciences, and adopted him as his heir. At the age of seventeen Aristotle went to Athens, and devoted himself to the study of philosophy in the school of Plato. The uncommon acuteness of his apprehension, and his indefatigable industry, soon attracted the attention of Plato, and obtained his applause. Plato used to call him the *Mind of the school;* and to say when he was absent, "Intellect is not here." His acquaintance with books was extensive and accurate, as sufficiently appears from the concise abridgment of opinions, and the numerous quotations which are found in his works. According to Strabo, he was the first person who formed a library. Aristotle continued in the academy till the death of Plato, that is, till the thirty-seventh year of his age. After the death of his master he erected a monument to his memory, on which he inscribed an epitaph expressive of the highest respect, as follows:—

> To Plato's sacred name this tomb is reared,
> A name by Aristotle long revered!
> Far hence, ye vulgar herd! nor dare to stain
> With impious praise this ever hallow'd fane.

He likewise wrote an oration and elegies in praise of Plato, and gave other proofs of respect for his memory. Little regard is therefore due to the improbable tale related by Aristoxenus, of a quarrel between Aristotle and Plato, which terminated in a temporary exclusion of Aristotle from the academy, and in his erection of a school in opposition to Plato during his life. We find no proof that Aristotle instituted a new system of philosophy before the death of Plato.

It is certain, however, that when Speusippus, upon the death of his uncle, succeeded him in the academy, Aristotle was so much displeased, that he left Athens, and paid a visit to Hermias, king of the Atarnenses, who had been his friend and fellow disciple, and who received him with every expression of regard. Here he remained three years, and during this interval diligently prosecuted his philosophical researches. At the close of this term, his friend Hermias was taken prisoner by Memnon, a Rhodian, and sent to Artaxerxes, king of Persia, who put him to death. Upon this, Aristotle placed a statue of his friend in the temple at Delphos, and, out of respect to his memory, married his sister, whom her brother's death had reduced to poverty and distress. Upon the death of Hermias, Aristotle removed to Mitylene, but from what inducement does not appear. After he had remained there two years, Philip, king of Macedon, having heard of his extraordinary abilities and merit, made choice of him as preceptor to his son Alexander, and wrote him the following letter:—

"PHILIP to ARISTOTLE, *wisheth health:*

"Be informed that I have a son, and that I am thankful to the gods, not so much for his birth, as that he was born in the same age with you; for if you will undertake the charge of his education, I assure myself that he will become worthy of his father, and of the kingdom which he will inherit."

Aristotle accepted the charge, and in the second year of the hundred and ninth Olympiad, when Alexander was in his fifteenth year, he took up his residence in the court of Philip. He had been himself well instructed, not only in the doctrines of the schools, but in the manners of the world, and therefore was excellently qualified for the office of preceptor to the young prince. Accordingly, we find that he executed his trust so perfectly to the satisfaction of Philip and Olympia, that they admitted him to their entire confidence, and conferred upon him many acceptable tokens of esteem. Philip allowed him no small share of influence in his public councils, and it reflected great honor upon Aristotle, that he made use of his interest with his prince rather for the benefit of his friends and the public, than for his own emolument. At his intercession, the town of Stagira, which had fallen into decay, was rebuilt, and the inhabitants were restored to their ancient privileges. In commemoration of their obligations to their fellow-citizen, and as a testimony of respect for his merit, they instituted an annual Aristotelian festival. Alexander entertained such an affection for his preceptor, that he professed himself more indebted to him than to his father; declaring that Philip had only given him life, but that Aristotle had taught him the art of living well. He is said, not only to have instructed his pupil in the principles of ethics and policy, but also to have communicated to him the most abstruse and concealed doctrines of philosophy. But it may be questioned whether a preceptor, who was himself so well trained by experience in the prudential maxims of life, would think of conducting a youth, who was destined to wield a sceptre, through the intricate mazes of metaphysics, or whether a pupil of Alexander's enterprising spirit would be able to bend his mind to such studies. What is related concerning the pains which Aristotle took to make his pupil acquainted with Homer, and to inspire him with a love of his writings, is much more credible; for he certainly could not have adopted a more judicious method of enriching the mind of the young prince with noble sentiments, or of inspiring him with ambition to distinguish himself by illustrious actions.

After Aristotle had left his pupil they carried on a friendly correspondence, in which the philosopher prevailed upon Alexander to employ his increasing power and wealth in the service of philosophy, by furnishing him, in his retirement, with the means of enlarging his acquaintance with nature. Alexander accordingly employed several thousand persons in different parts of Europe and Asia to collect animals of various kinds, birds, beasts, and fishes, and sent them to Aristotle, who from the information which this collection afforded him, wrote fifty volumes on the history of animated nature, only ten of which are now extant. Callisthenes, in the course of the

Asiatic expedition, incurred the displeasure of Alexander by the freedom with which he censured his conduct; the aversion was by a natural association transferred to Aristotle; and from that time a mutual alienation and jealousy took place between the philosopher and his prince. But there is no sufficient reason to believe that their attachment was converted into a settled enmity, which at length led them to form designs against each other's life.

Aristotle, upon his return to Athens, finding the Academy, in which he probably intended to preside, occupied by Xenocrates, resolved to acquire the fame of a leader in philosophy by founding a new sect in opposition to the Academy, and teaching a system of doctrines different from that of Plato. The place which he chose for his school was the Lyceum, a grove in the suburbs of Athens, which had hitherto been made use of for military exercises. Here he held daily conversations on subjects of philosophy with those who attended him, walking as he discoursed; whence his followers were called Peripatetics.

According to the long-established practice of philosophers among the Grecians, Egyptians, and other nations, Aristotle had his public and his secret doctrine, the former of which he called the Exoteric, and the latter the Acroamatic or Esoteric. Hence he divided his auditors into two classes, to one of which he taught his Exoteric doctrine, discoursing on the principal subjects of logic, rhetoric, and policy; the other he instructed in the Acroamatic, or concealed and subtle doctrine, concerning Being, Nature and God. His more abstruse discourses he delivered in the morning to his select disciples, whom he required to have been previously instructed in the elements of learning, and to have discovered abilities and dispositions suited to the study of philosophy. He delivered lectures to a more promiscuous auditory in the evening, when the Lyceum was open to all young men without distinction. The former he called his Morning Walk, the latter his Evening Walk. Both were much frequented.

Aristotle continued his school in the Lyceum twelve years; for, although the superiority of his abilities, and the novelty of his doctrines created him many rivals and enemies, during the life of Alexander the friendship of that prince protected him from insult. But after Alexander's death, which happened in the first year of the hundred and fourteenth Olympiad, the fire of jealousy, which had long been smothered, burst into a flame of persecution. His adversaries instigated Eurymedon, a priest, to accuse him of holding and propagating impious tenets. What these were, we are not expressly informed, but it is not improbable that the doctrine of Aristotle concerning fate might be construed into a denial of the necessity of prayers and sacrifices, and might consequently be resented as inimical to the public institutions of religion. This would doubtless be thought, on the part of the priesthood, a sufficient ground of accusation, and would be admitted by the judges of the Areopagus as a valid plea for treating him as a dangerous man. That Aristotle himself was apprehensive of meeting with the fate of Socrates, appears from the reason which he gave his friends for leaving Athens: "I am not willing," says he, "to give the Athenians an opportunity of committing a second offence against philosophy." It is certain that he retired, with a few of his disciples, to Chalcis, where he remained till his death. He left Athens in the second year of the hundred and fourteenth Olympiad, and died at Chalcis the third year of the same Olympiad, and the sixty-third year of his age. Many idle tales are related concerning the manner of his death. It was most likely that it was the effect of premature decay, in consequence of excessive watchfulness, and application to study. His body was conveyed to Stagira, where his memory was honored with an altar and a tomb.

Aristotle was twice married, first to Pythias, sister to his friend Hermias, and after her death to Herpyllis, a native of Stagira. By his second wife he had a son named Nichomachus, to whom he addressed his *Magna Moralia*, "Greater Morals." His person was slender; he had small eyes, and a shrill voice, and when he was young hesitated in his speech. He endeavored to supply the defects of his natural form by an attention to dress, and commonly appeared in a costly habit, with his beard shaven, and his hair cut, and with rings upon his fingers. He was subject to frequent indispositions, through a natural weakness of stomach; but he corrected the infirmities of his constitution by a temperate regimen.

Concerning the character of Aristotle nothing can be more contradictory than the statements of different writers. The above account of the Stagirite is from "Enfield's Brucker." A number of additional facts are furnished by Diogenes Laerties, from whom we select the following.

ARISTOTLE was the son of Nicomachus and Phæstias, a citizen of Stagira; he lived with Amyntas, the king of the Macedonians, as both a physician and a friend.

He was the most eminent of all the pupils of Plato. He had a lisping voice. He also had very thin legs, they say, and small eyes; but he used to indulge in very conspicuous dress, and rings, and used to dress his hair carefully.

He had also a son named Nicomachus, by Herpyllis his concubine, as we are told by Timotheus.

He seceded from Plato while he was still alive; so that they tell a story that he said, "Aristotle has kicked us off just as chickens do their mother after they have been hatched." But Hermippus says in his Lives, that while he was absent on an embassy to Philip, on behalf of the Athenians, Xenocrates became the president of the school and the Academy; and that when he returned and saw the school under the presidency of some one else, he selected a promenade in the Lyceum, in which he used to walk up and down with his disciples, discussing subjects of philosophy till the time for anointing themselves came; on which account he was called a Peripatetic.* But others

* From *peripateo*, "to walk about."

say that he got this name because once when Alexander was walking about after recovering from a sickness, he accompanied him and kept conversing with him. But when his pupils became numerous, he then gave them seats; saying:—

> It would be shame for me to hold my peace,
> And for Isocrates to keep on talking.

And he used to accustom his disciples to discuss any question which might be proposed, training them just as an orator might.

After that he went to Hermias the Eunuch, the tyrant of Atarneus, who, as it is said, allowed him all kinds of liberties; and some say that he formed a matrimonial connection with him, giving him either his daughter or his niece in marriage, as is recorded in Demetrius by Magnesia. And the same authority says that Hermias had been the slave of Eubulus, and a Bithynian by descent, and that he slew his master. But Aristippus, in the first book of his treatise on Ancient Luxury, says that Aristotle was enamored of the concubine of Hermias, and that, as Hermias gave his consent, he married her; and was so overjoyed that he sacrificed to her, as the Athenians do the Eleusinian Ceres. And he wrote a hymn to Hermias, which is given at length below.

After that he lived in Macedonia, at the court of Philip, and was entrusted by him with his son Alexander as a pupil; and he entreated him to restore his native city which had been destroyed by Philip, and had his request granted; and he also made laws for the citizens. And also he used to make laws in his schools, doing this in imitation of Xenocrates, so that he appointed a president every ten days. And when he thought that he had spent time enough with Alexander, he departed for Athens, having recommended to him his relation Callisthenes, a native of Olynthus; but as he spoke too freely to the king, and would not take Aristotle's advice, he reproached him and said:—

Alas! my child, in life's primeval bloom,
Such hasty words will bring thee to thy doom.

And his prophecy was fulfilled, for as he was believed by Hermolaus to have been privy to the plot against Alexander, he was shut up in an iron cage, covered with lice, and untended; and at last he was given to a lion, and so died.

Aristotle then having come to Athens, and having presided over his school there for thirteen years, retired secretly to Chalcis, as Eurymedon, the hierophant, had impeached him on an indictment for impiety, though Pharorinus, in his Universal History, says that his persecutor was Demophelus, on the ground of having written the hymn to the before-mentioned Hermias, and also the following epigram which was engraven on his statue at Delphi:—

The tyrant of the Persian archer race,
Broke through the laws of God to slay this man;
Not by the manly spear in open fight,
But by the treachery of a faithless friend.

And after that he died of taking a draught of aconite, as Eumelus says in the fifth book of his Histories, at the age of seventy years. And the same author says that he was thirty years old when he first became acquainted with Plato. But this is a mistake of his, for he did only live in reality sixty-three years, and he was seventeen years old when he first attached himself to Plato. And the hymn in honor of Hermias is as follows: —

O Virtue, won by earnest strife,
And holding out the noblest prize
That ever gilded earthly life,
Or drew it on to seek the skies!
For thee what son of Greece would not
Deem it an enviable lot,
To live the life, to die the death,
That fears no weary hour, shrinks from no fiery breath?

Such fruit hast thou of heavenly bloom,
A lure more rich than golden heap,
More tempting than the joys of home,
More bland than spell of soft-eyed sleep.

For thee Alcides, son of Jove,
And the twin boys of Leda strove,
With patient toil and sinewy might,
Thy glorious prize to grasp, to reach thy lofty height.

Achilles, Ajax, for thy love
Descended to the realms of night;
Atarneus' king thy vision drove,
To quit for aye the glad sun-light;
Therefore, to Memory's daughter dear,
His deathless name, his pure career,
Live shrined in song, and linked with awe,
The awe of Xenian Jove, and faithful friendship's law.

There is also an epigram of ours upon him, which runs thus: —

Eurymedon, the faithful minister
Of the mysterious Eleusinian Queen,
Was once about t' impeach the Stagirite
Of impious guilt. But he escaped his hands
By mighty draught of friendly aconite,
And thus defeated all his wicked arts.

Pharorinus, in his Universal History, says that Aristotle was the first person who ever composed a speech to be delivered in his own defence in a court of justice, and that he did so on the occasion of this prosecution, and said that at Athens,—

Pears upon pear-trees grow; on fig-trees, figs.

Apollodorus, in his Chronicles, says that he was born in the first year of the ninety-ninth Olympiad, and that he attached himself to Plato, and remained with him for twenty years, having been seventeen years of age when he originally joined him.

It is said also that he was offended with the king, because of the result of the conspiracy of Calisthenes against Alexander; and that the king, for the sake of annoying him, promoted Anaximenes to honor, and sent presents to Xenocrates. And Theocritus, of Chios, wrote an epigram upon him, to ridicule him, in the following terms, as it is quoted by Ambryon in his account of Theocritus: —

The empty-headed Aristotle raised
This empty tomb to Hermias the Eunuch,
The ancient slave of the ill-used Eubulus,
[Who, for his monstrous appetite, preferred
The Bosphorus to Academia's groves.]

And Timon attacked him too, saying of him: —

Nor the sad chattering of the empty Aristotle.

We have also met with his will, which we give as interesting to those who may desire to know the manner in which this distinguished philosopher disposed of his property. It contains some peculiar features: "May things turn out well; but if anything happens to him, in that case Aristotle has made the following disposition of his affairs: That Antipater shall be the general and universal executor. And until Nicanor marries my daughter, I appoint Aristomedes, Timarchus, Hipparchus, Dioteles, and Theophrastus, if he will consent and accept the charge, to be the guardians of my children and of Herpyllis, and the trustees of all the property I leave behind me; and I desire them, when my daughter is old enough, to give her in marriage to Nicanor; but if any thing should happen to the girl, which may God forbid, either before or after she is married, but before she has any children, then I will that Nicanor shall have the absolute disposal of my son, and of all other things, in the full confidence that he will arrange them in a manner worthy of me and of himself. Let him also be the guardian of my daughter and son Nicomachus, to act as he pleases with respect to them, as if he were their father or brother. But if anything should happen to Nicanor, which may God forbid, either before he receives my daughter in marriage, or after he is married to her, or before he has any children by her, then any arrangements which he may make by will shall stand. But if Theophrastus, in this case, should choose to take my daughter in marriage, then he is to stand exactly in the same position as Nicanor. And if not, then I will, that my trustees, consulting with Antipater concerning both the boy and girl, shall arrange everything respecting them as they shall think fit; and that my trustees and Nicanor, remembering both me and Herpyllis, and how well she has behaved to me, shall take care, if she be inclined to take a husband, that one be found for her that shall not be unworthy of us; and shall give her, in addition to all that has been already given her, a talent of silver, and three maid-servants, if she please to accept them, and the hand-maid whom she has now, and the boy Pyrrhæus. And if she likes to dwell at Chalcis, she shall have the house which joins the garden; but if she likes to dwell in Stagira, then she shall have my father's house. And whichever of these houses she elects to take, I will that my executors do furnish it with all necessary furniture, in such manner as shall seem to them and to Herpyllis to be sufficient. And let Nicanor be the guardian of the child Myrmex, so that he shall be conducted to his friends in a manner worthy of us, with all his property which I received. I also will that Aubracis shall have her liberty, and that there shall be given to her when her daughter is married, five hundred drachmas, and the hand-maid whom she now has. And I will that there be given to Thales, besides the hand-maiden whom she now has, who was bought for her, a thousand drachmas, and another hand-maid. And to Timon, in addition to the money that has been given to him before for another boy, an additional slave, or a sum of money which shall be equivalent I also will that Tychon shall have his liberty when his daughter is married, and Philon, and Olympius, and his son. Moreover, of those boys who wait upon me, I will that none shal be sold, but my executors may use them, and when they ar grown up, then they shall emancipate them if they deserve it. I desire too, that my executors will take under their care the statues which it has been entrusted to Gryllion to make, that when they are made they may be erected in their proper places; and so too shall the statues of Nicanor, and of Proxenus, which I was intending to give him a commission for, and also that of the mother of Nicanor. I wish them also to erect in its proper place the statue of Arimnestus, which is already made, that it may be a memorial of her, since she has died childless. I wish them also to dedicate a statue of my mother to Ceres at Nemea, or wherever else they think fit. And wherever they bury me, there I desire that they shall also place the bones of Pythias, having taken them up from the place where they now lie, as she herself enjoined. And I desire that Nicanor, as he has been preserved, will perform the vow which I made on his behalf, and dedicate some figures of animals in stone, four cubits high, to Jupiter the saviour, and Minerva the saviour, in Stagira."

And it is said that a great many dishes were found in his house; and that Lycon stated that he used to bathe in a bath of warm oil, and afterwards to sell the oil. But some say that he used to place a leather bag of warm oil on his stomach. And whenever he went to bed, he used to take a brazen ball in his hand, having arranged a brazen dish below it, so that, when the ball fell into the dish, he might be awakened by the noise.

The following admirable apophthegms are attributed to him.

He was once asked, what those who tell lies gain by it: "They gain this," said he, "that when they speak the truth they are not believed."

On one occasion he was blamed for giving alms to a worthless man, and he replied, "I did not pity the man, but his condition."

He was accustomed continually to say to his friends and pupils wherever he happened to be, "That sight receives the light from the air which surrounds it, and in like manner the soul receives the light from the science."

Very often, when he was inveighing against the Athenians, he would say that they had invented both wheat and laws, but that they used only the wheat and neglected the laws.

It was a saying of his that the roots of education were bitter, but the fruit sweet.

Once he was asked what grew old most speedily, and he replied, "Gratitude."

On another occasion the question was put to him, what hope is? and his answer was, "The dream of a waking man."

Diogenes once offered him a dry fig, and as he conjectured that if he did not take it the cynic had a witticism ready prepared, he accepted it, and then said that Diogenes had lost his joke and his fig too; and another time when he took one from him as he offered it, he held it up as a child does, and said, "O great Diogenes;" and then he gave it to him back again.

He used to say that there were three things necessary to education; natural qualifications, instruction, and practice.

Having heard that he was abused by some one, he said, "He may beat me too, if he likes, in my absence."

He used to say that beauty is the best of all recommendations, but others say that it was Diogenes who gave this description of it; and that Aristotle called beauty, "The gift of a fair appearance;" that Socrates called it "A short-lived tyranny;" Plato, "The privilege of nature;" Theophrastus "A silent deceit;" Theocritus, "An ivory mischief;" Carneades, "A sovereignty which stood in need of no guards."

On one occasion he was asked how much educated men were superior to those uneducated; "As much," said he, "as the living are to the dead."

It was a saying of his that education was an ornament in prosperity, and a refuge in adversity. And that those parents who gave their children a good education deserve more honor than those who merely beget them; for that the latter only enabled the children to live, but the former gave them the power of living well.

When a man boasted in his presence that he was a native

of an illustrious city, he said, "That is not what one ought to look at, but whether one is worthy of a great city."

He was once asked what a friend is; and his answer was, "One soul abiding in two bodies."

It was a saying of his that some men were as stingy as if they expected to live forever, and some as extravagant as if they expected to die immediately.

When he was asked why people like to spend a great deal of their time with handsome people, "That," said he, "is a question fit for a blind man to ask."

The question was once put to him, what he had gained by philosophy; and the answer he made was this, "That I do without being commanded, what others do from fear of the laws."

He was once asked what his disciples ought to do to get on, and he replied, "Press on upon those who are in front of them, and not wait for those who are behind to catch them."

A chattering fellow, who had been abusing him, said to him, "Have not I been jeering you properly?" "Not that I know of," said he, "for I have not been listening to you."

A man on one occasion reproached him for having given a contribution to one who was not a good man (for the story which I have mentioned before is also quoted in this way), and his answer was, "I gave not to the man, but to humanity."

The question was once put to him, how we ought to behave to our friends; and the answer he gave was, "As we should wish our friends to behave to us."

He used to define justice as "A virtue of the soul distributive of what each person deserved."

Another of his sayings was, that education was the best viaticum for old age.

Pharorinus, in the second book of his Commentaries, says that he was constantly repeating, "The man who has friends has no friend." And this sentiment is to be found also in the seventh book of the Ethics.

AURELIUS ANTONINUS.

The great and good emperor, Marcus Aurelius Antoninus, was a man not less distinguished by his learning, wisdom, and virtue, than by his imperial dignity. We shall here consider him only in the light of a philosopher, and a patron of philosophers.

Aurelius, who was born in the year one hundred and twenty-one, after having been early instructed in languages, eloquence, and liberal arts, followed the natural bias of his genius, in devoting himself to the study of philosophy under Sextus Junius, and other professors of the Stoic school. At the same time he omitted no opportunity of acquainting himself with the tenets of other sects. At twelve years of age he forsook the common pursuits and amusements of childhood, and assumed the habit of a Stoic philosopher. In order to inure himself to the hardiness of the Stoic character, he used to sleep upon the ground, with no other covering than his cloak; and it was with great difficulty that his mother prevailed upon him to make use of a leathern couch. So great was the respect which he always retained for his preceptors, that he honored their memory with statues, and kept their busts, or portraits, in his domestic temple.

The accomplishments and virtues of this excellent youth recommended him to the favor of the emperor Adrian, who conducted him rapidly through the several stages of advancement, and who appointed Antoninus Pius his successor upon the express condition that Aurelius should be next in succession. Aurelius, far from being elated with these honors, upon his removal from his father's house to the emperor's discovered great reluctance, and expressed strong apprehensions of the difficulties and hazards of government. After his advancement, he continued to treat his parents with the same respect, and to pay the same regard to their advice and authority, as he had before always done. Nor did he suffer the engagements or avocations of his high station to divert him from the prosecution of his studies. Under the direction of Apollonius the Chalcidian, a Stoic philosopher, he studied philosophy as the foundation of policy, in order to qualify himself for the offices of government.

During the life of Antoninus Pius, that emperor was greatly assisted in the affairs of government by Aurelius, who gave him every possible proof of probity, fidelity, and affection. After the death of the emperor, which happened in the year one hundred and sixty-one, Marcus Aurelius Antoninus was, with the unanimous concurrence of the senate and the people, advanced to the purple; and through the whole course of his reign he exercised his power under the direction of philosophy, and by his justice and clemency obtained the general love of his subjects.

It is much to be lamented that the mild and gentle spirit which this emperor unquestionably possessed should, with respect to the Christians, have so far yielded to the importunity of inferior governors, and the tumultuous complaints of the people, that in several provinces, particularly in Gaul, he permitted them to be harassed by persecution. Perhaps, too, that false notion of the character and conduct of the Christians, which led him, with many others, to mistake their meritorious perseverance for culpable obstinacy, might have some share in producing those severities which were continued through his whole reign.

An invasion from the north having been, not without great difficulty, repelled, the emperor devoted his attention to the institution of useful laws, and the correction of civil and moral disorders. He never failed to give encouragement to such as distinguished themselves by their talents or merit, and to recommend the strictest morality by his own example. Whilst he was indefatigable in his attention to public affairs, he filled up every hour of leisure with philosophical studies. He suffered no material incident to pass without writing such reflections upon it as might serve to establish in the mind the habit of virtuous fortitude. This practice produced those *Meditations*, which are deservedly reckoned among the most valuable remains of Stoic philosophy. Modesty, and humanity, the fairest fruits of wisdom, were virtues peculiarly conspicuous in the character of this amiable prince. He despised flattery, refused magnificent titles, and would suffer no temples or altars to be erected in honor of his name. When the rebellion in Syria was suppressed, and the head of Aulus Cassius, the leader of the revolt, was brought to Rome, the emperor received it with manifest tokens of regret, and ordered it to be buried.

During an interval of peace, Aurelius took a journey to Athens. His route was marked with actions worthy of his character; and when he arrived at the ancient seat of the Muses, he gave many welcome proofs of his love of learning and philosophy, by appointing public professors, liberally endowing the schools, conferring honors upon persons of distinguished merit, and performing other acts of imperial munificence.

Returning to Rome, the emperor retired to Lavinium, with the design of devoting himself to his favorite studies. But after a short interval, an irruption of Scythians, and other Northern people, obliged him to lead his forces against them. From this expedition he returned victorious; but, in his way home, he was seized at Vienna with a mortal disease. Aurelius met his end with great firmness; expressing, in the true spirit of Stoicism, indifference to life, and contempt of death. He died in the sixtieth year of his age.

Through his whole life, this illustrious philosopher exhibited a shining example of Stoic equanimity. His countenance remained unaltered by any emotions of joy or sorrow; he never suffered himself to be elated by victory, or depressed by defeat. The severity which the philosophical system he espoused was adapted to cherish, was, nevertheless, happily chastised by an innate benevolence of heart; and it is deservedly represented as his highest praise, that he was able, by the united influence of his precepts and example, to make bad citizens good, and the good still better.

AVERROËS.

Of all the Arabian philosophers and physicians, the most celebrated was Averroës, a philosopher whom Christians as well as Arabians esteemed equal, if not superior, to Aristotle himself. Averroës was born about the middle of the twelfth century, of a noble family at Corduba, the capital of the Saracen dominions in Spain. He was early instructed in the Islamitic law, and, after the usual manner of the Arabian schools, united with the study of Mahometan theology that of the Aristotelian philosophy. These studies he pursued under Thophail, and became a follower of the sect of the Asharites. Under Avenzoar he studied the science of medicine, and under Ibnu-Saig he made himself master of the mathematical sciences. Thus qualified, he was chosen, upon his father's demise, to the chief magistracy of Corduba. The fame of his extraordinary erudition and talents soon afterwards reached the Caliph Jacob Al-Mansor, king of Mauritania, the third of the Almohadean dynasty, who had built a magnificent school at Morocco; and that prince appointed him supreme magistrate and priest of Morocco and all Mauritania, allowing him still to retain his former honors. Having left a temporary substitute at Corduba, he went to Morocco, and remained there till he had appointed, through the kingdom, judges well skilled in the Mahometan law, and settled the whole plan of administration; after which he returned home, and resumed his offices.

This rapid advancement of Averroës brought upon him the

envy of his rivals at Corduba, and they conspired to lodge an accusation against him, for an heretical desertion of the true Mahometan faith. For this purpose, they engaged several young persons among their dependents, to apply to him for instruction in philosophy. Averroës, who was easy of access, and always desirous of communicating knowledge, complied with their request, and thus fell into the snare which had been laid for him. His new pupils were very industrious in taking minutes of every tenet or opinion advanced by their preceptor, which appeared to contradict the established system of Mahometan theology. These minutes they framed into a charge of heresy, and attested upon oath that they had been fairly taken from his lips. The charge was signed by a hundred witnesses. The Caliph listened to the accusation, and punished Averroës, by declaring him heterodox, confiscating his goods, and commanding him for the future to reside among the Jews, who inhabited the precincts of Corduba, where he remained an object of general persecution and obloquy. Even the boys in the streets pelted him with stones when he went up to the mosque in the city to perform his devotions. His pupil, Maimonides, that he might not be under the necessity of violating the laws of friendship and gratitude, by joining the general cry against Averroës, left Corduba. From this unpleasant situation Averroës at last found means to escape. He fled to Fez; but he had been there only a few days, when he was discovered by the magistrate, and committed to prison. The report of his flight from Corduba was soon carried to the king, who immediately called a council of divines and lawyers, to determine in what manner this heretic should be treated. The members of the council were not agreed in opinion. Some strenuously maintained, that a man who held opinions so contrary to the law of the prophet deserved death. Others thought that much mischief, arising from the dissatisfaction of those among the infidels who were inclined to favor him, might be avoided, by only requiring from the culprit a public penance and recantation of his errors. The milder opinion prevailed, and Averroës was brought out of prison to the gate of the mosque, and placed upon the upper step, with his head bare, at the time of public prayers, and every one, as he passed into the mosque, was allowed to spit upon his face. At the close of the service, the judge, with his attendants, came to the philosopher, and asked him whether he repented of his heresies. He acknowledged his penitence, and was dismissed without further punishment. With the permission of the king, Averroës returned to Corduba, where he experienced all the miseries of poverty and contempt. In process of time, the people became dissatisfied with the regent who had succeeded Averroës, and petitioned the king that their former governor might be restored. Jacob Al-Mansor, not daring to show such indulgence to one who had been infamous for heresy, without the consent of the priesthood, called a general assembly, in which it was debated, whether it would be consistent with the safety of religion, and the honor of the law, that Averroës should be restored to the government of Corduba. The deliberation terminated in favor of the penitent heretic, and he was restored, by the royal mandate, to all his former honors. Upon this fortunate change in his affairs, Averroës removed to Morocco, where he remained till his death, which happened, as some say, in the year 1195, or, according to others, in 1206.

Averroës is highly celebrated for his personal virtues. He practiced the most rigid temperance, eating only, once in a day, the plainest food. So indefatigable was his industry in the pursuit of science, that he often passed whole nights in study. In his judicial capacity, he discharged his duty with great wisdom and integrity. His humanity would not permit him to pass the sentence of death upon any criminal. He left this painful office to his deputies. He possessed so great a degree of self-command and patient lenity, that when one of his enemies, in the midst of a public discourse, sent a servant to him to whisper some abusive language in his ear, he took no other notice of what passed than if it had been a secret message of business. The next day the servant returned, and publicly begged pardon of Averroës for the affront he had offered him; upon which Averroës only appeared displeased that his patient endurance of injuries should be brought into public notice, and dismissed the servant with a gentle caution, never to offer that insult to another, which had in the present instance passed unpunished. Averroës spent a great part of his wealth in liberal donations to learned men, without making any distinction between his friends and his enemies; for which his apology was, that in giving to his friends and relations, he only followed the dictates of Nature; but in giving to his enemies he obeyed the commands of Virtue. With uncommon abilities and learning, Averroës united great affability and urbanity of manners. He may be justly regarded as one of the greatest men of his age.

AVICENNA.

Avicenna, or Ibn-Sina, was born at Bochara in the year 978. His first preceptor was Abu-Abdalla, a philosopher, whom his father engaged to instruct him in his own house; concerning whom Avicenna says, that he taught him the terms of logic, but was unacquainted with the nature of the art. Before he arrived at his eighteenth year, Avicenna, more, as it seems, through his own industry than by the assistance of preceptors, became well read in languages, in the Islamitic law, and in the sciences. In order, however, to render himself a more perfect master of the sublime doctrines of philosophy, and the subtle questions of dialectics, he became a student in the school of Bagdat. Here he prosecuted his studies with indefatigable industry, but at the same time with a fanatical spirit scarcely consistent with manly sense and sound judgment. When he was perplexed with any logical question, or could not discover a proper middle term for a syllogism, he used to repair to the mosque, and poured out prayers for divine illumination; after which he fancied that the arguments and proofs he had sought were communicated to him in his sleep.

As was usual among the philosophers of Bagdat, Avicenna united with the study of philosophy the practice of medicine; and he soon acquired such a degree of reputation, that the caliph consulted him with respect to his son, in a case which perplexed the physicians of the court. His prescription succeeded, and the success obtained him admission to the court, and access to the library of the prince. From this time he continued to prosecute his studies with diligence, and to practise medicine with great applause. During this tide of prosperity, Avicenna had no small degree of influence in public affairs, and rapidly increased his possessions. An unfortunate circumstance, however, suddenly turned the current of his fortune, and removed him from the court to a prison. The sultan Jasochbagh proposing to send his nephew as his representative into the native country of Avicenna, the young prince obtained the sultan's permission to take Avicenna with him, as his companion and physician. The sultan was, not long afterwards, informed that the young prince, with his brother, was meditating a rebellion. Upon this, he immediately sent secret orders to Avicenna, to take off the leader of the conspiracy by poison. The philosopher had too much fidelity to his master to fulfil the commission, but at the same time, through caution or fear, chose to conceal the order from the young prince. But when Avicenna's master became, by some unknown means, acquainted with the sultan's design against his life, he was so highly offended with Avicenna for his dishonest reserve, in not communicating to him so important a circumstance, that he ordered him to be imprisoned. Avicenna endeavored to justify himself, by pleading that he had concealed the sultan's order, from the hope of preventing those mischiefs which he foresaw must have arisen from the discovery. The prince, however, suffered him to remain in prison from this time to his death, which he is said to have hastened by incontinence. He died in the fifty-eighth year of his age.

BELUS.

There are those who ascribe the invention of Astronomy to Belus. Pliny says, there is yet standing the temple of Jupiter Belus; he was the inventor of the science of the stars. Alian gives the following relation: Xerxes, son of Darius, waking up the monument of ancient Belus, found an urn of glass, in which his dead body lay in oil; but the urn was not full; it wanted a hand-breadth of the top. Next the urn there was a little pillow, on which it was written that whosoever should open the sepulchre, and did not fill up the urn, should have ill fortune; which Xerxes reading, grew afraid, and commanded that they should pour oil into it with all speed; notwithstanding it was not filled. Then he commanded to pour into it a second time; but neither did it increase at all thereby. So that at last, failing of success, he gave over, and, shutting up the monument, departed very sad. Nor did the event foretold by the pillow deceive him; for he led an army of fifty myriads against Greece, where he received a great defeat, and returning home, died miserably, being murdered by his own son, in the night-time, abed. To this Belus, Semiramis, his daughter, erected a temple in the middle of Babylon, which was exceedingly high; and by the help thereof the Chaldeans, who addicted themselves to contemplation of the stars, did exactly observe their rising and setting.

BIAS.

Bias, who stands at the head of the seven wise men, was a citizen of Priene. Some say that he was the most wealthy man in the city, but others that he was only a settler. He ransomed some Messenian maidens, who had been taken prisoners, educated them as his own daughters, gave them dowries, and then sent them back to their father in Messina. When the tripod was found which bore the inscription, "For the wise," Satyrus says that the damsels (but others say it was their father) came into the assembly, and said that Bias was the wise man, recounting what he had done to them; and so the tripod was sent to him. But Bias, when he saw it, said that it was Apollo who was "the Wise," and consequently could not receive the tripod.

But others say that he consecrated it at Thebes to Hercules, because he himself was a descendant of the Thebans, who had sent a colony to Priene, as Phanodicus relates. It is said also than when Alyattes was besieging Priene, Bias fattened up two mules, and drove them into his camp; and that the king, seeing the condition that the mules were in, was astonished at their being able to spare food to keep the brute beasts so well, and so he desired to make peace with them, and sent an ambassador to them. On this Bias, having made some heaps of sand, and put corn on the top, showed them to the convoy; and Ályattes, hearing from him what he had seen, made peace with the people of Priene; and then, when he sent to Bias, desiring him to come quickly to him, "Tell Alyattes, from me," he replied, "to eat onions;"—which is the same as if he had said, "go and weep."

It is said that he was very energetic and eloquent when pleading causes; but that he always reserved his talents for the right side. In reference to which Demodicus of Alerius uttered the following enigmatical saying—"If you are a judge, give a Prienian decision." And Hipponax says, "More excellent in his decisions than Bias of Priene." Now he died in this manner:—

Having pleaded a cause for some one when he was exceedingly old, after he had finished speaking, he leaned back with his head on the bosom of his daughter's son; and after the advocate on the opposite side had spoken, and the judges had given their decision in favor of Bias's client, when the court broke up he was found dead on his grandson's bosom. And the city buried him in the greatest magnificence, and put over him this inscription—

Beneath this stone lies Bias, who was born
In the illustrious Prienian land,
The glory of the whole Ionian race.

And we ourselves have also written an epigram on him—

Here Bias lies, whom, when the hoary snow
Had crowned his aged temples, Mercury
Unpityingly led to Pluto's darken'd realms.
He pleaded his friend's cause, and then reclin'd
In his child's arms, repos'd in lasting sleep.

He also wrote about two thousand verses on Ionia, to show in what matter a man might best arrive at happiness; and of all his poetical sayings these have the greatest reputation:—

Seek to please all the citizens, even though
Your house may be in an ungracious city.
For such a course will favor win from all:
But haughty manners oft produce destruction

And this one too:—

Great strength of body is the gift of nature;
But to be able to advise whate'er
Is most expedient for one's country's good,
Is the peculiar work of sense and wisdom.

Another is:–

Great riches come to many men by chance.

He used also to say that that man was unfortunate who could not support misfortune; and that it is a disease of the mind to desire what was impossible, and to have no regard for the misfortunes of others. Being asked what was difficult, he said—"To bear a change of fortune for the worse with magnamity." Once he was on a voyage with some impious men, and the vessel was overtaken by a storm; so they began to invoke the assistance of the Gods; on which he said, "Hold your tongues, lest they should find out that you are in this ship." When he was asked by an impious man what piety was, he made no reply; and when his questioner demanded the reason of his silence, he said, "I am silent because you are putting questions about things with which you have no concern." Being asked what was pleasant to men, he replied, "Hope." It was a saying of his that it was more agreeable to decide between enemies than between friends; for that of friends, one was sure to become an enemy to him; but that of enemies, one was sure to become a friend. When the question was put to him, what a man derived pleasure in while he was doing, he said, "While acquiring gain." He used to say, too, that men ought to calculate life both as if they were fated to live a long and short time; and that they ought to love one another as if at a future time they would come to hate one another; for that most men were wicked. He used also to give the following pieces of advice:—Choose the course which you adopt with deliberation; but when you have adopted it, then persevere in it with firmness. Do not speak fast, for that shows folly. Love prudence. Speak of the Gods as they are. Do not praise an undeserving man because of his riches. Accept of things having procured them by persuasion, and not by force. Whatever good fortune befalls you, attribute it to the Gods. Cherish wisdom as a means of travelling from youth to old age, for it is more lasting than any other possession. The greatest infelicity is not to be able to endure misfortunes patiently. Great minds alone can bear a sudden reverse of fortune. The most pleasant state is to be always gaining. Be not unmindful of the miseries of others. If you are handsome, do handsome things. If you are deformed, supply the defects of nature by your virtues. Many men are dishonest, therefore love your friend with caution, for he may hereafter become your enemy.

During an invasion, whilst every one about him was collecting his most valuable effects, and preparing for flight, one of his friends observing with surprise that he took no pains to preserve anything, asked him the reason; Bias replied, "I carry all my treasures with me."

BION.

Bion was a native of the country around Borysthenes; but as to who his parents were, and to what circumstances it was owing that he applied himself to the study of philosophy, we know no more than what he himself told Antigonus. For when Antigonus asked him;—

> What art thou, say! from whence, from whom you came;
> Who are your parents? tell thy race, thy name;

he, knowing that he had been misrepresented to the king, said to him, "My father was a freedman, who used to wipe his mouth with his sleeve," (by which he meant that he used to sell salt fish.) "As to his race, he was a native of the district of the Borysthenes; having no countenance, but only a brand in his face, a token of the bitter cruelty of his master. My mother was such a woman as a man of that condition might marry, taken out of a brothel. Then, my father being in arrears to the tax-gatherers, was sold with all his family, and with me among them; and as I was young and good looking, a certain orator purchased me, and when he died he left me everything. And I, having burnt all his books, and torn up all his papers, came to Athens, and applied myself to the study of philosophy:—

> Such was my father, and from him I came,
> The honored author of my birth and name.

This is all that I can tell you of myself; so that Persæus and Philonides may give up telling these stories about me, and you may judge of me on my own merits."

Bion was truly a man of great versatility, and a very subtle philosopher, and a man who gave all who chose great opportunities of practising philosophy. In some respects he was of a gentle disposition, and very much inclined to indulge in vanity.

He left behind him many memorials of himself in the way of writings, and also many apoththegms full of useful sentiments. As, for instance, once when he was reproved for having failed to charm a young man, he replied, "You cannot possibly draw up cheese with a hook before it has got hard." On another occasion, he was asked who was the most miserable of men, and replied, "He who has set his heart on the greatest prosperity." When he was asked whether it was advisable to marry, (for this answer also is attributed to him,) he replied, "If you marry an ugly woman you will have a punishment (*poine*), and if a handsome woman you will have one that is common" (*koine*). He called old age "a port to shelter one from misfortune;" and accordingly, he said that every one fled to it. He said that "glory was the mother of years;" that "beauty was a good which concerned others rather than one's self;" that "riches were the sinews of business." To a man who had squandered his estate he said, "The earth swallowed up Amphiaraus, but you have swallowed up the earth." Another saying of his was, that it was a great evil not to be able to bear evil. And he condemned those who burnt the dead as though they felt nothing, and then mocked them as though they did feel. And he was always saying that it was better to put one's own beauty at the disposal of another, than to covet the beauty of others; for that one whc did so was injuring both his body and his soul. And he used to blame Socrates, saying, that if he derived no advantage from Alcibiades he was foolish, and if he never derived any advantage from him, he then deserved no credit. He used to say that the way to the shades below was easy, and accordingly, that people went there with their eyes shut. He used to blame Alcibiades, saying, that while he was a boy he seduced husbands from their wives, and when he had become a young man he seduced the wives from their husbands. While most of the Athenians at Rhodes practised rhetoric, he himself used to give lectures on philosophical subjects; and to one who blamed him for this he said, "I have bought wheat, and I sell barley."

It was a saying of his that the inhabitants of the shades below would be more punished if they carried water in buckets that were whole, than in such as were bored. To a chattering fellow, who was soliciting him for aid, he said, "I will do what is sufficient for you, if you will send deputies to me, and forbear to come yourself." Once when he was at sea, in the company of some wicked men, he fell into the hands of pirates; and when the rest said, "We are undone, if we are known." "But I," said he, "am undone if we are not known." He used to say that self-conceit was the enemy of progress. Of a rich man who was mean and niggardly, he said, "That man does not possess his estate, but his estate possesses him." He used to say that stingy men took care of their property as if it were their own, but derived no advantage from it, as if it belonged to other people. Another of his sayings was, that young men ought to display courage, but that old men ought to be distinguished for prudence.

And that prudence was as much superior to the other virtues as sight was to the other senses. And that it was not right to speak of old age, at which every one is desirous to arrive. To an envious man who was looking gloomy, he said, "I know not whether it is because some misfortune has happened to you, or some good fortune to some one else." One thing that he used to say was, that a mean extraction was a bad companion to freedom of speech. For:—

> It does enslave a man, however bold
> His speech may be.

And another was, that "we ought to keep our friends, whatever sort of people they may be, so that we may not seem to have been intimate with wicked men, or to have abandoned good men."

Very early in his career he abandoned the school of the Academy, and at the same time became a disciple of Crates. Then he passed over to the sect of the Cynics, taking their coarse cloak and wallet. For what else could ever have changed his nature into one of such apathy? After that, he adopted the Theodorean principles, having become a disciple of Theodorus the Atheist, who was used to employ every kind of reasoning in support of his system of philosophy. After leaving him he became a pupil of Theophrastus, the Peripatetic.

He was very fond of theatrical entertainments, and very skilful in distracting his hearers by exciting a laugh, giving things disparaging names. And because he used to avail himself of every species of reasoning, they relate that Eretosthenes said that Bion was the first person who had clothed philosophy in a flowery robe. He was also very ingenious in parodying passages, and adapting them to circumstances as they arose. And he jested on every part of music and geometry. He was a man of very expensive habits, and on that account he used to go from city to city, and at times he would contrive the most amazing devices. Accordingly, in Rhodes, he persuaded the sailors to put on the habiliments of philosophical students, and follow him about; and then he made himself conspicuous by entering the gymnasium with his train of followers. He was accustomed also to adopt young men as his sons, in order to derive assistance from them in his pleasures, and to be protected by their affection for him. But he was a very selfish man, and very fond of quoting the saying, "The property of friends is common;" owing to which it is said that no one is spoken of as a disciple of his, though so many men attended his school. And he made some very shameless; accordingly, Betion, one of his intimate acquaintances, is reported to have said once to Menedemus, "So Menedemus constantly spends the evening with Bion, and I see no harm in it." He used also to talk with great impiety to those who conversed with him, having derived his opinions on this subject from Theodorus.

At a later period he became afflicted with disease, as the people of Chalcis said, for he died there. He was persuaded to wear amulets and charms, and to show his repentance for the insults that he had offered to the Gods. But he suffered fearfully for want of proper people to attend him, until Antigonus sent him two servants. And he followed him in a litter, as Pharorinus relates in his Universal History. And the circumstances of his death we have ourselves spoken of in the following lines:—

We hear that Bion the Borysthenite,
Whom the ferocious Scythian land brought forth,
Used to deny that there were Gods at all.
Now, if he'd persevered in this opinion,
One would have said he speaks just as he thinks;
Though certainly his thoughts are quite mistaken.
But when a lengthened sickness overtook him,
And he began to fear lest he should die;
This man who heretofore denied the Gods,
And would not even look upon a temple,

And mocked all those who e'er approached the Gods
With prayer or sacrifice; who ne'er, not even
For his own hearth, and home, and household table,
Regaled the Gods with savory fat and incense,
Who never once said, "I have sinned, but spare me."
Then did this atheist shrink, and give his neck
To an old woman to hang charms upon,
And bound his arms with magic amulets,
With laurel branches blocked his doors and windows,
Ready to do and venture anything
Rather than die. Fool that he was, who thought
To win the Gods to come into existence,
Whenever he might think he wanted them.
So wise too late, when now mere dust and ashes,
He put his hand forth, Hail, great Pluto, Hail!

CALANUS.

Calanus was of the sect of Gymnosophists, called Brachman. The Brachmans were all of one tribe. From the time of their birth they were put under guardians, and, as they grew up, had a succession of instructors. They were in a state of pupilage till thirty-six years of age; after which they were allowed to live more at large, to wear fine linen and gold rings, to live upon the flesh of animals not employed in labor, and to marry as many wives as they pleased. Others submitted, through their whole lives, to stricter discipline, and passed their days upon the banks of the Ganges, with no other food than fruits, herbs, and milk. The Samanæans were a society formed of those who voluntarily devoted themselves to the study of divine wisdom. They gave up all private property, and committed their children to the care of the state, and their wives to the protection of their relations. They were supported at the public expense, and spent their time in contemplation, in conversation on divine subjects, or in acts of religion. A wonderful circumstance is related concerning these philosophers; that frequently, without any apparent reason from ill health or misfortunes, they formed a resolution to quit the world, and, when they had communicated their intention to their friends, immediately, without any expressions of regret on the one side, or of apprehension on the other, threw themselves into a fire which they had themselves prepared for the occasion. There was another sect, called the Hylobeons, who lived entirely in forests, upon leaves and wild fruits, wore no other clothing than the bark of trees, and practised the severest abstinence of every kind.

From this account of the Indian Gymnosophists, it is easy to perceive that they were more distinguished by severity of manners than by the cultivation of science, and that they more resembled modern monks than ancient philosophers.

In a conference which was held with Onesicritus, Calanus, when he saw Alexander's messengers clothed with fine linen garments, and elegantly adorned, laughed at their effeminacy, and requested them, if they wished to hold any conference with the Brachmans, to lay aside their ornaments, and, like them, recline upon the naked rocks. It is also related, that when he found the infirmities of age coming upon him, he devoted himself to voluntary death, and ascending the funeral pile, said, "Happy hour of departure from life, in which, as it happened to Hercules, after the mortal body is burned, the soul shall go forth into light!"

CALVISIUS TAURUS.

Calvisius Taurus flourished under the reign of Antoninus Pius. He is mentioned as a Platonist of some note. Among his pupils was Aulus Gellius, a man of various learning, who has preserved several specimens of his preceptor's method of philosophizing. He examined all sects, but preferred the Platonic, in which he had at least the merit of avoiding the infection of that spirit of confusion, which at this period seized almost the whole body of the philosophers, especially those of the Platonic school. He lived at Athens, and taught, not in the schools, but at his table. A. Gellius, who was frequently one of his guests, and whose *Noctis Atticæ*, "Attic Evenings," are doubtless much indebted to these philosophical entertainments, gives the following account of the manner in which they were conducted: "Taurus, the philosopher, commonly invited a select number of his friends to a frugal supper, consisting of lentils, and a gourd, cut into small pieces upon an earthen dish; and during the repast, philosophical conversation upon various topics was introduced. His constant disciples, whom he called his family, were expected to contribute their share towards the small expense which attended these simple repasts, in which interesting conversation supplied the place of luxurious provision. Every one came furnished with some new subject of inquiry, which he was allowed in his turn to propose, and which, during a limited time, was debated. The subjects of discussion, in these conversations, were not of the more serious and important kind, but such elegant questions as might afford an agreeable exercise of the faculties in the moments of convivial enjoyment; and these Taurus afterwards frequently illustrated more at large with sound erudition."

CATO.

Cato the younger was a Stoic in opinion and character. He is called Cato of Utica from the last memorable scene of his life. From his childhood he discovered in his countenance and language, and even in his sports, an inflexible spirit. He had such a natural gravity of aspect, that his features were scarcely ever relaxed into a smile. He was seldom angry, but when provoked was not without difficulty appeased. In acquiring learning, he was slow of perception, but his memory faithfully retained whatever it received. Being in early life elected to the office of a *flamen* of Apollo, he made choice of Antipater, a Tyrian, of the Stoic sect, as his preceptor in morals and jurisprudence, that in his sacred character he might exhibit an example of the most rigid virtue. His language, both in private and public, was a true image of his mind, free from all affectation of novelty or elegance; plain, concise, and somewhat harsh; enlivened with strokes of genius, which could not be heard without pleasure. He inured himself to endure, without injury, the extremes of heat and cold. To express his contempt of effeminate and luxurious manners, he refused to wear the purple robe which belonged to his rank, and often appeared in public without his tunic, and with his feet uncovered; and this he did, not for the sake of attracting admiration, but to teach his fellow-citizens that a wise man ought to be ashamed of nothing which is not in itself shameful.

In the civil war, Cato carried his virtues with him into military life, and exhibited before his fellow commanders an example of unusual moderation, sobriety, and magnanimity. Whilst he was in Macedonia, in the capacity of military tribune, it happened that his brother Cæpio, whom he had always loved, perished in shipwreck. Cato, upon this occasion, forgot his Stoical principles, and so far yielded to the impulse of nature, as to embrace, with many tears and lamentations, the dead body which had been cast upon the shore, and to bury it with splendid sepulchral honors. So difficult is it, by any artificial discipline of philosophy, to subdue the feelings of nature. During his residence in Greece, Cato having heard of an eminent Stoic, Athenodorus Cordyliones, who had rejected the proffered friendship of several princes, and was now passing his old age in retirement at Pergamus, resolved if possible to make him his friend; and, as he had no hopes of succeeding by message, undertook for this sole purpose a voyage into Asia. Upon the interview, Athenodorus found in Cato a soul so congenial with his own, that he was easily prevailed upon to accompany him into Greece, and, after the term of Cato's military service was expired, to reside with him, as his companion and friend, at Rome. Cato boasted of this acquisition more than of all his military exploits. After his return, he devoted his time either to the society of Athenodorus, and his other philosophical friends, or to the service of his fellow-citizens in the forum.

When Cato had, by diligent study, qualified himself for the duties of magistracy, he accepted of the office of questor. He corrected the abuses of this important trust, which negligence or dishonesty had introduced, and by his upright and steady administration of justice merited the highest applause. In every other capacity he manifested the same inviolable regard to truth and integrity. Whilst he was engaged in the business of the senate, he was indefatigable in the discharge of his senatorial duty; and even when he was among his philosophical friends at his farm in Lucania he never interrupted his attention to the welfare of the state. It was during a recess of this kind that he discovered the danger which threatened the republic from the machinations of Metellus; and, with a truly patriotic spirit, he instantly determined that private enjoyment should give way to public duty. That he might be in a capacity to oppose with effect the designs of Metellus, he offered himself candidate for the office of Tribune of the people; and being chosen, executed the office (notwithstanding the illiberal jests which Cicero, inconsistently enough with his general professions and character, on this occasion cast upon his Stoical virtue) with a degree of probity, candor and independence, which fully established the public opinion of his superior merit.

At a period when the Roman affairs were in the utmost confusion, and powerful factions were repeatedly formed against the state, Cato, withstood the assaults which were made upon liberty by Marcellus, Pompey, Cæsar, and others, with such a firm and resolute adherence to the principles of public virtue, that no apprehension of danger to himself or his family could ever induce him to listen to any proposal which implied a treacherous desertion of his country. Whilst some were supporting the interest of Cæsar, and others that of Pompey, Cato, himself a host, withstood them both, and convinced them that there was another interest still existing—that of the state. When he saw that the necessity of the times required it, in order that, of two impending evils, the least might be chosen, he persuaded the senate to create Pompey sole consul, that, if possible, he might crush the growing power of Cæsar, which threatened destruction to the freedom of the republic. It was with this design alone that, upon Cæsar's approach towards Rome, he declared himself on the side of Pompey, and that he afterwards became a companion of his flight, and at the head of an army supported his cause. The same public spirit afterwards prompted him to endeavor to save his country from the last extremities of civil war by proposing a reconciliation between the contending powers. And when Pompey treated the proposal with neglect, and seemed to distrust the adviser, Cato, still true to the cause of freedom, at the battle of Dyrrachium roused the languid spirit of the soldiers by an animated address; but afterwards when, in the course of the engagement, he saw his countrymen butchering one another, he bitterly lamented the fatal effects of ambition.

After the battle of Pharsalia, which at once cut off the hopes of Pompey, Cato, with a small band of select friends, and fifteen cohorts, of which Pompey had given him the command, still attempted to support the expiring cause of liberty. His determination was to follow Pompey into Egypt, and there share his fate; but when he arrived upon the African coast, he was met by Sextus, Pompey's younger son, who informed him of his father's death. Cato, upon hearing these tidings, marched the small force which was under his command into Libya, to meet Scipio, Pompey's father-in-law, and Varus, to whom Pompey had given the government in Africa, and who were paying their court to Juba. Though strongly importuned, he refused to take the command of the African forces from those officers, to whom it had been legally appointed; but, at the request of Scipio, and of the inhabitants, he took the charge of Utica.

The defeat of Scipio and Juba, in the battle of Thapsus, contracted the remaining strength of the Roman republic within the walls of this small city. Here Cato, as his last effort in the service of his country, convened his little senate to deliberate upon measures for the public good. Their consultations proved ineffectual; and Cato despaired of being longer able to serve his country. He therefore advised his friends to provide for their safety by flight, but, for his own part, resolved not to survive the liberties of Rome. At the close of an evening, in which he had conversed with more than usual spirit on topics of philosophy, he retired with great cheerfulness into his chamber, where, after reading a portion of Plato's *Phædo*, he ordered his sword to be brought. His attendants delayed; and his son and friends importuned him to desist from his purpose. The stern philosopher dismissed them from his apartment, and again took up the book. After a short interval, he executed his purpose by stabbing himself below the breast. By those who have been better instructed, this action will, doubtless, be deemed criminal, and will be imputed to rashness, or to weakness. But it should be remembered that the situation of Cato, in concurrence with his Stoical principles, strongly impelled him to this fatal deed; and that whatever censure he may deserve on this account, he supported, through his whole life, a character of inflexible integrity, and uncorrupted public spirit. Whilst he lived, he held up before his fellow-citizens a pattern of manly virtue; and when he died, he taught the conquerors of the world that the noble mind can never be subdued.

> I see the world subdued,
> All but the mighty soul of Cato.

CARNEADES.

Carneades, one of the most illustrious ornaments of the Academy, was an African, a native of Cyrene. The time of his birth has been a subject of much debate. It is probable that he was born in the third year of the hundred and forty-first Olympiad. He received his first knowledge of the art of reasoning from Diogenes, the Stoic; whence he used sometimes to say, in the course of a debate, "If I have reasoned right, I have gained my point; if not, let Diogenes return me my *minæ*," meaning the price he had paid him for his instruction. Afterwards, becoming a member of the Academy, he attended upon the lectures of Hegesinus, and by assiduous study became an eminent master of the method of disputing which Arcesilaus had introduced. He succeeded Hegesinus in the chair, and restored the declining reputation of the Academy. With Diogenes the Stoic, and Critolaus the Peripatetic, he was sent on an embassy from Athens to Rome, to complain of the severity of a fine inflicted upon the Athenians, under the authority of the Romans, by their neighbors, the Sicyonians, for having laid waste Oropus, a town in Bœotia. The Athenians would undoubtedly, upon this occasion, employ none but those in whose judgment, eloquence, and integrity, they could confide. The three philosophers whom they entrusted with their embassy, whilst they were in Rome, gave the Roman people many specimens of Grecian learning and eloquence, with which till then they had been unacquainted. Carneades excelled in the vehement and rapid, Critolaus in the correct and elegant, and Diogenes in the simple and modest kind of eloquence. Carneades particularly attracted the attention and admiration of his new auditors, by the subtlety of his reasoning, and the fluency of his language. Before Galba, and Cato the Censor, he harangued, with great variety of thought and copiousness of diction, in praise of justice. The next day, to establish his doctrine of the uncertainty of human knowledge, he undertook to refute all his former arguments. Many were captivated by his eloquence; but Cato, apprehensive lest the Roman youth should lose their military character in the pursuit of Grecian learning, persuaded the senate to send back these philosophers, without further delay, to their own schools.

From this incident, of which we shall afterwards have further occasion to take notice, it sufficiently appears that Carneades was an eminent orator and philosopher. He obtained such high reputation in his school, that other philosophers, when they had dismissed their scholars, frequently came to hear him. In application to study he was indefatigable. So intensely did he fix his thoughts upon the subject of his meditations, that even at meals he frequently forgot to take the food which was set before him. He strenuously opposed the Stoic Chrysippus, but was always ready to do justice to his merit. He used to say, that "if there were no Chrysippus, there would be no Carneades;" intimating, that he derived much of his reputation as a disputant from the abilities of his opponent. His voice was remarkably strong, and he had such a habit of vociferation, that the master of the gymnastic exercises, in the public field, desired him not to speak so loud. In return, he requested some measure to regulate his voice; to which the master very judiciously replied, "You have a measure, the number of your hearers." As Carneades grew old, he discovered strong apprehensions of dying, and frequently lamented that the same nature which had composed the human frame could dissolve it. He paid the last debt to nature in the eighty-fifth, or, according to Cicero and Valerius Maximus, in the ninetieth year of his age.

Diogenes Laertius relates of him, that he read all the books of the Stoics with great care, and especially those of Chrysippus; and then he wrote replies to them, but did it at the same time with such modesty, that he used to say, "If Chrysippus had not lived, I should never have existed." It is said that at night he was not aware when lights were brought in; and that once he ordered his servant to light the candles, and when he had brought them in and told him; "Well, then," said he, "read by the light of them."

He was a man of as great industry as ever existed; not, however, very much devoted to the investigation of subjects of natural philosophy, but more fond of the discussion of ethical topics, on which account he used to let his hair and his nails grow, from his entire devotion of all his time to philosophical pursuits.

He appears to have been beset with fears of death, as he was continually saying, "Nature, who has put this frame together, will also dissolve it." And learning that Antipater had died after having taken poison, he felt a desire to imitate the boldness of his departure, and said, "Give me some too." And when they asked "What?" "Some mead," said he. And it is said that an eclipse of the moon happened when he died, the most beautiful of all the stars, next to the sun, indicating (as any one might say) its sympathy with the philosopher. And Apollodorus, in his Chronicles, says that he died in the fourth year of the hundred and sixty-second Olympiad, being eighty-five years old.

I have written on him the following lines in logoædical Archebulian metre:—

Why now, O Muse, do you wish me Carneades to confute?
He was an ignoramus, as he did not understand

Why he should stand in fear of death. So once, when he 'd a cough,
The worst of all diseases that affect the human frame,
He cared not for a remedy; but when the news did reach him,
That brave Antipater had ta'en some poison, and so died,
"Give me," said he, "some stuff to drink." "Some what?" "Some luscious mead."
Moreover, he 'd this saying at all times upon his lips:
"Nature did make me, and she does together keep me still;
But soon the time will come when she will pull me all to pieces."
But still at last he yielded up the ghost; though long ago
He might have died, and so escaped the evils that befell him.

CHILO.

Chilo was a Lacedæmonian, the son of Damagetus. He composed verses in elegiac metre to the number of two hundred; and it was a saying of his that a foresight of future events, such as could be arrived at by consideration, was the virtue of a man. He also said once to his brother, who was indignant at not being an ephor, while he himself was one: "The reason is because I know how to bear injustice; but you do not." And he was made ephor in the fifty-fifth Olympiad; but Pamphila says that it was in the fifty-sixth. And he was made first ephor in the year of the archonship of Euthydemus, as we are told by Sosicrates.* Chilo was also the first person who introduced the custom of joining the ephors to the kings as their counsellors; though Satyrus attributes this institution to Lycurgus. He, as Herodotus says, when Hippocrates was sacrificing at Olympia, and the cauldrons began to boil of their own accord, advised him either to marry, or, if he were married already, to discard his wife, and disown his children.

They tell a story, also, of his having asked Æsop what Jupiter was doing, and that Æsop replied, "He is lowering

* An Ephor was a magistrate appointed by the people, and intended as a check upon the regal, or, as some say, upon the senatorial power.

what is high, and exalting what is low." Being asked in what educated men differed from those who were illiterate, he said, "In good hopes." Having had the question put to him, What was difficult, he said, "To be silent about secrets; to make good use of one's leisure, and to be able to submit to injustice." And besides these three things he added further, "To rule one's tongue, especially at a banquet, and not to speak ill of one's neighbors; for if one does so one is sure to to hear what one will not like." He advised, moreover, "To threaten no one; for that is a womanly trick. To be more prompt to go to one's friends in adversity than in prosperity. To make but a moderate display at one's marriage. Not to speak evil of the dead. To honor old age. To keep a watch upon one's self. To prefer punishment to disgraceful gain; for the one is painful but once, but the other for one's whole life. Not to laugh at a person in misfortune. If one is strong to be also merciful, so that one's neighbors may respect one rather than fear one. To learn how to regulate one's own house well. Not to let one's tongue outrun one's sense. To restrain anger. Not to dislike divination. Not to desire what is impossible. Not to make too much haste on one's road. When speaking, not to gesticulate with the hand; for that is like a madman. To obey the laws. To love quiet."

And of all his songs this one was the most approved:—

Gold is best tested by a whetstone hard,
Which gives a certain proof of purity;
And gold itself acts as the test of men,
By which we know the temper of their minds.

They say, too, that when he was old he said, that he was not conscious of having ever done an unjust action in his life; but that he doubted about one thing. For that once when judging in a friend's cause he had voted himself in accordance with the law, but had persuaded a friend to vote for his acquittal, in order that so he might maintain the law, and yet save his friend.

But he was most especially celebrated among the Greeks for having delivered an early opinion about Cythera an island belonging to Laconia. For having become acquainted with its nature, he said, "I wish it had never existed, or that, as it does exist, it were sunk at the bottom of the sea." And his foresight was proved afterwards. For when Demaratus was banished by the Lacedæmonians, he advised Xerxes to keep his ships at that island; and Greece would have been subdued, if Xerxes had taken the advice. And afterwards Nicias, having reduced the island at the time of the Peloponnesian war, placed in it a garrison of Athenians, and did a great deal of harm to the Lacedæmonians.

He was very brief in his speech. On which account Aristagoras, the Milesian, calls such conciseness, the Chilonean fashion; and says that it was adopted by Branchus, who built the temple among the Branchidæ. Chilo was an old man, about the fifty-second Olympiad, when Æsop, the fable writer, flourished. And he died, as Hermippus says, at Pisa, after embracing his son, who had gained the victory in boxing at the Olympic games. The cause of his death was excess of joy, and weakness caused by extreme old age. All the spectators who were present at the games attended his funeral, paying him the highest honors. And we have written the following epigram on him:—

I thank you brighest Pollux, that the son
Of Chilo wears the wreath of victory;
Nor need we grieve if at the glorious sight
His father died. May such my last end be!

And the following inscription is engraved on his statue:—

The warlike Sparta called this Chilo son,
The wisest man of all the seven sages.

One of his sayings was, "Suretyship, and then destruction." He was one of the seven wise men of Greece, and that important saying is ascribed to him—KNOW THYSELF.

CHRYSIPPUS.

CHRYSIPPUS was the son of Apollonius, a native of either Soli or Tarsus, and a pupil of Cleanthes, and while he was still living he abandoned him, and became a very eminent philosopher. He was a man of great natural ability, and of great acuteness in every way, so that on many points he dissented from Zeno, and also from Cleanthes, to whom he often used to say that he only wanted to be instructed in the dogmas of the school, and that he would discover the demonstrations for himself. But whenever he opposed him with any vehemence, he always repented, so that he used frequently to say:—

> In most respects I am a happy man,
> Excepting where Cleanthes is concerned;
> For in that matter I am far from fortunate.

And he had such a high reputation as a dialectician, that most people thought that if there were such a science as dialectics among the Gods, it would be in no respect different from that of Chrysippus. But though he was so eminently able in matter, he was not perfect in style.

He was industrious beyond all other men, as is plain from his writings; for he wrote more than seven hundred and five books. And he often wrote several books on the same subject, wishing to put down everything that occurred to him, and constantly correcting his previous assertions, and using a great abundance of testimonies. So that, as in one of his writings he had quoted very nearly the whole of the Medea of Euripides, and some one had his book in his hands; this latter, when he was asked what he had got there, made answer, "The Medea of Chrysippus." And Apollodorus, the Athenian, in his Collection of Dogmas, wishing to assert that what Epicurus had written out of his own head, and without any quotations to support his arguments, was a great deal more than all the books of Chrysippus, speaks thus (I give his exact words): "For if any one were to take away from the books of Chrysippus all the passages which he quotes from other authors, his paper would be left empty."

These are the words of Apollodorus; but the old woman who lived with him, as Dioles reports, used to say that he wrote five hundred lines every day. And Hecaton says, that he first applied himself to philosophy when his patrimony had been confiscated, and seized for the royal treasury.

He was slight in person, as is plain from his statue which is in the Ceramicus, which is nearly hidden by the equestrian statue near it; in reference to which circumstance, Carneades called him Cryxippus.* He was once reproached by some one for not attending the lectures of Ariston, who was drawing a great crowd after him at the time; and he replied, "If I had attended to the multitude I should not have been a philosopher." And once, when he saw a dialectician pressing hard on Cleanthes, and proposing sophistical fallacies to him, he said, "Cease to drag that old man from more important business, and propose those questions to us who are young." At another time, when some one wishing to ask him something privately, was addressing him quietly, but when he saw a multitude approaching began to speak more energetically, he said to him:—

> Alas, my brother! now your eye is troubled;
> You were quite sane just now; and yet how quickly
> Have you succumbed to frenzy.†

And at drinking parties he used to behave quietly, moving his legs about however, so that a female slave once said, "It is only the legs of Chrysippus that are drunk." And he had so high an opinion of himself, that once, when a man asked him, "To whom shall I entrust my son?" he said, "To me, for if

* From *krupto*, to hide, and *hippos*, a horse.

† These lines are from the Erestes of Euripides.

I thought that there was any one better than myself, I would have gone to him to teach me philosophy." In reference to which anecdote they report that people used to say of him:—

> He has indeed a clear and subtle head,
> The rest are forms of empty æther made.*

And also:—

> For if Chrysippus had not lived and taught,
> The Stoic school would surely have been nought.

But at last, when Arcesilaus and Lacydes, as Sotion records in his eighth book, came to the Academy, he joined them in the study of philosophy; from which circumstance he got the habit of arguing for and against a custom, and discussed magnitudes and quantities, following the system of the Academies.

Hermippus relates, that one day, when he was teaching in the Odeum, he was invited to a sacrifice by his pupils; and, that drinking some sweet unmixed wine, he was seized with giddiness, and departed this life five days afterwards, when he had lived seventy-three years; dying in the hundred and forty-third Olympiad, as Apollodorus says in his Chronicles. And we have written an epigram on him:—

> Chrysippus drank with open mouth some wine;
> Then became giddy, and so quickly died.
> Too little reck'd he of the Porch's weal,
> Or of his country's, or of his own dear life:
> And so descended to the realms of Hell.

But some people say that he died of a fit of immoderate laughter. For that seeing his ass eating figs, he told his old woman to give the ass some unmixed wine to drink afterwards, and then laughed so violently that he died.

He appears to have been a man of exceeding arrogance. Accordingly, though he wrote such numbers of books, he never dedicated one of them to any sovereign. And when

* This is a quotation from Homer.

Ptolemy wrote to Cleanthes, begging him either to come to him himself, or to send him some one, Sphærus went to him, but Chrysippus slighted the invitation. However, he sent for the sons of his sister, Aristocrea and Philocrates, and educated them; and he was the first person who ventured to hold a school in the open air in the Lyceum.

There was also another Chrysippus, a native of Cnidos, a physician, from whom Erasistratus testifies that he received great benefit. And another also, who was a son of his, and the physician of Ptolemy; who, having had a false accusation brought against him, was apprehended and punished by being scourged. There was also a fourth, who was a pupil of Erasistratus; and a fifth was an author of a work called Georgics.

Now this philosopher used to delight in proposing questions of this sort: The person who reveals the mysteries to the uninitiated commits a sin; the hierophant reveals them to the uninitiated; therefore the hierophant commits sin? Another was, that which is not in the city, is also not in the house; but a well is not in the city, therefore there is not a well in the house. Another was, there is a certain head; that head you have not got; there is then a head that you have not got; therefore you have not got a head. Again, if a man is in Megara, he is not in Athens; but there is a man in Megara, therefore there is not a man in Athens. Again, if you say anything, what you say comes out of your mouth; but you say "a waggon;" therefore a waggon comes out of your mouth. Another was, if you have not lost a thing, you have it; but you have not lost horns; therefore you have horns. Though some attribute this sophism to Eubulides.

There are people who run Chrysippus down as having written a great deal that is very shameful and indecent. And in his treatise on Polity, he allows people to marry their mothers, or their daughters, or their sons. And he repeats this doctrine in his treatise on those things which are not desirable for their own sake, in the very opening of it. And in the third book of his treatise on Justice, he devotes a thousand lines to bidding people to devour even the dead.

In the second book of his treatise on Life and Means of Support, where he is warning us to consider beforehand, how the wise man ought to provide himself with means, he says, "And yet why need he provide himself with means? for if it is for the sake of living, living at all is a matter of indifference; if it is for the sake of pleasure, that is a matter of indifference too; if it is for the sake of virtue, that is of itself sufficient for happiness. But the methods of providing one's self with means are ridiculous; for instance, some derive them from a king; and then it will be necessary to humor him. Some from friendship; and then friendship will become a thing to be bought with a price. Some from wisdom; and then wisdom will become mercenary, and these are the accusations which he brings."

The friends of the Stoic school complained that in the warmth of dispute, whilst he was attempting to load his adversary with the reproach of obscurity and absurdity, his own ingenuity often failed him, and he adopted such unusual and illogical modes of reasoning as gave his opponents great advantage against him. It was also a common practice with Chrysippus, at different times, to take the opposite sides of the same question, and thus furnish his antagonists with weapons which might easily be turned, as occasions offered, against himself. Carneades, who was one of his most able and skilful adversaries, frequently availed himself of this circumstance, and refuted Chrysippus by convicting him of inconsistency. Plutarch, in his piece, "On Stoic Contradictions," has collected many examples of inconsistent opinions, most of which are ascribed to Chrysippus.

CICERO.

Marcus Tullius Cicero was born at Arpinum, in the 647th year of the city. During his childhood he distinguished himself in literary contests with his companions, and studied under several masters, among whom he particularly mentions Plotius, a Greek preceptor, Phædras, an Epicurean philosopher, and Archias, the poet. He made several juvenile attempts in poetry; but, if we may judge from the few fragments of his verses which remain, with no great degree of success. After he had finished his puerile studies, he applied his mature judgment to philosophy under Philo of Larissa; a philosopher who was held in the highest esteem among the Romans, both for his learning and manners. From the same preceptor he also received instruction in rhetoric; for, from the first, Cicero made philosophy subservient to eloquence.

In the eighteenth year of his age Cicero studied law under the direction of Mucius Scævola, an eminent augur, to who he was introduced by his father, when he put on the manly dress, with this advice, never to lose an opportunity of conversing with that wise and excellent man. After a short interval, in which he engaged in military expeditions, first under Sylla, then under Pompey, he returned with great impatience to his studies. At this time he put himself under the constant tuition of Diodotus, a Stoic, chiefly for the sake of exercising himself in dialectics, which the Stoics considered as a restricted kind of eloquence, but not without an assiduous attention to many other branches of study, in which this learned philosopher was well qualified to instruct him. About the age of twenty years he translated into the Latin tongue Xenophon's *Œconomics*, and several books of Plato. A specimen of his version of the Timæus of Plato is preserved in his works.

Having thus prepared himself for his profession by indefatigable study, Cicero made his first appearance in public at twenty-six years of age, and pleaded in defence of Roscius against the accusation of Sylla. Soon afterwards, under the plea of recruiting his strength, which he had impaired by the violence of his oratorical exertions, but perhaps chiefly through fear of Sylla, whom he had opposed, he withdrew to Athens. Here he attended on Antiochus the Ascalonite; but not approving his doctrine, which differed from that of the Middle Academy, he became a hearer of Posidonius the Rhodian. By frequenting the schools of these and other preceptors, he acquired such a love of philosophy, that after his return to Rome, amidst the business of the forum and the senate, he always found leisure for the speculations of the schools. Upon his second appearance in public, he met with some discouragement from a prevalent opinion that he was better qualified for the study of philosophy than for the business of active life. But his superior powers of eloquence soon subdued every prejudice against him, and raised him to the highest distinction among his fellow-citizens. In the successive offices of questor, edile, and pretor, he acquitted himself with great reputation. In the consulate he obtained immortal honor by his bold and successful opposition to the machinations of Catiline and his party, and received the glorious title of Father of his Country.

The popularity which Cicero had acquired during his consulship exposed him to the envy of his rivals. Soon afterwards, his unsuccessful attempt to bring Clodius to public justice brought upon him the resentment of that daring and seditious profligate; and, notwithstanding all the efforts of the senate to protect him, the affair terminated in his banishment from Rome. Leaving Italy, he passed over into Greece, and visited his friend Plancius at Thessalonica, who afforded him a hospitable asylum. All good men lamented his disgrace, and many Grecian cities vied with each other in offering him tokens of respect. But nothing could alleviate the dejection which he suffered, whilst he lay under a sentence of banishment from the country which had been the seat of all his former honors. He remained inconsolable, till, after an interval of sixteen months, the Clodian party was suppressed by Pompey, and, by the unanimous voice of the senate and people, he was recalled.

In Cicero's subsequent questorship in Cilicia his conduct was highly meritorious; for he exercised his authority with exemplary mildness and integrity, and, in the midst of war, cultivated the arts of peace. On his return, he called at Rhodes, and made a short stay at Athens, where he had the satisfaction of revisiting the places in which his youthful feet had wandered in search of wisdom, and of conversing with many of his former preceptors and friends.

When the flames of civil dissension between Pompey and Cæsar began to burst forth, Cicero used his utmost influence with each party to bring them to terms of accommodation. Finding every attempt of this kind unsuccessful, he long remained in anxious deliberation, whether he should follow Pompey in a glorious and honorable, but ruined cause; or should consult his own safety, and that of his friends, by following the rising fortunes of Cæsar. Had the latter motive preponderated, he would have listened to the counsel of Cæsar, who advised him, if on account of his advancing years he were averse to military life, to retire into some remote part of Greece, and pass the remainder of his days in tranquillity. But he could not persuade himself to desert the ancient constitution of his country, which he had hitherto honestly defended, and therefore determined to join the party of Pompey. Afterwards, however, when he found that Pompey slighted his friendship, he repented of his resolution; and, after the memorable battle of Pharsalia, instead of accepting the charge of the armament, which lay at Dyrrachium, as Cato advised, he met Cæsar on his return from Asia, and accepted his friendship.

From this time Cicero, no longer able to serve his country

in the manner he wished, retired from public affairs, resolving to devote himself wholly to the study of philosophy. He employed the unwelcome leisure, which the ruin of the republic afforded him, in reading or writing; and he found more satisfaction in conversing with the dead in his valuable library at Tusculum, than in visiting Rome to pay homage to Cæsar. His tranquillity was, however, soon interrupted by domestic vexations and afflictions. From causes which are not fully explained, he divorced his wife Terentia; and his daughter Tullia, who was married to Lentulus, died in child-bed.

Soon after the death of Cæsar, although it does not appear that Cicero had any concern in the conspiracy, he fell a sacrifice to the resentment of Antony, who could not forget the severe Philippics which the orator had delivered against him. When the triumvirate was formed, and it was reciprocally agreed that some of the enemies of each party should be given up, Antony demanded the head of Cicero. Accordingly, after much contention, and on the part of Octavius a delay of three days, Cicero was registered among the hundred and thirty senators who were doomed to destruction by this sanguinary proscription. Apprized by his friends of the danger, he fled from place to place for safety; always thinking, as was natural in such a situation, any other place more secure than the present. His last retreat was to a small farm which he had at Caieta. The house was surrounded by the appointed executioners of the bloody commission. After an unsuccessful attempt of his attendants to save him by conveying him away on a litter towards the sea, Popilius Lænas, a military tribune, in whose behalf Cicero had formerly pleaded when he was accused of parricide, came up to the litter, and struck off his head, while some of the soldiers, who were standing by, cut off his hands. These mangled remains of this great man were conveyed to Antony, who, in triumphant revenge, placed them upon the *rostra* of that pulpit from which the orations against him had been delivered; not, however, without exciting much indignation in the populace, who bitterly lamented the tragical end of this father of his country. His death happened in the 710th* year of the city, and in the sixty-fourth year of his age.

From the whole history of the life of Cicero it appears that, though exceedingly ambitious of glory, he wanted strength of mind sufficient to sustain him in its pursuit. Perpetually fluctuating between hope and fear, he was unable to support with equanimity the convulsions of a disordered state and the commotions of a civil war; and therefore was always attempting to reconcile the contending parties, when he ought to have been maintaining, by vigorous measures, the cause which he approved. He was, in his natural temper, so averse to contention, that his spirits were depressed more than became a wise man, by private injuries and domestic vexations. On many public occasions he discovered an surprising degree of timidity. When under the immediate apprehension of danger from popular tumult, he undertook the defence of Milo, his panic was so great that he was seized with an universal tremor, and was scarcely able to speak; so that his client, notwithstanding his innocence, was sentenced to exile. His chief delight was in the society and conversation of learned men; and many elegant specimens remain of his ability in relating, or framing philosophical conferences. But in his private intercourse with his friends, as well as in the forum and the senate, he discovered a degree of vanity scarcely to be reconciled with true greatness of mind. From these circumstances, compared with the general character of his writings, it seems reasonable to conclude that Cicero's chief execellences were fertility of imagination and readiness of invention; and that his talents were better adapted to the splendid offices of eloquence, than to the accurate and profound investigations of philosophy.

* B. C. 43.

CLEANTHES.

CLEANTHES was a native of Assos, and the son of Phanias. He was originally a boxer. And he came to Athens, having but four drachmas, as some people say, and attaching himself to Zeno, he devoted himself to Philosophy in a most noble manner; and he adhered to the same doctrines as his master.

He was especially eminent for his industry, so that as he was a very poor man, he was forced to undertake mercenary employments, and he used to draw water in the gardens by night, and by day he used to exercise himself in philosophical discussions; on which account he was called Phreantles.* They also say that he was on one occasion brought before a court of justice, to be compelled to give an account what his sources of income were from which he maintained himself in such good condition; and that then he was acquitted, having produced as his witness the gardener in whose garden he drew the water; and a woman who was a mealseller, in whose establishment he used to prepare the meal. And the judges of the Areopagus admired him, and voted that ten minæ should be given to him; but Zeno forbade him to accept them.

They also say that Antigonus presented him three thousand drachmas. And once, when he was conducting some young men to some spectacle, it happened that the wind blew away his cloak, and it was seen then that he had nothing on under it; on which he was greatly applauded by the Athenians. And he was greatly admired by them on account of this circumstance.

They also say that Antigonus, who was a pupil of his, once asked him why he drew water; and that he made answer, "Do I do nothing beyond drawing water? Do I not also dig, and do I not water the land, and do all sorts of things for the sake of philosophy?" For Zeno used to accustom him to

* That is a well-drawer, from *phrear* a well, and *antleo* to draw water.

this, and used to require him to bring him an obol by way of tribute. And once he brought one of the pieces of money which he had collected in this way, into the middle of a company of his acquaintances, and said, "Cleanthes could maintain even another Cleanthes if he were to choose; but others who have plenty of means to support themselves, seek for necessaries from others; although they only study philosophy in a very lazy manner." And, in reference to these habits of his, Cleanthes was called a second Heracles.

He was then very industrious; but he was not well endowed by nature, and was very slow in his intellect. On which account Timon says of him:—

> What stately ram thus measures o'er the ground,
> And master of the flock surveys them round?
> What citizen of Assos, dull and cold,
> Fond of long words, a mouth-piece, but not bold.

And when he was ridiculed by his few pupils, he used to bear it patiently.

He did not even object to the name when he was called an ass; but only said that he was the only animal able to bear the burdens which Zeno put upon him. And once, when he was reproached as a coward, he said, "That is the reason why I make but few mistakes." He used to say, in justification of his preference of his own way of life to that of the rich, "That while they were playing at ball, he was earning money by digging hard and barren ground." And he very often used to blame himself. And once, Ariston heard him doing so, and said, "Who is it that you are reproaching?" and he replied, "An old man who has gray hair, but no brains."

When some one once said to him, that Arcesilaus did not do what he ought, "Desist," he replied, "and do not blame him; for if he destroys duty as far his words go, at all events he establishes it by his actions." Arcesilaus once said to him, "I never listen to flatterers." "Yes," rejoined Cleanthes, "I flatter you, when I say that though you say one thing, you do another." When some one once asked him what lesson he ought to inculcate on his son, he replied, "The warning of Electra:"—

Silence, silence, gently step.

When a Lacedæmonian once said in his hearing, that labor was a good thing, he was delighted, and addressed him:—

Oh, early worth, a soul so wise and young
Proclaims you from the sage Lycurgus sprung.

Once when he was conversing with a youth, he asked him if he felt; and as he said that he did, "Why is it then," said Cleanthes, "that I do not feel that you feel?"

When Sositheus, the poet, said in the theatre where he was present:—

Men whom the folly of Cleanthes urges;

He continued in the same attitude; at which the hearers were surprised, and applauded him, but drove Sositheus away. And when he expressed his sorrow for having abused him in this manner, he answered him gently, saying, "It would be a preposterous thing for Bacchus and Hercules to bear being ridiculed by the poets without any expression of anger, and for me to be indignant at any chance attack." He used also to say, "That the Peripatetics were in the same condition as lyres, which though they utter sweet notes, do not hear themselves." And it is said, that when he asserted that, on the principles of Zeno, one could judge of a man's character by his looks, some witty young men brought him a profligate fellow, having a hardy look from continual exercise in the fields, and requested him to tell them his moral character; and he, having hesitated a little, bade the man depart; and, as he departed, he sneezed, "I have the fellow now," said Cleanthes, "he is a debauchee."

He said once to a man who was conversing with him by

himself, "You are not talking to a bad man." And when some one reproached him with his old age, he rejoined, "I too wish to depart, but when I perceive myself to be in good health in every respect, and to be able to recite and read, I am content to remain." They say, too, that he used to write down all that he heard from Zeno on oyster shells, and on the shoulder-blades of oxen, from want of money to buy paper with.

He died in the following manner: His gums swelled very much; and, at the command of his physicians, he abstained from food for two days. And he got so well that his physicians allowed him to return to all his former habits; but he refused, and saying that he had now already gone part of the way, he abstained from food for the future, and so died; being, as some report, eighty years old, and having been a pupil of Zeno nineteen years. We have written a playful epigram on him also, which runs thus:—

I praise Cleanthes, but praise Pluto more;
Who could not bear to see him grown so old,
So gave him rest at last among the dead,
Who'd draw such loads of water while alive.

CLEOBULUS.

Cleobulus was a native of Lindus, and the son of Evagoras. But according to Duris he was a Carian; others again trace his family back to Hercules. He is reported to have been eminent for personal strength and beauty, and to have studied philosophy in Egypt. He had a daughter named Cleobulina, who used to compose enigmas in hexameter verse. They say also that he restored the temple of Minerva, which had been built by Danaus.

Cleobulus composed songs and obscure sayings in verse, to

the number of three thousand lines, and some say that it was he who composed the epigram on Midas:—

I am a brazen maiden lying here
Upon the tomb of Midas. And as long
As water flows, as trees are green with leaves,
As the sun shines, and eke the silver moon;
As long as rivers flow, and billows roar,
So long will I upon this much-wept tomb,
Tell passers by, "Midas lies buried here."

And as an evidence of this epigram being by him, they quote a song of Simonides, which runs thus:—

What men possessed of sense
Would ever praise the Lindian Cleobulus?
Who could compare a statue made by man
To overflowing streams,
To blushing flowers of spring,
To the sun's rays, to beams o' the golden morn,
And to the ceaseless waves of mighty ocean?
All things are trifling when compared to God.
While men beneath their hands can crush a stone;
So that such sentiments can only come from fools.

And the epigram cannot possibly be by Homer, for he lived many years, as it is said, before Midas.

There is also the following enigma quoted in the Commentaries of Pamphila, as the work of Cleobulus:—

There was one father, and he had twelve daughters,
Each of his daughters had twice thirty children,
But most unlike in figure and complexion;
For some were white, and others black to view,
And though immortal, they all taste of death.

And the solution is, "the year."

Of his apophthegms, the following are the most celebrated: Ignorance and talkativeness bear the chief sway among men. Opportunity will be the most powerful. Cherish not a thought. Do not be fickle, or ungrateful. He used to say, too, that men ought to give their daughters in marriage while they were girls in age, but women in sense; as indicating by this that girls ought to be well educated. Another of his sayings was, that one ought to serve a friend that he may become a greater friend; and an enemy, to make him a friend. And that one ought to guard against giving one's friends occasion to blame one, and one's enemies opportunity of plotting against one. Also, when a man goes out of his house, he should consider what he is going to do; and when he comes home again, he should consider what he has done. He used also to advise men to keep their bodies in health by exercise. To be fond of hearing rather than of talking. To be fond of learning rather than unwilling to learn. To speak well of people. To seek virtue and eschew vice. To avoid injustice. To give the best advice in one's power to one's country. To be superior to pleasure. To do nothing by force. To instruct one's children. To be ready for reconciliation after quarrels. Not to caress one's wife, nor to quarrel with her, when strangers are present; for that to do the one is a sign of folly, and to do the latter is downright madness. Not to chastise a servant while elated with drink; for so doing, one will appear to be drunk one's self. To marry from among one's equals; for if one takes a wife of a higher rank than one's self, one will have one's connexions for one's masters. Not to laugh at those who are being reproved; for so one will be detested by them. Be not haughty when prosperous. Be not desponding when in difficulties. Learn to bear the changes of fortune with magnanimity. Moderation is the best thing.

CRANTOR.

Crantor, a native of Soli, being admired very greatly in his own country, came to Athens and became a pupil of Xenocrates at the same time with Polemo. And he left behind him memorials, in the shape of writings, to the number of 30,000 lines, some of which, however, are by some writers attributed to Arcesilaus.

They say of him that when he was asked what it was that he was so charmed with in Polemo, he replied, "That he had never heard him speak in too high or too low a key." When he was ill he retired to the temple of Æsculapius, and there walked about, and people came to him from all quarters, thinking that he had gone thither, not on account of any disease, but because he wished to establish a school there.

And among those who came to him was Arcesilaus, wishing to be recommended by him to Polemo, although he was much attached to him. But when he got well he became a pupil of Polemo, and was excessively admired on that account. It is said, also, that he left his property to Arcesilaus, to the amount of twelve talents; and that, being asked by him where he would like to be buried, he said:

> It is a happy fate to lie entombed
> In the recesses of a well-lov'd land.

It is said also that he wrote poems, and that he sealed them up in the temple of Minerva, in his own country; and Meætetus the poet wrote thus about him:—

> Crantor pleased men; but greater pleasure still
> He to the Muses gave, ere he aged grew.
> Earth, tenderly embrace the holy man,
> And let him lie in quiet undisturb'd.

And of all writers, Crantor admired Homer and Euripides most; saying that the hardest thing possible was to write tragically and in a manner to excite sympathy, without departing from nature; and he used to quote this line out of the Bellerophon:—

> Alas! why should I say alas! for we
> Have only borne the usual fate of man.

The following verses of Antagoras the poet are also attributed to Crantor; the subject is love, and they run thus:—

My mind is much perplexed; for what, O Love,
Dare I pronounce your origin? May I
Call you chiefest of the immortal Gods,
Of all the children whom dark Erebus
And Royal Night bore on the billowy waves
Of widest Ocean? Or shall I bid you hail
As son of proudest Venus? or of Earth?
Or of the untamed winds? so fierce you rove,
Bringing mankind sad cares, yet not unmixed
With happy good, so two fold is your nature.

And he was very ingenious at devising new words and expressions; accordingly, he said that one tragedian had an unhewn voice, all over bark; and he said that the verses of a certain poet were full of moths; and that the propositions of Theophrastus had been written on an oyster shell.

CRATES.

Crates was a Theban by birth and the son of Ascondus. There are the following sportive lines of his quoted:—

The waves surround vain Peres' fruitful soil,
And fertile acres crown the sea-born isle;
Land which no parasite e'er dares invade,
Or lew'd seducer of a hapless maid;
It bears figs, bread, thyme, garlic's savory charms,
Gifts which ne'er tempt men to detested arms,
They'd rather fight for gold than glory's dreams.

There is also an account-book of his much spoken of, which is drawn up in such terms as these:—

Put down the cook for minas half a score,
Put down the doctor for a drachma more:
Five talents to the flatterer; some smoke
To the adviser, an obol and a cloak
For the philosopher; for the willing nymph,
A talent . . . . .

He was also nicknamed Door-opener, because he used to enter every house and give the inmates advice. These lines, too, are his :—

> All this I learnt and pondered in my mind,
> Drawing deep wisdom from the Muses kind,
> But all the rest is vanity.

There is a line, too, which tells us that he gained from philosophy :—

> A peck of lupins, and to care for nobody.

This, too, is attributed to him :—

> Hunger checks love ; and should it not, time does.
> If both should fail you, then a halter choose.

He flourished about the hundred and thirteenth Olympiad.

Antisthenes, in his Successions, says that he, having once, in a certain tragedy, seen Telephus holding a date basket, and in a miserable plight in other respects, betook himself to the Cynic philosophy; and having turned his patrimony into money (for he was of illustrious extraction), he collected three hundred talents by that means, and divided them among the citizens. And after that he devoted himself to philosophy with such eagerness, that even Philemon the comic poet mentions him. Accordingly he says :—

> And in the summer he 'd a shaggy gown,
> To inure himself to hardship; in the winter
> He wore mere rags.

But Diocles says that it was Diogenes who persuaded him to discard all his estate and his flocks, and to throw his money into the sea; and he says further, that the house of Crates was destroyed by Alexander, and that of Hipparchia under Philip. And he would very frequently drive away with his staff those of his relations who came after him, and endeavored to dissuade him from his design; and he remained immovable.

Demetrius, the Magnesian, relates that he deposited his money with a banker, making an agreement with him, that if his sons turned out ordinary ignorant people, he was then to restore it to them; but if they became philosophers, then he was to divide it among the people, for that they, if they were philosophers, would have no need of anything.

Pharorinus, in the second book of his Commentaries, relates a witty saying of his; for he says that once, when he was begging a favor of the master of a gymnasium, on the behalf of some acquaintance, he touched his thighs; and as he expressed his indignation at this, he said, "Why, do they not belong to you as well as your knees?" He used to say that it was impossible to find a man who had never done wrong, in the same way as there was always some worthless seed in a pomegranate. On one occasion, he provoked Nicodromus, the harp-player, and received a black eye from him; so he put a plaster on his forehead, and wrote on it, "Nicodromus did this." He used to abuse prostitutes designedly, for the purpose of practising himself in enduring reproaches. When Demetrius Phalereus sent him some loaves and wine, he attacked him for his present, saying, "I wish that the fountains bore loaves;" and it is notorious that he was a water drinker.

He was once reproved by the ædiles of the Athenians, for wearing fine linen, and so he replied, "I will show you Theophrastus also clad in fine linen." And as they did not believe him, he took them to a barber's shop, and showed him to them as he was being shaved. At Thebes he was once scourged by the master of the gymnasium (though some say it was by Euthycrates, at Corinth), and dragged out by the feet; but he did not care, and quoted the lines:—

> I feel, O mighty chief, your matchless might,
> Dragged, foot first, downward from th' ethereal height.*

But Diocles says that it was by Menedemus, of Eretria, that he was dragged in this manner, for that as he was a handsome man, and supposed to be very obsequious to Asclepiades, the

* This is a parody on Homer. Il. 591. Pope's Version, 760.

Phliasian, Crates touched his thighs, and said, "Is Asclepiades within?" And Menedemus was very much offended, and dragged him out, as has been already said; and then Crates quoted the above-cited line.

Zeno, the Cittiæan, in his Apophthegms, says that he once sewed up a sheep's fleece in his cloak, without thinking of it; and he was a very ugly man, and one who excited laughter when he was taking exercise. And he used to say, when he put up his hands, "Courage, Crates, as far as your eyes and the rest of your body is concerned; for you shall see those who now ridicule you, convulsed with disease, and envying your happiness, and accusing themselves of slothfulness." One of his sayings was, "That a man ought to study philosophy, up to the point of looking on generals and donkey-drivers in the same light." Another was, that "those who live with flatterers are as desolate as calves when in the company of wolves; for that neither the one nor the other are with those whom they ought to be, or their own kindred, but only with those who are plotting against them."

When he felt that he was dying, he made verses on himself, saying:—

> You 're going, noble hunchback, you are going
> To Pluto's realms, bent double by old age.

For he was hump-backed from age.

Alexander asked him "Whether he wished to see the restoration of his country?" To which he replied, "What would be the use of it? For perhaps some other Alexander would come at some future time, and destroy it again:—

> But poverty, and dear obscurity,
> Are what a prudent man should think his country."

He also said that he was

> A fellow-countryman of wise Diogenes,
> Whom even envy never hád attacked.

Menander, in his Twin-Sister, mentions him thus:—

For you will walk with me, wrapped in your cloak,
As his wife used to with the Cynic Crates.

He gave his daughter to his pupils, as he himself used to say:—

To have and keep on trial for a month.

There was another Crates, who was the son of Antigenes, and of the Thriasian burgh, and a pupil and attached friend of Polemo. He was also his successor as president of his school.

And they benefited one another so much, that not only did they delight while alive in the same pursuits, but almost to their latest breath did they resemble one another, and even after they were both dead they shared the same tomb. In reference to which circumstance, Antagoras has written an epigram on the pair, in which he expresses himself thus:—

Stranger, who passest by, relate that here
  The godlike Crates lies, and Polemo;
Two men of kindred nobleness of mind,
  Out of whose holy mouths pure wisdom flowed;
And they with upright lives did well display
  The strength of all their principles and teaching.

And they say, too, that it was in reference to this that Arcesilaus, when he came over to them from Theophrastus, said that they were some gods, or else a remnant of the golden race; for they were not very fond of courting the people, but had a disposition in accordance with the saying of Dionysodorus, the flute-player, who is reported to have said, with great exultation and pride, that no one had ever heard his music in a trireme or at a fountain, as they had heard Ismenius.

The following lines were written by a philosopher of this name:—

'T is not one town, nor one poor single house,
That is my country; but in every land
Each city and each dwelling seems to me
A place for my reception ready made.

DEMETRIUS.

Demetrius was a native of Phalerus, and the son of Phanostratus. He was a pupil of Theophrastus.

As a leader of the people at Athens, he governed the city for ten years, and was honored with three hundred and sixty brazen statues, the greater part of which were equestrian; and some were placed in carriages, or in pair-horse chariots, and the entire number were finished within three hundred days, so great was the zeal with which they were worked at. He governed his country for a long time in a most admirable manner. For he aggrandized the city by increased revenues and by new buildings, although he was a person of no distinction by birth.

He lived with a citizen of noble birth, named Lamia, as his mistress. Didymus, in his Banquets, says that he was called Beautiful Eyed, by some courtesan. It is said that he lost his eye-sight in Alexandria, and recovered it again by the favor of Serapis; on which account he composed the pæans which are sung and spoken of as his composition to this day.

He was held in the greatest honor among the Athenians, but nevertheless, he found his fame darkened by envy, which attacks everything; for he was impeached by some one on a capital charge, and, as he did not appear, he was condemned. His accusers, however, did not become masters of his person, but expended their venom on the brass, tearing down his statues, and selling some and throwing others into the sea, and some they cut up into chamber-pots. For even this is stated. And one statue alone of him is preserved, which is in the Acropolis. But Pharorinus, in his Universal History, says that the Athenians treated Demetrius in this manner at the command of the king; and they also impeached him as guilty of illegality in his administration. But Hermippus says, that after the death of Cassander, he feared the enmity of Antigonus, and on that account fled to Ptolemy Soter; and that he remained at his court for a long time, and, among other pieces of advice, counselled the king to make over the kingdom to his sons by Eurydice. And as he would not agree to this measure, but gave the crown to his son by Berenice, this latter, after the death of his father, commanded Demetrius to be kept in prison until he should come to some determination about him. And there he remained in great despondency; and while asleep on one occasion, he was bitten by an asp in the hand, and so he died. And he is buried in the district of Busiris, near Diospolis; and we have written the following epigram on him:—

An asp, whose tooth of venom dire was full,
  Did kill the wise Demetrius.
The serpent beamed not light from out his eyes,
  But dark and lurid hell.

But Heraclides, in his Epitome of the Successions of Sotion, says that Ptolemy wished to transmit the kingdom to Philadelphus, and that Demetrius persuaded him from doing so by the argument, "If you give it to another, you will not have it yourself." And when Menander, the comic poet, had an information laid against him at Athens (for this is a statement which I have heard), he was very nearly being convicted, for no other reason but that he was a friend of Demetrius. He was, however, successfully defended by Telesphorus, the son-in-law of Demetrius.

In the multitude of his writings, and the number of lines which they amount to, he exceeded nearly all the Peripatetics of his day, being a man of great learning and experience on every subject.

When he was told that the Athenians had thrown down his statues, he said, "But they have not thrown down my virtues, on account of which they erected them." He used to say that "The eyebrows were not an insignificant part of a man, for that they were able to overshadow the whole life."

Another of his sayings was, that "It was not Plutus alone who was blind, but Fortune also, who acted as his guide." Another, that "Reason had as much influence on government, as steel had in war." On one occasion, when he saw a debauched young man, he said, "There is a square Mercury with a long robe, a belly, and a beard." It was a favorite saying of his, that in the case of men elated with pride one ought to cut something off their height, and leave them their spirit. Another of his apophthegms was, that "At home young men ought to show respect to their parents, and in the streets to every one whom they met, and in solitary places to themselves." Another, that "Friends ought to come to others in good fortune only when invited, but to those in distress of their own accord."

Brucker states that he committed suicide. His account is that Demetrius, unable to support the repeated misfortunes he had met with, put an end to his life by the bite of an asp.

This fact is supported by the concurrent testimony of the ancients. Hence it has, not without reason, been questioned whether credit be due to the reports of Aristobulus, Philo, Josephus, and others, that Demetrius Phalereus was librarian to Ptolemy Philadelphus, and that it was by his advice that this prince gave orders for a version of the Jewish scriptures from the Hebrew into the Greek language. The truth is, that the whole story of a royal mandate for this undertaking is destitute of satisfactory proof, and probably first arose from Jewish vanity, and was afterwards hastily adopted by the Christian fathers. It is most probable that the Septuagint version was the private labor of the Jews who were at this time resident in Egypt.

DEMETRIUS, OF CORINTH.

There was another of the same name, Demetrius, of Corinth. So free and severe were his censures of the fashionable customs and vices of the day, that he was banished from Rome by Nero. After this emperor's death, he returned, but, by his freedom of speech, he soon offended the emperor Vespasian, who punished him by depriving him of his liberty. Seneca, who was an intimate friend of Demetrius, speaks of him in language of the highest praise for his masculine eloquence, sound judgment, intrepid fortitude, and inflexible integrity. "Leaving," says he, "the nobles clad in purple, I converse with and admire the half-naked Demetrius; and why do I admire him, but because I perceive that in the midst of his poverty he wants nothing! When I hear this excellent man discoursing from his couch of straw, I perceive in him not a preceptor only, but a witness of the truth; and I cannot doubt that Providence has endowed him with such virtues and talents that he might be an example and a monitor to the present age."

It was a prominent maxim with Demetrius, that "It is better to have a few precepts of wisdom always at hand for use, than to learn many things which cannot be applied to practice." He attended Thraseas Pætus in his last moments before his execution, and fortified his mind by conversing with him upon subjects of philosophy.

DEMOCRITUS.

Democritus was a native of Aldera, or as some say, a citizen of Miletus. He was a pupil of some of the Magi and Chaldeans whom Xerxes had left with his father as teachers, when he had been hospitably received by them.

He was one of three brothers who divided their patrimony among them; and the most common story is, that he took the smaller portion, as it was in money, because he required money for the purpose of travelling; though his brothers suspected him of entertaining some treacherous design. Demetrius says, that his share amounted to more than a hundred talents, and that he spent the whole of it.

He also says, that he was so industrious a man, that he cut off for himself a small portion of the garden which surrounded his house, in which there was a small cottage, and shut himself up in it. And on one occasion, when his father brought him an ox to sacrifice, and fastened it there, he for a long time did not discover it, until his father having roused him, on the pretext of the sacrifice, told him what he had done with the ox.

He further asserts, that it is well known that he went to Athens, and as he despised glory, he did not desire to be known; and that he became acquainted with Socrates, without Socrates knowing who he was. "For I came," says he, "to Athens, and no one knew me." He it was who was the author of the saying, "Speech is the shadow of action." But Demetrius Phalereus, in his defence of Socrates, affirms that he never came to Athens at all. And that is a still stranger circumstance than any, if he despised so important a city, not wishing to derive glory from the place in which he was, but preferring rather himself to invest the place with glory.

And Apollodorus, of Cyzicus, says he was intimate with Philolaus; "He used to practise himself," says Antisthenes, "in testing perceptions in various manners; sometimes retiring into solitary places, and spending his time even among tombs."

And he further adds, that when he returned from his travels, he lived in a most humble manner; like a man who had spent all his property, and that on account of his poverty, he was supported by his brother Damasus. But when he had foretold some future event, which happened as he had predicted, and had in consequence become famous, he was for all the rest of his life thought worthy of almost divine honors by the generality of people. And as there was a law, that a man who had squandered the whole of his patrimony, should not be allowed funeral rites in his country, Antisthenes says, that he, being aware of this law, and not wishing to be exposed to the calumnies of those who envied him, and would be glad to accuse him, recited to the people his work called the Great World, which is far superior to all his other writings, and that as a reward for it he was presented with five hundred talents; and not only that, but he also had some brazen statues erected in his honor. And when he died, he was buried at the public expense; after having attained the age of more than a hundred years. But Demetrius says, that it was his relations who read the Great World, and that they were presented with a hundred talents only; and Hippobotus coincides in this statement.

Athenodorus tells us, that once, when Hippocrates came to see him, he ordered some milk to be brought; and that, when he saw the milk, he said that it was the milk of a black goat, with her first kid; on which Hippocrates marvelled at his accurate knowledge.

And Hermippus relates, that Democritus died in the following manner: he was exceedingly old, and appeared at the point of death; and his sister was lamenting that he would die during the festival of the Thesmophoria,* and so prevent her from discharging her duties to the Goddess; and so he bade her be of good cheer, and desired her to bring him hot loaves every day. And, by applying these to his nostrils, he kept himself alive even over the festival. But when the days of the festival were passed (and it lasted three days), then he expired without any pain, as Hipparchus assures us, having lived a hundred and nine years. And we have written an epigram upon him in our collection of poems in every metre, which runs thus:—

* The Thesmophoria was a festival in honor of Ceres.

What man was e'er so wise, who ever did
So great a deed as this Democritus?
Who kept off death, though present for three days,
And entertained him with hot steam of bread

DEMONAX.

A Distinguished place among the genuine Cynics who were friends to virtue appears to be due to Demonax; whose history, though related only by Lucian, deserves credit, since it is not probable that the Satirist, who lived at the same period, would have ventured to give a false narrative of a well-known character, or that he would have gone so far out of his usual track of satire, merely to draw a fictitious portrait of a good man. Demonax, according to Lucian, was born in Cyprus. His parents were possessed of wealth and rank; but he aspired after higher honors in the study of wisdom, and the practice of virtue. Early in life he removed to Athens, where he afterwards continued to reside. In his youth he was intimately conversant with the poets, and committed the most valuable parts of their writings to memory. When he engaged in the study of philosophy, he did not lightly skim over the surface of subjects, but made himself perfect master of the several sects. In his habit and manner of living, Demonax resembled Diogenes, and is therefore properly ranked among the Cynics; but he imitated Socrates in making philosophy, not a speculative science, but a rule of life and manners. He never openly espoused the doctrines of any particular sect, but took from each whatever tenets he judged most favorable to moral wisdom. Avoiding all ridiculous singularity, disgusting severity, and forbidding haughtiness, he associated freely with all, and conversed with such graceful ease, that persuasion might be said to dwell upon his lips. He possessed the happy art of rendering even reproof acceptable; like a prudent physician, curing the disease without fretting the patient. His simple manner of living gave him perfect independence; and his virtues procured him such a degree of influence, that he was often employed in settling domestic dissensions. His philanthropy was universal; and he never withdrew his regard from any, but such as would not be persuaded to forsake their vices. So perfect was his equanimity, that nothing ever deeply affected him, except the sickness or death of a friend. He lived nearly to the age of a hundred years, without suffering pain or disease, or becoming burdensome to any one. In extreme old age he went from house to house wherever he pleased, and was everywhere received with respect. As he passed along the streets the sellers of bread would beg him to accept of some from their hands; and children would offer him fruits, and call him father. He died with the same placid countenance with which he had been accustomed to meet his friends. The Athenians honored his body with a public funeral, which was attended by a numerous train of philosophers and others, who lamented the loss of so excellent a man. If this picture, which is that of Lucian in miniature, was originally taken from real life, the biographer had some reason to speak of Demonax as the best philosopher he ever knew.

From the anecdotes of Demonax, related by Lucian, we shall select the following:—Soon after Demonax came to Athens, a public charge was brought against him for neglecting to offer sacrifice to Minerva, and to be initiated into the Eleusinian mysteries. Appearing before the assembly in a white garment, he pleaded that Minerva did not stand in need of his offerings; and that he declined initiation into the mysteries because, if they were bad he ought not to conceal them, and if they were good, his love to mankind would oblige him to disclose them; upon which he was acquitted. One of his companions proposing to go to the temple of Esculapius, to pray for the recovery of his son from sickness, Demonax said, "Do you suppose that Esculapius cannot hear you as well from this place?" Hearing two ignorant pretenders to philosophy conversing, and remarking that the one asked foolish questions, and the other made replies which were nothing to the purpose, he said, "One of these men is milking a he-goat, while the other is holding a sieve under him." Advising a certain rhetorician, who was a wretched declaimer, to perform frequent exercises, the rhetorician answered, "I frequently practise by myself." "No wonder," replied Demonax, "that you are so bad a speaker, when you practise before so foolish an audience." Seeing a Spartan beating his servant unmercifully, he said to him, "Why do you thus put yourself upon a level with your slave?" When Demonax was informed that the Athenians had thoughts of erecting an amphitheatre for gladiators, in imitation of the Corinthians, he went into the assembly, and cried out, "Athenians, before you make this resolution, go and pull down the Altar of Mercy."

DIOGENES.

Diogenes was a native of Sinope, the son of Tresius, a money-changer. And Diocles says that he was forced to flee from his native city, as his father kept the public bank there, and had adulterated the coinage. But Eubulides, in his essay on Diogenes, says, that it was Diogenes himself who did this, and that he was banished with his father. And, indeed, he himself, in his Perdalus, says of himself that he had adulterated the public money. Others say that he was one of the curators, and was persuaded by the artisans employed, and that he went to Delphi, or else to the oracle at Delos, and there consulted Apollo as to whether he should do what people were trying to persuade him to do; and that, as the God gave him permission to do so, Diogenes, not comprehending that the God meant that he might change the political customs* of his country if he could, adulterated the coinage; and being detected, was banished, as some people say, but as other accounts have it, took the alarm and fled away of his own accord. Some again, say that he adulterated the money which he had received from his father; and that his father was thrown into prison and died there; but that Diogenes escaped and went to Delphi, and asked, not whether he might tamper with the coinage, but what he could do to become very celebrated, and that in consequence he received the oracular answer which I have mentioned.

When he came to Athens he attached himself to Antisthenes; but as he repelled him, because he admitted no one, he at last forced his way to him by his pertinacity. And once, when he raised his stick at him, he put his head under it, and said, "Strike, for you will not find any stick hard enough to drive me away as long you continue to speak." And from this time forth he was one of his pupils; and being an exile, he naturally betook himself to a simple mode of life.

And when, as Theophrastus tells us in his Megaric Philosopher, he saw a mouse running about and not seeking for a bed, nor taking care to keep in the dark, nor looking for any of those things which appear enjoyable to such an animal, he found a remedy for his own poverty. He was, according to the account of some people, the first person who doubled up his cloak out of necessity, and who slept in it; and who carried a wallet, in which he kept his food; and who used whatever place was near for all sorts of purposes, eating and sleeping, and conversing in it. In reference to which habit he used to say, pointing to the Colonnade of Jupiter, and to the Public Magazine, "that the Athenians had built him places to live in." Being attacked with illness, he supported himself

* The passage is not free from difficulty; but the thing which misled Diogenes appears to have been that *nomisma*, the word here used, meant both "a coin, or coinage," and "a custom."

with a staff; and after that he carried it continually, not indeed in the city, but whenever he was walking in the roads, together with his wallet.

When he had written to some one to look out and get ready a small house for him, as he delayed to do it, he took a cask which he found in the Temple of Cybele, for his house, as he himself tells us in his letters. And during the summer he used to roll himself in the warm sand, but in winter he would embrace statues all covered with snow, practising himself, on every occasion, to endure anything.

He was very violent in expressing his haughty disdain of others. He said that the *schole* (school) of Euclides was *chole* (gall). And he used to call Plato's *diatribe* (discussions) *katatribe* (disguise). It was also a saying of his that the Dionysian games were a great marvel to fools; and that the demagogues were the ministers of the multitude. He used likewise to say, "that when in the course of his life he beheld pilots, and physicians, and philosophers, he thought man the wisest of all animals; but when again he beheld interpreters of dreams, and soothsayers, and those who listened to them, and men puffed up with glory or riches, then he thought that there was not a more foolish animal than man." Another of his sayings was, "that he thought a man ought oftener to provide himself with a reason than with a halter." On one occasion, when he noticed Plato at a very costly entertainment tasting some olives, he said, "O you wise man! why, after having sailed to Sicily for the sake of such a feast, do you not now enjoy what you have before you?" And Plato replied, "By the Gods, Diogenes, while I was there I ate olives and all such things a great deal." Diogenes rejoined, "What then did you want to sail to Syracuse for? Did not Attica at that time produce any olives?" But Phavorinus, in his Universal History, tells this story of Aristippus. At another time he was eating dried figs, when Plato met him, and he said to him, "You may have a share of these;" and as he took some and ate them, he said, "I said that you might have a share of them, not that you might eat them all." On one occasion Plato had invited some friends who had come to him from Dionysius to a banquet, and Diogenes trampled on his carpets, and said, "Thus I trample on the empty pride of Plato;" and Plato made him answer, "How much arrogance are you displaying, O Diogenes! when you think that you are not arrogant at all." But as others tell the story, Diogenes said, "Thus I trample on the pride of Plato;" and that Plato rejoined, "With quite as much pride yourself, O Diogenes." Sotion too, in his fourth book, states, that the Cynic made the following speech to Plato: Diogenes once asked him for some wine, and then for some dried figs; so he sent him an entire jar full; and Diogenes said to him, "Will you, if you are asked how many two and two make, answer twenty? In this way, you neither give with any reference to what you are asked for, nor do you answer with reference to the question put to you." He used also to ridicule him as an interminable talker. When he was asked where in Greece he saw virtuous men; "Men," said he, "nowhere; but I see good boys in Lacedæmon." On one occasion, when no one came to listen to him while he was discoursing seriously, he began to whistle. And then when people flocked round him, he reproached them for coming with eagerness to folly, but being lazy and indifferent about good things. One of his frequent sayings was, "That men contended with one another in punching and kicking, but that no one showed any emulation in the pursuit of virtue." He used to express his astonishment at the grammarians for being desirous to learn everything about the misfortunes of Ulysses, and being ignorant of their own. He used also to say, "That the musicians fitted the strings to the lyre properly, but left all the habits of their soul ill-arranged." And, "That mathematicians kept their eyes fixed on the sun and moon, and overlooked what was under their feet." "That orators were anxious to speak justly, but not at all about acting so." Also, "That misers blamed money, but were preposterously fond of it." He often condemned those who praise the just for being superior to money, but who at the same time are eager themselves for great riches. He was also very indignant at seeing men sacrifice to the Gods to procure good health, and yet at the sacrifice eating in a manner injurious to health. He often expressed his surprise at slaves, who, seeing their masters eating in a gluttonous manner, still do not themselves lay hands on any of the eatables. He would frequently praise those who were about to marry, and yet did not marry; or who were about to take a voyage, and yet did not take a voyage; or who were about to engage in affairs of state, and did not do so; and those who were about to rear children, yet did not rear any; and those who were preparing to take up their abode with princes, and yet did not take it up. One of his sayings was, "That one ought to hold out one's hand to a friend without closing the fingers."

Hermippus, in his Sale of Diogenes, says that he was taken prisoner and put up to be sold, and asked what he could do; and he answered, "Govern men." And so he bade the crier "give notice that if any one wants to purchase a master, there is one here for him." When he was ordered not to sit down, "It makes no difference," said he, "for fish are sold, be where they may." He used to say, that he "wondered at men always ringing a dish or jar before buying it, but being content to judge of a man by his look alone." When Xeniades bought him, he said to him that he ought to obey him even though he was his slave; for that a physician or a pilot would find men to obey them even though they might be slaves."

And Eubulus says, in his essay entitled, The Sale of Diogenes, that he taught the children of Xeniades, after their other lessons, to ride, and shoot, and sling, and dart. And then in the gymnasium he did not permit the trainer to exercise them after the fashion of athletes, but exercised them himself to just the degree sufficient to give them a good color and good health. And the boys retained in their memory many sentences of poets and prose writers, and of Diogenes himself; and he used to give them a concise statement of everything, in order to strengthen their memory; and at home he used to teach them to wait upon themselves, contenting themselves with plain food, and drinking water. He accustomed them to cut their hair close, and to eschew ornament, and to go without tunics or shoes, and to keep silent, looking at nothing except themselves as they walked along. He used also to take them out hunting; and they paid the greatest attention and respect to Diogenes himself, and spoke well of him to their parents.

And the same author affirms, that he grew old in the household of Xeniades, and that when he died he was buried by his sons. And that while he was living with him, Xeniades once asked him how he should bury him; and he said, "On my face;" and when he was asked why, he said, "Because in a little while everything will be turned upside down." And he said this because the Macedonians were already attaining power, and becoming a mighty people from having been very inconsiderable. Once, when a man had conducted him into a magnificent house, and had told him that he must not spit, after hawking a little, he spit in his face, saying that he could not find a worse place. But some tell this story of Aristippus. Once he called out, "Holloa, men." And when some people gathered round him in consequence, he drove them away with his stick, saying, "I called men, and not dregs." They also relate that Alexander said, that if he had not been Alexander, he should have liked to be Diogenes. On one occasion he went half shaved into an entertainment of young men, and so was beaten by them. And afterwards he wrote the names of all those who had beaten him on a white tablet, and went about with the tablet round his neck, so as to expose them to insult, as they were generally condemned and reproached for their conduct.

He used to say that he was "the hound of those who were praised; but that none of those who praised them dared to go out hunting with him." A man once said to him, "I conquered men at the Pythian games;" on which he said, "I conquer men, but you only conquer slaves." When some people said to him, "You are an old man, and should rest for the remainder of your life," "Why so?" replied he, "suppose I had run a long distance, ought I to stop when I was near the end, and not rather press on?" Once, when he was invited to a banquet, he said that he would not come: for that the day before no one had thanked him for coming. He used to go bare foot through the snow, and to do a number of other things which have been already mentioned. Once he attempted to eat raw meat, but he could not digest it. On one occasion he found Demosthenes, the orator, dining in an inn; and as he was slipping away, he said to him, "You will now be ever so much more in an inn."* Once, when some strangers wished to see Demosthenes, he stretched out his middle finger, and said, "This is the great demagogue of the Athenian people." When some one had dropped a loaf, and was ashamed to pick it up again, he wishing to give him a lesson, tied a cord round the neck of a bottle and dragged it all through the Ceramicus. He used to say, that he imitated the teachers of choruses, for that they spoke too loud, in order that the rest might catch the proper tone. Another of his sayings was, that "most men were within a finger's breadth of being mad. If, then, any one were to walk along, stretching out his middle finger, he will seem to be mad; but if he puts out his fore finger, he will not be thought so." Another of his sayings was, that, "things of great value were often sold for nothing, and *vice versâ*. Accordingly, that a statue would fetch three thousand drachmas, and a bushel of meal only two obols;" and when Xeniades had bought him, he said to him, "Come, do what you are ordered to." And when he said—

† This line is from Euripides, Medea,

"The streams of sacred rivers now
Run backwards to their source!"

"Suppose," rejoined Diogenes, "you had been sick, and had bought a physician, could you refuse to be guided by him, and tell him—

"The streams of sacred rivers now
Run backwards to their source?"

Once a man came to him, and wished to study philosophy as his pupil; and he gave him a saperda * and made him follow him. And as he from shame threw it away and departed, he soon afterwards met him and, laughing, said to him, "A saperda has dissolved your friendship for me." But Diocles tells this story in the following manner; that when some one said to him, "Give me a commission, Diogenes," he carried him off, and gave him a half-penny worth of cheese to carry. And as he refused to carry it, "See," said Diogenes, "a half-penny worth of cheese has broken off our friendship."

On one occasion he saw a child drinking out of its hands, and so he threw away the cup which belonged to his wallet, saying, "That child has beaten me in simplicity." He also threw away his spoon, after seeing a boy, when he had broken his vessel, take up his lentils with a crust of bread. And he used to argue thus,—"Everything belongs to the gods; and wise men are the friends of the gods. All things are in common among friends; therefore everything belongs to wise men." Once he saw a woman falling down before the Gods in an unbecoming attitude; he, wishing to cure her of her superstition, as Zoilus of Perga tells us, came up to her, and said, "Are you not afraid, O woman, to be in such an indecent attitude, when some God may be behind you, for every place is full of him?" He consecrated a man to Æsculapius, who was to run up and beat all those who prostrated themselves with their faces to the ground; and he was in the habit of saying that the tragic curse had come upon him, for that he was—

* The saperda was the coracinus (a kind of fish) when salted.

Houseless and citiless, a piteous exile
From his dear native land; a wandering beggar,
Scraping a pittance poor from day to day.

And another of his sayings was, that he "opposed confidence to fortune, nature to law, and reason to suffering." Once, while he was sitting in the sun in the Craneum, Alexander was standing by, and said to him, "Ask any favor you choose of me." And he replied, "Cease to shade me from the sun"—as some express it, "stand out of my light." On one occasion a man was reading some long passages, and when he came to the end of the book and showed there was nothing more written, "Be of good cheer, my friends," exclaimed Diogenes, "I see land." A man once proved to him syllogistically that he had horns, so he put his hand to his forehead and said, "I do not see them." And in a similar manner he replied to one who had been asserting that there was no such thing as motion, by getting up and walking away. When a man was talking about the heavenly bodies and meteors, "Pray, how many days," said he to him, "is it since you came down from heaven?"

A profligate eunuch had written on his house, "Let no evil thing enter in." "Where," said Diogenes, "is the master of the house going?" After having anointed his feet with perfume, he said that the ointment from his head mounted up to heaven, and that from his feet up to his nose. When the Athenians entreated him to be initiated in the Eleusinian mysteries, and said that in the shades below the initiated had the best seats; "It will," he replied, "be an absurd thing if Ægesilaus and Epaminondas are to live in the mud, and some miserable wretches, who have been initiated, are to be in the islands of the blest." Some mice crept up to his table, and he said, "See, even Diogenes maintains his favorites." Once, when he was leaving the bath, and a man asked him whether many men were bathing, he said "No;" but when a number of people came out, he confessed that there were a great many.

When Plato called him a dog, he said, "Undoubtedly, for I have come back to those who sold me."

Plato defined man thus: "Man is a two-footed, featherless animal," and was much praised for the definition; so Diogenes plucked a cock and brought it into his school, and said, "This is Plato's man." On which account this addition was made to the definition, "With broad flat nails." A man once asked him what was the proper time for supper, and he made answer, "If you are a rich man, whenever you please; and if you are a poor man, whenever you can." When he was at Megara he saw some sheep carefully covered over with skins, and the children running about naked; and so he said, "It is better at Megara to be a man's ram, than his son." A man once struck him with a beam, and then said, "Take care." "What," said he, "are you going to strike me again?" He used to say that "the demagogues were the servants of the people; and garlands the blossoms of glory." Having lighted a candle in the day time, he said, "I am looking for a man." On one occasion he stood under a fountain, and as the bystanders were pitying him, Plato, who was present, said to them, "If you wish really to show your pity for him, come away;" intimating that he was only acting thus out of a desire for notoriety. Once, when a man had struck him with his fist, he said, "O Hercules, what a strange thing that I should be walking about with a helmet on without knowing it!"

When Midias struck him with his fist and said, "There are three thousand drachmas for you;" the next day Diogenes took the cestus of a boxer and beat him soundly, and said, "There are three thousand drachmas for you."* When Lysias, the drug-seller, asked him whether he thought that there were any Gods: "How," said he, "can I help thinking so, when I consider you to be hated by them?" but some attribute this

* This is probably an allusion to a prosecution instituted by Demosthenes against Midias, which was afterwards compromised by Midias paying Demosthenes thirty minæ, or three thousand drachmæ.

reply to Theodorus. Once he saw a man purifying himself by washing, and said to him, "Oh, wretched man, do not you know that as you cannot wash away blunders in grammar by purification, so, too, you can no more efface the errors of a life in that same manner?"

He used to say that men were wrong for complaining of fortune; for that they ask of the Gods what appear to be good things, not what are really so. And to those who were alarmed at dreams he said, that they did not regard what they do while they are awake, but make a great fuss about what they fancy they see while they are asleep. Once, at the Olympic games, when the herald proclaimed, "Dioxippus is the conqueror of men;" he said, "He is the conqueror of slaves, I am the conqueror of men."

He was greatly beloved by the Athenians; accordingly, when a youth had broken his cask they beat him, and gave Diogenes another. And Dionysius, the Stoic, says that after the battle of Chæronea he was taken prisoner and brought to Philip; and being asked who he was, replied, "A spy, to spy upon your insatiability." And Philip marvelled at him and let him go. Once, when Alexander had sent a letter to Athens to Antipater, by the hands of a man named Athlias, he, being present, said, "Athlias from Athlius, by means of Athlias to Athlius.* When Perdiccas threatened that he would put him to death if he did not come to him, he replied, "That is nothing strange, for a scorpion or a tarantula could do as much: you had better threaten me that, if I kept away, you should be very happy." He used constantly to repeat with emphasis, that "An easy life had been given to man by the Gods, but that it had been overlaid by their seeking for honey, cheese-cakes, and unguents, and things of that sort." On which account he said to a man, who had his shoes put on by his servant, "You are not thoroughly happy, unless he

* There is a pun upon the similarity of Athlias's name to the Greek adjective *athlios*, which signifies miserable.

also wipes your nose for you; and he will do this, if you are crippled in your hands." On one occasion, when he had seen the hieromnemones* leading off one of the stewards who had stolen a goblet, he said, "The great thieves are carrying off the little thief." At another time, seeing a young man throwing stones at a cross, he said, "Well done, you will be sure to reach the mark." Once, too, some boys got round him and said, "We are taking care that you do not bite us;" but he said, "Be of good cheer, my boys, a dog does not eat beef." He saw a man giving himself airs because he was clad in a lion's skin, and said to him, "Do not go on disgracing the garb of nature." When people were speaking of the happiness of Calisthenes, and saying what splendid treatment he received from Alexander, he replied, "The man then is wretched, for he is forced to breakfast and dine whenever Alexander chooses." When he was in want of money, he said that he reclaimed it from his friends and did not beg for it.

On one occasion he was working with his hands in the market-place, and said, "I wish I could rub my stomach in the same way, and so avoid hunger." When he saw a young man going with some satraps to supper, he dragged him away and led him off to his relations, and bade them take care of him. He was once addressed by a youth beautifully adorned, who asked him some question; and he refused to give him any answer, till he satisfied him whether he was a man or a woman. And on one occasion, when a youth was playing the cottabus in the bath, he said to him, "The better you do it, the worse you do it." Once at a banquet, some of the guests threw him bones, as if he had been a dog; so he, as he went away, put up his leg against them as if he had been dog in reality. He used to call the orators, and all those who speak for fame, thrice men, instead of thrice miserable. He said

* The *hieromnemones* were the sacred secretaries or recorders sent by each Amphictyonic state to the council along with their actual deputy or minister.

that "A rich but ignorant man, was like a sheep with a golden fleece." When he saw a notice on the house of a profligate man, "To be sold." "I knew," said he, "that you who are so incessantly drunk, would soon vomit up your owner." To a young man, who was complaining of the number of people who sought his acquaintance, he said, "Do not make such a parade of your vanity."

Having been in a very dirty bath, he said, "I wonder where the people, who bathe here, clean themselves." When all the company was blaming an indifferent harp-player, he alone praised him, and being asked why he did so, he said, "Because, though he is such as he is, he plays the harp and does not steal." He saluted a harp-player who was always left alone by his hearers, with "Good morning, cock;" and when the man asked him, "Why so?" he said, "Because you, when you sing, make every one get up." When a young man was one day making a display of himself, he, having filled the bosom of his robe with lupins, began to eat them; and when the multitude looked at him, he said, "that he marvelled at their leaving the young man to look at him." And when a man, who was very superstitious, said to him, "With one blow I will break your head." "And I," he replied, "with one sneeze will make you tremble." When Hegesias entreated him to lend him one of his books, he said, "You are a silly fellow, Hegesias, for you will not take painted figs, but real ones; and yet you overlook the genuine practice of virtue, and seek for what is merely written." A man once reproached him with his banishment, and his answer was, "You wretched man, that is what made me a philosopher." And when on another occasion, some one said to him, "The people of Sinope condemned you to banishment," he replied, "And I condemned them to remain where they were." Once he saw a man who had been a victor at the Olympic games, feeding sheep, and he said to him, "You have soon come across my friend from the Olympic games, to the Nemean." When he was asked why athletes are insensible to pain, he said, "Because they are built up of pork and beef."

He once asked for a statue; and being questioned as to his reason for doing so, he said, "I am practising disappointment." Once he was begging of some one (for he did this at first out of actual want), he said, "If you have given to any one else, give also to me; and if you have never given to any one, then begin with me." On one occasion, he was asked by the tyrant, "What sort of brass was the best for a statue?" and he replied, "That of which the statues of Harmodius and Aristogiton are made." When he was asked how Dionysius treats his friends, he said, "Like bags; those which are full he hangs up, and those which are empty he throws away." A man who was lately married put an inscription on his house, "Hercules Callinicus, the son of Jupiter, lives here; let no evil enter." And so Diogenes wrote in addition, "An alliance is made after the war is over." He used to say that covetousness was the metropolis of all evils. Seeing on one occasion a profligate man in an inn eating olives, he said, "If you had dined thus, you would not have supped thus." One of his apophthegms was, that good men were the images of the Gods; another, that love was the business of those who had nothing to do. When he was asked what was miserable in life, he answered, "An indigent old man." And when the question was put to him, what beast inflicts the worst bite, he said, "Of wild beasts the sycophant, and of tame animals the flatterer."

On one occasion he saw two Centaurs very badly painted; he said, "Which of the two is the worst?"* He used to say that a speech, the object of which was solely to please, was a honeyed halter. He called the belly, the Charybdis of life. Having heard once that Didymon the adulturer, had been caught in the fact, he said, "He deserves to be hung by his

* Chiron was also the most celebrated of the Centaurs, the tutor of Achilles.

name."* When the question was put to him, why is gold of a pale color, he said, "Because it has so many people plotting against it." When he saw a woman in a litter, he said, "The cage is not suited to the animal." And seeing a runaway slave sitting on a well, he said, "My boy, take care you do not fall in." Another time, he saw a little boy who was a stealer of clothes from the baths, and said, "Are you going for unguents, or for other garments." Seeing some women hanging on some olive trees, he said, "I wish every tree bore similar fruit." At another time, he saw a clothes' stealer, and addressed him thus:—

What moves thee, say, when sleep has clos'd the sight,
To roam the silent fields in dead of night?
Art thou some wretch by hopes of plunder led,
Through heaps of coinage to despoil the dead.†

When he was asked whether he had any girl or boy to wait on him, he said, "No." And as his questioner asked further, "If then you die, who will bury you?" He replied, "Whoever wants my house." Seeing a handsome youth sleeping without any protection, he nudged him, and said, "Wake

Mix'd with the vulgar shall thy fate be found,
Pierc'd in the back, a vile dishonest wound."‡

And he addressed a man who was buying delicacies at a great expense:—

Not long, my son, will you on earth remain,
If such your dealings.§

When Plato was discoursing about his "ideas," and using the nouns "tableness" and "cupness;" "I, O Plato!" interrupted Diogenes, "see a table and a cup, but I see no tableness or cupness." Plato made answer, "That is natural

* There is a pun intended here.

† This is taken from Homer, Il. Pope's Version, 455.

‡ This is also from Homer, Il. Pope's Version, 120.

§ This is a parody on Homer.

enough, for you have eyes, by which a cup and a table are contemplated; but you have not intellect, by which tableness and cupness are seen."

On one occasion, he was asked by a certain person, "What sort of a man, O Diogenes, do you think Socrates?" and he said, "A madman." Another time, the question was put to him, when a man ought to marry? And his reply was, "Young men ought not to marry yet, and old men never ought to marry at all." When asked what he would take to let a man give him a blow on the head, he replied, "A helmet." Seeing a youth smartening himself up very carefully, he said to him, "If you are doing that for men, you are miserable; and if for women, you are profligate." Once he saw a youth blushing, and addressed him, "Courage, my boy, that is the complexion of virtue." Having once listened to two lawyers, he condemned them both, saying, "That the one had stolen the thing in question, and that the other had not lost it." When asked what wine he liked to drink, he said, "That which belongs to another." A man said to him one day, "Many people laugh at you." "But I," he replied, "am not laughed down." When a man said to him, that it was a bad thing to live; "Not to live," said he, "but to live badly." When some people were advising him to make search for a slave who had run away, he said, "It would be a very absurd thing for Manes to be able to live without Diogenes, but not for Diogenes to be able to live without Manes." When he was dining on olives, a cheese-cake was brought in, on which he threw the olive away, saying:—

Keep well aloof, O stranger, from all tyrants.*

And presently he added:—

He drove the olive off.†

* This is a line of the Phœnissæ of Euripides. v. 40.

† The pun here is on the similarity of the noun *elaan*, an olive, to the verb *elaan*, to drive.

When he was asked what sort of a dog he was, he replied, "When hungry, I am a dog of Melita; when satisfied, a Molossian; a sort which most of those who praise do not like to take out hunting with them, because of the labor of keeping up with them; and in like manner, you cannot associate with me, from fear of the pain I give you." The question was put to him, whether wise men ate cheese-cakes, and he replied, "They eat everything, just as the rest of mankind." When asked why people give to beggars and not to philosophers, he said, "Because they think it possible that they themselves may become lame and blind, but they do not expect ever to turn out philosophers." He once begged of a covetous man, and as he was slow to give, he said, "Man, I am asking you for something to maintain me, and not to bury me." When some one reproached him for having tampered with the coinage, he said, "There was a time when I was such a person as you are now; but there never was when you were such as I am now, and never will be." And to another person who reproached him on the same grounds, he said, "There were times when I did what I did not wish to, but that is not the case now." When he went to Myndus, he saw some very large gates, but the city was a small one, and so he said, "Oh men of Myndus, shut your gates, lest your city should steal out." On one occasion he saw a man who had been detected stealing purple, and so he said:—

A purple death, and mighty fate o'ertook him.*

When Craterus entreated him to come and visit him, he said, "I would rather lick up salt at Athens, than enjoy a luxurious table with Craterus." On one occasion, he met Anaximenes, the orator, who was a fat man, and thus accosted him: "Pray give us, who are poor, some of your belly; for by so doing you will be relieved yourself, and you will assist us." And once, when he was discussing some point, Diogenes

* This line occurs in Hom. Iliad.

held up a piece of salt-fish, and drew off the attention of his hearers; and as Anaximenes was indignant at this, he said, "See, one pennyworth of salt-fish has put an end to the lecture of Anaximenes." Being once reproached for eating in the market-place, he made answer, "I did, for it was in the market-place that I was hungry." Some authors also attribute the following repartee to him: Plato saw him washing vegetables, and so coming up to him, he quietly accosted him thus: "If you had paid court to Dionysius, you would not have been washing vegetables." "And," he replied with equal quietness, "if you had washed vegetables, you would never have paid court to Dionysius." When a man said to him once, "Most people laugh at you;" "And very likely," he replied, "the asses laugh at them; but they do not regard the asses, neither do I regard them." Once he saw a youth studying philosophy, and said to him, "Well done; inasmuch as you are leading those who admire your person to contemplate the beauty of your mind."

A certain person was admiring the offerings in the temple at Samothrace,* and he said to him, "They would have been much more numerous, if those who were lost had offered them instead of those who were saved;" but some attribute this speech to Diagoras the Thelian. Once he saw a handsome youth going to a banquet, and said to him, "You will come back worse (*cheiron*†);" and when he the next day after the banquet said to him, "I have left the banquet, and was no worse for it," he replied, "You were not Chiron, but Eurytion."‡ He was begging once of a very ill-tempered man, and as he said to him, "If you can persuade me, I will give

* The Samothracian Gods were Gods of the sea, and it was customary for those who had been saved from shipwreck to make them an offering of some part of what they had saved; and of their hair, if they had saved nothing but their lives.

† Cheiron signifies worse, and was also a name of one of the Centaurs.

‡ Eurytion was another of the Centaurs, who was killed by Hercules.

you something;" he replied, "If I could persuade you, I would beg you to hang yourself." He was on one occasion returning from Lacedæmon to Athens; and when some one asked him, "Whither are you going, and whence do you come?" he said, "I am going from the men's apartments to the women's." Another time he was returning from the Olympic games, and when some one asked him whether there had been a great multitude there, he said, "A great multitude, but very few men." He used to say that "Debauched men resembled figs growing on a precipice; the fruit of which is not tasted by men, but devoured by crows and vultures." When Phryne had dedicated a golden statue of Venus at Delphi, he wrote upon it, "From the profligacy of the Greeks."

Once Alexander the Great came and stood by him, and said, "I am Alexander, the great king." "And I," said he, "am Diogenes the dog." And when he was asked to what actions of his it was owing that he was called a dog, he said, "Because I fawn upon those who give me anything, and bark at those who give me nothing, and bite the rogues." On one occasion he was gathering some of the fruit of a fig-tree, and when the man who was guarding it told him a man hung himself on this tree the other day, "I, then," said he, "will now purify it." Once he saw a man who had been a conqueror at the Olympic games looking very often at a courtesan; "Look," said he, "at that warlike ram, who is taken prisoner by the first girl he meets." One of his sayings was, that good-looking courtesans were like poisoned mead.

On one occasion he was eating his dinner in the market-place, and the bystanders kept constantly calling out "Dog;" but he said, "It is you who are the dogs, who stand around me while I am at dinner." When two effeminate fellows were getting out of his way, he said, "Do not be afraid, a dog does not eat beetroot." Being once asked about a debauched boy, as to what country he came from, he said, "He is a Tegean."*

* This is a pun on the similarity of the sound, Tegea, to *tegos*, a brothel.

Seeing an unskilful wrestler professing to heal a man he said, "What are you about, are you in hopes now to overthrow those who formerly conquered you?" On one occasion he saw the son of a courtesan throwing a stone at a crowd, and said to him, "Take care, lest you hit your father." When a boy showed him a sword that he had received from one to whom he had done some discreditable service, he told him, "The sword is a good sword, but the handle is infamous." And when some people were praising a man who had given him something, he said to them, "And do not you praise me who was worthy to receive it?" He was asked by some one to give him back his cloak; but he replied, "If you gave it me, it is mine; and if you only lent it me, I am using it." A supposititious son of somebody once said to him, that he had gold in his cloak; "No doubt," said he, "that is the very reason why I sleep with it under my head." When he was asked what advantage he had derived from philosophy, he replied, "If no other, at least this, that I am prepared for every kind of fortune." The question was put to him what countryman he was, and he replied, "A Citizen of the world." Some men were sacrificing to the Gods to prevail on them to send them sons, and he said, "And do you not sacrifice to procure sons of a particular character?" Once he was asking the president of a society for a contribution, and said to him:—

"Spoil all the rest but keep your hands from Hector."

He used to say that courtesans were the queens of kings; for that they asked them for whatever they chose. When the Athenians had voted that Alexander was Bacchus, he said to them, "Vote, too, that I am Serapis." When a man reproached him for going into unclean places, he said, "The sun, too, penetrates into privies, but is not polluted by them." When supping in a temple, as some dirty loaves were set before him, he took them up and threw them away, saying that nothing dirty ought to come into a temple; and when some one said to him, "You philosophize without being possessed of any knowledge;" he said, "If I only pretend to wisdom, that is philosophizing." A man once brought him a boy, and said that he was a very clever child, and one of an admirable disposition. "What, then," said Diogenes, "does he want of me." He used to say that those who utter virtuous sentiments, but do not do them, are no better than harps, for that a harp has no hearing or feeling. Once when he saw a young man putting on effeminate airs, he said to him, "Are you not ashamed to have worse plans for yourself than nature had for you? For she has made you a man, but you are trying to force yourself to be a woman." When he saw an ignorant man tuning a psaltery, he said to him, "Are you not ashamed to be arranging proper sounds on a wooden instrument, and not arranging your soul to a proper life?" When a man said to him, "I am not calculated for philosophy," he said, "Why then do you live, if you have no desire to live properly?" To a man who treated his father with contempt, he said, "Are you not ashamed to despise him to whom you owe it that you have it in your power to give yourself airs at all?" Seeing a handsome young man chattering in an unseemly manner, he said, "Are you not ashamed to draw a sword cut of lead out of a scabbard of ivory?" Being once reproached for drinking in a vintner's shop, he said, "I have my hair cut, too, in a barber's." At another time he was attacked for having accepted a cloak from Antipater, but he replied:—

"Refuse not thou to heed
The gifts which from the mighty Gods proceed."*

A man once struck him with a broom, and said, "Take care;" so he struck him in return with his staff, and said, "Take care."

He once said to a man who was addressing anxious entreaties to a courtesan, "What can you wish to obtain, you

* Hom. Iliad.

wretched man, that you had not better be disappointed in?" Seeing a man reeking all over with unguents, he said to him, "Have a care, lest the fragrance of your head give a bad odor to your life." One of his sayings was, that servants serve their masters, and that wicked men are the slaves of their appetites. Being asked why slaves were called *andropoda* (men-footed), he replied, "Because they have the feet of men (*podas andron*), and a soul such as you who are asking this question." He once asked a profligate fellow for a mina; and when he put the question to him, why he asked others for an obol and him for a mina, he said, "Because I hope to get something from the others another time, but the Gods alone know whether I shall ever extract anything from you again." Once he was reproached for asking favors, while Plato never asked for any; and he said:—

> "He asks as well as I do, but he does it
> Bending his head, that no one else may hear."

One day he saw an unskilful archer, shooting; so he went and sat down by the target, saying, "Now I shall be out of harm's way." He used to say that those who were in love, were disappointed in regard of the pleasure they expected. When he was asked whether death was an evil, he replied, "How can that be an evil which we do not feel when it is present?" When Alexander was once standing by him, and saying, "Do not you fear me?" He replied, "No; for what are you, a good or an evil?" And as he said that he was good. "Who, then," said Diogenes, "fears the good?" He used to say that education was, for the young, sobriety; for the old, comfort; for the poor, riches; and for the rich, an ornament. When Didymus, the adulterer, was once trying to cure the eye of a young girl (*kores*), he said, "Take care, lest when you are curing the eye of the maiden, you do not hurt the pupil."* A man once said to him, that his friends laid

* There is a pun here; *kore* means both "a girl" and "the pupil of the eye." And *phtheiro*, "to destroy," is also especially used for "to seduce."

plots against him; "What, then," said he, "are you to do, if you must look upon both your friends and enemies in the same light?"

On one occasion he was asked, what was the most excellent thing among men; and he said, "Freedom of speech." He went once into a school, and saw many statues of the Muses, but very few pupils, and said, "Gods, and all my good schoolmaster, you have plenty of pupils." He was in the habit of doing everything in public, whether in respect of Venus or Ceres; and he used to put his conclusions in this way to people: "If there is nothing absurd in dining, then it is not absurd to dine in the market-place. But it is not absurd to dine, therefore it is not absurd to dine in the market-place." And as he was continually doing manual work in public, he said one day, "Would that by rubbing my belly I could get rid of hunger." Other sayings also are attributed to him, which it would take a long time to enumerate, there is such a multiplicity of them.

He used to say, that there were two kinds of exercise; that, namely, of the mind and that of the body; and that the latter of these created in the mind such quick and agile phantasies at the time of its performance, as very much facilitated the practice of virtue; but that one was imperfect without the other, since the health and vigor necessary for the practice of what is good, depend equally on both mind and body. And he used to allege as proofs of this, and of the ease which practice imparts to acts of virtue, that people could see that in the case of mere common working trades, and other employments of that kind, the artisans arrived at no inconsiderable accuracy by constant practice; and that any one may see how much one flute player, or one wrestler, is superior to another, by his own continued practice. And that if these men transferred the same training to their minds they would not labor in a profitless or imperfect manner. He used to say also, that there was nothing whatever in life which could be brought to perfection without practice, and that that alone was able to overcome every obstacle; that, therefore, as we ought to repudiate all useless toils, and to apply ourselves to useful labors, and to live happily, we are only unhappy in consequence of most exceeding folly. For the very contempt of pleasure, if we only inure ourselves to it, is very pleasant; and just as they who are accustomed to live luxuriously, are brought very unwillingly to adopt the contrary system; so they who have been originally inured to that opposite system, feel a sort of pleasure in the contempt of pleasure.

This used to be the language which he held, and he used to show in practice, really altering men's habits, and deferring in all things rather to the principles of nature than to those of law. He also argued about the law, that without it there is no possibility of a constitution being maintained; for without a city there can be nothing orderly, but a city is an orderly thing; and without a city there can be no law; therefore law is order. And he played in the same manner with the topics of noble birth, and reputation, and all things of that kind, saying that they were all veils, as it were, for wickedness; and that that was the only proper constitution which consisted in order. And he said, that all people's sons ought to belong to every one in common; and there was nothing intolerable in the idea of taking anything out of a temple, or eating any animal whatever, and that there was no impiety in tasting even human flesh; as is plain from the habits of foreign nations; and he said that this principle might be correctly extended to every case and every people. For he said that in reality, everything was a combination of all things. For that in bread there was meat, and in vegetables there was bread, and so there were some particles of all other bodies in everything communicating by invisible passages and evaporating.

And he bore being sold with a most magnanimous spirit. For as he was sailing to Ægina, and was taken prisoner by some pirates, under the command of Scirpalus, he was carried off to Crete and sold; and when the Circe asked him what art he understood, he said, "That of governing men." And presently pointing out a Corinthian, very carefully dressed, (the same Xeniades whom we have mentioned before,) he said, "Sell me to that man; for he wants a master." Accordingly Xeniades bought him and carried him away to Corinth; and then he made him tutor of his sons, and committed to him the entire management of his house. And he behaved himself in every affair in such a manner, that Xeniades, when looking over his property, said, "A good genius has come into my house." And Cleomenes, in his book which is called the Schoolmaster, says, that he wished to ransom all his relations, but that Diogenes told him they were all fools; for that lions did not become the slaves of those who kept them, but, on the contrary, those who maintained lions were their slaves. For that it was the part of a slave to fear, but that wild beasts were formidable to men.

And the man had the gift of persuasion in a wonderful degree; so that he could easily overcome any one by his arguments. Accordingly, it is said that an Æginetan of the name of Onesicritus, having two sons, sent to Athens one of them, whose name was Androsthenes, and that he, after having heard Diogenes lecture, remained there; and that after that, he sent the elder, Philiscus, who has been already mentioned, and that Philiscus was charmed in the same manner. And last of all, he came himself, and then he too remained no less than his son, studying philosophy at the feet of Diogenes. So great a charm was there in the discourses of Diogenes. Another pupil of his was Phocion, who was surnamed the Good; and Stilpon, the Megarian, and a great many other men of eminence as statesmen.

He is said to have died when he was nearly ninety years of age, but there are different accounts given of his death. For some say that he ate an ox's foot raw, and was in consequence seized with a bilious attack, of which he died; others, of whom Cercidas, a Megalopolitan or Cretan, is one, say that he died of holding his breath for several days; and Cercidas speaks thus of him in his Meliambics:—

He, that Sinopian who bore the stick,
Wore his cloak doubled, and in th' open air
Dined without washing, would not bear with life
A moment longer: but he shut his teeth,
And held his breath. He truly was the son
Of Jove, and a most heavenly-minded dog,
The wise Diogenes.

Others say that he, while intending to distribute a polypus to his dogs, was bitten by them through the tendon of his foot, and so died. But his own greatest friends, as Antisthenes tells us in his Successions, rather sanction the story of his having died from holding his breath. For he used to live in the Craneum, which was a Gymnasium at the gates of Corinth. And his friends came according to their custom, and found him with his head covered; and as they did not suppose that he was asleep, for he was not a man much subject to the influence of night or sleep, they drew away his cloak from his face, and found him no longer breathing; and they thought that he had done this on purpose, wishing to escape the remaining portion of his life.

On this there was a quarrel, as they say, between his friends, as to who should bury him, and they even came to blows; but when the elders and chief men of the city came there, they say that he was buried by them at the gate which leads to the Isthmus. And they placed over him a pillar, and on that a dog in Parian marble. And at a later period his fellow-citizens honored him with brazen statues, and put this inscription on them:—

E'en brass by lapse of time doth old become,
But there is no such time as shall efface,
Your lasting glory, wise Diogenes;

Since you alone did teach to men the art
Of a contented life; the surest path
To glory and a lasting happiness.

Some, however, say that when he was dying, he ordered his friends to throw his corpse away without burying it, so that every beast might tear it, or else to throw it into a ditch, and sprinkle a little dust over it. And others say that his injunctions were, that he should be thrown into the Ilissus; that so he might be useful to his brethren. But Demetrius, in his treatise on Men of the Same Name, says that Diogenes died in Corinth the same day that Alexander died in Babylon. And he was already an old man, as early as the hundred and thirteenth Olympiad.

DIOGENES, THE BABYLONIAN.

Diogenes, of Seleucia, called also the Babylonian, from the vicinity of Babylon to his native place, applied himself so diligently to the study and propagation of the Stoic doctrine, that Cicero calls him a great and respectable Stoic. This was unquestionably the reason for which he was sent with Carneades and Critolaus on the celebrated embassy from Athens to Rome. Seneca relates, that as he was one day discoursing upon anger, a foolish youth, in hope of raising a laugh against the philosopher by making him angry, spit in his face; upon which Diogenes meekly and prudently said, "I am not angry, but I am in doubt whether I ought not to be so." He lived to the age of eighty-eight years.

DIAGORAS.

Diagoras was a native of the island of Melos. He was sold as a captive in his youth, but was afterwards redeemed by Democritus, and trained up to the study of philosophy. He also cultivated polite learning, and distinguished himself in the art of poetry. His name, however, has been transmitted to posterity with infamy, in consequence of his atheistical principles. It is positively asserted that on one occasion, when he saw a perjured person escape punishment, he publicly avowed his disbelief of Divine Providence, and from that time spoke of the Gods, and of all religious ceremonies, with ridicule and contempt. He even attempted to lay open the sacred mysteries, and to dissuade the people from submitting to the rites of initiation. These public insults offered to religion brought upon him the general hatred of the Athenians; who, upon his refusing to obey a summons to appear in the courts of judicature, issued forth a decree, which was inscribed upon a brazen column, offering the reward of a talent to any one who should kill him, or two talents to any one who should bring him alive before the judges. This happened in the ninety-first Olympiad. From that time Diagoras became a fugitive in Attica, and at last fled to Corinth, where he died. It is said, that being on board a ship during a storm, the terrified sailors began to accuse themselves for having received into their ship a man so infamous for his impiety; upon which Diagoras pointed out to them other vessels, which were near them on the sea in equal danger, and asked them, whether they thought that each of these ships also carried a Diagoras; and that afterwards, when a friend, in order to convince him that the Gods are not indifferent to human affairs, desired him to observe how many consecrated tablets were hung up in the temples in grateful acknowledgment of the escapes from the dangers of the sea, he said in reply, "True; but here are no tablets of those who have suffered shipwreck, and perished in the sea." But there is reason to suspect that these tales are mere inventions; for similar stories have been told of Diogenes, the Cynic, and others.

EDDIN SADI.

Eddin Sadi, a Persian, about the middle of the thirteenth century, when the Turks invaded Persia, withdrew from his own country, and settled at Bagdat, for the purpose of prosecuting his studies. After experiencing much vicissitude of fortune, he returned home, and compiled a beautiful compendium of Oriental ethics, under the title of the Persian Rosary, which he completed in the year 1257. This work has been universally read in the East, and has been translated into Latin, and into several modern languages. From this Rosary, which is divided into eight chapters, we shall cull a few of the choicest flowers.

1. Paradise will be the reward of those kings who restrain their resentment, and know how to forgive. A king who institutes unjust laws, undermines the foundation of his kingdom. Let him who neglects to raise the fallen, fear lest, when he himself falls, no one will stretch out his hand to lift him up. Administer justice to your people, for a day of judgment is at hand. The dishonest steward's hand will shake, when he comes to render an account of his trust. Be just, and fear not. Oppress not thy subjects, lest the sighing of the oppressed should ascend to heaven. If you wish to be great, be liberal; for unless you sow the seed, there can be no increase. Assist and relieve the wretched, for misfortunes may happen to yourself. Wound no man unnecessarily; there are thorns enough in the path of human life. If a king take an apple from the garden of a subject, his servants will soon cut down the tree. The flock is not made for the shepherd, but the shepherd for the flock.

2. Excel in good works, and wear what you please; innocence and piety do not consist in wearing an old or coarse garment. Learn virtue from the vicious; and what offends you in their conduct, avoid in your own. If you have received

an injury, bear it patiently; by pardoning the offences of others, you will wash away your own. Him, who has been every day conferring upon you new favors, pardon, if, in the space of a long life, he should have once done you an injury. Respect the memory of the good, that your good name may live forever.

3. In your adversity, do not visit your friend with a sad countenance; for you will embitter his cup: relate even your misfortunes with a smile; for wretchedness will never reach the heart of a cheerful man. He who lives upon the fruits of his own labor, escapes the contempt of haughty benefactors. Always encounter petulance with gentleness, and perverseness with kindness: a gentle hand will lead the elephant itself by a hair. When once you have offended a man, do not presume that a hundred benefits will secure you from revenge: an arrow may be drawn out of a wound, but an injury is never forgotten. Worse than the venom of a serpent, is the tongue of an enemy who pretends to be your friend.

4. It is better to be silent on points we understand, than to be put to shame by being questioned upon things of which we are ignorant. A wise man will not contend with a fool. It is a certain mark of folly, as well as rudeness, to speak whilst another is speaking. If you are wise, you will speak less than you know.

5. Although you can repeat every word of the Koran, if you suffer yourself to be enslaved by love, you have not yet learned your alphabet. The immature grape is sour; wait a few days, and it will become sweet. If you resist temptation, do not assure yourself that you shall escape slander. The reputation which has been fifty years in building, may be thrown down by one blast of calumny. Listen not to the tale of friendship from the man who has been capable of forgetting his friends in adversity.

6. Perseverance accomplishes more than precipitation: the patient mule, which travels slowly night and day, will in the

end go further than an Arabian courser. If you are old, leave sports and jests to the young: the stream which has passed away, will not return into its channel.

7. Instruction is only profitable to those who are capable of receiving it: bring an ass to Mecca, and it will still return an ass. If you would be your father's heir, learn his wisdom: his wealth you may expend in ten days. He who is tinctured with good principles while he is young, when he is grown old will not be destitute of virtue. If a man be destitute of knowledge, prudence, and virtue, his door-keeper may say, Nobody is at home. Give advice where you ought; if it be not regarded, the fault is not yours.

8. Two kinds of men labor in vain: they who get riches, and do not enjoy them; and they who learn wisdom, and do not apply it to the conduct of life. A wise man who is not at the same time virtuous, is a blind man carrying a lamp: he gives light to others, whilst he himself remains in darkness. If you wish to sleep soundly, provide for to-morrow. Trust no man, not even your best friend, with a secret: you will never find a more faithful guardian of the trust than yourself. Let your misfortunes teach you compassion: he knows the condition of the wretched, who has himself been wretched. Excessive vehemence creates enmity; excessive gentleness, contempt: be neither so severe as to be hated, nor so mild as to be insulted. He who throws away advice upon a conceited man, himself wants an adviser. In a single hour you may discover whether a man has good sense; but it will require many years to discover whether he has good temper. Three things are unattainable: riches without trouble, science without controversy, and government without punishment. Clemency to the wicked is an injury to the good. If learning were banished from the earth, there would, notwithstanding, be no one who would think himself ignorant.

The whole work from which these specimens are selected is an elegant specimen of Arabian morals.

EMPEDOCLES.

Empedocles was a citizen of Agrigentum. He was a pupil of Pythagoras, saying that he was afterwards convicted of having divulged his doctrines, in the same way as Plato was, and therefore that he was forbidden from thenceforth to attend his school. And they say that Pythagoras himself mentions him when he says:—

> And in that band there was a learned man,
> Of wondrous wisdom ; one, who of all men
> Had the profoundest wealth of intellect.

But some say that when the philosopher says this, he is referring to Parmenides.

Satyrus says that he practiced magic, and that he professes a knowledge of this art in the following lines:—

> And all the drugs which can relieve disease,
> Or soften the approach of age, shall be
> Revealed to your inquiries ; I do know them,
> And I to you alone will them disclose.
> You shall restrain the fierce unbridled winds,
> Which, rushing o'er the earth, bow down the corn,
> And crush the farmer's hopes. And when you will,
> You shall recall them back to sweep the land:
> Then you shall learn to dry the rainy clouds,
> And bid warm summer cheer the heart of men.
> Again, at your behest, the draught shall yield
> To wholesome show'rs: when you give the word
> Hell shall restore its dead.

And Timæus, in his eighteenth book, says, that this man was held in great esteem on many accounts; for that once, when the Etesian gales were blowing violently, so as to injure the crops, he ordered some asses to be flayed, and some bladders to be made of their hides, and these he placed on the hills and high places to catch the wind. And so, when the wind ceased, he was called wind-forbidder.

It is also said that he kept the corpse of a dead woman free from corruption thirty days, on which account he professed to be a physician and a prophet. Empedocles, seeing the people immersed in luxury, said, "The men of Agrigentum devote themselves wholly to luxury as if they were to die to-morrow, but they furnish their houses as if they were to live forever."

And Aristotle says, that he was a most liberal man, and far removed from anything like a domineering spirit; since he constantly refused the sovereign power when it was offered to him, as Xanthus assures us in his account of him, showing plainly that he preferred a simple style of living. And Timæus tells the same story, giving at the same time the reason why he was so very popular. For he says that when on one occasion, he was invited to a banquet by one of the magistrates, the wine was carried about, but the supper was not served up. And as every one else kept silence, he, disapproving of what he saw, bade the servants bring in the supper; but the person who had invited him said that he was waiting for the secretary of the council. And when he came he was appointed master of the feast, at the instigation of the giver of it, and then he gave a plain intimation of his tyrannical inclinations, for he ordered all the guests to drink, and those who did not drink were to have the wine poured over their heads. Empedocles said nothing at the moment, but the next day he summoned them before the court, and procured the execution of both the entertainer and the master of the feast.

And this was the beginning of his political career. But there are two accounts of the manner of his death.

For Heraclides, relating the story about the dead woman, how Empedocles got great glory from sending away a dead woman restored to life, says that he celebrated a sacrifice in the field of Pisianax, and that some of his friends were invited, among whom was Pausanias. And then, after the banquet, they lay down, some going a little way off, and some lying under the trees close by in the field, and some wherever they happened to choose. But Empedocles himself remained in the place where he had been sitting. But when day broke, and they arose, he alone was not found. And when he was sought for, and the servants were examined and said that they did not know, one of them said, that at midnight he had heard a loud voice calling Empedocles; and that then he himself rose up and saw a great light from heaven, but nothing else. And as they were all amazed at what had taken place, Pausanias descended and sent some people to look for him; but afterwards he was commanded not to busy himself about the matter, as he was informed that what had happened was deserving of thankfulness, and that they behoved a sacrifice to Empedocles as to one who had become a God.

Hermippus says also, that a woman of the name of Panthea, a native of Agrigentum, who had been given over by the physicians, was cured by him, and that it was on this account that he celebrated a sacrifice; and that the guests invited were about eighty in number. But Hippobotus says that he rose up and went away as if he were going to mount Ætna; and that when he arrived at the crater of fire he leaped in, and disappeared, wishing to establish a belief that he had become a God. But afterwards the truth was detected by one of his slippers having been dropped. For he used to wear slippers with brazen soles. Pausanias, however, contradicts this statement.

But Diodorus, of Ephesus, writing about Anaximander, says that Empedocles imitated him; indulging in the tragic sort of pride, and wearing magnificent apparel. And when a pestilence attacked the people of Selinus, by reason of the bad smells arising from the adjacent river, so that the men died and the women bore dead children, Empedocles contrived a plan, and bought into the same channel two other rivers at his own expense; and so, by mixing their waters with that of the other river, he sweetened the stream. And as the pestilence was removed in this way, when the people of Selinus were on one occasion holding a festival on the bank of the river, Empedocles appeared among them; and they rising up, offered him adoration, and prayed to him as to a God. And he, wishing to confirm this idea which they had adopted of him, leaped into the fire.

But Timæus contradicts all these stories; saying expressly, that he departed into Peloponnesus, and never returned at all, on which account the manner of his death is uncertain. And he especially denies the tale of Heraclides in his fourth book; for he says that Pisianax was a Syracusan, and had no field in the district of Agrigentum; but that Pausanias erected a monument in honor of his friend, since such a report had got about concerning him; and, as he was a rich man, made it a statue and little chapel, as one might erect to a God. "How then," adds Timæus, "could he have leaped into a crater, of which, though they were in the neighborhood, he had never made any mention? He died then in Peloponnesus; and there is nothing extraordinary in there being no tomb of his to be seen; for there are many other men who have no tomb visible." These are the words of Timæus; and he adds further, "But Heraclides is altogether a man fond of strange stories, and one who would assert that a man had fallen from the moon."

Hippobotus says, that there was a clothed statue of Empedocles which lay formerly in Agrigentum, but which was afterwards placed in front of the Senate House of the Romans, divested of its clothing, as the Romans had carried it off and erected it there. And there are traces of some inscriptions or reliefs still discernible on it.

Neanthes, of Cyzicus, who also wrote about the Pythagoreans, says, that when Meton was dead, the seeds of tyrannical power began to appear; and that then Empedocles persuaded the Agrigentines to desist from their factious disputes, and to establish political equality. And besides, as there were many of the female citizens destitute of dowry, he portioned them out of his own private fortune. And relying on these actions of his, he assumed a purple robe and wore a golden circlet on his hand, as Phavorinus relates in the first book of his Commentaries. He also wore slippers with brazen soles, and a Delphian garland. His hair was let grow very long, and he had boys to follow him; and he himself always preserved a solemn countenance, and a uniformly grave deportment. And he marched about in such style, that he seemed to all the citizens, who met him and who admired his deportment, to exhibit a sort of likeness to kingly power. And afterwards, it happened that as on the occasion of some festival he was going in a chariot to Messene, he was upset and broke his thigh; and he was taken ill in consequence, and so died, at the age of seventy-seven. His tomb is in Megara.

He flourished about the eighty-fourth Olympiad. Demetrius, of Træzon, in his book against the Sophists, reports that as the lines of Homer say:—

> He now, self-murdered, from a beam depends,
> And his mad soul to blackest hell descends.*

But in the letter of Telauges, which has been mentioned before, it is said that he slipped down through old age, and fell into the sea, and so died.

There is a jesting epigram of ours upon him, in our collection of Poems in all Metres, which runs thus:—

> You too, Empedocles, essayed to purge
> Your body in the rapid flames, and drank
> The liquid fire from the restless crater;
> I say not that you threw yourself at once
> Into the stream of Ætna's fiery flood.
> But seeking to conceal yourself you fell,
> And so you met with unintended death.

And another:—

> 'Tis said the wise Empedocles did fall
> Out of his chariot, and so broke his thigh:
> But if he leapt into the flames of Ætna,
> How could his tomb be shown in Megara?

* This is slightly parodied from Homer. Od. xi. 278. Pope's Version, 337.

In addition to the above account by D. Laertius, we insert the following from Brucker:

After the death of his father Meto, who was a wealthy citizen of Agrigentum, Empedocles acquired great weight among his fellow-citizens by espousing the popular party and favoring democratic measures. He employed a large share of his paternal estate in giving dowries to young women, and marrying them to men of superior rank. His consequence in the state became at length so great, that he ventured to assume several of the distinctions of royalty, particularly a purple robe, a golden girdle, a Delphic crown, and a train of attendants, always retaining a grave and commanding aspect. He was a determined enemy to tyranny, and is said to have employed his influence in establishing and defending the rights of his countrymen.

The skill which Empedocles possessed in medicine and natural philosophy enabled him to perform many wonders, which he passed upon the superstitious and credulous multitude for miracles. He pretended to drive away noxious winds from his country, and hereby put a stop to epidemical diseases. He is said to have checked, by the power of music, the madness of a young man, who was threatening his enemy with instant death; to have cured Pantha, a woman of Agrigentum, whom all the physicians had declared incurable; to have restored a woman to life, who had lain breathless for thirty days; and to have done many other things equally astonishing, after the manner of Pythagoras; on account of which he was an object of universal admiration, so that when he came to the Olympic games, the eyes of all the people were fixed upon him.

EPICTETUS.

An illustrious ornament of the Stoic school, who claims respectful attention, both for his wisdom and virtues, is Epictetus. This eminent philosopher was born at Hierapolis, in Phrygia, in a servile condition, and was sold as a slave to Epaphroditus, one of Nero's domestics. Ancient writers are agreed that Epictetus was lame, but differ with respect to the cause of his lameness. Suidas says that he lost one of his legs when he was young, in consequence of a defluxion; Simplicius asserts that he was born lame; Celsus relates, that when his master, in order to torture him, bended his leg, Epictetus, without discovering any sign of fear, said to him, "You will break it;" and when his tormentor had broken the leg, he only said, "Did I not tell you you would break it?" Others ascribe his lameness to the heavy chains with which his master loaded him.

Having at length, by some means which are not related, obtained his manumission, Epictetus retired to a small hut within the city of Rome, where, with nothing more than the bare necessaries of life, he devoted himself to the study of philosophy. Here he passed his days entirely alone, till his humanity led him to take the charge of a child, whom a friend of his had through poverty exposed, and to provide it with a nurse. Having furnished himself, by diligent study, with a competent knowledge of the principles of the Stoic philosophy, and having received instructions in rhetoric from Rufus, who is said to have been himself a bold and successful corrector of public manners, Epictetus, notwithstanding his poverty, became a popular moral preceptor. He was an acute and judicious observer of manners. His eloquence was simple, majestic, nervous, and penetrating. His doctrine inculcated the purest morals; and his life was an admirable pattern of sobriety, magnanimity, and the most rigid virtue.

Neither his humble station, nor his singular merit, could, however, screen Epictetus from the tyranny of the monster Domitian. With the rest of the philosophers, he was banished, under a mock decree of the senate, from Italy. But he bore his exile with a degree of firmness worthy of a philosopher who called himself a citizen of the world, and could boast that, wherever he went, he carried his best treasures along with him. At Nicopolis, the place which he chose for his residence, he prosecuted his design of correcting vice and folly by the precepts of philosophy. Wherever he could obtain an auditory, he discoursed concerning the true way of attaining contentment and happiness; and the wisdom and eloquence of his discourses were so highly admired, that it became a common practice among the more studious of his hearers to commit them to writing.

Epictetus flourished from the time of Nero to the latter end of the reign of Adrian; but it is improbable, notwithstanding the assertion of Themistius and Suidas, that his life was protracted to the reign of the Antonines; for Aulus Gellius, who wrote in their time, speaks of Epictetus as lately dead, whereas, had he been living when that prince engaged preceptors of different sects, it is not likely that he would have overlooked the first ornament of the Porch, or preferred his disciple, Junius Rusticus. The memory of Epictetus was so highly respected, that, according to Lucian, the earthen lamp by which he used to study was sold for three thousand drachms. His beautiful Moral Manual, or *Enchiridion*, and his "Dissertations," collected by Arrian, were drawn up from notes which his disciples took from his lips.

EPICURUS.

Epicurus was an Athenian, and the son of Neocles. After the death of Alexander, when the Athenians were driven out of Samos by Perdiccas, he went to Colophon, to his father. And when he had spent some time there, and collected some disciples, he again returned to Athens, in the time of Anaxicrates, and for some time studied philosophy, mingling with the rest of the philosophers; but, subsequently, he somehow or other established the school which was called after his name. And he used to say, that he began to study philosophy when he was fourteen years of age; but Apollodorus, the Epicurean, in the first book of his account of the life of Epicurus says, that he came to the study of philosophy, having conceived a great contempt for the grammarians, because they could not explain to him the statements in Hesiod respecting Chaos.

Diotimus, the Stoic, was very hostile to him, and calumniated him in a most bitter manner, publishing fifty obscene letters, and attributing them to Epicurus, and also giving him the credit of the letters, which generally go under the name of Chrysippus. And Posidonius, the Stoic, and Nicolaus, and Sotion, in the twelfth of these books, which are entitled the Refutations of Diocles, of which there are altogether twenty-four volumes, and Dionysius, of Halicarnassus, have also attacked him with great severity; for they say that he used to accompany his mother when she went about the small cottages, performing purifications, and that he used to read the formula, and that he used also to keep a school with his father at very low terms. Also, that he, as well as one of his brothers, was a most profligate man in his morals, and that he used to live with Leontium, the courtesan. Moreover, that he claimed the books of Democritus on Atoms, and that of Aristippus on Pleasure, as his own; and that he was not a legitimate citizen; and this last fact is asserted also by Timocrates, and by Herodotus, in his treatise on the Youth of Epicurus.

They also say that he used to flatter Mithras, the steward of Lysimachus, in a disgraceful manner, calling him in his letters Pæan, and King; and also that he flattered Idomeneus, and Herodotus, and Timocrates who had revealed all his secret practices, and that he flattered them on this very account. And in his letters to Leontium, he says, "O king Apollo, my dear Leontium, what transports of joy did I feel when I read your charming letter." And to Themista, the wife of Leontius, he writes, "I am ready and prepared, if you do not come to me, to roll myself to wherever you and Themista invite me." And he addresses Pythocles, a beautiful youth, thus, "I will sit quiet," says he, "awaiting your longed-for and god-like approach." And at another time, writing to Themista, he says, "That he had determined to make his way with her."

He also wrote to many other courtesans, and especially to Leontium, with whom Metrodorus also was in love. And in his treatise on the Chief Good, he writes thus, "For I do not know what I can consider good, if I put out of sight the pleasures which arise from favors, and those which are derived from amatory pleasures, and from music, and from the contemplation of beauty." And in his letter to Pythocles, he writes, "And, my dear boy, avoid all sorts of education."

Epictetus also attacks him as a most debauched man, and reproaches him most vehemently, and so does Timocrates, the brother of Metrodorus, in his treatise entitled the Merry Guests, and this Timocrates had been a disciple in his school, though he afterwards abandoned it; and he says that he used to vomit twice a day, in consequence of his intemperance; and that he himself had great difficulty in escaping from this nocturnal philosophy, and that mystic kind of re-union. He also accuses Epicurus of shameful ignorance in his reasoning, and still more especially in all matters relating to the conduct of life. And says that he was in a pitiable state of health, so that he could not for many years rise up from his sofa; and that he used to spend a minæ a day on his eating, as he himself states in his letter to Leontium, and in that to the philosophers at Mitylene. He also says that many courtesans used to live with him and Metrodorus; and among them Marmaricem, and Hedea, and Erotium, and Nicidium.

And in the thirty-seven books which he wrote about natural philosophy, they say that he says a great many things of the same kind over and over again, and that in them he writes in contradiction of other philosophers, and especially of Nausiphanes, and speaks as follows, word for word: "But if any one else ever was afflicted in such a manner, then certainly this man had a continual labor, striving to bring forth the sophistical boastfulness of his mouth, like many other slaves." And Epicurus also speaks of Nausiphanes in his letters, in the following terms: "These things led him on to such arrogance of mind, that he abused me and called me a schoolmaster." He used also to call him Lungs, and Blockhead, and Humbug, and Fornicator. And he used to call Plato's followers Flatterers of Dionysius, but Plato himself he called Golden. Aristotle he called a debauchee and a glutton, saying that he joined the army after he had squandered his patrimony, and sold drugs. He used also to call Protagoras a porter, and the secretary of Democritus, and to say that he taught boys their letters in the streets. Heraclitus he called a disturber; Democritus, he nicnamed Lerocrates;* and Antidorus, Sænidorus.† The Cynics he called enemies of Greece; and the Dialecticians he charged with being eaten up with envy. Pyrrho, he said, was ignorant and unlearned.

But these men who say this are all wrong, for there are plenty of witnesses of the unsurpassable kindness of the man to everybody; both his own country which honored him with brazen statues, and his friends who were so numerous that they could not be contained in whole cities; and all his acquaintances who were bound to him by nothing but the charms of his doctrine, none of whom ever deserted him, èxcept Me-

* That is "trifler," from *krino*, to judge; and *leros*, nonsensical talk.

† That is, flattering for gifts; from *saino*, to wag the tail as a dog, to caress; and *doron*, a gift.

trodorus, the son of Stratoniceus, who went over to Carneades, probably because he was not able to bear with equanimity the unapproachable excellence of Epicurus. Also, the perpetual succession of his school, which, when every other school decayed, continued without any falling off, and produced a countless number of philosophers, succeeding one another without any interruption. We may also speak here of his gratitude towards his parents, and his beneficence to his brothers, and his gentleness to his servants (as is plain from his will, and from the fact too, that they united with him in his philosophical studies, and the most eminent of them was the one whom I have mentioned already, named Inus); and his universal philanthropy towards all men.

His piety towards the Gods, and his affection for his country was quite unspeakable; though, from an excess of modesty, he avoided affairs of state. And though he lived when very difficult times oppressed Greece, he still remained in his own country, only going two or three times across to Ionia to see his friends, who used to throng to him from all quarters, and to live with him in his garden, as we are told by Apollodorus. (This garden he bought for eighty minæ.)

And Diocles, in the third book of his Excursion, says that they all lived in the most simple and economical manner; "They were content," says he, "with a small cup of light wine, and all the rest of their drink was water." He also tells us that Epicurus would not allow his followers to throw their property into a common stock, as Pythagoras did, who said that the possessions of friends were held in common. For he said that such a doctrine as that was suited rather for those who distrusted one another; and that those who distrusted one another were not friends. But he himself in his letters, says that he is content with water and plain bread, and adds, "Send me some Cytherean cheese, that if I wish to have a feast, I may have the means." This was the real character of the man who laid down the doctrine that pleasure was the chief good; whom Athenæus thus mentions in an epigram:—

O men, you labor for pernicious ends;
And out of eager avarice, begin
Quarrels and wars. And yet the wealth of nature
Fixes a narrow limit for desires,
Though empty judgment is insatiable.
This lesson the wise child of Neocles
Had learnt by heart, instructed by the Muses,
Or at the sacred shrine of Delphi's God.

And as we advance further, we shall learn this fact from his dogmas, and his apophthegms.

He uses in his works plain language with respect to anything he is speaking of, for which Aristophanes, the grammarian, blames him, on the ground of that style being vulgar. But he was such an admirer of perspicuity, that even in his treatise on Rhetoric, he aims at and recommends nothing but clearness of expression. And in his letters, instead of the usual civil expressions, "Greeting," "Farewell," and so on, he substitutes, "May you act well," "May you live virtuously," and expressions of that sort.

He came to Athens, and he died there in the second year of the hundred and twenty-seventh Olympiad, in the archonship of Pytharatus, when he had lived seventy-two years.

He died of the stone, after having been ill a fortnight; and at the end of the fortnight, Hermippus says that he went into a brazen bath, properly tempered with warm water, and asked for a cup of pure wine, and drank it; and having recommended his friends to remember his doctrines, he expired. And there is an epigram of ours on him, couched in the following language:—

Now fare ye well, remember all my words;
This was the dying charge of Epicurus:
Then to the bath he went, and drank some wine,
And sank beneath the cold embrace of Pluto.

And when he was at the point of death, he wrote the following letter to Idomeneus:—

"We have written this letter to you on a happy day to us, which is also the last day of our life. For strangury has attacked me, and also a dysentery so violent, that nothing can be added to the violence of my sufferings. But the cheerfulness of my mind, which arises from the recollection of all my philosophical contemplations, counterbalances all these afflictions. And I beg you to take care of the children of Metrodorus, in a manner worthy of the devotion shown by the youth to me, and to philosophy."

In his last will and testament he bequeathed freedom to four of his slaves.

Epicurus was a most voluminous author, exceeding all men in the number of his books, for there are more than three hundred volumes of them; and in the whole of them there is not one citation from other sources, but they are filled wholly with the sentiments of Epicurus himself. In the quantity of his writings he was rivalled by Chrysippus, as Carneades asserts, who calls him a parasite of the books of Epicurus; for if ever this latter wrote anything, Chrysippus immediately set his heart on writing a book of equal size; and in this way he often wrote the same thing over again, putting down whatever came into his head; and he published it all without any corrections, by reason of his haste. And he quotes such numbers of testimonies from other authors, that his books are entirely filled with them alone; as one may find also in the works of Aristotle and Zeno.

His description of a wise man is as follows: He said that injuries existed among men, either in consequence of hatred, or of envy, or of contempt, all of which the wise man overcomes by reason. Also, that a man who has once been wise can never receive the contrary disposition, nor can he of his own accord invent such a state of things as that he should be subjected to the dominion of the passions; nor can he hinder himself in his progress towards wisdom. That the wise man, however, cannot exist in every state of body, nor in every nation. That even if the wise man were to be put to the torture, he would still be happy. That the wise man will only feel gratitude to his friends, but to them equally whether they are present or absent. Nor will he groan and howl when he is put to the torture. Nor will he marry a wife whom the laws forbid, as Diogenes says in his epitome of the Ethical Maxims of Epicurus. He will punish his servants, but also pity them, and show indulgence to any that are virtuous. They do not think that the wise man will ever be in love, nor that he will be anxious about his burial, nor that love is a passion inspired by the Gods, as Diogenes says in his twelfth book. They also assert that he will be indifferent to the study of oratory. Marriage, say they, is never any good to a man, and we must be quite content if it does no harm; and the wise man will never marry or beget children, as Epicurus himself lays it down in his Doubts, and in his treatises on Nature. Still, under certain circumstances of life, he will forsake these rules, and marry. Nor will he ever indulge in drunkenness, says Epicurus in his Banquet, nor will he entangle himself in affairs of state. Nor will he become a tyrant. Nor will he become a Cynic. Nor a beggar. And even though he should lose his eyes, he will still partake of life.

The wise man will be subject to grief, as Diogenes says, he will also not object to go to law. He will leave books and memorials of himself behind him, but he will not be fond of frequenting assemblies. He will take care of his property, and provide for the future. He will like being in the country, he will resist fortune, and will grieve none of his friends. He will show a regard for a fair reputation to such an extent as to avoid being despised; and he will find more pleasure than other men in speculations.

All faults are not equal. Health is good for some people but a matter of indifference to others. Courage is a quality which does not exist by nature, but which is engendered by a consideration of what is suitable. Friendship is caused by one's wants; but it must be begun on one side. For we sow the earth; and friendship arises from a community of, and participation in, pleasure. Happiness must be understood in two senses; the highest happiness, such as is that of God, which admits of no increase; and another kind, which admits of the addition or abstraction of pleasures. The wise man may raise statues if it suits his inclination, if it does not it does not signify. The wise man is the only person who can converse correctly about music and poetry; and he can realize poems, but not become a poet.

It is possible for one wise man to be wiser than another. The wise man will also, if he is in need, earn money, but only by his wisdom; he will propitiate an absolute ruler when occasion requires, and will humor him for the sake of correcting his habits; he will have a school, but not on such a system as to draw a crowd about him; he will also recite in a multitude, but that will be against his inclination; he will pronounce dogmas, and will express no doubts; he will be the same man asleep and awake; and he will be willing even to die for a friend.

Amongst his fundamental maxims are the following:—

No pleasure is intrinsically bad: but the efficient causes of some pleasures bring with them a great many perturbations of pleasure.

Irresistible power and great wealth may, up to a certain point, give us security as far as men are concerned; but the security of men in general depends upon the tranquillity of their souls, and their freedom from ambition.

He who desires to live tranquilly without having anything to fear from other men, ought to make himself friends; those whom he cannot make friends of, he should, at least, avoid rendering enemies; and if that is not in his power, he should, as far as possible, avoid all intercourse with them, and keep them aloof, as far as it is for his interest to do so.

Of all the things which wisdom provides for the happiness of the whole life, by far the most important is the acquisition of friendship.

It is not possible to live pleasantly without living prudently, and honorably, and justly: nor to live prudently, and honorably, and justly, without living pleasantly. But he to whom it does not happen to live prudently, honorably, and justly, cannot possibly live pleasantly.

Thus much concerning this philosopher, we have taken from Laertius. Brucker adds the following:

During the siege of Athens by Demetrius, which happened when Epicurus was forty-four years of age, while the city was severely harassed by famine, Epicurus is said to have supported himself and his friends on a small quantity of beans, which he shared equally with them.

The luxurious refinement which prevailed in Athens, while it rendered every rigid scheme of philosophy, as well as all grossness of manners, unpopular, inclined the younger citizens to listen to a preceptor, who smoothed the stern and wrinkled brow of philosophy, and, under the notion of conducting his followers to enjoyment in the bower of tranquillity, led them unawares into the paths of moderation and virtue. Hence his school became exceedingly popular, and disciples flocked into the garden, not only from different parts of Greece, but from Egypt and Asia. Seneca, though a Stoic philosopher, bears this testimony to Epicurus: "I the more freely quote the excellent maxims of Epicurus, in order to convince those who become his followers from the hope of screening their vices, that to whatever sect they attach themselves, they must live virtuously. Even at the entrance of the garden they will find this inscription 'the hospitable keeper of this mansion, where you will find pleasure the highest good, will present you liberally with barley cakes and water from the spring.

These gardens will not provoke your appetite by artificial dainties, but satisfy it with natural supplies. Will you not then be well entertained?'"

Those disciples who were regularly admitted into the school of Epicurus, lived together, not in the manner of the Pythagorians, who cast their possessions into a common stock, for this, in his opinion, implied mutual distrust, rather than friendship; but upon such a footing of friendly attachment, that each individual cheerfully supplied the necessities of his brother. And this was no difficult task, not only on account of the smallness of the expenses attending their frugal manner of living, but because the most cordial affection subsisted among them. The friendship of the Epicurean fraternity is described by Cicero as unequalled in the history of mankind; and Valerius Maximus relates a memorable example of indissoluble friendship between Polycrates and Hippoclides, two philosophers of the garden.

Epicurus, that he might prosecute his philosophical labors with the less interruption, lived in a state of celibacy. In his own conduct he was exemplary for temperance and continence, and he inculcated upon his followers serenity of manners, and the strict government of the passions, as the best means of passing a tranquil and happy life. Notwithstanding his regular manner of living, towards the close of his days, probably in consequence of his close application to study, his constitution became infirm, and he was afflicted with the stone, of which, after great suffering, he died.

Not only did the immediate followers of Epicurus adorn the memory of their master with the highest honors, but many eminent writers, who have disapproved his philosophy, have expressed great respect for his personal merit. Nevertheless, it cannot be denied, that from the time when this philosopher appeared to the present day, an uninterrupted course of censure has fallen upon his memory; so that the name of his sect has almost become a proverbial expression for everything corrupt in principles, and infamous in character. The charges brought against Epicurus are, that he superseded all religious principles, by dismissing the Gods from the care of the world; that, if he acknowledged their existence, it was only in conformity to popular prejudice, since, according to his system, nothing exists in nature but material atoms; that he discovered great insolence and vanity in the disrespect with which he treated the memory of former philosophers, and the characters and persons of his cotemporaries; that both the master and the whole fraternity were addicted to the vilest and most infamous vices, so that the school ought not to have been called a garden, but a sty; and, in short, that this philosopher and his followers relinquished all liberal studies and manly pursuits, that they might devote themselves to the grossest impieties and debaucheries. These accusations against the Epicurean school have been not only the voice of common rumor, but have been more or less confirmed by men distinguished for their wisdom and virtue; Zeno, Cicero, Plutarch, Galen, and a long train of Christian Fathers. So that if the question were to be determined by the number of accusers, there can be no doubt that Epicurus and his followers must be condemned. But if the cause be examined with impartiality; if the credit of the witnesses against Epicurus be thoroughly canvassed; if the causes of the spirit of invective raised against him be duly considered; and if the evidences on the other side be allowed a fair hearing, it will perhaps be found that this philosopher, though in some respects highly censurable, has been in several others severely and unjustly condemned.

Calumny never appeared with greater effrontery than in accusing Epicurus of intemperance and incontinence. That his character was distinguished by the contrary virtues, appears not only from the numerous attestations adduced by Laertius, but even from the confession of the more respectable opponents of his doctrine, particularly Cicero, Plutarch, and

Seneca. And indeed, without any external evidence, this is sufficiently clear, from the particulars which are related concerning his usual manner of living. Chrysippus himself, one of his most violent enemies among the Stoics, acknowledged that Epicurus discovered little inclination towards sexual pleasures. Nothing can be a greater proof that his adversaries had little to allege against his innocence, than that they were obliged to have recourse to forgery. The infamous letters which Diotimus, or according to Athenæus, Theotimus, ascribed to him, were proved in a public court, to have been fraudulently imposed upon the world, and the author of the imposition was punished. Whatever might be the case afterwards, there is little reason to doubt that during the life of Epicurus his garden was rather a school of temperance, than a scene of riot and debauchery.

After the death of Epicurus, his followers celebrated his birth-day as a festival. They preserved his image on their rings or cups, or in pictures, which they carried about their persons, or hung up in their chambers. So great was their reverence for his authority, and their regard to his dying advice, that they committed his maxims, and some of them the whole body of his instructions, to memory. For several ages they adhered with wonderful unanimity to his system, yielding as implicit submission to his decisions as the Athenians or Spartans ever yielded to the laws of Solon or Lycurgus. They carried this point so far, that it was deemed a kind of impiety to innovate upon his doctrine; so that the Epicureans formed a Philosophical Republic, regulated by one judgment, and animated by one soul.

EPIMENIDES.

Epimenides was a Cretan by birth, but, because he allowed his hair to grow long, he did not resemble a Cretan. It is said of him that he was sent by his father into the fields to look for a sheep, and he turned out of the road at midday, and lay down in a certain cave and fell asleep, and slept there fifty-seven years; and after that, when he awoke, he went on looking for the sheep, thinking that he had been taking a short nap; but as he could not find it, he went on to the field, and there he found every thing changed, and the estate in another person's possession, and so he came back again to the city in great perplexity; and as he was going into his own house he met some people, who asked him who he was, until at last he found his younger brother, who had now become an old man, and from him he learnt all the truth.

When he was recognized, he was considered by the Greeks as a person especially beloved by the Gods, on which account, when the Athenians were afflicted by a plague, and the priestess at Delphi enjoined them to purify their city, they sent a ship and Nicias, the son of Niceratus, to Crete, to invite Epimenides to Athens; and he, coming there in the forty-sixth Olympiad, purified the city, and eradicated the plague for that time. He took some black sheep and some white ones, and led them up to the Areopagus, and from thence he let them go wherever they chose, having ordered the attendants to follow them; and wherever any one of them lay down, they were to sacrifice him to the God who was the patron of the spot, and so the evil was stayed; and owing to this, one may even now find in the different boroughs of the Athenians, altars without names, which are a sort of memorial of the propitiation of the Gods that then took place. Some said that the cause of the plague was the pollution contracted by the city in the matter of Cylon, and that Epimenides pointed out to the Athenians how to get rid of it; and that in consequence, they put to death two young men, Cretinus and Ctesilius, and that thus the pestilence was put an end to.

And the Athenians passed a vote to give him a talent and a ship to convey him back to Crete; but he would not accept the money, but made a treaty of friendship and alliance between the Gnossians and Athenians.

Not long after he had returned home he died, as Phlegon relates in his book on long-lived people, after he had lived a hundred and fifty-seven years; but, as the Cretans report, he had lived two hundred and ninety-nine; but, as Xenophones, the Colophonian, states that he had heard it reported, he was a hundred and fifty-four years old when he died.

The story of his long sleep is denied by some, who assert, that during that period he was absent from his country, pursuing botanical studies.

Brucker refers to him in the following language: Another idle story of this Cretan is, that he had the power of sending his soul out of his body, and recalling it at pleasure. It is added, that he had familiar intercourse with the Gods, and possessed the powers of prophecy. During a plague in Attica, the Athenians sent for him to perform a sacred lustration, in consequence of which, it is said that the Gods were appeased, and the plague ceased. He is reported to have lived, after his return to Crete, to the age of one hundred and fifty-seven years. We probably owe most of these tales to the Cretans, who were, to a proverb, famous for their powers of invention. All that is credible concerning Epimenides is, that he was a man of superior talents, who pretended to intercourse with the Gods, and, to support his pretensions, lived in retirement upon the spontaneous productions of the earth, and practised various arts of imposture. Perhaps, in his hours of pretended inspiration, he had the art of appearing totally insensible and entranced, which would easily be mistaken by ignorant spectators for a power of dismissing and recalling his spirit. Solon, in whose time the lustration above named was performed, seems to have been no stranger to the true character of Epimenides; for we find that he greatly disapproved of the conduct of the Athenians in employing him to perform this ceremony. Divine honors were paid him, after his death, by the superstitious Cretans.

ERIGENA.

Joannes Scotus, surnamed Erigena, is said by some writers to have been a native of the town of Ayr in Scotland, and by others to have been born in Herefordshire. For his profound knowledge of philosophy, he obtained among the writers of the Middle Age the appellation of Scotus the Wise. The fame of his learning reached Charles the Bald, who invited him into France, admitted him to his intimacy, and gave him the direction of the University of Paris. But a circumstance soon afterwards arose, which brought upon him much obloquy and persecution. The Greek emperor, Michael the Stammerer, had, in the year 824, sent over, as a present of inestimable value to the Western emperor, Lewis the Mild, the treatises of the supposed Dionysius the Areopagite, which had long been held in great veneration among the Greek Christians. This book, Charles the Bald, who could not read Greek, was earnestly desirous of perusing in a Latin translation. This desire was doubtless increased by the opinion which at this time universally prevailed, though without any proof, that Dionysius the Areopagite, or St. Denys, was the first Christian teacher, or apostle, in France. At the request of the emperor, Joannes Scotus undertook the task of translating the books of this Dionysius, "On the Celestial Monarchy;" "On the Ecclesiastical Hierarchy;" "On Divine Names;" and "On Mystic Theology." These books were received with great eagerness by the Western churches. The translation, however, being made without the pope's license, and containing many things contrary to the received faith of the Church of Rome, the pope, Nicholas the First, was highly displeased, and wrote a threatening letter to the emperor, requiring that Scotus should be banished from the University of Paris, and sent to Rome. The emperor had too much respect for Scotus to obey the pope's order; but Scotus thought it advisable for his safety to retire from Paris, and after the death of the emperor is said to have returned into England.

It was the translation of this book which revived the knowledge of Alexandrian Platonism in the West, and laid the foundation of the mystical system of theology which afterwards so generally prevailed. Thus philosophical enthusiasm, born in the East, nourished by Plato, educated by Alexandria, matured in Asia, and adopted into the Greek church, found its way, under the pretext and authority of an apostolic name, into the Western church, and there produced innumerable mischiefs.

EUBULIDES.

Eubulides, of Miletus, has handed down a great many arguments or dialectics, such as the Lying one; the Concealed one; the Electra; the Sorites; the Horned one; the Bald one, &c.

The *Lying* one is this:—Is the man a liar who says that he tells lies. If he is, then he does not tell lies; and if he does not tell lies, is he a liar?

The *Concealed* one:—Do you know this man who is concealed? If you do not, you do not know your own father; for he it is who is concealed.

The *Electra* is a quibble of the same kind as the two preceding ones: Electra sees Orestes: she knows that Orestes is her brother, but does not know that the man she sees is Orestes; therefore she does know, and does not know, her brother at the same time.

The *Sorites* is universally known.

The *Bald* one is a kind of Sorites; pulling one hair out of a man's head will not make him bald, nor two, nor three, and so on till every hair in his head is pulled out.

The *Horned* one:—You have what you have not lost. You have not lost horns, therefore you have horns.

A different translation of some of these is given as follows: *The Lying:* if, when you speak the truth, you say you lie, you lie; but you say you lie when you speak the truth; therefore, in speaking the truth, you lie. *The Occult.* Do you know your father? Yes. Do you know this man who is veiled? No. Then you do not know your father; for it is your father who is veiled. *Electra.* Electra, the daughter of Agamemnon, knew her brother, and did not know him: she knew Orestes to be her brother, but she did not know that person to be her brother who was conversing with her. *Sorites.* Is one grain a heap? No. Two grains? No. Three grains? No. Go on, adding one by one; and, if one grain be not a heap, it will be impossible to say what number of grains make a heap. *The Horned.* You have what you have not lost; you have not lost horns; therefore you have horns.—In such high repute were these silly inventions for perplexing plain truth, that Chrysippus wrote six books upon the first of these sophisms; and Philetas, a Coan, died of a consumption which he contracted by the close study which he bestowed upon it. The inscription upon his tomb was, "The deceived." A serious attempt to expose the futility of these disputes would now be justly deemed an idle waste of time and words.

EUCLID.

Euclid of Megara, endued by nature with a subtle and penetrating genius, early applied himself to the study of philosophy. Hearing of the fame of Socrates, Euclid determined to attend upon his instructions, and for this purpose removed from Megara to Athens. Here he long remained a constant hearer and zealous disciple of the Moral Philosopher; and when, in consequence of the enmity which subsisted between the Athenians and Megareans, a decree was passed by the former, that any inhabitant of Megara who should be seen in Athens should forfeit his life, he frequently came to Athens by night, from the distance of about twenty miles, concealed in a long female cloak and veil, to visit his master. Not finding his natural propensity to disputation sufficiently gratified in the tranquil method of philosophising adopted by Socrates, he frequently engaged in the business and disputes of the civil courts. Socrates, who despised forensic contests, expressed some dissatisfaction with his pupil for indulging a fondness for controversy. This circumstance probably proved the occasion of a separation between Euclid and his master; for we find him, after this time, at the head of a school in Megara, in which his chief employment was to teach the art of disputation. Debates were conducted with so much vehemence among his pupils, that Timon said of Euclid, that he had carried the madness of contention from Athens to Megara. That he was, however, capable of commanding his temper, appears from his reply to his brother, who in a quarrel had said, "Let me perish if I be not revenged on you!" "And let *me* perish," returned Euclid, "if I do not subdue your resentment by forbearance, and make you love me as much as ever!" His kind reception of the disciples of Socrates, after the death of their master, has been already noticed. Euclid of Megara is not to be confounded with Euclid the mathematician, who flourished at a later period under Ptolemy Lagus, and died in the hundred and twenty-third Olympiad.

In disputation Euclid was averse to the analogical method of reasoning, and judged, that legitimate argumentation consists in deducing fair conclusions from acknowledged premises. It is said that when Euclid was asked his opinion concerning the gods, he replied, "I know nothing more of them than this, that they hate inquisitive persons." If this apophthegm be justly ascribed to Euclid, it may serve to prove, either that he had learned from the precepts of Socrates to think soberly and respectfully concerning the divine nature, or that the fate of that good man had taught him caution in declaring his opinions.

EUDOXUS.

Eudoxus, a native of Cnidos, was an astronomer, a geometrician, a physician and a law-giver.

It is said that he introduced the fashion of sitting in a semicircle, at an entertainment given by Plato.

He composed among other works a book entitled, "Dialogues of Dogs."

He flourished about the hundred and third Olympiad; and was the inventor of the theory of crooked lines. And he died in his fifty-third year. But when he was in Egypt with Conuphis, of Heliopolis, Apis * licked his garment; and so the priests said that he would be short-lived, but very illustrious, as it is reported by Phavorinus in his Commentaries. And we have written an epigram on him, that runs thus:—

'Tis said, that while at Memphis wise Eudoxus
Learnt his own fate from th' holy fair-horned bull;
He said indeed no word, bulls do not speak;
Nor had kind nature e'er calf Apis gifted
With an articulately speaking mouth.
But standing on one side he lick'd his cloak,
Showing by this most plainly—in brief time
You shall put off your life. So death came soon,
When he had just seen three and fifty times
The Pleiads rise to warn the mariners.

EUSEBIUS.

Eusebius, of Myndus in Caria, though one of the disciples of Ædesius, appears from a conference with which he had

* The sacred bull of the Egyptians.

with Julian, to have considered all pretensions to intercourse with demons, or inferior divinities, as illusions of the fancy, or tricks of imposture, and to have discouraged them as unworthy of the purity and sublimity of true philosophy. His design seems to have been to restore the contemplation of Intelligibles, or Ideas, as the only real and immutable natures, according to the doctrine of Porphyry, and of Plato himself; but the fanatical doctrine of an intercourse between demons and men, and the arts of theurgy founded upon this doctrine, were now too generally established, and found too useful, to be dismissed. Eusebius of Myndus was, therefore, less acceptable to the emperor Julian than another disciple of Ædesius, Maximus of Ephesus.

FAVORINUS.

Favorinus, a native of Arles, lived in the reigns of Trajan and Adrian. The latter esteemed him highly for his learning and eloquence, and frequently disputed with him, after his usual manner, upon subjects of literature and philosophy. To many other learned men who were inclined to do justice to their own talents, this unequal contest proved injurious, and to some even fatal; but to Favorinus, who perceived that it was the emperor's foible not to endure a defeat in disputation, upon every occasion of this nature prudently ceded to the purple the triumph of conquest. One of his friends reproaching him for having so tamely given up the point in a debate with the emperor, concerning the authority of a certain word, (for the emperor was a great philologist,) Favorinus replied, "Would you have me contest a point with the master of fifty legions?"

GERBERT.

One of the most celebrated among the learned was Gerbert, a native of Orleans, archbishop of Rheims, and afterwards Pope Sylvester II. He merits a distinguished place in the list of natural philosophers, on account of the skill which he acquired in mathematics, mechanics, hydraulics, and astronomy. Dithmar, writing concerning Gerbert, says: "He was well skilled in astronomical observations, and far excelled his contemporaries in various kinds of knowledge. After his banishment from France, he fled to the emperor Otho, and during his stay with him at Madgeburg, he made a clock, which he corrected by observing through a tube a certain star by which sailors are guided in navigation." The knowledge of nature which Gerbert possessed, so far surpassed that of his contemporaries, that they thought him possessed of magical power; and Benno, a cardinal who owed him a grudge for his opposition to the see of Rome, invented and circulated a tale of his holding converse with the devil. His Epistles, of which one hundred and sixty-one are still extant, contain many curious particulars respecting natural philosophy. Sylvester II. died in the year 1003.

HEGESIAS.

Hegesias was a disciple of the Cyrenaic sect, founded by Aristippus of Cyrene. His temper was too gloomy to find enjoyment upon his master's plan, and his principles furnished him with no other sources of happiness. He was so thoroughly dissatisfied with life, that he thought it the only concern of man to avoid misery, and wrote a book to prove that death, as the cure of all evil, is the greatest good. Hence he obtained the appellation of *peisithanatos*, "Advocate for death."

He was called "Death's Orator," because of a book he wrote upon a certain person who had nearly famished himself to death, but was restored by his friends. In this book he described the evils of life with so much power, as to beget in many persons a desire to die voluntarily, many of whom committed suicide. On which account he was prohibited by King Ptolemy from discoursing upon the subject in the schools.

HERACLIDES.

Heraclides was the son of Euthyphron, and was born at Heraclea, in Pontus. He was also a wealthy man. After he came to Athens, he was at first a disciple of Speusippus, but he also attended the schools of the Pythagorean philosophers, and he adopted the principles of Plato. Last of all, he became a pupil of Aristotle. He used to wear delicate garments, and was a man of great size, so that he was nicknamed by the Athenians, Pompicus, instead of Ponticus. But he was of quiet manners and noble aspect.

He appears to have delivered his country when it was under the yoke of tyrants, by slaying the monarch, as Demetrius of Magnesia tells us, in his treatise on People of the Same Name.

And he gives the following account of him: That he brought up a young serpent, and kept it till it grew large; and that when he was at the point of death, he desired one of his faithful friends to hide his body, and to place the serpent in his bed, that he might appear to have migrated to the Gods. And all this was done; and while the citizens were all attending his funeral, and extolling his character, the serpent, hearing the noise, crept out of his clothes and threw the multitude into confusion. And afterwards everything was revealed, and Heraclides was seen, not as he hoped to have been, but as he really was. And we have written an epigram on him, which runs thus:—

> You wish'd, O Heraclides, when you died,
> To leave a strange belief among mankind,
> That you, when dead, a serpent had become.
> But all your calculations were deceived,
> For this your serpent was indeed a beast,
> And you were thus discovered and pronounced another.

But Hermippus says, that once, when a famine oppressed the land, the people of Heraclea consulted the Pythian oracle for the way to get rid of it; and that Heraclides corrupted the ambassadors who were sent to consult the oracle, and also the priestess, with bribes; and that she answered that they would obtain a deliverance from their distresses, if Heraclides, the son of Euthyphron, was presented by them with a golden crown, and if when he was dead they paid him honors as a hero. Accordingly, this answer was brought back from the oracle to Heraclea, but they who brought it got no advantage from it; for as soon as Heraclides had been crowned in the theatre, he was seized with apoplexy, and the ambassadors who had been sent to consult the oracle were stoned, and so put to death; and at the very same moment the Pythian priestess was going down to the inner shrine, and while standing there, was bitten by a serpent, and died immediately. This then is the account given of his death.

And Aristoxenus, the musician, says, that he composed tragedies, and inscribed them with the name of Thespis. And Chamæleon says, that he stole essays from him on the subject of Homer and Hesiod, and published them as his own. And Aretodorus, the Epicurean, reproaches him, and contradicts all the arguments which he advanced in his treatise on Justice. Moreover, Dionysius, called the Deserter, or, as some say, Spentharus, wrote a tragedy called Parthenopæus, and forged the name of Sophocles to it. And Heraclides was so much deceived, that he took some passages out of one of his works, and cited them as the words of Sophocles. And Dionysius, when he perceived it, gave him notice of the real truth; and as he would not believe it, and denied it, he sent him word to examine the first letters of the first verses of the book, and they formed the name of Panculus, who was a friend of Dionysius. And as Heraclides still refused to believe it, and said that it was possible that such a thing might happen by chance, Dionysius sent him back word once more, "You will find this passage too:—

'An aged monkey is not easily caught;
He 's caught indeed, but only after a time.'"

And he added, "Heraclides knows nothing of letters, and has no shame."

There were fourteen persons of the name of Heraclides.

HERACLITUS.

Heraclitus was the son of Blyson, or, as some say, of Heraceon, and a citizen of Ephesus. He flourished about the sixty-ninth Olympiad.

He was above all men of a lofty and arrogant spirit, as is plain from his writings, in which he says, "Abundant learning does not form the mind; for if it did, it would have instructed Hesiod, and Pythagoras, and likewise Xenophanes, and Hecatæus. For the only piece of real wisdom is to know that idea, which by itself will govern everything on every occasion." He used to say, too, that Homer deserved to be expelled from the games and beaten, and Archilochus likewise. He used also to say, "It is more necessary to extinguish insolence, than to put out a fire." Another of his sayings was, "The people ought to fight for the law, as for their city." He also attacks the Ephesians for having banished his companion Hermodorus, when he says, "The Ephesians deserve to have all their youth put to death, and all those who are younger still banished from their city, inasmuch as they have banished Hermodorus, the best man among them, saying, 'Let no one of us be pre-eminently good; and if there be any such person, let him go to another city and another people.'"

And when he was requested to make laws for them, he refused, because the city was already immersed in a thoroughly bad constitution. And having retired to the temple of Diana with his children, he began to play at dice; and when all the Ephesians flocked round him, he said, "You wretches, what are you wondering at? is it not better to do this, than to meddle with public affairs in your company?"

And at last, becoming a complete misanthrope, he used to live, spending his time in walking about the mountains; feeding on grasses and plants, and in consequence of these habits, he was attacked by the dropsy, and so then he returned to the city, and asked the physicians, in a riddle, whether they were able to produce a drought after wet weather. And as they did not understand him, he shut himself up in a stable for oxen, and covered himself with cow-dung, hoping to cause the wet to evaporate from him, by the warmth that this produced. And as he did himself no good in this way, he died, having lived seventy years; and we have written an epigram upon him which runs thus:—

I've often wondered much at Heraclitus,
That he should choose to live so miserably,
And die by such a miserable fate.
For fell disease did master all his body,
With water quenching all the light of his eyes,
And bringing darkness o'er his mind and body.

But Hermippus states that what he asked the physicians was this, whether any one could draw off the water by depressing his intestines? and when they answered that they could not, he placed himself in the sun, and ordered his servants to plaster him over with cow-dung; and being stretched out in that way, on the second day he died, and was buried in the market-place. But Neanthes, of Cyzicus says, that as he could not tear off the cow-dung, he remained there, and on account of the alteration in his appearance, he was not discovered, and so was devoured by the dogs.

And he was a wonderful person, from his boyhood, since, while he was young, he used to say that he knew nothing; but when he had grown up, he then used to affirm that he knew everything. And he was no one's pupil, but he used to say, that he himself had investigated everything, and had learned everything of himself. But Sotion relates, that some people affirmed that he had been a pupil of Xenophanes. And that Ariston stated in his account of Heraclitus, that he was cured of the dropsy, and died of some other disease. And Hippobotus gives the same account.

There is a book of his extant, which is about nature generally, and it is divided into three discourses; one on the Universe; one on Politics; and one on Theology. And he deposited this book in the temple of Diana, as some authors report, having written it intentionally in an obscure style, in order that only those who were able men might comprehend it, and that it might not be exposed to ridicule at the hands of the common people. Timon attacks this man also, saying: —

Among them came that cuckoo Heraclitus
The enigmatical obscure reviler
Of all the common people.

Theophrastus asserts, that it was out of melancholy that he left some of his works half finished, and wrote several in completely different styles; and Antisthenes, in his Successions, adduces as a proof of his lofty spirit, the fact, that he yielded to his brother the title and privileges of royalty.* And his book had so high a reputation, that a sect arose in

* According to Strabo, the descendants of Androclus, the founder of Ephesus (of which family Heraclitus came), bore the title of king, and had certain prerogatives and privileges attached to the title.

consequence of it, who were called after his own name, Heraclitean.

The following may be set down in a general manner as his main principles: that everything is created from fire, and is dissolved into fire; that everything happens according to destiny, and that all existing things are harmonized, and made to agree together by opposite tendencies; and that all things are full of souls and dæmones. He also discussed all the passions which exist in the world, and used also to contend that the sun was of that precise magnitude of which he appears to be. One of his sayings too was, that no one, by whatever road he might travel, could ever possibly find out the boundaries of the soul, so deeply hidden are the principles which regulate it. He used also to call opinion the sacred disease; and to say that eye-sight was often deceived. Sometimes, in his writings, he expressed himself with great brilliancy and clearness; so that even the most stupid man may easily understand him, and receive an elevation of soul from him. And his conciseness, and the dignity of his style, are incomparable.

They say that when he was asked why he preserved silence, he said, "That you may talk."

Darius was very desirous to enjoy his conversation; and wrote thus to him:—

KING DARIUS, THE SON OF HYSTASPES, ADDRESSES HERACLITUS, OF EPHESUS, THE WISE MAN, GREETING HIM.

"You have written a book on Natural Philosophy, difficult to understand and difficult to explain. Accordingly, if in some parts it is explained literally, it seems to disclose a very important theory concerning the universal world, and all that is contained in it, as they are placed in a state of most divine motion. But commonly, the mind is kept in suspense, so that those who have studied your work the most, are not able precisely to disentangle the exact meaning of your expressions. Therefore, King Darius, the son of Hystaspes, wishes to enjoy the benefit of hearing you discourse, and of receiving some Grecian instruction. Come, therefore, quickly to my sight, and to my royal palace; for the Greeks, in general, do not accord to wise men the distinction which they deserve, and disregard the admirable expositions delivered by them, which are, however, worthy of being seriously listened to and studied; but with me you shall have every kind of distinction and honor, and you shall enjoy every day honorable and worthy conversation, and your pupil's life shall become virtuous, in accordance with your precepts."

HERACLITUS, OF EPHESUS, TO KING DARIUS, THE SON OF HYSTASPES, GREETING.

"All the men that exist in the world, are far removed from truth and just dealings; but they are full of evil foolishness, which leads them to insatiable covetousness and vain-glorious ambition. I, however, forgetting all their worthlessness, and shunning satiety, and who wish to avoid all envy on the part of my countrymen, and all appearance of arrogance, will never come to Persia, since I am quite contented with a little, and live as best suits my own inclination."

This was the way in which the man behaved even to the king. And Demetrius, in his treatise on People of the Same Name, says that he also despised the Athenians, among whom he had a very high reputation. And that though he was himself despised by the Ephesians, he nevertheless preferred his own home. Demetrius Phaleruus also mentions him in his Defence of Socrates:—

I who lie here am Heraclitus, spare me
Ye rude unlettered men: 'Twas not for you
That I did labor, but for wiser people.
One man may be to me a countless host,
And an unnumbered multitude be no one;
And this I still say in the shades below.

And there is another expressed thus:—

Be not too hasty, skimming o'er the book
Of Heraclitus; 'tis a difficult road,
For mist is there, and darkness hard to pierce.
But if you have a guide who knows his system,
Then everything is clearer than the sun.

HIPPARCHIA.

Hipparchia and her brother Metrocles, were natives of Meronea. She fell in love with both the doctrines and the manners of Crates, and could not be diverted from her regard for him by either the wealth or the high birth or personal beauty of any of her suitors; but Crates was everything to her; and she threatened her parents to make away with herself, if she were not given in marriage to him. Crates, accordingly, being entreated by her parents to dissuade her from this resolution, did all he could; and at last, as he could not persuade her, he rose up, and placing all his furniture before her, he said, "This is the bridegroom whom you are choosing, and this is the whole of his property; consider these facts, for it will not be possible for you to become his partner, if you do not also apply yourself to the same studies, and conform to the same habits that he does." But the girl chose him; and assuming the same dress that he wore, went about with him as her husband, and appeared with him in public everywhere, and went to all entertainments in his company.

And once, when she went to sup with Lysimachus, she attacked Theodorus, who was surnamed the Atheist, proposing to him the following sophism: "What Theodorus could not be called wrong for doing, that same thing Hipparchia ought not to be called wrong for doing. But Theodorus does no wrong when he beats himself; therefore Hipparchia does no wrong when she beats Theodorus." He made no reply to what she said, but only pulled her clothes about; but Hipparchia was neither offended nor ashamed, as many a woman would have been; but when he said to her,

> "Who is the woman who has left the shuttle
> So near the warp?"*

"I, Theodorus, am that person," she replied; "but do I appear to you to have come to a wrong decision, if I devote that time to philosophy, which I otherwise should have spent at the loom?" And these and many other sayings are reported of this female philosopher.

HIEROCLES.

TOWARDS the close of the fifth century flourished HIEROCLES, who was born and taught in Alexandria. He suffered severely for his adherence to the Pagan superstitions. At Constantinople he was cruelly scourged; and, in the midst of his torture, receiving some of the blood into his own hand, he threw it upon the face of his judge, repeating the following verse from Homer:—

> Cyclops, since human flesh has been thy feast,
> Now drain this goblet, potent to digest.

HILLEL.

HILLEL, surnamed Hassaken, was born at Babylon, of poor parents, but of the royal stock of David, in the year one hundred and twelve before Christ. After residing forty years in Babylon, where he married and had a son, he removed with his family to Jerusalem, for the purpose of studying the law. Shemaiah and Abdalion were at that time eminent doctors

* This line is from the Bacchæ of Euripides.

in Jerusalem. Hillel, unable on account of his poverty to gain a regular admission to their lectures, spent a considerable part of the profits of his daily labor in bribing the attendants to allow him a place at the door of the public hall, where he might gather up the doctrine of these eminent masters by stealth; and when this expedient failed him, he found means to place himself at the top of the building, near one of the windows. By unwearied perseverance, Hillel acquired a profound knowledge of the most difficult points of the law, in consequence of which his reputation rose to such a height, that he became the master of the chief school in Jerusalem. In this station he was universally regarded as an oracle of wisdom scarcely inferior to Solomon, and had many thousand followers. He had such command of his temper, that no one ever saw him angry. The name of Hillel is in the highest esteem among the Jews, for the pains which he took to perpetuate the knowledge of the traditionary law. He arranged its precepts under six general classes, and thus laid the foundation of that digest of the Jewish law which is called the Talmud. Hillel is said to have lived to the great age of one hundred and twenty years.

HYPATIA.

Hypatia was the daughter of Theon, a celebrated mathematician of Alexandria. Her extensive learning, elegant manners, and tragical end, have rendered her name immortal. She possessed an acute and penetrating judgment, and great sublimity and fertility of genius, and her talents were cultivated with assiduity by her father and other preceptors. After she had made herself mistress of polite learning, and of the sciences of geometry and astronomy, as far as they were then understood, she entered upon the study of philosophy.

She prosecuted this study with such uncommon success, that she was importuned to become a public preceptress in the school where Plotinus and his successors had taught; and her love of science enabled her so far to subdue the natural diffidence of the sex, that she yielded to the public voice, and exchanged her female decorations for the philosopher's cloak. In the schools, and in other places of public resort, she discoursed upon philosophical topics, explaining, and endeavoring to reconcile, the systems of Plato, Aristotle, and other masters. A ready elocution, and graceful address, united with rich erudition and sound judgment, procured her numerous followers and admirers; among whom was Synesius. But that which reflects the highest honor upon her memory is, that, though she excelled most of the philosophers of her age in mathematical and philosophical science, she discovered no pride of learning; and though she was in person exceedingly beautiful, she never yielded to the impulse of female vanity, or gave occasion to the slightest suspicion against her chastity.

The extraordinary combination of accomplishments and virtues which adorned the character of Hypatia, rendered her house the general resort of persons of learning and distinction. But it was impossible that so much merit should not excite envy. The qualifications and attainments to which she was indebted for her celebrity, proved in the issue the occasion of her destruction. It happened that at this time the patriarchal chair of Alexandria was occupied by Cyril, a bishop of great authority, but of great haughtiness and violence of temper. In the vehemence of his bigoted zeal, he had treated the Jews with severity, and at last banished them out of Alexandria. Orestes, the prefect of the city, a man of a liberal spirit, highly resented this expulsion as an unpardonable stretch of ecclesiastical power, and a cruel act of oppression and injustice against a people who had inhabited Alexandria from the time of its founder. He reported the affair to the emperor. The bishop, on his part, complained to the prince of the seditious temper of the

Jews, and attempted to justify his proceedings. The emperor declined to interpose his authority; and the affair rapidly advanced to the utmost extremity. A body of about five hundred monks, who espoused the cause of Cyril, came into the city with a determination to support him by force. Meeting the prefect, as he was passing through the street in his carriage, they stopped him, and loaded him with reproaches; and one of them threw a stone at his head, and wounded him. The populace, who were by this time assembled on the part of the prefect, routed the monks, and seized one of their leaders. Orestes ordered him to be put to death. Cyril buried his body in the church, and gave instructions that his name should be registered among the sacred martyrs. Hypatia, who had always been highly respected by the prefect, and who had, at this time, frequent conferences with him, was supposed by the partisans of the bishop to have been deeply engaged in the interest of Orestes. Their resentment at length rose to such a height, that they formed a design against her life. As she was one day returning home from the schools, the mob seized her, forced her from her chair, and carried her to the Cæsarean church; where stripping off her garments, they put her to death with extreme barbarity; and having torn her body limb from limb, committed it to the flames. Cyril himself has, by some writers, been suspected of secretly promoting this horrid act of violence. And if the haughtiness and severity of his temper, his persecution of the Jews, his oppressive and iniquitous treatment of the Novatian sect of Christians and their bishop, the vehemence of his present indignation against Orestes and his party, and, above all, the protection which he is said to have afforded to the immediate perpetrators of the murder of Hypatia, be duly considered, it will perhaps appear that this suspicion is not wholly without foundation. Hypatia was murdered under the reign of the emperor Theodosius II. in the year four hundred and fifteen. Hence it is certain that she could not have been, as Suidas, with his usual precipitation, relates, the wife of Isidorus: it is probable that through her whole life she remained in a state of celibacy.

JULIAN.

THE emperor JULIAN is generally acknowledged to have been not only a patron of philosophers, but himself a philosopher. Referring to the civil historians for the particulars of his political conduct, we shall mention such incidents as more immediately respect his philosophical character.

Julian, in the early part of his life, was carefully instructed in literature and science by Christian preceptors. Whilst he was pursuing his studies at Nicomedia, his uncle Constantius strictly charged him not to attend upon the lectures of the celebrated Pagan Sophist, Libanius. This prohibition had no other effect than to awaken the young man's curiosity, and kindle an earnest desire of visiting the Pagan schools. Notwithstanding every precaution, he conversed freely with philosophers, and grew fond of the fanciful system taught by the Alexandrian Platonists. His natural disposition, which was tinctured with enthusiasm, favored this attachment; and it was confirmed by the intimacy which, during his residence at Nicomedia, he formed with Maximus, of Ephesus. Under his instructions, and those of Chrysanthius and others, he became a great proficient in the abstruse speculations, and in the theurgic arts of this school. With the permission of his uncle, he finished his studies at Athens, where he acquired great reputation in learning and philosophy, and was initiated in the Eleusinian mysteries.

When Julian was called by Constantius to exchange the school of philosophy for the field of war, he made great use of the magic arts, which he had learned from Maximus, in executing his political purposes. Whilst he was at Vienna, he reported that, in the middle of the night, he had been visited by a celestial form, which had in heroic verse promised him the possession of the imperial dignity.

As soon as Julian reached the summit of his wishes, he employed his power in restoring the heathen superstition. He at this time, however, used no violent measures to compel the Christians to forsake their religion, rightly judging that "false opinions can never be corrected by fire and sword." His principal favorites were the Pagan philosophers of the school of Ædesius; but learned men of every class were encouraged in his court. When he afterwards shut up the Christian schools, it was in the hope of suppressing the Christian religion by involving its professors in ignorance and barbarism.

This prince not only encouraged letters by his patronage, but was himself a learned writer. It is easy to perceive, from a slight inspection of his works, that he strictly adhered to the Alexandrian, or Eclectic school. He professes himself a warm admirer of Pythagoras and Plato, and recommends a union of their tenets with those of Aristotle. The later Platonists of his own period he loads with encomiums, particularly Jamblicus, whom he calls the Light of the World, and the Physician of the Mind. Amidst the numerous traces of an enthusiastic and bigoted attachment to Pagan theology and philosophy, and of an inveterate enmity to Christianity, which are to be found in his writings, the candid reader will discern many marks of genius and erudition.

Concerning the manners of Julian, Libanius writes that no philosopher, in the lowest state of poverty, was ever more temperate, or more ready to practice rigorous abstinence from food, as the means of preparing his mind for conversing with the Gods. Like Plotinus, Porphyry, Jamblicus, and others of this fanatical sect, he dealt in visions and ecstasies, and pretended to a supernatural intercourse with divinities. Suidas relates, probably from some writings of the credulous Eunapius, now lost, an oracular prediction concerning his death.

His philosophical character attended him in his military exploits, and accompanied him to the last. After he had received his mortal wound, he held a conference with the philosophers Maximus and Priscus, concerning the soul, in the midst of which he expired, in the thirty-second year of his age.

On the whole, although the emperor Julian must not be denied the place which has long been allowed him among philosophers, it must be owned that his philosophy was neither able to preserve him from superstition and enthusiasm, nor to raise his mind above the influence of the narrowest and most pernicious prejudices.

LACYDES.

Lacydes, the son of Alexander, was a native of Cyrene. He was the founder of the New Academy, having succeeded Arcesilaus. He was a man of great gravity of character and deportment, and one who had many imitators. He was industrious from his very childhood, and poor, but very pleasing and sociable in his manners.

They say he had a pleasant way of managing his housekeeping affairs. For when he had taken anything out of his store-chest, he would seal it up again, and throw in his seal through the hole, so that it should be impossible for anything of what he had laid up there, to be stolen from him or carried off. But his servants learning this contrivance of his, broke the seal, and carried off as much as they pleased, and then they put the ring back through the hole in the same manner as before; and though they did this repeatedly, they were never detected. Lacydes now used to hold his school in the garden, which had been laid out by Attalus, the king, and it was called Lacydeum, after him.

This witty saying is attributed to Lacydes: They say that when Attalus sent for him, he answered that "Statues ought to be seen at a distance." On another occasion, as it is reported, he was studying geometry very late in life, and some said to him, is it then a time for you to be learning now? "If it is not," he replied, "when will it be?"

He died in the fourth year of the hundred and thirty-fourth Olympiad, of a paralysis brought on by drinking. Diogenes L. jests upon him in the following manner:—

'Tis an odd story that I heard of you
Lacydes, that you went with hasty steps,
Spurred on by Bacchus, to the shades below.
Now then, if this be true, can it be said
That Bacchus e'er trips up his votaries' feet?
'Tis a mistake, his being named Lyæus.*

LYCON.

LYCON, was native of the Troas, the son of Astyanax, a man of great eloquence, and of especial ability in the education of youth. For he used to say that it was fit for boys to be harnessed with modesty and rivalry, as much as for horses to be equipped with a spur and a bridle. And his eloquence and energy in speaking is apparent, from this instance. For he speaks of a virgin who was poor in the following manner: "A damsel, who, for want of a dowry, goes beyond the seasonable age, is a heavy burden to her father;" on which account they say that Antigonus said with reference to him, that the sweetness and beauty of an apple could not be transferred to anything else, but that one might see, in the case of this man, all these excellencies, in as great perfection as on a

* From *luo* to relax or weaken the limbs.

tree; and he said this, because he was a surpassingly sweet speaker. On which account, some people prefixed a G to his name.* But as a writer, he was very unequal to his reputation. And he used to jest in a careless way, upon those who repented that they had not learnt when they had the opportunity, and who now wished that they had done so, saying, that "they were accusing themselves, showing by a prayer which could not possibly be accomplished, their misplaced repentance for their idleness." He used also to say, that "those who deliberated without coming to a right conclusion, erred in their calculations, like men who investigate a correct nature by an incorrect standard, or who look at a face in disturbed water, or a distorted mirror." Another of his sayings was, that "many men go in pursuit of the crown to be won in the forum, but few or none seek to attain the one to be gained at the Olympic games."

As he in many instances gave much advice to the Athenians, he was of exceedingly great service to them.

He was also a person of great neatness in his dress, wearing garments of an unsurpassable delicacy, as we are told by Hermippus. He was at the same time exeeedingly devoted to the exercises of the Gymnasium, and a man who was always in excellent condition as to his body, displaying every quality of an athlete (though Antigonus of Carystus, pretends that he was bruised about the ears and dirty); and in his own country he is said to have wrestled and played at ball at the Iliæan games.

He was exceedingly beloved by Eumenes and Attalus, who made him great presents; and Antigonus also tried to seduce him to his court, but was disappointed. He was so great an enemy to Hieronymus the Peripatetic, that he was the only person who would not go to see him on the anniversary festival which he used to celebrate, and which we have mentioned in our life of Arcesilaus. He presided over his school forty-

* So as to make it appear connected with glukus, sweet.

four years, as Strato had left it to him in his will, in the hundred and twenty-seventh Olympiad.

He was also a pupil of Panthoides, the dialectician. He died when he was seventy-four years of age, having been a great sufferer with the gout, and there is an epigram of ours upon him:—

Nor shall wise Lycon be forgotten, who
Died of the gout, and much I wonder at it.
For he who ne'er before could walk alone,
Went the long road to hell in a single night.

He left the following singular will: "I make the following disposition of my property; if I am unable to withstand this disease:—All the property in my house I leave to my brothers Astyanax and Lycon; and I think that they ought to pay all that I owe at Athens, and that I may have borrowed from any one, and also all the expenses that may be incurred for my funeral, and for other customary solemnities. And all that I have in the city, or in Ægina, I give to Lycon, because he bears the same name that I do, and because he has spent the greater part of his life with me, showing me the greatest affection, as it was fitting that he should do, since he was in the place of a son to me. And I leave my garden walk to those of my friends who like to use it; to Bulon, and Callinus, and Ariston, and Amplicon, and Lycon, and Python, and Aristomachus, and Heracleus, and Lycomedes, and Lycon my nephew. And I desire that they will elect as president him whom they think most likely to remain attached to the pursuit of philosophy, and most capable of holding the school together. And I entreat the rest of my friends to acquiesce in their selection, for my sake and that of the place. And I desire that Bulon, and Callinus, and the rest of my friends, will manage my funeral and the burning of my body, so that my obsequies may not be either mean or extravagant. And the property which I have in Ægina shall be divided by Lycon after my decease among the young men there, for the purpose of anointing themselves, in order that the memory of me and of him who honored me, and who showed his affection by useful presents, may be long preserved. And let him erect a statue of me; and as for the place for it, I desire that Diophantus and Heroclides the son of Demetrius, shall select that, and take care that it be suitable for the proposed erection. With the property that I have in the city let Lycon pay all the people of whom I have borrowed anything since his departure; and let Bulon and Callinus join him in this, and also in discharging all the expenses incurred for my funeral, and for all other customary solemnities, and let him deduct the amount from the funds which I have left in my house, and bequeathed to them both in common. Let him also pay the physicians, Pasithemis and Medias, men who, for their attention to me and for their skill, are very deserving of still greater honor. And I give to the son of Callinus my pair of Thericlean cups; and to his wife I give my pair of Rhodian cups, and my smooth carpet, and my double carpet, and my curtains, and the two best pillows of all that I leave behind me; so that as far as the compliment goes, I may be seen not to have forgotten them. And with respect to those who have been my servants, I make the following disposition:—To Demetrius who has long been freed, I remit the price of his freedom, and I further give five minæ, and a cloak, and a tunic, that as he has a great deal of trouble about me, he may pass the rest of his life comfortably. To Criton, the Chalcedonian, I also remit the price of his freedom, and I further give him four minæ. Micras I hereby present with his freedom; and I desire Lycon to maintain him, and instruct him for six years from the present time. I also give his freedom to Chares, and desire Lycon to maintain him. And I further give him two minæ, and all my books that are published; but those which are not published, I give to Callinus, that he may publish them with due care. I also give to Syrus, whom I have already emancipated, four minæ, and Menedora; and if he owes me anything I acquit him of the debt. And I give to Hilaras four minæ, and a double carpet, and two pillows, and a curtain, and any couch which he chooses to select. I also hereby emancipate the mother of Micras, and Noemon, and Dion, and Theon, and Euphranor, and Hermeas; and I desire that Agathon shall have his freedom when he has served two years longer; and that Ophelion, and Poseideon, my litter-bearers, shall have theirs when they have waited four years more. I also give to Demetrius, and Criton, and Syrus, a couch apiece, and coverlets from those which I leave behind me, according to the selection which Lycon is hereby authorized to make. And these are to be their rewards for having performed the duties to which they were appointed well. Concerning my burial, let Lycon do as he pleases, and bury me here or at home, just as he likes; for I am sure that he has the same regard for propriety that I myself have. And I give all the things herein mentioned, in the confidence that he will arrange everything properly. The witnesses to this my will are Callinus of Hermione, Ariston of Ceos, and Euphronius of Pæania."

As he then was thoroughly wise in everything relating to education, and every branch of philosophy, he was no less prudent and careful in the framing of his will. So that in this respect too, he deserves to be admired and imitated.

MAXIMUS.

Maximus was appointed by Constantius preceptor to Julian. According to the Christian historians, he introduced himself to Julian during his Asiatic expedition to Nicomedia. By accommodating his predictions to the wishes and hopes of the emperor, and by other parasitical arts, he gained entire possession of his confidence. The courtiers, as usual, followed the example of their master, and Maximus was daily loaded with new honors. He accompanied Julian in his expedition into Persia, and there, by the assistance of divination and flattery, persuaded him that he would rival Alexander in the glory of conquest. The event, however, proved as unfortunate to the philosopher as to the hero; for Julian being slain in battle, after the short reign of Jovian, Maximus fell under the displeasure of the emperors Valentinian and Valens, and, for the imaginary crime of magic, underwent a long course of confinement and suffering, which was not the less truly persecution because they were inflicted upon a Pagan. Maximus was finally sent into his native country, and there fell a sacrifice to the cruelty of the pro-consul, Festus.

MENEDEMUS.

Menedemus was one of those who belonged to the school of Phædo; and he was one of those who are called Theoprobidæ, being the son of Clisthenes, a man of noble family, but a poor man, and a builder. And some say that he was a tent-maker, and that Menedemus himself learnt both trades. On which account, when he on one occasion brought forward a motion for some decree, a man of the name of Alexinius attacked him, saying that a wise man had no need to draw a tent nor a decree.

But when Menedemus was sent by the Eretrians to Megara, as one of the garrison, he deserted the rest, and went to the Academy, to Plato; and, being charmed by him, he abandoned the army altogether. And when Asclepiades, the Phliasian, drew him over to him, he went and lived in Megara, near Stilpo, and they both became his discipies. And from thence they sailed to Elis, where they joined Anchipylus and Moschus, who belonged to Phædo's school. And up to this time, they were called Eleans; and they were also called Eretrians, from the native country of Menedemus, of whom I am now speaking.

Now Menedemus appears to have been a very severe and rigid man, on which account Crates, parodying a description, speaks of him thus :—

> And Asclepiades, the sage of Phlius,
> And the Eretrian bull.

And Timon mentions him thus :—

> Rise up, you frowning, bristling, frothy sage.

And he was a man of such excessive rigor of principle, that when Eurylochus, of Cassandra, had been invited by Antigonus to come to him in company with Cleippides, a youth of Cyzicus, he refused to go, for he was afraid lest Menedemus should hear of it; for he was very severe in his reproofs, and very free spoken. Accordingly, when a young man behaved with boldness towards him, he did not say a word, but took a bit of stick and drew on the floor an insulting picture; until the young man, perceiving the insult that was meant in the presence of numbers of people, went away. And when Hierocles, the governor of the Piræus, attacked him in the temple of Amphiaraus, and said a great deal about the taking of Eretria, he made no other reply beyond asking what Antigonus object was in treating him as he did.

On another occasion, he said to a profligate man who was giving himself airs, "Do not you know that the cabbage is not the only plant that has a pleasant juice, but that radishes have it also?" And once, hearing a young man talk very loudly, he said, "See whom you have behind you." When Antigonus consulted him whether he should go to a certain revel, he made no answer beyond desiring those who brought him the message, to tell him that he was the son of a king. When a stupid fellow once said something at random to him, he asked him whether he had a farm; and when he said that he had, and a large stock of cattle, he said, "Go then and look after them, lest, if you neglect them, you lose them, and that elegant rusticity of yours with them." He was once asked whether a good man should marry, and his reply was, "Do I seem to you to be a good man, or not?" And when the other said he did; "Well," said he, "and I am married." On one occasion, a person said that there were a great many good things, so he asked him how many; and whether he thought that there were more than a hundred. And as he could not bear the extravagance of one man who used frequently to invite him to dinner, once when he was invited he did not say a single word, but admonished him of his extravagance in silence, by eating nothing but olives.

On account then of the great freedom of speech in which he indulged, he was very near, while in Cyprus, at the court of Nicorreon, being in great danger with his friend Asclepiades. For when the king was celebrating a festival at the beginning of the month, and had invited them as he did all the other philosophers, Menedemus said, "If the assemblage of such men as are met here to-day is good, a festival like this ought to be celebrated every day; but if it is not good, even once is too often." And as the tyrant made answer to this speech, "that he kept this festival in order to have leisure in it to listen to the philosophers," he behaved with even more austerity than usual, arguing, even while the feast was going on, that it was right on every occasion to listen to philosophers; and he went on this way till, if a flute-player had not interrupted their discussion, they would have been put to death. In reference to which, when they were overtaken by a storm in a ship, they say that Asclepiades said, "that the fine playing of a flute-player had saved them, but the freedom of speech of Menedemus had ruined them."

But he was, they say, inclined to depart a good deal from the usual habits and discipline of a school, so that he never regarded any order, nor were the seats arranged around properly, but every one listened to him while lecturing, standing up or sitting down, just as he might chance to be at the moment, Menedemus himself setting the example of this irregular conduct. But in other respects, it is said that he was a nervous man, and very fond of glory; so that, as previously he and Asclepiades had been fellow journeymen of a builder, when Asclepiades was naked on the roof carrying mortar, Menedemus would stand in front of him to screen him when he saw any one coming.

When he applied himself to politics he was so nervous, that once, when setting down the incense, he actually missed the incense burner. And on one occasion, when Crates was standing by him, and reproaching him for meddling with politics, he ordered some men to put him in prison. But he, even then, continued not the less to watch him as he passed, and to stand on tiptoe and call him Agamemnon and Hegesipolis. He was also in some degree superstitious. Accordingly, once, when he was at an inn with Asclepiades, and had unintentionally eaten some meat that had been thrown away, when he was told of it he became sick, and turned pale, until Asclepiades rebuked him, telling him that it was not the meat itself which disturbed him, but only the idea that he had adopted. But in other respects he was a high-minded man, with notions such as became a gentleman.

As to his habit of body, even when he was an old man he retained all the firmness and vigor of an athlete, with firm flesh, and a ruddy complexion, and very stout and fresh looking. In stature he was of moderate size; as is plain from the statue of him which is at Eretria, in the Old Stadium. For he is there represented seated almost naked, undoubtedly for the purpose of displaying the greater part of his body.

He was very hospitable and fond of entertaining his friends; and because Eretria was unhealthy, he used to have a great many parties, particularly of poets and musicians. And he was very fond of Aratus and Lycophon the tragic poet, and

Antagoras of Rhodes. And above all he applied himself to the study of Homer; and next to him to that of the Lyric poets; then to Sophocles, and also to Achæus, to whom he assigned the second place as a writer of satiric dramas, giving Æschylus the first. And it is from Achæus that he quoted these verses against the politicians of the opposite party:—

A speedy runner once was overtaken
By weaker men than he. An eagle too,
Was beaten by a tortoise in a race.

And these lines are out of the satiric play of Achæus, called Omphale; so that they are mistaken who say that he had never read anything but the Medea of Euripides, which is found, they add, in the collection of Neophron, the Sicyonian.

Menedemus was not easy to be understood, and in his conversation he was hard to argue against. He spoke on every subject, and had a great deal of invention and readiness. But he was very disputatious, as Antisthenes says in his Successions; and he used to put questions of this sort: "Is one thing different from another thing?" "Yes." "And is benefiting a person something different from the good?" "Yes." "Then the good is not benefiting a person." And he, as it is said, discarded all negative axioms, using none but affirmative ones; and of these, he only approved of the simple ones, and rejected all that were not simple; saying that they were intricate and perplexing. But Heraclides says, that in his doctrines he was a thorough disciple of Plato, and that he scorned dialectics; so that once, when Alexinus asked him whether he had left off beating his father, he said, "I have not beaten him, and I have not left off;" and when he said further that he ought to put an end to the doubt by answering explicitly, yes or no, "It would be absurd," he rejoined, "to comply with your conditions when I can stop you at the entrance."

When Bion was attacking the soothsayers with great perseverance, he said that he was killing the dead over again. And once, when he heard some one assert that the greatest good was to succeed in everything that one desires; he said, "It is a much greater good to desire what is proper." But Antigonus, of Carystus, tells us, that he never wrote or composed any work, and never maintained any principle tenaciously. But in cross-questioning he was so contentious as to get quite black in the face before he went away. But though he was so violent in his discourse, he was wonderfully gentle in his actions. Accordingly, though he used to mock and ridicule Alexinus very severely, still he conferred great benefits on him, conducting his wife from Delphi to Chalcis for him, as she was alarmed about the danger of robbers and banditti in the road.

And he was a very warm friend, as is plain from his attachment to Asclepiades, which was hardly inferior to the friendship of Pylades and Orestes. But Asclepiades was the elder of the two, so that it was said that he was the poet, and Menedemus the actor. And they say, that on one occasion, Archipolis bequeathed them three thousand pieces of money between them, they had such a vigorous contest as to which should take the smaller share, that neither of them would receive any of it.

It is said that they were both married, and that Asclepiades was married to the mother, and Menedemus to the daughter; and when Asclepiades' wife died, he took the wife of Menedemus; and Menedemus, when he became the chief man of the state, married another, who was rich; and as they still maintained one house in common, Menedemus entrusted the whole management to his former wife. Asclepiades died first at Eretria, being of great age; having lived with Menedemus with great economy, though they had ample means. So that, when on one occasion, after the death of Asclepiades, a friend of his came to a banquet, and when the slaves refused him admittance, Menedemus ordered them to admit him, saying that Asclepiades opened the door for him, even now that he was under the earth. And the men who chiefly supported them, were Hyporicus, the Macedonian, and Agetor, the Lamian. And Agetor gave each of them thirty minæ, and Hyporicus gave Menedemus two thousand drachmas to portion his daughters with; and he had three, as Heraclides tells us, the children of his wife, who was a native of Oropus.

And he used to give banquets in this fashion: First of all, he would sit at dinner, with two or three friends, till late in the day, and then he would invite in any one who came to see him, even if they had already dined; and if any one came too soon, they would walk up and down, and ask those who came out of the house what there was on the table, and what o'clock it was; and then, if there were only vegetables and salt-fish, they would depart; but if they heard it was meat, they would go in. And during the summer, mats of rushes were laid upon the couches, and in winter, soft cushions; and each guest was expected to bring a pillow for himself. And the cup that was carried round did not hold more than a cotyla. And the second course consisted of lupins or beans, and sometimes fruits, such as pears, pomegranates, pulse, and sometimes, by Jove, dried figs. And all these circumstances are detailed by Lycophron, in his satiric dramas, which he inscribed with the name of Menedemus, making his play a panegyric on the philosopher. And the following are some of the lines:—

> After a temperate feast, a small-sized cup
> Is handed round with moderation due;
> And conversation wise makes the dessert.

At first, now, he was not thought much of, being called cynic and trifler by the Eretrians; but subsequently, he was so much admired by his countrymen, that they entrusted him with the chief government of the State. And he was sent cn embassies to Ptolemy and Lysimachus, and was greatly honored everywhere. He was sent as envoy to Demetrius; and, as the city used to pay him two hundred talents a year, he persuaded him to remit fifty. And having been falsely accused to him, as having betrayed the city to Ptolemy, he defended himself from the charge, in a letter. And the tradition is, that a man of the name of Æschylus, who was one of the opposite party in the State, was in the habit of making these false charges. It is well known, too, that he was sent on a most important embassy to Demetrius, on the subject of Oropus.

Antigonus was greatly attached to him, and professed himself his pupil; and when he defeated the barbarians, near Lysimachia, Menedemus drew up a decree for him, in simple terms, free from all flattery.

From these circumstances, and because of his friendship for him, as shown in other matters, he was suspected of betraying the city to him; and being impeached by Aristodemus, he left the city, and returned to Oropus, and there took up his abode in the temple of Amphiaraus; and as some golden goblets which were there were lost, he was ordered to depart by a general vote of the Bœotians. Leaving Oropus, and being in a state of great despondency, he entered his country secretly; and taking with him his wife and daughters, he went to the court of Antigonus, and there died of a broken heart.

But Heraclides gives an entirely different account of him; saying, that while he was the chief councillor of the Eretrians, he more than once preserved the liberties of the city from those who would have brought in Demetrius the tyrant; so that he never could have betrayed the city to Antigonus, and the accusation must have been false; and that he went to the court of Antigonus, and endeavored to effect the deliverance of his country; and as he could make no impression on him, he fell into despondency, and starved himself for seven days, and so he died. And Antigonus of Carystus gives a similar account; and Persæus was the only man with whom he had an implacable quarrel; for he thought that when Antigonus himself was willing to re-establish the democracy among the Eretrians for his sake, Persæus prevented him. And on this account Menedemus once attacked him at a banquet, saying many other things, and among them, "He may, indeed, be a philosopher, but he is the worst man that lives or that ever will live."

And he died, according to Heraclides, at the age of seventy-four. And we have written the following epigram on him:—

> I 've heard your fate, O Menedemus, that of your own accord
> You starved yourself for seven days and died;
> Acting like an Eretrian, but not much like a man,
> For spiritless despair appears your guide.

We add the following from Enfield's Brucker:—

Menedemus, though well descended, was obliged through poverty to submit to the manual employment of an house-builder. He formed an early intimacy with Asclepiades, a Phliasian, who was a fellow-laborer with him in his humble occupation. Having minds more formed for study than for labor, they determined to devote themselves to the pursuit of philosophy. For this purpose they left their native country, and went to Athens, where Plato then presided in the Academy. It was soon observed that these strangers had no visible means of subsistence; and, according to a law of Solon, they were cited before the court of Areopagus, to give an account of the manner in which they were supported. The master of one of the public prisons was, at their request, sent for, and attested that, every night, these two youths went among the criminals, and, by grinding with them, earned two drachmas, which enabled them to spend the day in the study of philosophy. The magistrates, struck with admiration at such an extraordinary proof of an indefatigable thirst after knowledge, dismissed them with high applause, and presented them with two hundred drachmas.* They met with several other friends, who liberally supplied them with whatever was necessary to enable them to prosecute their studies.

By the advice of his friend, and probably in his society,

* About six pounds.

Menedemus went from Athens to Megara, to attend upon the instructions of Stilpo. He expressed his approbation of the manner in which this philosopher taught, by giving him the appellation of The Liberal. He next visited Elis, where he became a disciple of Phædo, and afterwards his successor. Transferring the Eliac school from Elis to his native city, he gave it the name of Eretrian. In his school he neglected those forms which were commonly observed in places of this kind: his hearers were not, as usual, placed on circular benches around him; but every one attended him in whatever posture he pleased, standing, walking, or sitting.

At first Menedemus was received by the Eretrians with contempt; and, on account of the vehemence with which he disputed, he was often branded with the appellations of cur, and madman. But afterwards he rose into high esteem, and was intrusted with a public office, to which was annexed an annual stipend of two hundred talents. He discharged the trust with fidelity, but accepted only a fourth part of the appointment.

Menedemus possessed great readiness and versatility of genius, and was able to dispute on every subject with keenness and fluency. He declared his opinions with freedom, inveighed with severity against the vices of others, and by the purity of his own manners commanded universal respect. He observed the strictest moderation in his manner of living. His entertainments, which were frequented by many philosophers and men of distinction, were simple and frugal, consisting chiefly of vegetables, and were always enlivened by liberal conversation. He died about the hundred and twenty-fourth Olympiad.

There was another Menedemus, of whom the following is related. He was a disciple of Celotes of Lampsacus:

He proceeded, as Hippobotus tells, to such a great degree of superstition, that he assumed the garb of a fury, and went about saying that he had come from hell to take notice of all who did wrong, in order that he might descend thither again and make his report to the deities who abode in that country. And this was his dress: a tunic of a dark color reaching to his feet, and a purple girdle round his waist, an Arcadian hat on his head with the twelve signs of the zodiac, embroidered on it, tragic buskins, a preposterously long beard, and an ashen staff in his hand.

MONIMUS.

Monimus was a Syracusan, and also a slave of some Corinthian money-changer. Xeniades, who bought Diogenes, used often to come to him, extolling the excellency of Diogenes, both in actions and words, till he excited a great affection for the man in the mind of Monimus. For he immediately feigned madness, and threw about all the money and all the coins that were on the table, until his master discarded him, and then he straightway went to Diogenes and became his pupil. He also followed Crates the Cynic, a good deal, and devoted himself to the same studies as he did. His master regarded this conduct as additional evidence of his madness.

Monimus became a very eminent man, so that even Menander, the comic poet, speaks of him in the Hippocomus thus:—

> There is a man, O Philo, named Monimus,
> A wise man, though but little known, and one
> Who bears a wallet at his back, and is not
> Content with one but three. He never spoke
> A single sentence, by great Jove I swear,
> Like this one, "know thyself," or any other
> Of the oft-quoted proverbs; all such sayings
> He scorned, as he did beg his way through dirt;
> Teaching that all opinion is but vanity.

He was a man of such gravity that he despised glory and sought only for truth.

MUSONIUS.

Musonius a Babylonian (confounded by Suidas with Musonius the Tuscan, a Stoic philosopher) is ranked by Eunapius among the most virtuous and excellent of the Modern Cynics. Philostratus speaks of him as next to Apollonius in wisdom, and as an eminent philosopher. His cynical spirit would not permit him to spare the vices of Nero; and the resentment of that tyrant consigned him to prison. Whilst he was in confinement he formed a friendship with Apollonius, and held a correspondence with him, some specimens of which are preserved by Philostratus. He was at last banished to the Isthmus of Greece, and condemned to remain a slave, and to labor daily with the spade. His friend Demetrius, seeing him in this condition, expressed great concern at his misfortunes; upon which Musonius, striking his spade firmly in the ground, said, "Why, Demetrius, do you lament to see me digging in the Isthmus? You might indeed lament if you saw me, like Nero, playing upon the harp." Julian speaks with admiration of his magnanimity. The time of his death is uncertain; and none of his writings remain.

PITTACUS.

Pittacus was a native of Mitylene, and son of Hyrradius. But Duris says, that his father was a Thracian. He in union with the brothers of Alcæus, put down Melanchrus the tyrant of Lesbos. In the battle which took place between the Athenians and Mitylenæans on the subject of the district of Achilis, he was the Mitylenæan general; the Athenian commander being Phrynon, a Pancratiast, who had gained the victory at Olympia. Pittacus agreed to meet him in single combat, and having a net under his shield, he entangled, Phrynon without his being aware of it beforehand, and so, having killed him, he preserved the district in dispute to his countrymen. But Appollodorus, in his Chronicles, says, that subsequently, the Athenians had a trial with the Mitylenæans about the district, and that the cause was submitted to Periander, who decided it in favor of the Athenians.

In consequence of this victory the Mitylenæans held Pittacus in the greatest honor, and committed the supreme power into his hands which he held for ten years, and then, when he had brought the city and constitution into good order, he resigned the government. He lived ten years after that, and the Mitylenæans assigned him an estate, which he consecrated to the God, and to this day it is called the Pittacian land. But Sosicrates says that he cut off a small portion of it, saying that half was more than the whole; and when Crœsus offered him some money he would not accept it, as he said he had already twice as much as he wanted; for that he had succeeded to the inheritance of his brother, who had died without children.

But Pamphila says, in the second book of his Commentaries, that he had a son named Tyrrhæus, who was killed while sitting in a barber's shop, at Cyma, by a brazier, who threw an axe at him; and that the Cymæans sent the murderer to Pittacus, who when he had learnt what had been done, dismissed the man, saying, "Pardon is better than repentance." But Heraclitus says that the true story is, that he had got Alcæus into his power, and that he released him, saying, "Pardon is better than punishment." He was also a law-giver; and he made a law that if a man committed a crime while drunk, he should have double punishment; in the hope of deterring men from getting drunk, as wine was very plentiful in the island.

It was a saying of his that it was a hard thing to be good, and this apophthegm is quoted by Simonides, who says, "It was a saying of Pittacus, that it is a hard thing to be really a good man." Plato also mentions it in his Protagorus. Another of his sayings was, "Even the Gods cannot strive against necessity." Another was, "Power shows the man." Being once asked what was best, he replied, "To do what one is doing at the moment well." When Crœsus put the question to him, "What is the greatest power?" "The power," he replied, "of the variegated wood," meaning the wooden tablets of the laws. He used to say too, that there were some victories without bloodshed. He said once to a man of Phocæa, who was saying that we ought to seek out a virtuous man, "But if you seek ever so much you will not find one." Some people once asked him what thing was very grateful? and he replied, "Time."—What was uncertain? "The future."—What was trusty? "The land."—What was treacherous? "The sea." Another saying of his was, that it was the part of wise men, before difficult circumstances arose, to provide for their not arising; but that it was the part of brave men to make the best of existing circumstances. He used to say too, "Do not say before hand what you are going to do; for if you fail, you will be laughed at." "Do not reproach a man with his misfortunes, fearing lest Nemesis may overtake you." "If you have received a deposit, restore it." "Forbear to speak evil not only of your friends, but also of your enemies." "Practice piety, with temperance." "Cultivate truth, good faith, experience, cleverness, sociability, and industry." "Watch your opportunity."

He wrote also some songs, of which the following is the most celebrated one:—

> The wise will only face the wicked man,
> With bow in hand well bent,
> And quiver full of arrows—
> For such a tongue as his says nothing true,
> Prompted by a wily heart
> To utter double speeches.

He also composed six hundred verses in elegiac metre; and

he wrote a treatise in prose, on Laws, addressed to his countrymen.

He flourished about the forty-second Olympiad; and he died when Aristomenes was Archon, in the third year of the fifty-second Olympiad; having lived more than seventy years, being a very old man. On his tomb is this inscription:—

Lesbos who bore him here, with tears doth bury
Hyrradius' worthy son, wise Pittacus.

There was also another Pittacus, a law-giver, who was called Pittacus the less.

But it is said that the wise Pittacus once, when a young man consulted him on the subject of marriage, made him the following answer, which is thus given by Callimachus in his Epigrams:—

Hyrradius' prudent son, old Pittacus,
The pride of Mitylene, once was asked
By an Atarnean stranger; "Tell me, sage,
I have two marriages proposed to me;
One maid my equal is in birth and riches;
The other 's far above me;—which is best?
Advise me now which shall I take to wife?"
Thus spoke the stranger; but the aged prince,
Raising his old man's staff before his face,
Said, "These will tell you all you want to know;"
And pointed to some boys, who with quick lashes
Were driving whipping tops along the street.
"Follow their steps," said he; so he went near them
And heard them say, "Let each now mind his own."
So when the stranger heard the boys speak thus,
He pondered on their words, and laid aside
Ambitious thoughts of an unequal marriage,
As then he took to shame the poorer bride,
So too do you, O reader, mind thy own.

It seems that he may have here spoken from experience, for his own wife was of more noble birth than himself, since she was the sister of Draco, the son of Penthilus; and she gave herself great airs, and tyrannized over him.

Alcæas calls Pittacus, *splay-footed draggler*, because he was splay-footed, and used to drag his feet in walking; he also called him *chap-footed*, because he had scars on his feet which were called chaps. And *supercilious*, implying that he gave himself airs without reason. And *paunch* and *belly* because, he was fat. He also called him *eater-in-the-dark* because he had weak eyes, and *the lazy and dirty*. He used to grind corn for the sake of exercise, as Clearchus, the philosopher, relates.

There is a letter of his extant, which runs thus:—

PITTACUS TO CRŒSUS.

You invite me to come to Lydia in order that I may see your riches; but, I, even without seeing them, do not doubt that the son of Alyattes is the richest of monarchs. But I should get no good by going to Sardis; for I do not want gold myself, but what I have is sufficient for myself and my companions. Still, I will come, in order to become acquainted with you as a hospitable man.

PERIANDER.

PERIANDER was a Corinthian, the son of Cypselus, of the family of the Heraclidæ. He married Lyside (whom he himself called Melissa), the daughter of Procles the tyrant of Epidaurus, and of Eristhenea the daughter of Aristocrates, and sister of Aristodemus, who governed nearly all Arcadia, and had by her two sons Cypselus and Lycophron, the younger of whom was a clever boy, but the elder was deficient in intellect. At a subsequent period he in a rage either kicked or threw his wife down stairs when she was pregnant, and so killed her, being wrought upon by the false accusations of his concubines, whom he afterwards burnt alive. And the child, whose name was Lycophron, he sent away to Corcyra because he grieved for his mother.

But afterwards, when he was now extremely old, he sent for him back again, in order that he might succeed to the tyranny. But the Corcyreans, anticipating his intention, put him to death, at which he was greatly enraged, and sent their children to Corcyra to be made eunuchs of; and when the ship came near to Samos, the youths, having made supplications to Juno, were saved by the Samians. And he fell into despondency and died, being eighty years old. Sosicrates says that he died forty-one years before Crœsus, in the last year of the forty-eighth Olympiad. Herodotus, in the first book of his History, says that he was connected by ties of hospitality with Thrasybulus the tyrant of Miletus. And Aristippus, in the first book of his Treatise on Ancient Luxury, tells the following story of him; that his mother Cratea fell in love with him, and introduced herself secretly into his bed; and he was delighted; but when the truth was discovered he became very oppressive to all his subjects, because he was grieved at the discovery. Ephorus relates that he made a vow that, if he gained the victory at Olympia in the chariot race, he would dedicate a golden statue to the God. Accordingly he gained the victory; but being in want of gold, and seeing the women at some national festival beautifully adorned, he took away their golden ornaments, and then sent the offering which he had vowed.

But some writers say that he was anxious that his tomb should not be known, and that with that object he adopted the following contrivance. He ordered two young men to go out by night, indicating a particular road by which they were to go, and to kill the first man they met, and bury him; after them he sent out four other men who were to kill and bury them. Again he sent out a still greater number against these four, with similar instructions. And in this manner he put himself in the way of the first pair, and was slain, and the Corinthians erected a cenotaph over him with the following inscription:—

> The sea-beat land of Corinth in her bosom,
> Doth here embrace her ruler Periander,
> Greatest of all men for his wealth and wisdom.

We ourselves have also written an epigram upon him:—

> Grieve not when disappointed of a wish,
> But be content with what the Gods may give you—
> For the great Periander died unhappy,
> At failing in an object he desired.

It was a saying of his that we ought not to do anything for the sake of money; for that we ought only to acquire such gains as are allowable. He composed apophthegms in verse to the number of two thousand lines; and said that those who wished to wield absolute power in safety, should be guarded by the good will of their countrymen, and not by arms. And once, being asked why he assumed tyrannical power, he replied, "Because, to abdicate it voluntarily, and to have it taken from one, are both dangerous." The following sayings also belong to him:—Tranquillity is a good thing.—Rashness is dangerous.—Gain is disgraceful.—Democracy is better than tyranny.—Pleasures are transitory, but honor is immortal.—Be moderate when prosperous, but prudent when unfortunate.—Be the same to your friends when they are prosperous, and when they are unfortunate.—Whatever you agree to do, observe.—Do not divulge secrets.—Punish not only those who do wrong, but those who intend to do so.

This prince was the first who had body-guards, and who changed a legitimate power into a tyranny; and he would not allow any one who chose to live in his city.

And he flourished about the thirty-eighth Olympiad, and enjoyed absolute power for forty years. But Sotion, and Heraclides, and Pamphila, in the fifth book of her Commentaries, says that there were two Perianders; the one a tyrant, and the other a wise man and a native of Ambracia. And Neanthes of Cyzicus makes the same assertion, adding that the two men were cousins to one another. And Aristotle says, that it was the Corinthian Periander who was the wise one; but Plato contradicts him. The saying—"Practice does everything," is his. He it was, also, who proposed to cut through the Isthmus.

The following letter of his is quoted:—

PERIANDER TO THE WISE MEN.

I give great thanks to Apollo of Delphi that my letters are able to determine you all to meet together at Corinth; and I will receive you all, as you may be well assured, in a manner that becomes free citizens. I hear also that last year you met at Sardis, at the court of the King of Lydia. So now do not hesitate to come to me, who am the tyrant of Corinth; for the Corinthians will all be delighted to see you come to the house of Periander.

There is this letter too:—

PERIANDER TO PROCLES.

The injury of my wife was unintended by me; and you have done wrong in alienating from me the mind of my child. I desire you, therefore, either to restore me to my place in his affections, or I will revenge myself on you; for I have myself made atonement for the death of your daughter, by burning on her tomb the clothes of all the Corinthian women.*

Thrasybulus also wrote him a letter in the following terms:—

I have given no answer to your messenger; but having taken him into a field, I struck with my walking-stick all the highest ears of corn, and cut off their tops, while he was walking with me. And he will report to you, if you ask him, everything which he heard or saw while with me; and do you act accordingly if you wish to preserve your power safely,

* Herodotus mentions the case of Periander's children, iii. 50, and the death of his wife, and his burning the clothes of all the Corinthian women, v. 92.

taking off the most eminent of the citizens, whether he seems an enemy to you or not, as even his companions are deservedly objects of suspicion to a man possessed of supreme power.

PHERECYDES.

PHERECYDES was a Syrian, the son of Babys, and a pupil of Pittacus. Theopompus says that he was the first person who ever wrote among the Greeks on the subject of Natural Philosophy and the Gods. And there are many marvellous stories told of him. For it is said that he was walking along the sea-shore at Samos, and that seeing a ship sailing by with a fair wind, he said that it would soon sink; and presently it sank before their eyes. At another time he was drinking some water which had been drawn up out of a well, and he foretold that within three days there would be an earthquake; and there was one. And as he was going up to Olympia, and had arrived at Messene, he advised his entertainer, Perilaus, to migrate from the city with all his family, but that Perilaus would not be guided by him; and afterwards Messene was taken.

He is said to have told the Lacedæmonians to honor neither gold nor silver, as Theopompus says in his Marvels; and it is reported that Hercules laid this injunction on him in a dream, and that the same night he appeared also to the kings of Sparta, and enjoined them to be guided by Pherecydes; but some attribute these stories to Pythagoras.

Hermippus relates that when there was a war between the Ephesians and Magnesians, he, wishing the Ephesians to conquer, asked some one, who was passing by, from whence he came? and when he said, "From Ephesus," "Drag me now," said he, "by the legs, and place me in the territory of the Magnesians, and tell your fellow countrymen to bury me there after they have got the victory; and that he went and reported that Pherecydes had given him this order. And so they went forth the next day and defeated the Magnesians; and as Pherecydes was dead, they buried him there and paid him very splendid honors.

But some writers say that he went to Delphi, and threw himself down from the Corycian hill; Aristoxenus, in his History of Pythagoras and his Friends, says that Pherecydes fell sick and died, and was buried by Pythagoras in Delos. But others say that he died of the lousy disease; and when Pythagoras came to see him, and asked him how he was, he put his finger through the door, and said, "You may see by my skin." And from this circumstance that expression passed into a proverb among the philosophers, when affairs are going on badly; and those who apply it to affairs that are going on well, make a blunder. He used to say, also, that the Gods call their table *thuros*, i. e. a social table. It also means, money-changer's table.

And I myself have composed an epigram on him in the Pherecratean metre:—

The story is reported,
That noble Pherecydes,
Whom Syros calls her own,
Was eaten up by lice;
And so he bade his friends,
Convey his corpse away
To the Magnesian land,
That he might victory give
To holy Ephesus.
For well the God had said,
(Though he alone did know
Th' oracular prediction),
That this was fate's decree.
So in that land he lies.
This then is surely true,
That those who 're really wise
Are useful while alive,
And e'en when breath has left them.

He flourished about the fifty-ninth Olympiad. There is a letter of his extant in the following terms:—

PHERECYDES TO THALES.

May you die happily when fate overtakes you. Disease has seized upon me at the same time that I received your letter. I am all over lice, and suffering likewise under a low fever. Accordingly, I have charged my servants to convey this book of mine to you, after they have buried me. And do you, if you think fit, after consulting with the other wise men, publish it; but if you do not approve of doing so, then keep it unpublished, for I am not entirely pleased with it myself. The subject is not one about which there is any certain knowledge, nor do I undertake to say that I have arrived at the truth; but I have advanced arguments, from which any one who occupies himself with speculations on the divine nature, may make a selection; and as to other points, he must exercise his intellect, for I speak obscurely throughout. I, myself, as I am afflicted more severely by this disease every day, no longer admit any physicians, or any of my friends. But when they stand at the door, and ask me how I am, I put out my finger to them through the opening of the door, and show them how I am eaten up with the evil; and I desired them to come to-morrow to the funeral of Pherecydes.

PLATO.

PLATO was the son of Ariston and Perictione or Petone, and a citizen of Athens; and his mother traced her family back to Solon; Plato being the sixth in descent from Solon. And Solon traced his pedigree up to Neleus and Neptune. They say, too, that on the father's side he was descended from Codrus, the son of Melanthus, and they, too, are said by Thrasylus to derive their origin from Neptune. The report at Athens was that Perictione was very beautiful, and that Ariston endeavored to violate her and did not succeed; and that he, after he had desisted from his violence, saw a vision of Apollo in a dream, in consequence of which he abstained from approaching his wife till after her confinement.

Plato was born, as Apollodorus says in his Chronicles, in the eighty-eighth Olympiad, on the seventh day of the month Thargelion, on which day the people of Delos say that Apollo also was born. And he died, as Hermippus says, at a marriage feast, in the first year of the hundred and eighth Olympiad, having lived eighty-one years. But Neanthes says that he was eighty-four years of age at his death.

He was of the borough of Colytus, as Antileon tells us in his second book on Dates. And he was born, according to some writers, in Ægina, in the house of Phidiades, the son of Thales. His father had been sent thither with several others as a settler, and returned again to Athens when the settlers were driven out by the Lacedæmonians, who came to the assistance of the Æginetans. And he served the office of choregus at Athens, when Dion was at the expense of the spectacle exhibited, as Theodorus relates in the eighth book of his Philosophical Conversations.

He was taught learning in the school of Dionysius, whom he mentions in his Rival Lovers. And he learnt gymnastic exercises under the wrestler Ariston of Argos. And it was by him that he had the name of Plato given to him instead of his original name, on account of his robust figure, as he had previously been called Aristocles, after the name of his grandfather, as Alexander informs us in his Successions. But some say that he derived this name from the breadth (*Platutes*, broad) of his eloquence, or else because he was very wide (*Platus*, width) across the forehead, as Neanthes affirms.

It is also said that he applied himself to the study of painting, and that he wrote poems, dithyrambics at first, and afterwards lyric poems and tragedies.

But he had a very weak voice, they say; and the same fact is stated by Timotheus the Athenian, in his book on Lives. And it is said that Socrates in a dream saw a cygnet on his knees, who immediately put forth feathers, and flew up on high, uttering a sweet note, and that the next day Plato came to him, and that he pronounced him the bird which he had seen.

He used to philosophize at first in the Academy, and afterwards in the garden near Colonus; and subsequently, though he was about to contend for the prize in tragedy in the theatre of Bacchus, after he had heard the discourse of Socrates, he learnt his poems, saying:—

> Vulcan, come here; for Plato wants your aid.

Having fallen sick at Eurytus, he was cured by the priests by the application of sea water, in reference to which he said:—

> The sea doth wash away all human evils.

And he said too, that, according to Homer, all the Egyptians were physicians. Plato had also formed the idea of making the acquaintance of the Magi; but he abandoned it on account of the wars in Asia.

When he returned to Athens, he settled in the Academy, and that is a suburban place of exercise planted like a grove, so named from an ancient hero named Hecademus.

> In the well-shaded walks, protected well
> By Godlike Academus.

Timon, with reference to Plato, says:—

> A man did lead them on, a strong stout man,
> A honeyed speaker, sweet as melody
> Of tuneful grasshopper, who, seated high
> On Hecademus' tree, unwearied sings.

For the word Academy was formerly spelt with E. He was three times engaged in military expeditions; once against

Tanagra; the second time against Corinth, and the third time at Delium; and that in the battle of Delium he obtained the prize of pre-eminent valor. He combined the principles of the schools of Heraclitus, and Pythagoras and Socrates; for he used to philosophize on those things which are the subjects of sensation, according to the system of Heraclitus; on those with which intellect is conversant, according to that of Pythagoras; and on politics, according to that of Socrates.

Plato made three voyages to Sicily, first of all for the purpose of seeing the island and the craters of volcanoes, when Dionysius, the son of Hermocrates, being the tyrant of Sicily, pressed him earnestly to come and see him; and he, conversing about tyranny, and saying that that is not the best government which is advantageous for one individual alone, unless that individual is pre-eminent in virtue, had a quarrel with Dionysius, who got angry, and said, "Your words are those of an old dotard:" to which Plato replied, "And your language is that of a tyrant." And on this the tyrant became very indignant, and at first was inclined to put him to death; but afterwards, being appeased by Deni and Aristimenes, he forebore to do that, but gave him to Pollis, the Lacedæmonian, who happened to have come to him on an embassy just at that time, to sell as a slave. And he took him to Ægina and sold him; and Charmander, the son of Charmandrides, instituted a capital prosecution against him, in accordance with the law which was in force, in the island of Ægina, that the first Athenian who landed on the island should be put to death without a trial; and he himself was the person who had originally proposed that law, as Pharorinus says, in his Universal History. But when some one said, though he said it only in joke, that it was a philosopher who had landed, the people released him. But some say that he was brought into the assembly and watched; and that he did not say a word, but stood prepared to submit to whatever might befall him; and that they determined not to put him to death, but to sell him after the fashion of prisoners of war. And it happened by chance that Anniceris, the Cyrenean, was present, who ransomed him for twenty minæ, or, as others say, for thirty, and sent him to Athens, to his companions, and they immediately sent Anniceris his money: but he refused to receive it, saying that they were not the only people in the world who were entitled to have a regard for Plato. Some writers again say, that it was Deni who sent the money, and that he did not refuse it, but bought him the garden in the Academy. And with respect to Pollis it is said that he was defeated by Chabrias, and that he was afterwards drowned in Helia, in consequence of the anger of the deity at his treatment of this philosopher. And this is the story told by Pharorinus in the first book of his Commentaries. Dionysius, however, did not remain quiet; but when he had heard what had happened he wrote to Plato not to speak ill of him, and he wrote back in reply that he had not leisure enough to think at all of Dionysius.

But he went a second time to Sicily to the younger Dionysius, and asked him for some land and for some men whom he might make live according to his own theory of a constitution. And Dionysius promised to give him some, but never did it. And some say that he was in danger himself, having been suspected of exciting Dion and Thetas to attempt the deliverance of the island; but that Archytas, the Pythagorean, wrote a letter to Dionysius, and begged Plato off and sent him back safe to Athens.

In his own country he did not meddle with state affairs, although he was a politician as far as his writings went. And the reason was that the people were accustomed to a form of government and constitution different from what he approved of. And Pamphile, in the twenty-fifth book of his Commentaries, says that the Arcadians and Thebans, when they were founding a great city, appointed him its law-giver; but that he, when he had ascertained that they would not consent to an equality of rights, refused to go thither.

It is said also, that he defended Chabrias the general, when he was impeached in a capital charge; when no one else of the citizens would undertake the task; and as he was going up towards the Acropolis with his client, Crobylus the sycophant met him and said, "Are you come to plead for another, not knowing that the hemlock of Socrates is waiting also for you?" But he replied, "And also, when I fought for my country I encountered dangers; and now too I encounter them in the cause of justice and for the defence of a friend."

He was the first author who wrote treatises in the form of dialogues, as Pharorinus tells us in the eight book of his Uni versal History. And he was also the first person who introduced the analytical method of investigation, which he taught to Leodamus of Thasos. He was also the first person in philosophy who spoke of antipodes, and elements, and dialectics, and actions and oblong numbers, and plane surfaces, and the providence of God. He was likewise the first of the philosophers who contradicted the assertion of Lysias, the son of Cephalus, setting it out word for word in his Phædrus. And he was also the first person who examined the subject of grammatical knowledge scientifically. And as he argued against almost every one who had lived before his time, it is often asked why he has never mentioned Democritus.

Neanthes of Cyzicus says, that when he came to the Olympic games all the Greeks who were present turned to look at him; and that it was on that occasion that he held a conversation with Dion, who was on the point of attacking Dionysius. Moreover, in the first book of the Commentaries of Pharorinus, it is related that Mithridates, the Persian, erected a statue of Plato in the Academy, and put on it this inscription: "Mithridates, the son of Rhodobates, a Persian, consecrated an image of Plato to the Muses, which was made by Silanion."

Heraclides says, that even while a young man, he was so modest and well regulated, that he was never once seen to laugh excessively. But though he was of such a grave character himself, he was nevertheless ridiculed by the comic poets Accordingly, Theopompus, in his Pleasure-seeker, says:—

For one thing is no longer only one,
But two things now are scarcely one; as says
The solemn Plato.

And Anaxandrides in his Theseus, says:—

When he ate olives like our worthy Plato.

And Timon speaks of him in this way, punning on his name:—

As Plato placed strange platitudes on paper.

Alexis says in his Mesopis:—

You 've come in time: since I' ve been doubting long,
And walking up and down some time, like Plato;
And yet have hit upon no crafty plan,
But only tir'd my legs.

And in his Analion, he says:—

You speak of what you do not understand,
Running about like Plato: hoping thus,
To learn the nature of saltpetre and onions.

Amphis says in his Amphicrates:—

But what the good is, which you hope to get
By means of her, my master, I no more
Can form a notion of, than of the good
Of Plato.

And in his Dexidemus he speaks thus:—

O Plato! how your learning is confined
To gloomy looks, and wrinkling up your brows
Like any cockle.

Cratinas, in his Pseudripobolimæus, says:—

You clearly are a man, endued with sense,
And so, as Plato says, I do not know;
But I suspect.

Alexis, in his Olympiodorus, speaks thus:—

My mortal body became dry and withered:
But my immortal part rose to the sky.
Is not this Plato's doctrine?

And in his Parasite he says :—

> Or to converse alone, like Plato.

Anaxilas also laughs at him in his Botrylion, and Circe, and his Rich Women.

Aristippus, in the fourth book of his treatise upon Ancient Luxury, says that he was much attached to a youth of the name of Aster, who used to study astronomy with him ; and also to Dion, whom we have already mentioned. And some say that he was also attached to Phædrus, and that the following epigrams which he wrote upon them are evidences of the love he felt for them :—

> My Aster,* you 're gazing on the stars (*asteres*),
> Would that I were the heavens, that so I might
> Gaze in return with many eyes on thee.

Another of his epigrams is :—

> Aster, you while among the living shone,
> The morning star. But now that you are dead,
> You beam like Hesperus, in the shades below.

And he wrote thus on Dion :—

> Once, at their birth, the Fates did destine tears
> To be the lot of all the Trojan women,
> And Hecuba, their Queen—to you, O Dion,
> As the deserved reward for glorious deeds,
> They gave extensive and illustrious hopes.
> And now you lie beneath your native soil ;
> Honored by all your countrymen, O Dion,
> And loved by me with ardent, lasting love.

And they say that this epigram is inscribed upon his tomb at Syracuse. They say, also, that he was in love with Alexis, and with Phædrus, as I have already mentioned, and that he wrote an epigram on them both, which runs thus :—

> Now when Alexis is no longer aught,
> Say only how beloved, how fair he was,
> And every one does turn his eyes at once.
> Why, my mind, do you show the dogs a bone?
> You 're but preparing trouble for yourself :
> Have we not also lost the lovely Phædrus !

* *Aster* signifies star.

There is also a tradition that he had a mistress named Archianassa, on whom he wrote the following lines :—

I have a mistress fair from Colophon,
Archianassa, on whose very wrinkles
Sits genial love: hard must have been the fate
Of him who met her earliest blaze of beauty,
Surely he must have been completely scorched.

He also wrote this epigram on Agathon :—

While kissing Agathon, my soul did rise,
And hover'd o'er my lips; wishing perchance,
O'er anxious that it was, to migrate to him.

Another of his epigrams is :—

I throw this apple to you. And if you
Love me who love you so, receive it gladly,
And let me taste your lovely virgin charms.
Or if that may not be, still take the fruit,
And in your bosom cherish it, and learn
How fleeting is all gracefulness and beauty.

And another :—

I am an apple, and am thrown to you,
By one who loves you: but consent, Xanthippe;
For you and I shall both with time decay.

They also attribute to him the following epigram on the Eretrians who had been surprised in an ambuscade :—

We were Eretrians, of Eubæan race?
And now we lie near Susa, here entomb'd,
Far from my native land.

And this one also :—

Thus Venus to the muses spoke:
Damsels submit to Venus' yoke,
  Or dread my Cupid's arms.
Those threats, the Virgins nine replied,
May weigh with Mars, but we deride
  Love's wrongs, or darts, or charms.

Another is :-

A certain person found some gold,
Carried it off, and in its stead
Left a strong halter neatly roll'd.

The owner found his treasure fled;
And powerless to endure his fortune s wreck,
Fitted the halter to his hapless neck.

It is said also, that Antisthenes, being about to recite some thing that he had written, invited him to be present; and that Plato having asked what he was going to recite, he said that it was an essay on the impropriety of contradicting. "How then," said Plato, "can you write on this subject?" and then he showed him that he was arguing in a circle. But Antisthenes was annoyed, and composed a dialogue against Plato, which he entitled Sothon; after which they were always enemies to one another; and they say that Socrates having heard Plato read the Lysis, said, "O Hercules! what a number of lies the young man has told about me." For he had set down a great many things as sayings of Socrates which he never said.

Pharorinus says, when Plato read his treatise on the Soul, Aristotle was the only person who sat it out, and that all the rest rose up and went away. And some say that Philip the Opuntian copied out the whole of his books upon Laws, which were written on waxen tablets only.

A story is told, that Plato, having seen a man playing at dice, reproached him for it, and that he said he was playing for a trifle: "But the habit," rejoined Plato, "is not a trifle." On one occasion he was asked whether there would be any monument of him, as of his predecessors in philosophy? and he answered, "A man must first make a name, and the monument will follow." Once, when Xenocrates came into his house, he desired him to scourge one of his slaves for him, for that he himself could not do it because he was in a passion; and that at another time he said to one of his slaves, "I should beat you if I were not in a passion." Having got on horseback he dismounted again immediately, saying that he was afraid that he should be infected with horse-pride. He used to advise people who got drunk to look in the glass, and then they would abandon their unseemly habit; and he said it was never decorous to drink to the degree of drunkenness, except at the festivals of the God who had given men wine. He also disapproved of much sleeping: accordingly, in his Laws he says, "No one while sleeping is good for anything." Another saying of his was, "That the pleasantest of all things to hear was the truth;" but others report this saying thus, "That the sweetest of all things was to speak truth." And of truth he speaks thus in his Laws: "Truth, my friend, is a beautiful and a durable thing; but it is not easy to persuade men of this fact."

He used also to wish to leave a memorial of himself behind, either in the hearts of his friends, or in his books. He also used to travel a good deal, as some authors inform us.

He died in the thirteenth year of the reign of Philip of Macedon; and Theopompus relates that Philip on one occasion reproached him. But Mysonianus, in his Resemblances, says that Philo mentions some proverbs that were in circulation about Plato's lice; implying that he had died of that disease.

He was buried in the Academy, where he spent the greater part of his time in the practice of philosophy, from which his was called the Academic school; and his funeral was attended by all the pupils of that sect. He made his will in the following terms:—"Plato left these things, and has bequeathed them as follows:—The farm in the district of the Hephæstiades, bounded on the north by the road from the temple of the Cephiciades, and on the south by the temple of Hercules, which is in the district of the Hephæstiades; and on the east by the estate of Archestratus the Phreanian, and on the west by the farm of Philip the Challidian, shall be incapable of being sold or alienated, but shall belong to my son Ademantus as far as possible. And so likewise shall my farm in the district of the Eiresides, which I bought of Callimachus, which is bounded on the north by the property of Eurymedon the Myrrhinusian, on the south by that of Demostratus of Xypeta, on the east by that of Eurymedon the Myrrhinusian, and on the west by the Cephisus;—I also leave him three minæ of silver, a silver goblet weighing a hundred and sixty-five drachms, a cup weighing forty-five drachms, a golden ring and a golden ear-ring, weighing together four drachms and three obols. Euclides the stone-cutter owes me three minæ. I leave Diana her liberty. My slaves Sychon, Bictas, Apolloniades, and Dionysius, I bequeath to my son; and I also give him all my furniture, of which Demetrius has a catalógue. I owe no one anything. My executors shall be Tozthenes, Speusippus, Demetrius, Hegias, Eurymedon, Callimachus, and Thrasippus." This was his will. And on his tomb the following epigrams were inscribed. First of all:—

Here, first of all men for pure justice famed,
And moral virtue, Aristocles lies;
And if there e'er has lived one truly wise,
This man was wiser still; too great for envy.

A second is:—

Here in her bosom does the tender earth
Embrace great Plato's corpse. His soul aloft
Has ta'en its place among the immortal Gods.
Ariston's glorious son—whom all good men,
Though in far countries, held in love and honor,
Remembering his pure and god-like life.

We add the following from Brucker:

Plato gave early indications of an extensive and original genius. While he was young, he was instructed in the rudiments of letters by the grammarian Dionysius, and trained in athletic exercises by Aristo of Argos. He applied, with great diligence, to the study and practice of the arts of painting and poetry. In the latter he made such proficiency as to produce an epic poem, which, however, on comparing it with Homer, he committed to the flames. At the age of twenty years he composed a dramatic piece, which he gave to the performers, to be represented upon the stage; but the day before the intended exhibition, happening to attend upon a discourse of Socrates, he was captivated by his eloquence, and from that moment determined to relinquish all pretensions to poetical distinction, and to turn his ambition into the channel of philosophy. He forsook the muses, burned his poems, and applied himself wholly to the study of wisdom.

It is probable that Plato received the first tincture of philosophy from Cratylus and Hermogenes, who taught the systems of Heraclitus and Parmenides. When he was twenty years old he became a stated disciple of Socrates, and remained with him in that relation eight years. During this period he frequently displeased the followers of Socrates, and sometimes gave Socrates himself occasions of complaint, by mixing foreign tenets with those of his master, and grafting upon the Socratic system opinions which were taken from some other stock. Plato, nevertheless, retained a zealous attachment to Socrates. When that great and good man was summoned before the senate, Plato, as we have seen, undertook to plead his cause, and began a speech in his defence; but the partiality and violence of the judges would not permit him to proceed. After the condemnation, he presented his master with money sufficient to redeem his life, which, however, Socrates refused to accept. During his imprisonment, Plato attended him, and was present at a conversation which he held with his friends concerning the immortality of the soul, the substance of which he afterwards committed to writing in the beautiful dialogue entitled Phædo, not, however, without interweaving his own opinions and language. Upon the death of his master, he withdrew, with several other friends of Socrates, to Megara, where they were hospitably entertained by Euclid, and remained till the ferment at Athens subsided. Under Euclid he studied the art of reasoning, and probably increased his fondness for disputation.

Desirous of making himself master of all the wisdom and learning which the age could furnish, Plato travelled into every country which was so far enlightened as to promise him any recompense for his labor. That he might travel with safety, he assumed the character of a merchant, and as a seller of oil passed through the whole kingdom of Artaxerxes Mnemon. Wherever he came, he obtained information from the Egyptian priests concerning their astronomical observations and calculations. "Whilst studious youth," (says Valerius Maximus, rather indeed in the style of oratory than history, for Plato had not instituted his school at Athens) "were crowding to Athens from every quarter in search of Plato for their master, that philosopher was wandering along the winding banks of the Nile, or the vast plains of a barbarous country, himself a disciple to the old men of Egypt."

It has been asserted, that it was in Egypt that Plato acquired his opinions concerning the origin of the world, and learnt the doctrines of transmigration, and the immortality of the soul ; but it is more probable that he learned the latter doctrine from Socrates, and the former from Pythagoras. It is not likely that Plato, in the habit of a merchant, could have gained access to the sacred mysteries of Egypt; for we see, in the case of Pythagoras, that the Egyptian priests were so unwilling to communicate their secrets to strangers, that even a royal mandate was scarcely sufficient, in a single instance, to procure this indulgence.

From the particulars which we have related concerning the manner in which Plato acquired his knowledge, we are enabled to ascertain with some degree of precision, the sources of his philosophy. His dialectics he borrowed from Euclid of Megara: the principles of natural philosophy he learned in the Eleatic school from Hermogenes and Cratylus; and combining these with the Pythagorean doctrine of natural causes, he framed from both his system of metaphysics. Mathematics and astronomy he was taught in the Cyrenaic school, and by the Egyptian priests. From Socrates he imbibed the pure principles of moral and political wisdom ; but he afterwards obscured their simplicity by Pythagorean speculations.

Returning home richly stored with knowledge of various kinds, Plato settled in Athens, and executed the design, which he had doubtless long had in contemplation, of forming a new school for the instruction of youth in the principles of philosophy. The place which he made choice of for this purpose was a public grove called the Academy, from Academus, who left it to the citizens for the purpose of gymnastic exercises. Adornéd with statues, temples, and sepulchres, surrounded with high trees, and intersected by a gentle stream, it afforded a delightful retreat for philosophy and the muses. Of this retreat Horace speaks:

'Midst Academic groves to search for truth.

How much Plato valued mathematical studies, and how necessary a preparation he thought them for higher speculations, appears from the inscription which he placed over the door of his school: "Let no one, who is unacquainted with geometry, enter here."

This new school soon became famous, and its master was ranked among the most eminent philosophers. His travels into distant countries, where learning and wisdom flourished, gave him celebrity among his brethren of the Socratic sect. Not only did young men crowd to his school from every quarter, but people of the first distinction, in every department, frequented the Academy. Even females, disguised in men's clothes, often attended his lectures. Among the illustrious names which appear in the catalogue of his followers are Dion, the Syracusan prince, and the orators Hyperides, Lycurgus, Demosthenes, and Isocrates.

Such distinguished reputation naturally produced among the companions of Plato, formerly the disciples of Socrates, a spirit of emulation, which soon degenerated into envy, and loaded him with detraction and obloquy. It can only be ascribed to mutual jealousy, that Xenophon and Plato, though they relate the discourses of their common master, studiously avoid mentioning one another. Diogenes the Cynic ridiculed Plato's doctrine of ideas, and other abstract speculations. In the midst of these private censures, however, the public fame of Plato daily increased. His political wisdom was in such high estimation, that several States solicited his assistance in new-modelling their respective forms of government. Applications of this kind from the Arcadians, and from the Thebans, he rejected, because they refused to adopt the plan of his republic, which required an equal distribution of property. He gave his advice in the affairs of Elis, and other Grecian States, and furnished a code of laws for Syracuse. Plato was in high esteem with several princes, particularly Archelaus, king of Macedon, and Dionysius, tyrant of Sicily. At three different periods he visited the court of this latter prince, and made several bold, but unsuccessful attempts to subdue his haughty and tyrannical spirit. A brief relation of the particulars of these visits to Sicily may serve to cast some light upon the character of our philosopher.

The professed object of Plato's first visit to Sicily, which happened in the fortieth year of his age, during the reign of the elder Dionysius, the son of Hermocrates, was, to take a survey of the island, and particularly to observe the wonders of Mount Ætna. Whilst he was resident at Syracuse, he was employed in the instruction of Dion, the king's brother-in-law, who possessed excellent abilities, though hitherto restrained by the terrors of a tyrannical government, and relaxed by the luxuries of a licentious court. Disgusted by the debauched manners of the Syracusans, he endeavored to rescue his pupil from the general depravity. Nor did Dion disappoint his preceptor's expectations. No sooner had he received a taste of that philosophy which leads to virtue than he was fired with an ardent love of wisdom. Entertaining a hope that philosophy might produce the same effect upon Dionysius, he took great pains to procure an interview between Plato and the tyrant. In the course of the conference, whilst Plato was discoursing on the security and happiness of virtue, and the miseries attending injustice and oppression, Dionysius, perceiving that the philosopher's discourse was levelled against the vices and cruelties of his reign, dismissed him with high displeasure from his presence, and conceived a design against his life. It was not without great difficulty that Plato, by the assistance of Dion, made his escape. A vessel which had brought over Pollis, a delegate from Sparta, was fortunately at that time returning to Greece. Dion engaged Pollis to take the charge of the philosopher, and land him safely in his native country; but Dionysius discovered the design, and obtained a promise from Pollis that he would either put him to death, or sell him as a slave upon the passage. Pollis, accordingly, sold him in the island of Ægina, the inhabitants of which were then at war with the Athenians. Plato could not long remain unnoticed: Anicerris, a Cyrenaic philosopher, who happened to be at that time in the island, discovered the stranger, and thought himself happy in an opportunity of showing his respect for so illustrious a philosopher; he purchased his freedom for thirty *minæ*, and sent him home to Athens. Repayment being afterwards offered to Anicerris by Plato's relations, he refused the money, saying, with that generous spirit which true philosophy always inspires, that he saw no reason why the relations of Plato should engross to themselves the honor of serving him.

After a short interval, Dionysius repented of his ill-placed resentment, and wrote to Plato, earnestly requesting him to repair his credit by returning to Syracuse; to which Plato gave this high-spirited answer, that philosophy would not allow him leisure to think of Dionysius. Dion, who, through the influence of Plato's instructions, had become a determined votary of virtue, was earnestly desirous of inspiring others with the same sentiments. In hope of making an advantageous impression upon the mind of the younger Dionysius, he took every occasion of making him acquainted with the doctrines and precepts of his master. The effect was such as Dion wished—the youth soon expressed an earnest desire to became acquainted with the philosopher. Letters were immediately despatched to Plato, from the tyrant, from Dion, and from several followers of Pythagoras, who were at that time resident in Sicily, importuning him to return to Syracuse, and take upon him the education of the young prince. After some hesitation, apprehending lest a refusal might seem to imply an unworthy neglect of the interest of philosophy, and entertaining some hope, that by cleansing the fountain of public manners in Sicily, he should be able to purify the stream, he consented. It has also been said, and not without plausibility, that he was induced to undertake this second journey to Syracuse by a promise, on the part of Dionysius, that he would adopt the philosopher's plan of government. In the meantime, the enemies of Dion prevailed upon Dionysius to recall from exile Philistus, a man of tyrannical principles and spirit, from whom they hoped for a powerful opposition to the doctrine and the measures of Plato. The philosopher was conducted to Syracuse with public honors; the king himself received him in his chariot, and sacrifices were offered in congratulation of his arrival. New regulations were immediately introduced; the licentiousness of the court was restrained; moderation reigned in all public festivals; the king assumed an air of benignity; philosophy was studied by his courtiers; and every good man assured himself of a happy revolution in the state of public manners. But Philistus and his adherents, envious of the philosopher's increasing influence with the tyrant, soon found means to rekindle his jealousy. Through their intrigues, Dion became so obnoxious to Dionysius, that he ordered him to be imprisoned, and afterwards banished him into Italy. Plato, and the friends of Dion, were exceedingly alarmed at this measure, and began to be apprehensive for their own safety. Dionysius, however, continued to treat them courteously. Under the pretence of friendship, he allotted Plato an apartment in his palace, but at the same time placed a secret guard about him, that no one might visit him without his knowledge. At length, upon the commencement of a war, Dionysius sent Plato back into his own country, but not without a promise that he would recall both him and Dion upon the return of peace.

Dion, who now resided in Athens, diligently attended upon the lectures of his master, and so far profited by his moral precepts, as to lay aside everything effeminate and luxurious in his manner of living. The tyrant, in the meantime, that he might, if possible, obliterate the ignominy which he had brought upon himself by the banishment of Plato, invited philosophers from every quarter to his court. Their discourses recalled his attention to philosophy, and he again became exceedingly desirous of Plato's return. The philosopher received his solicitations with coolness, pleaded in excuse his advanced age, and reminded the tyrant of the violation of his promise, that on the return of peace Dion should be restored. It was not till the request of Dionysius was seconded by the intreaties of the wife and sister of Dion, and by the importunities of Archytas of Tarentum, and other Pythagorean philosophers, to whom the tyrant had pledged himself for the performance of his promises, that he could be prevailed upon to return.

When Plato arrived the third time at Syracuse, the king met him in a magnificent chariot, and conducted him to his palace. The Sicilians, too, whose hatred of Philistus inclined them to favor the party of Dion, rejoiced in his return, for they hoped that the wisdom of Plato would at length triumph over the tyrannical spirit of the prince. Dionysius seemed wholly divested of his former resentments, listened with apparent pleasure to the philosopher's doctrine, and, among other expressions of regard, presented him with eighty talents of gold. In the midst of a numerous train of philosophers, Plato now possessed the chief influence and authority in the court of Syr-

20*

acuse. Whilst Aristippus was enjoying himself in splendid luxury, whilst Diogenes was freely indulging his acrimonious humor, and whilst Æschines was gratifying his thirst after riches, Plato supported the credit of philosophy with an air of dignity, which his friends regarded as an indication of superior wisdom, but which his enemies imputed to pride. After all, it was not in the power of Plato to prevail upon Dionysius to adopt his system of policy, or to recall Dion from his exile. Mutual distrust, after a short interval, arose between the tyrant and the philosopher; each suspected the other of evil designs, and each endeavored to conceal his suspicion under the disguise of respect. Dionysius attempted to impose upon Plato by condescending attentions, and Plato to deceive Dionysius by an appearance of confidence. At length the philosopher became so much dissatisfied with his situation, that he earnestly requested permission to return to Greece.

After some opposition on the part of the tyrant, permission was granted and a vessel of convoy was provided. But before the ship set sail Dionysius repented, and detained Plato in Syracuse against his inclination. From this time the freedom of the philosopher's complaints and reproofs became offensive to the tyrant, and Dionysius dismissed Plato from his court, and put him under a guard of soldiers, whom false rumors had incensed against him. His Pythagorean friends at Tarentum, being informed of his dangerous situation, immediately despatched an embassy to Dionysius, demanding an instant completion of his promise to Archytas. The tyrant, not daring to refuse this demand, but at the same time desirous to save himself, as much as possible, from the disgrace of having banished from his court the first philosopher of the age, gave Plato a magnificent entertainment, and sent him away loaded with rich presents. On his way to Athens, passing through Elis during the celebration of the Olympic games, he was present at this general assembly of the Greeks, and engaged universal attention.

From this narrative it appears, that if Plato visited the courts of princes, it was chiefly from the hope of seeing his ideal plan of a republic realized; and that his talents and attainments rather qualified him to shine in the academy than in the council or the senate.

Plato, now restored to his country and his school, devoted himself to science, and spent the last years of a long life in the instruction of youth. Having enjoyed the advantage of an athletic constitution, and lived all his days temperately, he arrived at the eighty-first, or according to some writers, the seventy-ninth year of his age, and died, through the mere decay of nature, in the first year of the hundred and eighth Olympiad. He passed his whole life in a state of celibacy, and therefore left no natural heirs, but transferred his effects by will to his friend Adimantus. The grove and garden, which had been the scene of his philosophical labors, at last afforded him a sepulchre. Statues and altars were erected to his memory; the day of his birth long continued to be celebrated as a festival by his followers; and his portrait is to this day preserved in gems; but the most lasting monuments of his genius are his writings, which have been transmitted, without material injury, to the present times.

The personal character of Plato has been very differently represented. On the one hand, his encomiasts have not failed to adorn him with every excellence, and to express the most superstitious veneration for his memory. His enemies, on the other, have not scrupled to load him with reproach, and charge him with practices shamefully inconsistent with the purity and dignity of the philosophical character.

Several anecdotes are preserved, which reflect honor upon the moral principles and character of Plato. Such was his command of temper that, when he was lifting up his hand to correct his servant for some offence, perceiving himself angry, he kept his arm fixed in that posture, and said to a friend, who, coming in that instant, asked him what he was doing, "I am punishing a passionate man." At the Olympic games he happened to pass a day with some strangers, who were much delighted with his easy and affable conversation, but were no farther informed concerning him than that his name was Plato; for he had purposely avoided saying anything concerning Socrates or the Academy. At parting, he invited them, when they should visit Athens, to take up their residence at his house. Not long afterwards they accepted his invitation, and were courteously entertained. During their stay they requested that he would introduce them to his namesake, the famous philosopher, and show them his Academy. Plato, smiling, said, "I am the person you wish to see." The discovery surprised them exceedingly; for they could not easily persuade themselves that so eminent a philosopher would condescend to converse so familiarly with strangers. When Plato was told that his enemies were busily employed in circulating reports to his disadvantage, he said, "I will live so, that none shall believe them." One of his friends remarking, that he seemed as desirous to learn himself, as to teach others, asked him how long he intended to be a scholar? "As long," said he, "as I am not ashamed to grow wiser and better."

PLINY THE ELDER.

Caius Plinius Secundus, called Pliny the Elder, to distinguish him from his nephew Caius Plinius Cæcilius, was born in the reign of Tiberius, about the year twenty-three, and is commonly said to have been a native of Verona. In his youth, he took upon him the military character, and served in the army in the German war; but he soon turned the course of his ambition into the channel of learning, and by the indefatigable use of excellent talents acquired extensive and profound erudition. During the life of Nero his dread of the savage spirit of that tyrant induced him to prosecute his studies in private. Towards the close of the reign of that emperor, he wrote a political work on ambiguity of expression. Under the more favorable auspices of Vespasian, the superior abilities of Pliny had an opportunity of displaying themselves, not only in literary speculations, but in public affairs; for that emperor admitted him to his confidence, and employed him in important posts. In the midst of innumerable avocations, he prosecuted his studies with a degree of industry and perseverance scarcely to be paralleled. What his nephew relates on this head must not be omitted. After enumerating his writings, he says:

"You will wonder how a man of business could find time to write so much, and often upon such difficult subjects. You will be still more surprised when you are informed, that for some time he engaged in the profession of an advocate; that he died in his fifty-sixth year; and that, from the time of his quitting the bar to his death, he was busily occupied in the execution of the highest posts, and in the service of his prince. But he had a quick apprehension, joined to unwearied application. In summer he always began his studies as soon as it was night; in winter, generally at one in the morning, but never later than two, and sometimes at midnight. He slept little, and this often without retiring to his chamber. After a short and light repast at noon, according to the custom of our ancestors, he would frequently, in summer, if he was disengaged from business, recline in the sun: some author, in the meantime, being read to him, from which he made extracts and observations. This indeed was his constant practice in reading; for he used to say, that no book was so bad, but something might be learned from it. When this was over, he commonly went into the cold bath, and as soon as he came out of it, took a slight refreshment, and then reposed himself for a short time. After which, as if it had been a new day, he resumed his studies till supper time, when a book was again read to him, upon which he made some cursory remarks. In summer, he rose from supper by day-light, and in winter, as soon as it was dark, and this was an invariable rule with him. Such was his manner of life, amidst the noise and hurry of the town. But in the country, his whole time was devoted to study. Even in the bath, while he was rubbed and wiped, either some book was read to him, or he dictated himself. When he was travelling, he attended to no other object. A secretary constantly attended him in his chariot. For the same reason, he was always, at Rome, conveyed from one place to another in a chair. I remember he once reproved me for walking: 'You need not,' says he, 'lose so much time:' for he thought all time lost, which was not devoted to study. It was this intense application which enabled my uncle to write so many volumes, besides a hundred and sixty, which he left me, containing extracts and observations, written in a very small character."

Out of all the rich fruits of Pliny's industry, one work only has escaped the ravages of time, his "Natural History of the World:" a valuable treasury of ancient knowledge; concerning which, notwithstanding all its errors and extravagancies, we do not scruple, with some allowance for rhetorical decoration, to subscribe to the judgment of the Younger Pliny, who calls it "a comprehensive and learned work scarcely less various than Nature herself."

The insatiable desire which this philosopher always discovered to become acquainted with the wonders of Nature at last proved fatal to him. An eruption of the volcano of Mount Vesuvius happening while Pliny lay with the fleet under his command, at Misenum, his curiosity induced him to approach so near to the mountain, that he was suffocated by the gross and noxious vapors which it sent forth. An interesting account of this tragical event is given b Pliny the Younger. It happened in the year 79.

POLEMO.

Polemo was an Athenian of distinction, who in his youth had been addicted to infamous pleasures. The manner in which he was reclaimed from his licentious course of life, and brought under the discipline of philosophy, affords a memorable example of the power of eloquence when it is employed in the cause of virtue. As he was one morning, about the rising of the sun, returning home from the revels of the night, clad in a loose robe, crowned with garlands, strongly perfumed, and intoxicated with wine, he passed by the school of Xenocrates, and saw him surrounded with his disciples. Unable to resist so fortunate an opportunity of indulging his sportive humor, he rushed, without ceremony, into the school, and took his place among the philosophers. The whole assembly was astonished at this rude and indecent intrusion, and all but Xenocrates discovered signs of resentment. Xenocrates, however, preserved the perfect command of his countenance, and, with great presence of mind, turned his discourse from the subject on which he was treating to the topics of temperance and modesty, which he recommended with such strength of argument, and energy of language, that Polemo was constrained to yield to the force of conviction. Instead of turning the philosopher and his doctrine to ridicule, as he at first intended, he became sensible of the folly of his former conduct, was heartily ashamed of the contemptible figure which he made in so respectable an assembly, took his garland from his head, concealed his naked arm under his cloak, assumed a sedate and thoughtful aspect, and, in short, resolved from that hour to relinquish his licentious pleasures, and devote himself to the pursuit of wisdom. Thus was this young man, by the powerful energy of truth and eloquence, in an instant converted from an infamous libertine to a respectable philosopher. In such a sudden change of character it is difficult to avoid passing from one extreme to another. Polemo, after his reformation, in order to brace up his mind to the tone of rigid virtue, constantly practiced the severest austerity and most hardy fortitude. From the thirtieth year of his age till his death he drank nothing but water. When he suffered violent pain, he showed no external sign of anguish. In order to preserve his mind undisturbed by passion, he habituated himself to speak in an uniform tone of voice, without elevation or depression. The austerity of his manners was, however, tempered with urbanity and generosity. He was fond of solitude, and passed much of his time in a garden near his school. He died at an advanced age, of consumption.

Diogenes Laertius says of him, that after his reformation he always continued the same in appearance and never even changed his voice, on which account, Cranton was charmed by him. Accordingly on one occasion, when a dog was mad and had bitten his leg, he was the only person who did not turn pale; and once, when there was a great confusion in the city, he, having heard the cause, remained where he was without fleeing. In the theatres too, he was quite immovable; accordingly, when Nicostratus the poet was once reading something to him and Crates, and the latter was excited to sympathy, he behaved as though he heard nothing.

He was a well-bred and high-spirited man, avoiding what Aristophanes says of Euripides, speeches of vinegar and assafœtida, such as he says himself:—

Are base delights compared with better things!

He was accustomed to lecture and discuss propositions not sitting, but whilst walking. He was much honored because of his noble sentiments. After he had been walking about, he would rest in his garden; and his pupils erected little cabins near it, and dwelt near his school and corridor. He left behind him a great number of writings. And there is this epigram of ours upon him:—

Do you not hear, we 've buried Polemo,
Whom sickness, worst affliction of mankind,
Attacked, and bore off to the shades below;
Yet Polemo lies not here, but Polemo's body,
And that he did himself place here on earth,
Prepared in soul to mount up to the skies.

PROCLUS.

Proclus, according to his biographer Marinus, was a native of Constantinople, and was born in the year four hundred and twelve. His parents having been inhabitants of Xanthus in Lycia, he is commonly spoken of as a Lycian. He received the first rudiments of learning at Xanthus, and afterwards studied eloquence and polite literature under Isaurus at Alexandria, with a view to qualify himself for the profession of the law. This design, however, he soon relinquished, and wholly devoted himself to philosophy. From Olympiodorus he learned the Aristotleian system combined with the Platonic; and he was instructed in Mathematics by Hero. His facility of conception and strength of memory were such, that when his master's lectures, through the rapidity of his utterance, or the abstruse nature of his subject, were not clearly understood by the rest of the pupils, he was able to give an accurate summary of the arguments, in the order in which they had been delivered; a circumstance which gained him great credit and esteem among his fellow-students.

Having spent several years in the Alexandrian schools, Proclus determined to visit Athens. Here he first became acquainted with Syrian, who introduced him to Plutarch the son of Nestorius. The old man was delighted with the attainments of this young stranger, and undertook to conduct him into the more recondite mysteries of philosophy. Plutarch, dying two years afterwards, left Proclus to the care of his successor, Syrian, under whose direction the young man prosecuted his studies with indefatigable industry. He reaped great benefit from the practice recommended to him by Plutarch, of writing, from his own recollection, compendious abridgements of the lectures which he had heard from his preceptor. At the age of twenty-eight, he had written, besides many other pieces, his "Commentary on the Timæus of Plato," full of that kind of learning which at this time prevailed in the Platonic schools. In order to reach the point, which was in these schools esteemed the summit of wisdom, Proclus diligently studied the theology of the sect, both that which respects the contemplation of the Supreme Deity, and that which was supposed to lead to an intercourse with inferior divinities. He was instructed in the Chaldean arts of divination, and in the use of mystical words, and other charms, by Plutarch's daughter, Asclepigenia, who inherited from her father many secrets of this kind. He was also initiated into the Eleusinian mysteries. By these helps, and by diligent study of the writings of Plotinus, Porphyry, and Jamblicus, he became, if Marinus may be credited, a complete master, not only of divine science, but of theurgic powers.

Thus accomplished, Proclus was judged by Syrian worthy to share with him the honors and profits of the Platonic chair. And there can be no doubt, after what has been related, that he was eminently qualified for the office of preceptor in the Alexandrian philosophy. His biographer may be easily credited when he asserts, that Proclus excelled all his predecessors in the knowledge of this system, and that he improved it by many new dicoveries, and was the author of many opinions which had never before entered into the mind of man, both on the subject of physics, and in the sublime science of Ideas. The lectures which Proclus delivered in his school were obscure and enthusiastic ; but they suited the genius and taste of the age, and he had many followers.

The piety of Proclus is highly extolled by his biographer.

Of what sort it was may be learned from the superstitious manner in which he conducted his devotions. Besides his general abstinence from animal food, in which he followed the Pythagorean discipline, he often practiced rigorous fastings; and he spent whole days and nights in repeating prayers and hymns, that he might prepare himself for immediate intercourse with the gods. He observed with great solemnity the new moons and all public festivals, and on these occasions pretended, or fancied, that he conversed with superior beings, and was able by his sacrifices, prayers, and hymns, to expel diseases, to command rain, to stop an earthquake, and to perform other similar wonders. Marinus does not scruple to assert that, on these occasions, Proclus partook of divine inspiration, and that a celestial glory irradiated his countenance. He even relates, that God himself appeared to him in a human form, and with an audible voice hailed him as the glory of the city. In his old age his mental infirmities, as might naturally be expected, increased with those of his body; and he fancied, between sleeping and waking (the season in which these visions commonly happen), that Esculapius approached him in the form of a dragon, and relieved his pain. Without attempting accurately to determine how much of these tales is to be ascribed to the invention of Marinus, and how much to the fanaticism of his master, we may perceive in them proofs of superstitious weakness, of artful hypocrisy, or of a strange union of both, abundantly sufficient to justify us in ranking Proclus among enthusiasts or impostors, rather than among philosophers.

PROTAGORAS.

PROTAGORAS of Abdera, was the most celebrated disciple of Democritus. In his youth his poverty obliged him to perform the servile offices of a porter, and he was frequently employed in carrying logs of wood from the neighboring fields to Abdera. It happened, that as he was one day going on briskly towards the city under one of those loads, he was met by Democritus, who was particularly struck with the neatness and regularity of the bundle. Desiring him to stop and rest himself, Democritus examined more closely the structure of the load, and found that it was put together with mathematical exactness; upon which he asked the youth whether he himself had made it up. The youth assured him that he had, and immediately took it to pieces, and with great ease replaced every log in the same exact order as before. Democritus expressed much admiration of his ingenuity, and said to him, "Young man, follow me, and your talents shall be employed upon greater and better things." The youth consented, and Democritus took him home, maintained him at his own expense, and taught him philosophy.

Protagoras afterward acquired reputation at Athens, among the sophists for his eloquence, and among the philosophers for his wisdom. His public lectures were frequented, and he had many disciples, from whom he received the most liberal rewards; so that, as Plato relates, he became exceedingly rich. At length, however, he brought upon himself the displeasure of the Athenian state, by teaching doctrines favorable to impiety. In one of his books he said, "Concerning the gods, I am wholly unable to determine whether they have any existence or not; for the weakness of the human understanding, and the shortness of human life, with many other causes, prevent us from attaining this knowledge." On account of this and several other similar expressions, his writings were ordered to be diligently collected by the common crier, and burnt in the market-place, and he himself was banished from Attica. He wrote many pieces upon logic, metaphysics, ethics, and politics, none of which are at present extant. After having lived many years in Epirus, he was lost by sea on his passage from that country to Sicily.

PYRRHO.

Pyrrho was a citizen of Elis and the son of Pleistarchus. He was originally a painter. He asserted that there was no such thing as downright truth, but that men did everything in consequence of custom and law. His life corresponded to his principles; for he never shunned anything and never guarded against anything, encountering everything, even waggons, precipices, dogs, and things of that sort, committing nothing whatever to his senses. So that he used to be saved by his friends who accompanied him. He studied philosophy on the principle of suspending his judgment on all points. He used to walk out into the fields and seek solitary places, very rarely appearing to his family at Rome; and he did this in consequence of having heard some Indian reproaching Anaxarchus for never teaching any one else any good, but for devoting all his time to paying court to princes in palaces. He relates of him too, that he always maintained the same demeanor, so that if any one left him in the middle of his delivery of a discourse, he remained and continued what he was saying; although, when a young man, he was of a very excitable temperament. Often too, says Antigonus, he would go away for a time, without telling any one beforehand, and taking any chance persons whom he chose for his companions. And once, when Anaxarchus had fallen into a pond, he passed by without assisting him; and when some one blamed him for this, Anaxarchus himself praised his indifference and absence of all emotion.

On one occasion he was detected talking to himself, and when he was asked the reason, he said that he was studying how to be good. In his investigations he was never despised by any one, because he always spoke explicitly and straight to the question that had been put to him. On which account Nausiphanes was charmed by him even when he was quite young. And he used to say that he should like to be endowed with the disposition of Pyrrho, without losing his own power of eloquence. And he said too, that Epicurus, who admired the conversation and manner of Pyrrho, was frequently asking him about him.

He was so greatly honored by his country, that he was appointed a priest; and on this account all the philosophers were exempted from taxation. He had a great many imitators of his impassiveness; in reference to which Timon speaks thus of him in his Python, and in his Silli:—

> Now, you old man, you Pyrrho, how could you
> Find an escape from all the slavish doctrines
> And vain imaginations of the Sophists?
> How did you free yourself from all the bonds
> Of sly chicane, and artful deep persuasion?
> How came you to neglect what sort of breeze
> Blows round your Greece, and what's the origin
> And end of everything?

And again, in his Images, he says:—

> These things, my heart, O Pyrrho, longs to hear,
> How you enjoy such ease of life and quiet,
> The only man as happy as a God.

The Athenians presented him with the freedom of their city, as Diocles tells us, because he had slain Cotys, the Thracian.

He also lived in a most blameless manner with his sister, who was a midwife, as Eratosthenes relates, in his treatise on Riches and Poverty; so that he himself used to carry poultry, and pigs too if he could get any, into the market place and sell them. He used to clean all the furniture of the house without expressing any annoyance. It is said that he carried his indifference so far that he even washed a pig. Once, when he was very angry about something connected with his sister (and her name was Philista), and some one took him up, he said, "The display of my indifference does not depend on a woman." On another occasion, when he was driven back by a dog which was attacking him, he said to some one who blamed him for being discomposed, "That it was a difficult thing entirely to put off humanity; but that a man ought to strive with all his power to counteract circumstances with his actions if possible, and at all events with his reason." They also tell a story that once, when some medicines of a consuming tendency, and some cutting and cautery was applied to him for some wound, that he never even contracted his brow. Timon intimates his disposition plainly enough in the letters which he wrote to Python. Moreover, Philo, the Athenian, who was a friend of his, said that he was especially fond of Democritus; and next to him of Homer; whom he admired greatly, and was continually saying:—

> But as the race of falling leaves decay,
> Such is the fate of man.

He used also, as it is said, to compare men to wasps, and flies, and birds, and to quote the following lines:—

> Die then, my friend, what boots it to deplore?
> The great, the good Patroclus is no more.
> He, far thy better, was foredoom'd to die;
> And thou, doest thou bewail mortality?

And so he would quote anything that bore on the uncertainty and emptiness and fickleness of the affairs of man. Posidonius tells the following anecdote about him: that when some people who were sailing with him were looking gloomy because of a storm, he kept a calm countenance, and comforted their minds, exhibiting himself on deck eating a pig, and saying that it became a wise man to preserve an untroubled spirit in that manner.

He had many eminent disciples, and among them Eurylochus, of whom the following defective characteristic is related; for, they say, that he was once worked up to such a pitch of rage that he took up a spit with the meat on it, and chased the cook as far as the market-place. And once in Elis he was so harassed by some people who put questions to him in the middle of his discourses, that he threw down his cloak and swam across the Alpheus. He was the greatest possible enemy to the Sophists, as Timon tells us. But Philo, on the contrary, was very fond of arguing; on which account Timon speaks of him thus:—

> Avoiding men to study all devoted,
> He ponders with himself; and never heeds
> The glory or disputes which harass Philo.

All these men were called Pyrrhoneans from their master; and also doubters, and sceptics, and ephectics, or suspenders of their judgment, and investigators, from their principles. And their philosophy was called investigatory, from their investigating or seeking the truth on all sides; and sceptical from their being always doubting (*skeptemai*), and never finding; and ephectic, from the disposition which they encouraged after investigation, I mean the suspending of their judgment (*epochè*); and doubting, because they asserted that the dogmatic philosophers only doubted, and that they did the same.

Some say that Homer was the original founder of this school; since he at different times gives different accounts of the same circumstance, as much as any one else ever did; and since he never dogmatizes definitively respecting affirmation; they also say that the maxims of the seven wise men were sceptical; such as that, "Seek nothing in excess," and that "Suretyship is near calamity;" which shows that calamity follows a man who has given positive and certain surety; they also argue that Archilochus and Euripides were Sceptics; and Archilochus speaks thus:—

> And now, O Glaucus, son of Leptines,
> Such is the mind of mortal man, which changes
> With every day that Jupiter doth send.

And Euripides says:—

> Why then do men assert that wretched mortals
> Are with true wisdom gifted; for on you
> We all depend; and we do everything
> Which pleases you.

Moreover, Xenophanes, and Zeno the Eleatic, and Democritus were also Sceptics; of whom Xenophanes speaks thus:—

> And no man knows distinctly anything,
> And no man ever will.

Zeno endeavors to put an end to the doctrine of motion by saying: "The object moved does not move either in the place in which it is, or in that in which it is not." Democritus, too, discards the qualities, where he says: "What is cold is cold in opinion, and what is hot is hot in opinion; but atoms and the vacuum exist in reality." And again he says: "But we know nothing really; for truth lies in the bottom." Plato, too, following them, attributes the knowledge of the truth to the Gods and to the sons of the Gods, and leaves men only the investigation of probability. And Euripides says:—

> Who now can tell whether to live may not
> Be properly to die. And whether that
> Which men do call to die, may not in truth
> Be but the entrance into real life?

Empedocles speaks thus:—

> These things are not perceptible to sight,
> Nor to the ears, nor comprehensible
> To human intellect.

In a preceding passage he says:—

> Believing nothing, but such circumstances
> As have befallen each.

Heraclitus, too, says, "Let us not form conjectures at random, about things of the greatest importance." And Hippocrates delivers his opinion in a very doubtful manner, such as becomes a man; and before them all Homer has said:—

> Long in the field of words we may contend,
> Reproach is infinite and knows no end.

And immediately after:—

> Armed, or with truth or falsehood, right or wrong,
> (So voluble a weapon is the tongue),
> Wounded we wound, and neither side can fail,
> For every man has equal strength to rail:

Intimating the equal vigor and antethetical force of words. And the Sceptics persevered in overthrowing all the dogmas of every sect, while they themselves asserted nothing dogmatically; and contented themselves with expressing the opinions of others, without affirming anything themselves, not even that they did affirm nothing.

PYTHAGORAS.

There is a great uncertainty as to the parentage, the birthplace, and the time of the birth of Pythagoras.

The account of Diogenes Laertius is that he was a pupil of Pherecydes and after his death, of Hermodamas.

As he was a young man, devoted to learning, he quitted his country and got initiated into all the Grecian and barbarian sacred mysteries. Accordingly he went to Egypt, on which occasion Polycrates gave him a letter of introduction to Amasis; and he learnt the Egyptian language, and he associated with the Chaldeans and with the Magi.

Afterwards he went to Crete, and in company with Epimenides, he descended into the Idæan cave, (and in Egypt too, he entered into the holiest parts of their temples), and learned all the most secret mysteries that relate to their Gods. Then he returned back again to Samos, and finding his country reduced under the absolute dominion of Polycrates, he set sail, and fled to Crotona in Italy. And there, having given laws to the Italians, he gained a very high reputation, together with his scholars, who were about three hundred in number, and governed the republic in a most excellent manner; so that the constitution was very nearly an aristocracy.

Heraclides Ponticus says, that he was accustomed to speak of himself in this manner; that he had formerly been Æthalides, and had been accounted the son of Mercury; and that Mercury had desired him to select any gift he pleased except immortality. And that he accordingly had requested that, whether living or dead, he might preserve the memory of what had happened to him. While, therefore, he was alive, he recollected everything; and when he was dead, he retained the same memory. And at a subsequent period he passed into Euphorbus, and was wounded by Menelaus. And while he was Euphorbus, he used to say that he had formerly been Æthalides; and that he had received as a gift from Mercury the perpetual transmigration of his soul, so that it was constantly transmigrating and passing into whatever plants or animals it pleased; and he had also received the gift of knowing and recollecting all that his soul had suffered in hell, and what sufferings too are endured by the rest of the souls.

But after Euphorbus died, he said that his soul had passed into Hermotimus; and when he wished to convince people of this he went into the territory of the Branchidæ, and going into the temple of Apollo, he showed his shield which Menelaus had dedicated there as an offering. For he said that he, when he sailed from Troy, had offered up his shield* which was already getting worn out, to Apollo, and that nothing remained but the ivory face which was on it. And when Hermotimus died, then he said that he had become Pyrrhus,

* This resembles the account which Ovid puts into the mouth of Pythagoras, in the last book of his Metamorphoses, where he makes him say :—

Death has no power th' immortal soul to slay;
That, when its present body turns to clay,
Seeks a fresh home, and with unminish'd might,
Inspires another frame with life and light.
So I myself, (well I the past recall)
When the fierce Greeks begirt Troy's holy wall,
Was brave Euphorbus; and in conflict drear,
Poured forth my blood beneath Atrides' spear:
The shield this arm did bear I lately saw
In Juno's shrine, a trophy of that war.

a fisherman of Delos; and he still recollected everything, how he had been formerly Æthalides, then Euphorbus, then Hermotimus, and then Pyrrhus. And when Pyrrhus died, he became Pythagoras, and still recollected all the circumstances that I have been mentioning.

Now, some people say that Pythagoras did not leave behind him a single book; but they talk foolishly; for Heraclitus the natural philosopher, speaks plainly enough of him, saying, "Pythagoras, the son of Mnesarchus, was the most learned of all men in history; and having selected from these writings, he thus formed his own wisdom and extensive learning, and mischievous art." And he speaks thus, because Pythagoras, in the beginning of his treatise on Natural Philosophy, writes in the following manner: "By the air which I breathe, and by the water which I drink, I will not endure to be blamed on account of this discourse."

Aristoxenus asserts that Pythagoras derived the greater part of his ethical doctrines from Themistocles, the priestess at Delphi. And Ion, of Chios, in his Victories, says that he wrote some poems and attributed them to Orpheus. They also say that the poem called the Scopeadæ is by him, which begins thus:—

Behave not shamelessly to any one.

And Sosicrates, in his Successions, relates that he, having been asked by Leon, the tyrant of the Phliasians, who he was, replied, "A philosopher." And adds, that he used to compare life to a festival. "And as some people came to a festival to contend for the prizes, and others for the purposes of traffic, and the best as spectators; so also in life, the men of slavish dispositions," said he, "are born hunters after glory and covetousnesss, but philosophers are seekers after truth." And thus he spoke on this subject. But in the three treatises above mentioned, the following principles are laid down by Pythagoras generally.

He forbids men to pray for anything in particular for themselves, because they do not know what is good for them. He calls drunkenness an expression identical with ruin, and rejects all superfluity, saying, "That no one ought to exceed the proper quantity of meat and drink." And on the subject of venereal pleasures, he speaks thus:—"One ought to sacrifice to Venus in the winter, not in the summer; and in autumn and spring in a lesser degree. But the practice is pernicious at every season, and is never good for the health." And once when he was asked when a man might indulge in the pleasures of love, he replied, "Whenever you wish to be weaker than yourself."

He divides the life of man thus. A boy for twenty years; a young man for twenty years; a middle-aged man for twenty years; an old man for twenty years. And these different ages correspond proportionably to the seasons: boyhood answers to spring; youth to summer; middle age to autumn; and old age to winter.

He was the first person, as Timæus says, who asserted that the property of friends is common, and that friendship is equality. And his disciples used to put all their possessions together into one store, and use them in common; and for five years they kept silence, doing nothing but listen to discourses, and never once seeing Pythagoras, until they were approved; and after that time they were admitted into his house, and allowed to see him. They also abstained from the use of cypress coffins, because the sceptre of Jupiter was made of that wood.

He is said to have been a man of the most dignified appearance, and his disciples adopted an opinion respecting him, that he was Apollo who had come from the Hyperboreans; and it is said, that once when he was stripped naked, he was seen to have a golden thigh. And there were many people who affirmed, that when he was crossing the river Nessus it addressed him by his name.

Timæus, in the tenth book of his Histories, tells us, that he used to say that women who were married to men had the names of the Gods, being successively called virgins, then nymphs, and subsequently mothers.

It was Pythagoras also who carried geometry to perfection, after Mœris had first found out the principles of the elements of that science, as Aristiclides tells us in the second book of his History of Alexander; and the part of the science to which Pythagoras applied himself above all others was arithmetic. He also discovered the numerical relation of sounds on a single string; he also studied medicine. And Apollodorus, the logician, records of him, that he sacrificed a hecatomb, when he had discovered that the square of the hypotheneuse of a right-angled triangle is equal to the squares of the sides containing the right angle. And there is an epigram which is couched in the following terms:—

> When the great Samian sage his noble problem found,
> A hundred oxen dyed with their life-blood the ground.

He is also said to have been the first man who trained athletes on meat; and Eurymenes was the first man who ever did submit to this diet, as before that time men used to train themselves on dry figs and moist cheese, and wheaten bread. But some authors state, that a trainer of the name of Pythagoras certainly did train his athletes on this system, but that it was not our philosopher; for that he even forbade men to kill animals at all, much less would have allowed his disciples to eat then, as having a right to live in common with mankind. And this was his pretext; but in reality, he prohibited the eating of animals, because he wished to train and accustom men to simplicity of life, so that all their food should be easily procurable, as it would be, if they ate only such things as required no fire to dress them, and if they drank plain water; for from this diet they would derive health of body and acuteness of intellect.

The only altar at which he worshipped was that of Apollo the Father, at Delos, which is at the back of the altar of Ceratinus, because wheat, and barley, and cheese-cakes are the only offerings laid upon it, being not dressed by fire; and no victim is ever slain there. They say, too, that he was the first person who asserted that the soul went a necessary circle, being changed about and confined at different times in different bodies. He was also the first person who introduced measures and weights among the Greeks. Parmenides, too, assures us, that he was the first person who asserted the identity of Hesperus and Lucifer.

He was so greatly admired, that they used to say that his friends looked on all his sayings as the oracles of God.* And he himself says in his writings, that he had come among men after having spent two hundred and seven years in the shades below. Therefore the Lucanians and the Peucetians, and the Messapians, and the Romans, flocked around him, coming with eagerness to hear his discourses; but until the time of Philolaus, there were no doctrines of Pythagoras ever divulged; and he was the first person who published the three celebrated books which Plato wrote to have purchased for him for a hundred minæ. Nor were the number of his scholars who used to come to him by night fewer than six hundred. And if any of them had ever been permitted to see him, they wrote of it to their friends, as if they had gained some great advantage.

And the rest of the Pythagoreans used to say, according to the account given by Aristoxenus, in the tenth book of his Laws on Education, that his precepts ought not to be divulged to all the world; and Xenophilus, the Pythagorean, when he

* This passage has been interpreted in more ways than one. Casaubon thinks with great probability that there is a hiatus in the text. I have endeavored to extract a meaning out of what remains. Compare Samuel ii. 16, 23. "And the counsel of Ahitophel, which he counselled in those days, was as if a man had inquired at the oracle of God; so was all the counsel of Ahitophel both with David and with Absalom."

was asked what was the best way for a man to educate his son, said, "That he must first of all take care that he was born in a city which enjoyed good laws."

Pythagoras, too, formed many excellent men in Italy, by his precepts, and among them Zaleucus,* and Charondas, the lawgivers. For he was very eminent for his power of attracting friendships; and among other things, if ever he heard that any one had any community of symbols with him, he at once made him a companion and a friend.

Now, what he called his symbols were such as these. "Do not stir the fire with a sword." "Do not sit down on a bushel." "Do not devour your heart." "Do not aid men in discarding a burden, but in increasing one." "Always have your bed packed up." "Do not bear the image of a God on a ring." "Efface the traces of a pot in the ashes." "Do not wipe a seat with a lamp." He also announced the following: "Do not walk in the main street." Do not offer your right hand lightly." "Do not cherish swallows under your roof." "Do not cherish birds with crooked talons." "Do not defile; and do not stand upon the parings of your nails, or the cuttings of your hair." "Avoid a sharp sword." "When you are travelling abroad, look not back at your own borders." Now the precept not to stir fire with a

* Zaleucus was the celebrated lawgiver of the Epizephyrian Locrains, and is said to have been originally a slave employed by a shepherd, and to have been set free and appointed lawgiver by the direction of an oracle, in consequence of his announcing some excellent laws, which he represented Minerva as having communicated to him in a dream. Diogenes is wrong, however, in calling him a disciple of Pythagoras (see Bentley on Phalaris), as he lived about a hundred years before his time; his true date being 660 B.C. The code of Zaleucus is stated to have been the first collection of written laws that the Greeks possessed. Their character was that of great severity. They have not come down to us. His death is said to have occurred thus. Among his laws was one forbidding any citizen to enter the senate house in arms, under the penalty of death. But in a sudden emergency, Zaleucus himself, in a moment of forgetfulness, transgressed his own law: on which he slew himself, declaring that he would vindicate his law. (Eustath. ad. Il. i. p. 60). Diodorus, however, tells the same story of Charondas.

sword meant, not to provoke the anger or swelling pride of powerful men; not to violate the beam of the balance meant, not to transgress fairness and justice; not to sit on a bushel is to have an equal care for the present and for the future, for by the bushel is meant one's daily food. By not devouring one's heart, he intended to show that we ought not to waste away our souls with grief and sorrow. In the precept that a man when travelling abroad should not turn his eyes back, he recommended those who were departing from life not to be desirous to live, and not to be too much attracted by the pleasures here on earth. And the other symbols may be explained in a similar manner, that we may not be too prolix here.

And above all things, he used to prohibit the eating of the erythinus, and the melanurus; and also, he enjoined his disciples to abstain from the hearts of animals, and from beans. And Aristotle informs us, that he sometimes used also to add to these prohibitions paunches and mullet. And some authors assert that he himself used to be contented with honey and honeycomb, and bread, and that he never drank wine in the daytime. And his desert was usually vegetables, either boiled or raw; and he very rarely ate fish. His dress was white, very clean, and his bed-clothes were also white, and woollen, for linen had not yet been introduced into that country. He was never known to have eaten too much, or to have drunk to much, or to indulge in the pleasures of love. He abstained wholly from laughter, and from all such indulgences as jests and idle stories. And when he was angry, he never chastised any one, whether slave or freeman. He used to call admonishing, feeding storks.

He used to practice divination, as far as auguries and auspices go, but not by means of burnt offerings, except only the burning of frankincense. And all the sacrifices which he offered consisted of inanimate things. But some, however, assert that he did sacrifice animals, limiting himself to cocks, and sucking kids, but that he very rarely offered lambs. Aristoxenus, however, affirms that he permitted the eating of all other animals, and only abstained from oxen used in agriculture, and from rams.

And Hieronymus says, that when he descended to the shades below, he saw the soul of Hesoid bound to a brazen pillar, and gnashing its teeth; and that of Homer suspended from a tree, and snakes around it, as a punishment for the things that they had said of the Gods. And that those people also were punished who refrained from commerce with their wives; and that on account of this he was greatly honored by the people of Crotona.

But Aristippus, of Cyrene, in his Account of Natural Philosophers, says that Pythagoras derived his name from the fact of his speaking (*agoreuein*) truth no less than the God at Delphi (*tou puthiou*).

It is said that he used to admonish his disciples to repeat these lines to themselves whenever they returned home to their houses :—

> In what have I transgressed? What have I done?
> What that I should have done have I omitted?

And that he used to forbid them to offer victims to the Gods, ordering them to worship only at those altars which were unstained with blood. He forbade them also to swear by the Gods; saying, "That every man ought so to exercise himself, as to be worthy of belief without an oath" He also taught men that it behooved them to honor their elders, thinking that which was precedent in point of time more honorable: just as in the world, the rising of he sun was more so than the setting; in life, the beginning more so than the end; and in animals, production more so than destruction.

Another of his rules was that men should honor the Gods above the dæmons, heroes above men; and of all men parents were entitled to the highest degree of reverence. Another, that people should associate with one another in such a way as not to make their friends enemies, but to render their enemies friends. Another was that they should think nothing exclusively their own. Another was to assist the law, and to make war upon lawlessness. Not to destroy or injure a cultivated tree, nor any animal either which does not injure men. That modesty and decorum consisted in never yielding to laughter, and yet not looking stern. He taught that men should avoid too much flesh, that they should in travelling let rest and exertion alternate; that they should exercise memory; that they should never say or do anything in anger; that they should not pay respect to every kind of divination; that they should use songs set to the lyre; and by hymns to the Gods and to eminent men, display a reasonable gratitude to them.

He also forbade his disciples to eat beans, because, as they were flatulent, they greatly partook of animal properties [he also said that men kept their stomachs in better order by avoiding them]; and that such abstinence made the visions which appear in one's sleep gentle and free from agitation.

He also taught that the sun and the moon, and the stars, were all Gods; for in them the warm principle predominates which is the cause of life. And that the moon derives its light from the sun. And that there is a relationship between men and the Gods, because men partake of the divine principle: on which account also, God exercises his providence for our advantage. Also, that fate is the cause of the arrangement of the world both generally and particularly. And that the soul is a something torn off from the æther, both warm and cold, from its partaking of the cold æther. And that the soul is something different from life. Also, that it is immortal, because that from which it has been detached is immortal.

Also, that animals are born from one another by seeds, and that it is impossible for there to be any spontaneous production by the earth. And that seed is a drop from the brain which contains in itself a warm vapor; and that when this is applied to the womb, it transmits virtue, and moisture, and blood from the brain, from which flesh, and sinews, and bones, and hair, and the whole body are produced. And from the vapour is produced the soul, and also sensation.

And Aristotle says, in his treatise on Beans, that Pythagoras enjoined his disciples to abstain from beans, either because they resemble some part of the human body, or because they are like the gates of hell (for they are the only plants without parts); or because they dry up other plants, or because they are representatives of universal nature, or because they are used in elections in oligarchical governments. He also forbade his disciples to pick up what fell from the table, for the sake of accustoming them not to eat immoderately, or else because such things belong to the dead.

But Aristophanes says, that what falls belongs to the heroes; saying, in his Heroes:—

> Never taste the things which fall
> From the table on the floor.

He also forbade his disciples to eat white poultry, because a cock of that color was sacred to Month, and was also a suppliant. He was also accounted a good animal; * and he was sacred to the God Month, for he indicates the time.

The Pythagoreans were also forbidden to eat of all fish that were sacred; on the ground that the same animals ought not to be served up before both Gods and men, just as the same things do not belong to freemen and to slaves. Now, white is an indication of a good nature, and black of a bad one. Another of the precepts of Pythagoras was, that men ought not to break bread; because in ancient times friends used to assemble around one loaf, as they even now do among the barbarians. Nor would he allow men to divide bread which unites them. Some think that he laid down this rule in refer-

* There is a great variety of suggestions as to the proper reading here. There is evidently some corruption in the text.

ence to the judgment which takes place in hell; some because this practice engenders timidity in war. According to others, what is alluded to is the Union, which presides over the government of the universe.

Another of his doctrines was, that of all solid figures the sphere was the most beautiful; and of all plane figures, the circle. That old age and all diminution were similar, and also increase and youth were identical. That health was the permanence of form, and disease the destruction of it. Of salt his opinion was, that it ought to be set before people as a reminder of justice; for salt preserves everything which it touches, and it is composed of the purest particles of water and sea.

These are the doctrines which Alexander asserts that he discovered in the Pythagorean treatises; and Aristotle gives a similar account of them.

Timon, in his Silli, has not left unnoticed the dignified appearance of Pythagoras, when he attacks him on other points. And his words are these:—

> Pythagoras, who often teaches
> Precepts of magic, and with speeches
> Of long high-sounding diction draws,
> From gaping crowds, a vain applause.

Respecting his having been different people at different times, Xenophanes adds his evidence in an elegiac poem which commences thus:—

> Now I will on another subject touch,
> And lead the way.

The passage in which he mentions Pythagoras is as follows:—

> They say that once, as passing by he saw
> A dog severely beaten, he did pity him,
> And spoke as follows to the man who beat him:—
> "Stop now, and beat him not; since in his body,
> Abides the soul of a dear friend of mine,
> Whose voice I recognized as he was crying."

These are the words of Xenophanes.

Cratinus also ridiculed him in his Pythagorean Woman; but in his Tarentines, he speaks thus:—

They are accustomed, if by chance they see
A private individual abroad,
To try what powers of argument he has,
How he can speak and reason; and they bother him
With strange antithesis and forced conclusions,
Errors, comparisons, and magnitudes,
Till they have filled and quite perplex'd his mind.

And Innesimachus says in his Alcmæon:—

As we do sacrifice to the Phœbus whom
Pythagoras worships, never eating aught
Which has the breath of life.

Austophon says in his Pythagorean:—

A. He said that when he did descend below
Among the shades in Hell, he there beheld
All men who e'er had died; and there he saw,
That the Pythagoreans differ'd much
From all the rest; for that with them alone
Did Pluto deign to eat, much honoring
Their pious habits.
B. He 's a civil God,
If he likes eating with such dirty fellows.

And again, in the same play, he says:

They eat
Nothing but herbs and vegetables, and drink
Pure water only. But their lice are such,
Their cloaks so dirty, and their unwash'd scent
So rank, that no one of our younger men
Will for a moment bear them.

Pythagoras died in this manner. When he was sitting with some of his companions in Milo's house, some one of those whom he did not think worthy of admission into it, was excited by envy to set fire to it. But some say that the people of Crotona themselves did this, being afraid lest he might aspire to the tyranny. And that Pythagoras was caught as he was trying to escape; and coming to a place full of beans, he stopped there, saying that it was better to be caught than to trample on the beans, and better to be slain than to speak; and so he was murdered by those who were pursuing him. And in this way, also, most of his companions were slain; being in number abouty forty; but that a very few did escape, among whom were Archippus, of Tarentum, and Lysis, whom I have mentioned before.

But Dicæarchus relates that Pythagoras died afterwards, having escaped as far as the temple of the Muses, at Metapontum, and that he died there of starvation, having abstained from food for forty days. And Heraclides says, in his abridgment of the life of Satyrus, that after he had buried Pherecydes in Delos, he returned to Italy, and finding there a superb banquet prepared at the house of Milo, of Crotona, he left Crotona, and went to Metapontum, and there put an end to his life by starvation, not wishing to live any longer. But Hermippus says, that when there was war between the people of Agrigentum and the Syracusans, Pythagoras went out with his usual companions, and took the part of the Agrigentines; and as they were put to flight, he ran all round a field of beans, instead of crossing it, and so was slain by the Syracusans; and that the rest, being about five-and-thirty in number, were burnt at Tarentum, when they were trying to excite a sedition in the state against the principal magistrates.

Hermippus also relates another story about Pythagoras. For he says that when he was in Italy, he made a subterraneous apartment, and charged his mother to write an account of everything that took place, marking the time of each on a tablet, and then to send them down to him, until he came up again; and that his mother did so; and that Pythagoras came up again after a certain time, lean, and reduced to a skeleton; and that he came into the public assembly, and said that he had arrived from the shades below, and then he recited to them all that had happened during his absence. And they, being charmed by what he told them, wept and lamented, and believed that Pythagoras was a divine being; so that they even entrusted their wives to him, as likely to learn some good from him; and that they too were called Pythagoreans. This is the story of Hermippus.

And Pythagoras had a wife, whose name was Theano; the daughter of Brontinus, of Crotona. But some say that she was the wife of Brontinus, and only a pupil of Pythagoras. And he had a daughter named Damo, as Lysis mentions in his letter to Hipparchus; where he speaks thus of Pythagoras: "And many say that you philosophize in public, as Pythagoras also used to do; who, when he had entrusted his Commentaries to Damo, his daughter, charged her to divulge them to no person out of the house. And she, though she might have sold his discourses for much money, would not abandon them, for she thought poverty and obedience to her father's injunctions more valuable than gold; and that too, though she was a woman."

He had also a son, named Telauges, who was the successor of his father in his school, and who, according to some authors, was the teacher of Empedocles. At least Hippobotus relates that Empedocles said:—

> "Telauges, noble youth, whom in due time
> Theano bore to wise Pythagoras."

But there is no book extant, which is the work of Telauges, though there are some extant which are attributed to his mother Theano. And they tell a story of her, that once, when she was asked how long a woman ought to be absent from her husband to be pure, she said, the moment she leaves her own husband, she is pure; but she is never pure at all, after she leaves any one else. And she recommended a woman, who was going to her husband, to put off her modesty with her clothes, and when she left him, to resume it again with her clothes; and when she was asked, "What clothes?" she said, "Those which cause you to be called a woman."

Now Pythagoras, as Heraclides, the son of Sarapian, relates, died when he was eighty years of age, according to his own account of his age, but according to the common account, he was more than ninety. And we have written a sportive epigram on him which is couched in the following terms :—

You 're not the only man who has abstained
From living food, for so likewise have we;
And who, I 'd like to know did ever taste
Food while alive, most sage Pythagoras?
When meat is boil'd, or roasted well and salted,
I don't think it can well be called living.
Which, therefore, without scruple then we eat it,
And call it no more living flesh, but meat.

And another, which runs thus :—

Pythagoras was so wise a man, that he
Never eat meat himself, and called it sin,
And yet he gave good joints of beef to others
So that I marvel at his principles;
Who others wronged, by teaching them to do
What he believed unholy for himself.

And another as follows :—

Should you Pythagoras' doctrine wish to know,
Look on the centre of Euphorbus' shield.
For he asserts there lived a man of old,
And when he had no longer an existence,
He still could say that he had been alive,
Or else he would not still be living now.

And this one too :—

Alas! alas! why did Pythagoras hold
Beans in such wondrous honor? Why, besides,
Did he thus die among his choice companions?
There was a field of beans; and so the sage
Died in the common road of Agrigentum,
Rather than trample down his favorite beans.

He flourished about the sixteenth Olympiad; and his system lasted for nine or ten generations.

There were four men of the name of Pythagoras, about the same time, at no great distance from one another. But

Eratosthenes says, as Phavorinus quotes him, in the eighth book of his Universal History, that this philosopher, of whom we are speaking, was the first man who ever practiced boxing in a scientific manner, in the forty-eighth Olympiad, having his hair long, and being clothed in a purple robe, and that he was rejected from the competition among boys, and being ridiculed for his application, he immediately entered among the men, and came off victorious. And this statement is confirmed among other things, by the epigram which Theætetus composed:—

> Stranger, if e'er you knew Pythagoras,
> Pythagoras the man with flowing hair,
> The celebrated boxer, erst of Samos;
> I am Pythagoras. And if you ask
> A citizen of Elis of my deeds,
> You 'll surely think he is relating fables.

Phavorinus says, that he employed definitions, on account of the mathematical subjects to which he applied himself. And that Socrates and those who were his pupils, did so still more; and that they were subsequently followed in this by Aristotle and the Stoics.

He, too, was the first person who ever gave the name of *kosmos* to the universe, and the first who called the earth round; though Theophrastus attributes this to Parmenides, and Zeno to Hesiod. They say, too, that Cylon used to be a constant adversary of his, as Antidicus was of Socrates. And this epigram also used to be repeated, concerning Pythagoras the athlete:—

> Pythagoras of Samos, son of Crates,
> Came while a child to the Olympic games,
> Eager to battle for the prize in boxing.

Brucker says that the history of Pythagoras, beyond that of any other ancient philosopher, abounds with difficulties and contradictions, and is enveloped in fable and mystery. Pythagoras himself, and his followers through a long succession, were so far from committing their doctrines to writing, for the information of posterity, that they made use of every expedient to conceal them from their contemporaries. Hence the first records of the life and doctrines of this philosopher, which were only such as could be casually gathered up from tradition, were not less defective in probable and well-authenticated facts than they were abundant in absurd fictions. It was not till many ages after the time in which Pythagoras flourished that Porphyry and Jamblicus undertook to digest these scattered materials into a regular narrative. And these writers themselves were too credulous, too careless, and too much biased by prejudice, to to be capable of giving a judicious and impartial representation of what was at that time known concerning Pythagoras. They were of the school of Ammonius and Plotinus; in which, as we shall afterwards find, it was the common practice to misrepresent and falsify everything, and to obtrude upon the world marvellous tales, instead of real facts, for the sake of supporting the credit of their sect in opposition to Christianity. It follows, that the statements which are made concerning him, must be received with considerable allowance. He further says: Pythagoras, returning from Egypt to his native island, after an absence of more than twenty years, was desirous that his fellow-citizens should reap the benefit of his travels and studies, and for this purpose attempted to institute a school for their instruction in the elements of science, but chose to adopt the Egyptian method of teaching, and communicate his doctrines under a symbolical form. The Samians were either too indolent, or too stupid, to profit by his instructions. The number of his followers was so inconsiderable, that he was obliged for the present to relinquish his design. Loath, however, entirely to abandon the project, he determined, if possible, to find other means of engaging the attention of his countrymen. With this idea he repaired to Delos, and after presenting an offering of cakes to Apollo, then received, or pretended to receive, moral dogmas from the priestess, which he afterwards delivered to his disciples under the character of divine precepts. With the same design he also visited the island of Crete, so celebrated in mythological history, where he was conducted by the Corybantes, or priests of Cybele, into the cave of Mount Ida, in which Jupiter is said to have been buried. Here he conversed with Epimenides, an eminent pretender to prophetic powers, and was by him initiated into the most sacred mysteries of Greece. About the same time he visited Sparta and Elis, and was present during the celebration of the Olympic games, where he is said to have exhibited a golden thigh to Abaris, in order to convince him that he was Apollo. Amongst the places which he visited during his stay in Greece, was Phlius, the residence of Leon, king of the Phliasians. Here he first assumed the appellation of philosopher.

Thus furnished, not only with fresh stores of learning, but with a kind of authority which was still more liikely to procure him respect, he returned to Samos, and made a second more successful attempt to institute among his countrymen a school of philosophy. The place which he chose for his purpose was a semi-circular building, in which the Samians had been accustomed to meet for public business. Here he chiefly employed himself in delivering, with an air of sacred authority, popular precepts of morality, which might contribute to the general benefit of the people. Besides this, he provided himself with a secret cave, into which he retired with his intimate friends and professed disciples, and here, not without a wonderful parade of mystery, gave them daily instructions in the more abstruse parts of philosophy. These arts, which unquestionably rank this celebrated philosopher among impostors, proved successful, and procured him a great multitude of followers. What he had been unable to effect by the mere force of learning and ability, he soon accomplished by concealing his doctrines under the veil of mysterious symbols, and by issuing forth his precepts as responses from a divine oracle.

Having for some time successfully executed his plan of instruction in Samos, whether the Samians began to detect his frauds, or to be apprehensive of his increasing popularity, or whether Pythagoras wished to escape the tyranny of the governor, Syloson, the brother of Polycrates, he suddenly left Samos, and passing over into Italy, attempted to establish his school among the colonies of *Magna Græcia.* The time of this expedition is uncertain; but it seems most probable that it happened about the beginning of the fifty-ninth Olympiad. It is more certain that when Pythagoras arrived in this country, in order to obtain credit with the populace, he pretended to a power of performing miracles, and practiced many arts of imposture.

The first place at which Pythagoras arrived was Crotona, a city in the bay of Tarentum, whose inhabitants were at this time exceedingly corrupted in their manners. Upon his first arrival, Plutarch and Apuleius relate, that observing a large draught of fishes, which had just been taken, he bought the whole capture of the fishermen, and ordered them to throw them again into the water, as a lesson to the spectators to spare the lives of fishes, and to refrain from this, as well as every other kind of animal food. Porphyry and Jamblicus relate the same story, with the addition of this marvellous circumstance, that Pythagoras, while the fishermen were drawing up the net, told them the exact number of fishes which it contained.

By these and other arts, Pythagoras obtained such a degree of respect and influence in Crotona, that people of all classes assembled to hear his discourses. The effect was, that an entire change was produced in the manners of the citizens; so that, from great luxury and licentiousness, they were converted to strict sobriety and frugality of manners. It is asserted that in Crotona there were not less than six hundred persons (some say two thousand) who were prevailed upon to submit to the strict discipline which he required, and to throw their effects into a common stock for the benefit of the whole fraternity.

Pythagoras did not confine the influence of his philosophy to Crotona. He taught his doctrine in many other cities of *Magna Græcia* with so much energy and effect, that he established a large and extensive interest through the country, and obtained from his followers a degree of respect little short of adoration.

Had Pythagoras contented himself with issuing forth oracular precepts of wisdom, and instructing his select disciples in the speculative doctrines of philosophy, it is probable he might have continued his labors, without molestation, to the end of his life. But he discovered on many occasions a strong propensity towards political innovations. Not only at Crotona, but at Metapontus, Rhegium, Agrigentum, and many other places, he obtained great influence over the people, and employed it in urging them to the strenuous assertion of their rights against the encroachments of their tyrannical governors.

These attempts, together with the singularities of his school, excited a general spirit of jealousy, and raised a powerful opposition against him. At the head of this opposition was Cylo, a man of wealth and distinction in Crotona, who had been refused admission into the society of the Pythagoreans, and whose temper was too haughty and violent to endure with patience such an indignity. The party thus raised against the Pythagoreans hearing that they were assembled in a large body at the house of Milo, one of their chief friends, surrounded the house, and set it on fire. About forty persons perished in the flames. Archippus and Lysis, two natives of Tarentum, alone escaped: the former withdrew to his own city; the latter fled to Thebes.

Pythagoras himself, if he was not present at the assembly, was probably in Crotona at the time when this fatal attack was made upon his school; for the report of his having been then upon a journey to Delos, to visit his master Pherecydes, is inconsistent with chronology, that philosopher having died before Pythagoras left Samos. He was, however, wholly incapable of resisting the torrent of jealousy and enmity which rushed upon him. His remaining friends fled to Rhegium, and he was himself obliged to retire to Metapontum, after having in vain sought for protection from the Locrians. At Metapontum Pythagoras found himself still surrounded with enemies, and was obliged to take refuge in the temple of the Muses, where, not being able to procure from his friends the necessary supply of food, he perished with hunger. This is the most probable account we are able to collect of the last incidents in the life of Pythagoras. The time of his death is uncertain. According to the Chronicon of Eusebius, which we are inclined to follow, he died in the third year of the sixty-eight Olympiad, after having lived, according to the most probable statement of his birth, to the age of eighty years. After his death his disciples paid a superstitious respect to his memory, They erected statues in honor of him, converted his house in Crotona into a temple of Ceres, and appealed to him as a divinity, swearing by his name.

Many tales are related of Pythagoras, which carry with them their own refutation. That, by speaking a word, he tamed a Daunian bear which had laid waste the country; that he prevented an ox from eating beans, by whispering in his ear; that he called down an eagle from the sky; that he was, on the same day, present, and discoursed in public, at Metapontum in Italy, and at Tauromenium in Sicily; that he predicted earthquakes, storms, and other future events; and that a river, as he passed over it with his friends, cried out, Hail, Pythagoras! are wonders, which would require much clearer and better evidence to gain them credit, than the testimony of Apollonius, Porphyry, and Jamblicus, or even of Laertius and Pliny. It appears, upon the face of the history of this philosopher, that he owed much of his celebrity and authority to imposture. Why did he so studiously court the society of Egyptian priests, so famous in ancient times for their arts of deception? why did he take so much pains to be initiated in religious mysteries? why did he retire into a subterraneous cavern in Crete? why did he assume the character of Apollo, at the Olympic games? why did he boast that his soul had lived in former bodies, and that he had been first Æthalides the son of Mercury, then Euphorbus, then Pyrrhus of Delos, and at last Pythagoras, but that he might the more easily impose upon the credulity of an ignorant and superstitious people? His whole manner of life, as far as it is known, confirms this opinion. Clothed in a long white robe, with a flowing beard, and, as some relate, with a golden crown on his head, he preserved among the people, and in the presence of his disciples, a commanding gravity and majesty of aspect. He made use of music to promote the tranquillity of his mind, frequently singing, for this purpose, hymns of Thales, Hesiod, and Homer. He had such an entire command of himself, that he was never seen to express, in his countenance, grief, or joy, or anger. He refrained from animal food, and confined himself to a frugal vegetable diet, excluding from his simple bill of fare, for sundry mystical reasons, pulse or beans By this artificial demeanor, Pythagoras passed himself upon the vulgar as a being of an order superior tc the common condition of humanity, and persuaded them that he had received his doctrine from heaven.

Pythagoras married Theano of Crotona, or, as some relate, of Crete, by whom he had two sons, Telauges and Mnesarchus, who, after his death, took the charge of his school.

Whether Pythagoras left behind him any writings, is a point much disputed. Laertius enumerates many pieces which appeared under his name; and Jamblicus and Pliny increase the list. But Plutarch, Josephus, Lucian, and others, confess that there were no genuine works of Pythagoras extant; and, from the pains which Pythago:as took to confine his doctrine to his own school during his life, it appears highly probable that he never committed his philosophical system to writing, and that those pieces to which his name was early affixed were written by some of his followers, according to the principles and tenets which they had learned in his school. Among the pieces attributed to Pythagoras, no one is more famous than the Golden Verses, which Hierocles has illustrated with a Commentary. It is generally believed that they were not written by Pythagoras: perhaps they are to be ascribed to Epicharmus, or Empedocles. They may be considered as a brief summary of his popular doctrines.

The method of instruction adopted by Pythagoras was twofold, exoteric and esoteric, or public and private. This distinction he had seen introduced with great advantage by the Egyptian priests, who found it admirably adapted to strengthen their authority, and increase their emolument. He therefore determined as far as circumstances would admit, to form his school upon the Egyptian model. For the general benefit of the people, he held public assemblies, in which he delivered discourses in praise of virtue, and against vice; and in these he gave particular instructions, in different classes, to husbands and wives, parents and children, and others who filled the several relations of society. The auditors who attended these public lectures did not properly belong to his school, but continued to follow their usual mode of living. Besides these he had a select body of disciples whom he called his companions and friends, who submitted to a peculiar plan of discipline, and were admitted by a long course of instruction into all the mysteries of his esoteric doctrine.

Before any one could be admitted into this fraternity Pythagoras examined his features and external appearance; inquired in what manner he had been accustomed to behave towards his parents and friends; remarked his manner of conversing, laughing, and keeping silence; and observed what passions he was most inclined to indulge, with what kind of company he chose to associate, how he passed his leisure moments, and what incidents appeared to excite in him the strongest emotions of joy or sorrow. From these and other circumstances, Pythagoras formed an accurate judgment of the qualifications of the candidate; and he admitted no one into his society till he was fully persuaded of the docility of his dispositions, the gentleness of his manners, his power of retaining in silence what he was taught, and, in fine, his capacity of becoming a true philosopher.

Upon the first probationary admission, the fortitude and self-command of the candidate was put to the trial by a long course of severe abstinence and rigorous exercise. In order to subdue every inclination towards luxurious enjoyment, Pythagoras accustomed those who were admitted to this initiatory discipline to abstain from animal food, except the remains of the sacrifices, and to drink nothing but water, unless in the evening, when they were allowed a small portion of wine. That he might effectually inure them to self-denial, he sometimes ordered a table richly covered with dainties to be spread before them, and, when they were impatiently expecting to gratify their appetites, commanded the whole entertainment to be taken away, and dismissed them without any refreshment. He suffered them to wear no other garments but such as were suited to express the utmost purity and simplicity of manners. Of sleep he required them to be exceedingly frugal; and, in short, indulged them in nothing which could be supposed to inflame their passions, or cherish voluptuous desires. To correct an effeminate dread of labor or suffering, he prescribed them exercises which could not be performed without pain and fatigue. To teach them humility and industry, he exposed them, for three years, to a continued course of contradiction, ridicule, and contempt, among their fellows. The powerful passion of avarice he opposed, by requiring his disciples to submit to voluntary poverty. He not only taught them to be contented with a little, but even deprived them of all command over their own property, by casting the possessions of each individual into a common stock, to be distributed by proper officers, as occasion should require. From the time of this sequestration of their goods, as long as they continued members of this society, they lived upon the footing of perfect equality, and sat down together daily at a common table. If any one, however, repented of the connection, he was at liberty to depart, and might reclaim, from the general fund, his whole contribution.

That he might give his disciples a habit of entire docility, Pythagoras also enjoined upon them, from their first admission, a long term of silence called *echemuthia*, i. e., silence, or taciturnity. This exoteric silence is not to be confounded with that sacred reserve, with which all the disciples of Pythagoras were bound, upon oath, to receive the doctrines of their master, that they might, from no inducement whatever, suffer them to pass beyond the limits of the sect. The initiatory silence probably consisted in refraining from speech, not only during the hours of instruction, but through the whole term of initiation. It continued from two to five years, according to the degree of propensity which the pupil discovered towards conceit and loquacity. The restraint which Pythagoras thus put upon the "winged words" of his pupils, might possibly be of great use to them; it was certainly a judicious expedient with respect to himself, as it restrained impertinent curiosity, and prevented every inconvenience of contradiction. Accordingly, we find that his disciples silenced all doubts, and refuted all objections, by appealing to his authority. *Ipse dixit*, decided every dispute. Nor was this preparatory discipline deemed sufficiently severe, without adding, during the years of initiation, an entire prohibition of seeing their master, or hearing his lectures, except from behind a curtain. And even this privilege was too great to be commonly allowed; for in this stage of tuition they were usually instructed by some inferior preceptor, who barely recited the doctrines of Pythagoras, without assigning the reasonings or demonstrations upon which they were grounded, and required the obedient pupil to receive them as unquestionable truths, upon their master's word. Those who had sufficient perseverance to pass these several steps of probation were at last admitted among the esoterics, and allowed to hear and see Pythagoras behind the curtain. But if it happened that any one, through impatience of such rigid discipline, chose to withdraw from the society before the expiration of his term of trial, he was dismissed with a share of the common stock, the double of that which he had advanced; a tomb was erected for him as for a dead man, and he was to be as much forgotten by the brethren as if he had been actually dead.

It was the peculiar privilege of the members of the esoteric school (who were called genuine disciples) to receive a full explanation of the whole doctrine of Pythagoras, which to others was delivered in brief precepts and dogmas, under the concealment of symbols. They were also permitted to take minutes of their master's lectures in writing, and to propose questions, and offer remarks upon every subject of discourse. These disciples were particularly distinguished by the appellation of the Pythagoreans; they were also called Mathematicians, from the studies upon which they entered immediately after their initiation. After they had made a sufficient progress in geometrical science, they were conducted to the study of nature, the investigation of primary principles, and the knowledge of God. Those who pursued these sublime speculations were called Theorists; and such as more particularly devoted themselves to theology were styled Religious. Others, according to their respective abilities and inclinations, were engaged in the study of Morals, Œconomics and Policy; and were afterwards employed in managing the affairs of the fraternity, or sent into the cities of Greece, to instruct them in the principles of government, or assist them in the institution of laws.

The brethren of the Pythagorean college at Crotona, who were about six hundred in number, lived together, as one family, with their wives and children, in a public building called the common auditory. The whole business of the society was conducted with the most perfect regularity. Every day was begun with a distinct deliberation upon the manner in which it should be spent, and concluded with a careful retrospect of the events which had occurred, and the business which had been transacted. They rose before the sun, that they might pay him homage, after which they repeated select verses from Homer, and other poets, and made use of music, both vocal and instrumental, to enliven their spirits and fit them for the duties of the day. They then employed several hours in the study of science. These were succeeded by an interval of leisure, which was commonly spent in a solitary walk for the purpose of contemplation. The next portion of the day was allotted to conversation. The hour immediately before dinner was filled up with various kinds of athletic exercises. Their dinner consisted chiefly of bread, honey, and water; for, after they were perfectly initiated, they wholly denied themselves the use of wine. The remainder of the day was devoted to civil and domestic affairs, conversation, bathing, and religious ceremonies.

The exoteric disciples of Pythagoras were taught after the Egyptian manner by images and symbols, which must have been exceedingly obscure to those who were not initiated into the mysteries of the school. And they who were admitted to this privilege were trained from their first admission, to observe invariable silence with respect to the recondite doctrines of their master. That the wisdom of Pythagoras might not pass into the ears of the vulgar, they committed it chiefly to memory, and where they found it necessary to make use of writing, they were careful not to suffer their minutes to pass beyond the limits of the school.

QUINTIUS TUBERO.

Quintius Tubero, a nephew of Scipio Africanus, who was one of the most celebrated masters of civil law, was also conversant with philosophical learning, and professed himself a follower of the Stoic sect. The moral doctrine of this sect was peculiarly suitable to his natural temper, and to the habits of temperance and moderation which he had learned from his father, one of those excellent Romans, who, in the highest offices of the State, retained the simplicity of rustic manners. Confirmed in these habits by the precepts of Panætius, when Tubero was called upon, as pretor, to give a public entertainment in honor of his uncle, he provided only wooden couches covered with goat skins, earthen vessels, and a frugal repast. The people, who expected a splendid feast, were dissatisfied, and dismissed him from his office: but the action reflected no discredit either upon the lawyer or the philosopher; for it was, as Seneca remarks, an instructive lesson of moderation to the Romans, who, when they saw the sacred tables of Jupiter served with earthen vessels, would learn that men ought to be contented with such things as the Gods themselves did not disdain to use.

SENECA.

Lucius Annæus Seneca was a native of Corduba, an ancient and flourishing Roman settlement in Spain. His father, Marcus Annæus Seneca, a man of equestrian rank, was a celebrated orator; his mother's name was Helvia. He was born about fifteen years before the death of Augustus, or the year before the commencement of the Christian era, and was brought to Rome while a child, probably for education, by his aunt, who accompanied him on account of the delicate state of his health. His first studies were devoted by his father to eloquence, but his mind, naturally disposed towards serious and weighty pursuits, soon passed over from words to things; and he chose rather to reason with the philosophers than to declaim with the rhetoricians. This propensity was displeasing to his father, who, having himself no taste for philosophy, thought it a frivolous study, and had no other object of ambition, either for himself or his children, than eloquence. His son Junius Gallio succeeded in this pursuit, and was celebrated for the melody of his elocution; but Lucius was not to be diverted from his purpose of devoting himself to wisdom. Sotion, a philosopher, who, though of the Pythagorean sect, inclined to the Stoic doctrine concerning morals, was fixed upon as his preceptor. But whether it was that Seneca was disgusted with the severity of the Pythagoric discipline, or that he was dissatisfied with the obscure dogmas of this school, he soon forsook Sotion, and became a disciple of Attalus, a Stoic; at the same time, occasionally conversing with philosophers of other sects, and freely examining the writings, or doctrines, of the several founders of the Grecian schools. Through his father's importunity, he for a short time interrupted his philosophical studies to engage in the business of the courts; and we are assured by so good a judge as Quintilian, that, whilst he continued to plead, his speeches, if deficient in some of the graces of oratory, abounded with that good sense and strength of thought which are the basis of eloquence.

Thus furnished with plentiful stores of learning, and with a competent skill in the art of speaking, Seneca, as soon as he arrived at the age of manhood, aspired to the honors of the

State. The first office with which he was invested was that of questor; but at what time he obtained it is uncertain. From this time his good fortune made rapid advances; and he soon rose to distinction in the court of Claudius. But the particulars of his public life, during this period, are nowhere preserved. Hence it is impossible to discover with certainty the cause of the charge, which was publicly brought against him, of adultery with Julia, the daughter of Germanicus, and wife of Venicius. It is probable, however, from the infamous character of Messalina, who instigated the prosecution, that he was accused without any sufficient ground. The affair, notwithstanding, terminated in his banishment; and Seneca, after having for many years enjoyed the favor of the emperor, and been distinguished among the great, was obliged to remain eight years an exile in the island of Corsica. Here, if we are to credit his own account, he passed his time agreeably, devoting himself entirely to the study of philosophy and elegant learning. In a letter to his mother, he says, "Be assured that I am as cheerful and happy as in the days of my greatest prosperity; I may indeed call my present days such; since my mind, free from care, is at leisure for its favorite pursuits, and can either amuse itself with lighter studies, or, in its eager search after truth, rise to the contemplation of its own nature and that of the universe." But it may be questioned whether Stoic ostentation had not some share in dictating this report; for we find him, in another place, expressing much distress on account of his misfortune, and courting the emperor in a strain of servile adulation, little worthy of so eminent a philosopher.

Agrippina, the second wife of Claudius, whose character was the reverse of that of Messalina, employed her interest with the emperor in favor of Seneca; and not only obtained his recall from banishment, but prevailed upon Claudius to confer upon him the honorable office of pretor. Her inducement to this measure appears to have been a desire of engaging a philosopher of so much distinction and merit to undertake the education of her son. Probably, too, she hoped, by attaching Seneca to her family, to strengthen Nero's interest in the state; for the Roman people would, of course, entertain high expectations from a prince educated under such a master. Afranius Burrhus, a pretorian prefect, was joined with Seneca in this important charge; and these two preceptors, who were entrusted with equal authority, and had each his respective department, executed their trust with perfect harmony, and with some degree of success; Burrhus instructing his pupil in the military art, and inuring him to wholesome discipline; Seneca furnishing him with the principles of philosophy, and the precepts of wisdom and eloquence; and both endeavoring to confine their pupil within the limits of decorum and virtue. Whilst these preceptors united their authority, Nero was restrained from indulging his natural propensities; but after the death of Burrhus, the influence of Seneca declined, and the young prince began to disclose that depravity which afterwards stained his character with eternal infamy.

Still, however, Seneca enjoyed the favor of his prince; and, after Nero was advanced to the empire, he long continued to load his preceptor with honors and riches. Partly from inheritance and marriage, but chiefly through imperial munificence, he possessed a large estate, and lived in great splendor. Juvenal speaks of

The gardens of the wealthy Seneca.

A superb mansion at Rome, delightful country seats, rich furniture, including, as Dio particularly mentions, five hundred cedar tables with ivory feet, uniform, and of excellent workmanship, were articles of luxury hitherto unusual among philosophers, and were thought by many not very consistent with that high tone of indifference, in which the Stoics, and among the rest Seneca himself, spoke of external good. Suilius, one of his enemies, asked by what wisdom, or by what precepts of philosophy, Seneca had been able, during four years of imperial favor, to amass the immense sum of three hundred thousand *sestertia*.*

Seneca perceived the gathering clouds of jealousy and envy, and saw that his sovereign himself, whose vices were now becoming too imperious to endure restraint, was disposed to listen to the whispers of obloquy. In hopes of escaping the destruction which threatened him, he earnestly requested the emperor's permission to withdraw from the court, and devote the remainder of his days to philosophy; he even offered to refund the immense treasures which royal bounty had lavished upon him, and to retire with a bare competency. Nero rejected his proposal, and assured him of the continuance of his favor; but the philosopher knew the emperor's disposition too well to rely upon his promises. From this time Seneca declined all ceremonious visits, avoided company, and, under the pretence of indisposition, or a desire of prosecuting his studies, confined himself almost entirely to his own house.

It was not long before Seneca was convinced that in distrusting a tyrant, whose mind was wholly occupied by suspicion, he had acted prudently. Antonius Natalis, who had been concerned in the conspiracy of Piso, upon his examination, in order to court the favor of Nero, or perhaps even at his instigation, mentioned Seneca among the number of the conspirators. This single evidence was by the tyrant deemed sufficient against the man to whom he had been indebted for his education, and whom he had called his friend. To give some color to the accusation, Natalis pretended that he had been sent by Piso to visit Seneca whilst he was sick, and to complain of his having refused to see Piso, who as a friend might have expected free access to him upon all occasions; and that Seneca in reply, had said, that frequent conversa-

* £2,421,875.

tions could be of no service to either party; but that he considered his own safety as involved in that of Piso. Granius Sylvanus, tribune of the pretorian cohort, was sent to ask Seneca whether he recollected what had passed between himself and Natalis. Seneca, whether by accident or design is uncertain, had that day left Campania, and was at his country seat, about four miles from the city. In the evening, while he was at supper with his wife Paulina and two friends, the tribune, attended by a military band, came to the house, and after giving the soldiers orders to surround it, delivered the emperor's message. Seneca's answer was, that he had received a complaint from Piso, of his having refused to see him; and that the state of his health, which required repose, had been his apology. He added, that he saw no reason why he should prefer the safety of any other individual to his own; and that no one was better acquainted than Nero with his independent spirit.

This reply kindled the emperor's indignation, and he asked the messenger whether Seneca discovered any intention of putting an end to his own life. The tribune assured him that there was no appearance either of terror or of distress in his countenance or language. Upon this the tyrant, who felt his own pusillanimity reproached by the constancy of the philosopher, ordered him to return without delay to Seneca, with his peremptory command immediately to put himself to death. Sylvanus, who had himself been one of the conspirators, had not the courage to meet the face of Seneca upon such an embassy, but sent the fatal message by one of his centurions. The philosopher received it with perfect composure, and asked permission of the officer to alter his will. This indulgence being refused him, he turned to his friends, and requested, that, since he was not allowed to leave them any other legacy, they would preserve in their memory a portrait of his life, as a perpetual monument of friendship. At the same time he restrained their tears, and exorted them to exercise that fortitude which they had professed to learn in the school of philosophy. "Where are now," said he, "our boasted precepts of wisdom? where the armor which we have been so many years providing against adverse fate? Who among us has been a stranger to the savage spirit of Nero? After murdering his mother and his brother, it was not to be expected that he would spare his preceptor."

Having conversed in this manner for some time with his friends, Seneca embraced his wife, and earnestly entreated her to moderate her grief, and after his death to console herself with the recollection of his virtues; but Paulina refused every consolation, except that of dying with her husband, and earnestly solicited the friendly hand of the executioner. Seneca, after expressing his admiration of his wife's fortitude, proceeded to obey the emperor's fatal mandate, by opening a vein in each arm; but, through his advanced age, the vital stream flowed so reluctantly, that it was necessary also to open the veins of his legs. Still finding his strength exhausted without any prospect of a speedy release, in order to alleviate, if possible, the anguish of his wife, who was a spectator of the scene, and to save himself the torture of witnessing her distress, he persuaded her to withdraw to another chamber. In this situation, Seneca, with wonderful recollection and self-command, dictated many philosophical reflections to his secretary. After a long interval, his friend Statius Annæus, to whom he complained of the tedious delay of death, administered to him a strong dose of poison; but even this, through the feeble state of his vital powers, produced little effect. At last, he ordered the attendants to convey him into a warm bath; and, as he entered, he sprinkled those who stood near, saying, "I offer this libation to Jupiter the Deliverer." Then, plunging into the bath, he was soon suffocated. His body was consumed, according to his own express order in a will which he had made in the height of his prosperity, without any funeral pomp.

Such was the end of Seneca, an end not unworthy the purest and best principles of the Stoic philosophy.

SIMON.

Simon, was an Athenian leather-dresser. Whenever Socrates came into his workshop and conversed, he used to make memorandums of all his sayings that he recollected. From this circumstance people have called his dialogues leathern ones.

He is, as some people say, the first writer who reduced the conversations of Socrates into the form of dialogues. And when Pericles offered to provide for him, and invited him to come to him, he said he would not sell his freedom of speech.

SIMON MAGUS.

Simon Magus, who is commonly understood to have been the person mentioned in the Acts of the Apostles, was by birth a Samaritan, and in his native country practiced magical arts, which procured him many followers. According to the usual practice of the Asiatics at this time, he visited Egypt, and there, probably, became acquainted with the sublime mysteries taught in the Alexandrian school, and learned those theurgic or magical operations, by means of which it was believed that men might be delivered from the power of evil demons. Upon his return into his own country, the author of the "Clementine Recognitions" relates that he imposed upon his countrymen by his pretensions to supernatural powers. And St. Luke attests, that this artful fanatic, using sorcery, had bewitched the people of Samaria, giving out that he was some Great One; and that he obtained such general attention and reverence in Samaria, that the people all gave heed to him from the least to the greatest, saying, "This man is the Great Power of God."

From the nature of the philosophy which, at this period, was taught both in Asia and Egypt, and in which Simon had, doubtless, been instructed, it may be reasonably concluded that he pretended to be an Æon of the first order, or one of the most exalted of those substantial powers, or divine immortal natures, which were supposed to have emanated from the eternal fountain of the Supreme Deity. He boasted, that he was sent down from heaven, among men, to chastise and subdue those evil demons, by whose malignant influence the disorders and miseries of human nature were produced, and to conduct them to the highest felicity. To his wife Helena he also ascribed a similar kind of divine nature, pretending that a female Æon inhabited the body of this woman, to whom he gave the name of Wisdom; whence some Christian fathers have said, that he called her the Holy Spirit.

SOCRATES.

Socrates was the son of Sophronicus, a statuary, and of Phænarete, a midwife. He was a citizen of Athens.

Some people believed that he assisted Euripides in his poems; in reference to which idea, Moresimachus speaks as follows:—

> The Phrygians are a new play of Euripides,
> But Socrates has laid the main foundation.

And again he says:—

> Euripides: patched up by Socrates.

And Callias, in his Captives, says:—

> *A.* Are you so proud, giving yourself such airs?
> *B.* And well I may, for Socrates is the cause.

And Aristophanes says, in his Clouds:—

> This is Euripides, who doth compose
> Those argumentative wise tragedies.

But, having been a pupil of Anaxagoras, as some people say, but of Damon as the other story goes, related by Alexander in his Successions, after the condemnation of Anaxagoras, he became a disciple of Archelaus, the natural philosopher. And, indeed, Aristoxenus says that he was very intimate with him.

But Duris says that he was a slave, and employed in carving stones. And some say that the Graces in the Acropolis are his work; and they are clothed figures. And that it is in reference to this that Timon says, in his Silli :—

From them procceded the stone polisher,
The reasoning legislator, the enchanter
Of all the Greeks, making them subtle arguers,
A cunning pedant, a shrewd Attic quibbler.

For he was very clever in all rhetorical exercises, as Idomeneus also assures us. But the thirty tyrants forbade him to give lessons in the art of speaking and arguing, as Xenophon tells us. And Aristophanes turns him into ridicule in his Comedies, as making the worse appear the better reason. For he was the first man, as Phavorinus says in his Universal History, who, in conjunction with his disciple Æschines, taught men how to become orators. And Idomeneus makes the same assertion in his essay on the Socratic School. He, likewise, was the first person who conversed about human life; and also was the first philosopher who was condemned to death and executed. And Aristoxenus, the son of Spintharas, says that he lent money in usury; and that he collected the interest and principal together, and then, when he had got the interest, he lent it out again. And Demetrius, of Byzantium, says that it was Criton who made him leave his workshop and instruct men, out of the admiration which he conceived for his abilities.

He then, perceiving that natural philosophy had no immediate bearing on our interests, began to enter upon moral speculations, both in his workshop and in the market-place. And he said that the objects of his search were—

> Whatever good or harm can man befall
> In his own house.

And very often, while arguing and discussing points that arose, he was treated with great violence and beaten, and pulled about, and laughed at and ridiculed by the multitude. But he bore all this with great equanimity. So that once, when he had been kicked and buffeted about, and had borne it all patiently, and some one expressed his surprise, he said, "Suppose an ass had kicked me, would you have had me bring an action against him?" And this is the account of Demetrius.

But he had no need of travelling (though most philosophers did travel), except when he was bound to serve in the army. But all the rest of his life he remained in the same place, and in an argumentative spirit he used to dispute with all who would converse with him, not with the purpose of taking away their opinions from them, so much as of learning the truth, as far as he could do so, himself. And they say that Euripides gave him a small work of Heraclitus to read, and asked him afterwards what he thought of it, and he replied, "What I have understood is good; and so, I think, what I have not understood is; only the book requires a Delian diver to get at the meaning of it." He paid great attention also to the training of the body, and was always in excellent condition himself. Accordingly, he joined in the expedition to Amphipolis, and he it was who took up and saved Xenophon in the battle of Delian, when he had fallen from his horse; for when all the Athenians had fled, he retreated quietly, turning round slowly, and watching to repel any one who attacked him. He also joined in the expedition to Potidæa, which was undertaken by sea; for it was impossible to get there by land, as the war impeded the communication. And they say that on this occasion he remained the whole night in one place; and that though he had deserved the prize of pre-eminent valor, he yielded it to Alcibiades, to whom Aristippus, in the fourth book of his treatise on the Luxury of the Ancients, says that he was greatly attached.

He was a man of great firmness of mind, and very much attached to the democracy, as was plain from his not submitting to Critias, when he ordered him to bring Leon of Salamis, a very rich man, before the thirty, for the purpose of being murdered. And he alone voted for the acquittal of the ten generals;* and when it was in his power to escape out of prison he would not do it; and he reproved those who bewailed his fate, and even while in prison, he delivered those beautiful discourses which we still possess.

He was a contented and venerable man. And once, when Alcibiades offered him a large piece of ground to build a house upon, he said, "But if I wanted shoes, and you had given me a piece of leather to make myself shoes, I should be laughed at if I took it." And often, when he beheld the multitude of things which were being sold, he would say to himself, "How many things there are which I do not want." And he was continually repeating these iambics:—

For silver plate and purple useful are
For actors on the stage, but not for men.

And he showed his scorn of Archelaus the Macedonian, and Scopas the Crononian, and Eurylochus of Larissa, when he refused to accept their money, and to go and visit them. And he was so regular in his way of living, that it happened more than once when there was a plague at Athens, that he was the only person who did not catch it.

Aristotle says that he had two wives. The first was Xanthippe, by whom he had a son named Lamprocles; the second was Myrto, the daughter of Aristides the Just; and he took her without any dowry, and by her he had two sons,

* After the battle of Arginusæ.

Sophroniscus and Menexenus. But some say that Myrto was his first wife. And some, among whom are Satyrus, and Hieronymus, of Rhodes, say that he had them both at the same time. For they say that the Athenians, on account of the scarcity of men, passed a vote with the view of increasing the population, that a man might marry one citizen, and might also have children by another who should be legitimate; on which account Socrates did so.

And he was a man able to look down upon any who mocked him. And he prided himself upon the simplicity of his way of life; and never exacted any pay from his pupils. And he used to say, that the man who ate with the greatest appetite, had the least need of delicacies; and that he who drank with the greatest appetite, was the least inclined to look for a draught which is not at hand; and that those who want fewest things are nearest to the Gods. And thus much, indeed, one may learn from the comic poets; who, without perceiving it, praise him in the very matters for which they ridicule him. Aristophanes speaks thus:—

> Prudent man, who thus with justice long for mighty wisdom,
> Happiness will be your lot in Athens, and all Greece too;
> For you 've a noble memory, and plenty of invention,
> And patience dwells within your mind, and you are never tired,
> Whether you 're standing still or walking; and you care not for cold,
> Nor do you long for breakfast time, nor e'er give in to hunger,
> But wine and gluttony you shun, and all such kind of follies.

And Ameipsias introduces him on the stage in a cloak, and speaks thus of him:—

> O Socrates, among few men the best,
> And among many vainest; here at last
> You come to us courageously—but where,
> Where did you get that cloak? so strange a garment,
> Some leather cutter must have given you
> By way of joke: and yet this worthy man,
> Though ne'er so hungry, never flatters any one.

Aristophanes, too, exposes his contemptuous and arrogant disposition, speaking thus:—

You strut along the streets, and look around you proudly,
And barefoot many ills endure, and hold your head above us.

And yet, sometimes he adapted himself to the occasion and dressed handsomely. As, for instance, in the banquet of Plato, where he is represented as going to find Agathon.

He was a man of great ability, both in exhorting men to, and dissuading them from, any course; as, for instance, having discoursed with Thætetus on the subject of knowledge, he sent him away almost inspired, as Plato says. When Euthyphron had commenced a prosecution against his father for having killed a foreigner, he conversed with him on the subject of piety, and turned him from his purpose; and by his exhortations he made Lysis a most moral man. For he was very ingenious at deriving arguments from existing circumstances. And so he mollified his son Lamprocles when he was very angry with his mother, and he wrought upon Glauson, the brother of Plato, who was desirous to meddle with affairs of State, and induced him to abandon his purpose, because of his want of experience in such matters. And, on the contrary, he persuaded Charmidas to devote himself to politics, because he was a man very well calculated for such business. He also inspired Iphicrates, the general, with courage, by showing him the gamecocks of Midias the barber, pluming themselves against those of Callias; and Glauernides said, that the State ought to keep him carefully, as if he were a pheasant or a peacock. He used also to say, that "it was a strange thing that every one could easily tell what property he had, but was not able to name all his friends, or even to tell their number; so careless were men on that subject." Once when he saw Euclid exceedingly anxious about some dialectic arguments, he said to him, "O Euclid, you will acquire a power of managing sophists, but not of governing men." For he thought that subtle hair-splitting on those subjects was quite useless.

When Charmidas offered him some slaves, with the view

to his making a profit of them, he would not have them; and as some people say, he paid no regard to the beauty of Alcibiades.

He used to praise leisure as the most valuable of possessions. And it was a saying of his that there was one only good, namely, knowledge; and one only evil, namely, ignorance; that riches and high birth had nothing estimable in them, but that, on the contrary, they were wholly evil. Accordingly, when some one told him that the mother of Antisthenes was a Thracian woman, "Did you suppose," said he, "that so noble a man must be born of two Athenians?" And when Phædo was reduced to a state of slavery, he ordered Crito to ransom him, and taught him, and made him a philosopher.

He used to learn to play on the lyre when he had time, saying, "It is not absurd to learn anything that one does not know;" and further, he used frequently to dance, thinking such an exercise good for the health of the body.

He used also to say that the dæmon foretold the future to him;* and that to begin well was not a trifling thing, but yet not far from a trifling thing; and that he knew nothing, except the fact of his ignorance. Another saying of his was, that "those who bought things out of season, at an extravagant price, expected never to live till the proper season for them." Once, when he was asked what was the virtue of a young man, he said, "To avoid excess in everything." And he used to say, that it was necessary to learn geometry only so far as might enable a man to measure land for the purposes of buying and selling. And when Euripides, in his Augur, had spoken thus of virtue:—

'T is best to leave these subjects undisturbed;

---

* "This is not quite correct. Socrates believed that the demon which attended him, limited his warnings to his own conduct; preventing him from doing what was wrong, but not prompting him to do right."—*See Grote's admirable chapter on Socrates. History of Greece*, vol. v.

he rose up and left the theatre, saying that "It was an absurdity to think it right to seek for a slave if one could not find him, but to let virtue be altogether disregarded." The question was once put to him by a man whether he would advise him to marry or not? And he replied, "Whichever you do, you will repent it." He often said, that he wondered at those who made stone statues, when he saw how careful they were that the stone should be like the man it was intended to represent, but how careless they were of themselves, as to guarding against being like the stone. He used also to recommend young men to be constantly looking in the glass, in order that, if they were handsome, they might be worthy of their beauty; and if they were ugly, they might conceal their unsightly appearance by their accomplishments. He once invited some rich men to dinner, and when Xanthippe was ashamed of their insufficient appointments, he said, "Be of good cheer; for if our guests are sensible men, they will bear with us; and if they are not, we need not care about them." He used to say,' "That other men lived to eat, but that he ate to live." Another saying of his was, "That to have a regard for the worthless multitude, was like the case of a man who refused to take one piece of money of four drachmas as if it were bad, and then took a heap of such coin and admitted them to be good." When Æschines said, "I am a poor man, and having nothing else, but I give you myself;" "Do you not," he replied, "perceive that you are giving me what is of the greatest value?" He said to some one, who was expressing indignation at being overlooked when the thirty had seized on the supreme power, "Do you, then, repent of not being a tyrant too?" A man said to him, "The Athenians have condemned you to death." "And nature," he replied, "has condemned them." But some attribute this answer to Anaxagoras. When his wife said to him, "You die undeservedly." "Would you, then," he rejoined, "have had me deserve death?" He thought once that some one appeared to him in a dream, and said:—

On the third day you 'll come to lovely Phthia.

And so he said to Æschines, "In three days I shall die." And when he was about to drink the hemlock, Apollodorus presented him with a handsome robe, that he might expire in it; and he said, "Why was my own dress good enough to live in, and not good enough to die in?" When a person said to him, "Such an one speaks ill of you;" "To be sure," said he, "for he has never learnt to speak well." When Antisthenes turned the ragged side of his cloak to the light, he said, "I see your silly vanity through the holes in your cloak." When some one said to him, "Does not that man abuse you?" "No," said he, "for that does not apply to me." It was a saying of his, too, "That it is a good thing for a man to offer himself cheerfully to the attacks of the comic writers; for then, if they say anything worth hearing, one will be able to mend; and if they do not, then all they say is unimportant."

He said once to Xanthippe, who first abused him, and then threw water at him, "Did I not say that Xanthippe was thundering now, and would soon rain?" When Alcibiades said to him, "The abusive temper of Xanthippe is intolerable;" "But I," he rejoined, "am used to it, just as I should be if I were always hearing the noise of a pulley; and you yourself endure to hear geese cackling." To which Alcibiades answered, "Yes, but they bring me eggs and goslings." "Well," rejoined Socrates, "and Xanthippe brings me children." Once, she attacked him in the market-place, and tore his cloak off; his friends advised him to keep her off with his hands; "Yes, by Jove," said he, "that while we are boxing you may all cry out, 'Well done, Socrates, well done, Xanthippe.'" And he used to say, that one ought to live with a restive woman, just as horsemen manage violent-tempered horses; "and as they," said he, "when they have once mastered them, are easily able to manage all others; so I, after managing Xanthippe, can easily live with any one else whatever."

It was in consequence of such sayings and actions as these, that the priestess at Delphi was witness in his favor, when she gave Chærephon this answer, which is so universally known:—

Socrates of all mortals is the wisest.

In consequence of which answer, he incurred great envy; and he brought envy also on himself, by convicting men who gave themselves airs of folly and ignorance, as undoubtedly he did to Antyus; and as is shown in Plato's Meno. For he, not being able to bear Socrates' jesting, first of all set Aristophanes to attack him, and then persuaded Melitus to institute a prosecution against him, on the ground of impiety and of corrupting the youth of the city. Accordingly, Melitus did institute a prosecution; Polyeuctus pronounced the sentence. Polycrates, the sophist, wrote the speech which was delivered. And Lycon, the demagogue, prepared everything necessary to support the impeachment; but Antisthenes in his Successions of the Philosophers, and Plato in his Apology, say that these men brought the accusation:—Anytus, and Lycon, and Melitus; Anytus, acting against him on behalf of the magistrates, and because of his political principles; Lycon, on behalf of the orators; and Melitus on behalf of the poets, all of whom Socrates used to pull to pieces. But Phavorinus, in the first book of his Commentaries, says, that the speech of Polycrates against Socrates is not the genuine one; for in it there is mention made of the walls having been restored by Conon, which took place six years after the death of Socrates; and certainly this is true.

But the sworn informations, on which the trial proceeded, were drawn up in this fashion; for they are preserved to this day, says Phavorinus, in the temple of Cybele:—"Melitus, the son of Melitus, of Pittea, impeaches Socrates, the son of Sophroniscus, of Alopece: Socrates is guilty, inasmuch as he does not believe in the Gods whom the city worships, but introduces other strange deities; he is also guilty, inasmuch as he corrupts the young men, and the punishment he has incurred is death."

But the philosopher, after Lysias had prepared a defence for him, read it through, and said—"It is a very fine speech, Lysias, but is not suitable for me; for it was manifestly the speech of a lawyer, rather than of a philosopher." And when Lysias replied, "How is it possible, that if it is a good speech, it should not be suitable to you?" he said, "Just as fine clothes and handsome shoes would not be suitable to me." And when the trial was proceeding, Justus, of Tiberias, in his Garland, says that Plato ascended the tribune and said, "I, men of Athens, being the youngest of all those who have mounted the tribune . . ." and that he was interrupted by the judges, who cried out, "Come down."

So when he had been condemned by two hundred and eighty-one votes, being six more than were given in his favor, and when the judges were making an estimate of what punishment or fine should be inflicted on him, he said that he ought to be fined five and twenty drachmas; but Eubulides says that he admitted that he deserved a fine of one hundred. And when the judges raised an outcry at this proposition, he said, "My real opinion is, that as a return for what has been done by me, I deserve a maintenance in the Prytaneum for the rest of my life." So they condemned him to death, by eighty votes more than they had originally found him guilty. And he was put into prison, and a few days afterwards he drank the hemlock, having held many admirable conversations in the meantime, which Plato has recorded in the Phædo.

So he died; but the Athenians immediately repented* of their action, so that they closed all the palæstræ and gymnasia; and they banished his accusers, and condemned Melitus to death; but they honored Socrates with a brazen statue, which

* Grote gives good reasons for disbelieving this.

they erected in the place where the sacred vessels are kept; and it was the work of Lysippus. But Anytus had already left Athens; and the people of Heraclea banished him from that city the day of his arrival. But Socrates was not the only person who met with this treatment at the hands of the Athenians, but many other men received the same; for they fined Homer fifty drachmas as a madman, and they said that Iystæus was out of his wits. But they honored Astydamas, before Æschylus, with a brazen statue. And Euripides reproaches them for their conduct in his Palamedes, saying—

> Ye have slain, ye have slain,
> O Greeks, the all-wise nightingale,
> The favorite of the Muses, guiltless all.

But Philochorus says that Euripides died before Socrates.

Aristotle tells us that a certain one of the magi came from Syria to Athens and blamed Socrates for many parts of his conduct, and also foretold that he would come to a violent death; and we ourselves have written this epigram on him:—

> Drink now, O Socrates, in the realms of Jove,
> For truly did the God pronounce you wise,
> And he who said so is himself all wisdom;
> You drank the poison which your country gave,
> But they drank wisdom from your God-like voice.

Brucker's account of this distinguished man is as follows:

Socrates, by his penetrating judgment, exalted views, and liberal spirit, united with exemplary integrity, and purity of manners, is acknowledged, by the unanimous suffrage of antiquity, to have obtained the first place among philosophers. He was born at Alopeces, a village near Athens, in the fourth year of the seventy-seventh Olympiad. His parents were of low rank. Sophroniscus brought up his son, contrary to his inclination, in his own manual employment; in which Socrates, though his mind was continually aspiring after higher objects, was not unsuccessful. Whilst he was a young man, he is said to have formed statues of the habited Graces, which were allowed a place in the citadel of Athens. Upon the death of his father, he was left with no other inheritance than the small sum of eighty *minæ*, which, through the dishonesty of a relation, to whom Sophroniscus left the charge of his affairs, he soon lost. This laid him under the necessity of supporting himself by labor; and he continued to practice the art of statuary in Athens; at the same time, however, devoting all the leisure he could command to the study of philosophy.

Crito, a wealthy Athenian, remarking the strong propensity towards study which this young man discovered, and admiring his ingenious disposition and distinguished abilities, generously took him under his patronage, and entrusted him with the instruction of his children. The opportunities which Socrates by this means enjoyed of attending the public lectures of the most eminent philosophers, so far increased his thirst after wisdom, that he determined to relinquish his occupation, and every prospect of emolument which that might afford, in order to devote himself entirely to his favorite pursuits. His first preceptor in philosophy was Anaxagoras. After this eminent master in the Ionic school left Athens, Socrates attached himself to Archelaus. Under these instructors he diligently prosecuted the study of nature, in the usual manner of the philosophers of the age, and became well acquainted with their doctrines. Prodicus, the sophist, was his preceptor in eloquence, Evenus in poetry, Theodorus in geometry, and Damo in music. Aspasia, a woman no less celebrated for her intellectual than her personal accomplishments, whose house was frequented by the most celebrated characters, had also some share in the education of Socrates.

Thus furnished with preceptors of every kind, Socrates acquired that knowledge at home, which the Greeks had hitherto sought in foreign countries; but for which, after all, they were more indebted to their own ingenuity and industry, than to the instructions of the Oriental or Egyptian priests. It cannot be reasonably doubted that, with such advantages, he became master of every kind of learning, which the age in which he lived could afford.

With these uncommon endowments, both natural and acquired, Socrates appeared in Athens, under the respectable characters of a good citizen and a true philosopher. Being called upon by his country to take up arms in the long and severe struggle between Athens and Sparta, he signalized himself at the siege of Potidæa, both by his valor, and by the hardiness with which he endured fatigue. During the severity of a Thracian winter whilst others were clad in furs, he wore only his usual clothing, and walked barefoot upon the ice. In an engagement in which he saw Alcibiades (a young man of noble rank whom he accompanied during this expedition) falling down wounded, he advanced to defend him, and saved both him and his arms; and though the prize of valor was, on this occasion, unquestionably due to Socrates, he generously gave his vote that it might be bestowed upon Alcibiades, to encourage his rising merit. Several years afterwards, Socrates voluntarily entered upon a military expedition against the Bœotians, during which, in an unsuccessful engagement at Delium, he retired with great coolness from the field; when, observing Xenophon lying wounded upon the ground, he took him upon his shoulders and bore him out of the reach of the enemy. Soon afterwards he went out a third time, in a military capacity, in the expedition for the purpose of reducing Amphipolis; but this proving unsuccessful, he returned to Athens, and remained there till his death.

It was not till Socrates was upwards of fifty-six years of age that he undertook to serve his country in any civil office. At that age, he was chosen to represent his own district in the *senate of five hundred.* In this office, though he at first exposed himself to some degree of ridicule from the want of experience in the forms of business, he soon convinced his colleagues that he was superior to them all in wisdom and integrity. Whilst they, intimidated by the clamors of the populace, passed an unjust sentence of condemnation upon the commanders who, after the engagement at the Arginusian islands, had been prevented by a storm from paying funeral honors to the dead, Socrates stood forth singly in their defence, and, to the last, refused to give his suffrage against them, declaring that no force should compel him to act contrary to justice and the laws. Under the subsequent tyranny, he never ceased to condemn the oppressive and cruel proceedings of the Thirty Tyrants; and when his boldness provoked their resentment, so that his life was in hazard, fearing neither treachery nor violence, he still continued to support, with undaunted firmness, the rights of his fellow-citizens. The tyrants, probably that they might create some new ground of complaint against Socrates, sent an order to him, with several other persons, to apprehend a wealthy citizen of Salamis; the rest executed the commission; but Socrates refused, saying that he would rather himself suffer death than be instrumental in inflicting it unjustly upon another.

These proofs of public virtue, both in a military and civil capacity, are sufficient to entitle the name of Socrates to a distinguished place in the catalogue of good citizens. But his first honors arise from the manner in which he supported the character of a philosopher, and discharged the duties of a moral preceptor.

Observing, with regret, how much the opinions of the Athenian youth were misled, and their principles and taste corrupted by philosophers, who spent all their time in refined speculations upon nature and the origin of things, and by sophists, who taught in their schools the arts of false eloquence and deceitful reasoning, Socrates formed the wise and generous design of instituting a new and more useful method of instruction. He justly conceived the true end of philosophy to be, not to make an ostentatious display of superior learning and ability in subtle disputations or ingenious conjectures, but to free mankind from the dominion of pernicious prejudices; to correct their vices; to inspire them with the love of virtue, and thus conduct them in the path of wisdom to true felicity. He therefore assumed the character of a moral philosopher; and, looking upon the whole city of Athens as his school, and all who were disposed to lend him their attention as his pupils, he seized every occasion of communicating moral wisdom to his fellow-citizens. He passed his time chiefly in public. It was his custom in the morning to visit the places made use of for walking and public exercises; at noon, to appear among the crowds in the markets or courts, and to spend the rest of the day in those parts of the city which were most frequented. Sometimes he collected an audience about him in the Lyceum, (a pleasant meadow on the border of the river Ilyssus,) where he delivered a discourse from the chair, whilst his auditors were seated on benches around him. At other times he conversed, in a less formal way, with any of his fellow-citizens in places of common resort, or with his friends at meals, or in their hours of amusement; thus making every place to which he came a school of virtue. Not only did young men of rank and fortune attend upon his lectures, but he sought for disciples even among mechanics and laborers.

The method of instruction which Socrates chiefly made use of, was to propose a series of questions to the person with whom he conversed, in order to lead him to some unforeseen conclusion. He first gained the consent of his respondent to some obvious truths, and then obliged him to admit others, from their relation, or resemblance, to those to which they had already assented. Without making use of any direct argument or persuasion, he chose to lead the person he meant to instruct to deduce the truths of which he wished to convince him as a necessary consequence from his own concessions. He commonly conducted these conferences with such address, as to conceal his design till the respondent had advanced too far to recede. On some occasions he made use of ironical language, that vain men might be caught in their own replies, and be obliged to confess their ignorance. He never assumed the air of a morose and rigid preceptor, but communicated useful instruction with all the ease and pleasantry of polite conversation.

Socrates was not less distinguished by his modesty than by his wisdom. His discourses betray no marks of arrogance or vanity. He professed "to know only this, that he knew nothing." In this declaration, which he frequently repeated, he had no other intention than to convince his hearers of the narrow limits of the human understanding. Nothing was farther from his thoughts than to encourage universal scepticism: on moral subjects he always expressed himself with confidence and decision; but he was desirous of exposing to contempt the arrogance of those pretenders to science who would acknowledge themselves ignorant of nothing. The truth was, that Socrates, though eminently furnished, as we have already seen, with every kind of learning, preferred moral to speculative wisdom. Convinced that philosophy is valuable, not as it furnishes questions for the schools, but as it provides men with a law of life, he censured his predecessors for spending all their time in abstruse researches into nature, and taking no pains to render themselves useful to mankind. His favorite maxim was, "Whatever is above us, doth not concern us." He estimated the value of knowledge by its utility, and recommended the study of geometry, astronomy, and other sciences, only so far as they admit of a practical application to the purposes of human life. His great object, in all his conferences and discourses, was to lead men into an acquaintance with themselves; to convince them of their follies and vices; to inspire them with the love of virtue; and to furnish them with useful moral instruction. Cicero might, therefore, very justly say to Socrates, that he was the first who called down Philosophy from heaven to earth, and introduced her into the public walks and domestic retirements of men, that she might instruct them concerning life and manners.

The moral lessons which Socrates taught, he himself diligently practiced; whence he excelled other philosophers in personal merit no less than in his method of instruction. His conduct was uniformly such as became a teacher of modern wisdom.

Through his whole life, this good man discovered a mind superior to the attractions of wealth and power. Contrary to the general practice of the preceptors of his time, he instructed his pupils without receiving from them any gratuity. He frequently refused rich presents, which were offered him by Alcibiades and others, though importunately urged to accept them by his wife. The chief men of Athens were his stewards; they sent him in provisions, as they apprehended he wanted them: he took what his present wants required, and returned the rest. With Socrates moderation supplied the place of wealth. In his clothing and food he consulted only the demands of nature. He commonly appeared in a neat, but plain cloak, with his feet uncovered. Though his table was only supplied with simple fare, he did not scruple to invite men of superior rank to partake of his meals. He found by experience that temperance is the parent of health. It was owing to his perfect regularity in this respect that he escaped infection in the midst of the plague, which proved so fatal to his fellow-citizens.

Socrates was a great admirer of a fair external form, as the index of a mind possessed, or at least capable, of moral beauty, and conversed freely with young persons, of both sexes, in order to assist their progress in wisdom and virtue; but his enemies have never been able to fix upon him the stain of incontinence. Modern calumnies, which impute to this great man vices, with which he was never charged by his contemporaries, ought to be treated with universal contempt.

Though Socrates was exceedingly unfortunate in his domestic connection, he converted this infelicity into an occasion of exercising his virtues. Xanthippe, concerning whose ill-humor ancient writers relate many amusing tales, was certainly a woman of a high and unmanageable spirit. But Socrates, whilst he endeavored to curb the violence of her temper, improved his own. When Alcibiades expressed his surprise that his friend could bear to live in the same house with so perverse and quarrelsome a companion, Socrates replied, "That being daily inured to ill-humor at home, he was the better prepared to encounter perverseness and injury abroad." After all, however, it is probable that the infirmities of this good woman have been exaggerated, and that calumny has had some hand in finishing her picture; for Socrates himself, in a dialogue with his son Lamprocles, allows her many domestic virtues; and we find her afterwards expressing great affection for her husband during his imprisonment. She must have been as deficient in understanding, as she was froward in disposition, if she had not profited by the daily lessons which for twenty years she received from such a master.

In the midst of domestic vexations and public disorders, Socrates retained such an unruffled serenity, that he was never seen either to leave his own house, or to return home, with a disturbed countenance. If upon any occasion he felt a propensity towards anger, he checked the rising storm by lowering the tone of his voice, and resolutely assuming a more than usual gentleness of aspect and manner. He not only refrained from acts of revenge, but triumphed over his adversaries, by despising the insults and injuries which they offered him. In all situations, as will more fully appear in the sequel, he exercised that self-command which is founded on virtuous principles, and strengthened by reflection and habit.

In acquiring this entire dominion over his passions and appetites, Socrates had the greater merit, as it was not effected without a violent struggle against his natural propensities.

Zopyrus, an eminent physiognomist, declared that he discovered in the features of the philosopher evident traces of many vicious inclinations. The friends of Socrates, who were present, ridiculed the ignorance of this pretender to extraordinary sagacity. But Socrates himself ingenuously acknowledged his penetration, and confessed that he was, in his natural disposition, prone to vice, but that he had subdued his inclination by the power of reason and philosophy.

Through the whole course of his life, Socrates gave himself up to the direction of the divine power of reason. And this is, perhaps, all that we are to understand by the genius, or dæmon, which is said to have, from time to time, given him instruction; though his disciples, who admitted the ancient doctrine of the existence of dæmons, or spirits of a middle order between God and man, probably from obscure or figurative expressions which he had made use of, imagined that there was, in this matter, something supernatural; a notion which they would the more easily admit, and be the more ready to propagate, as they would naturally conceive it to reflect great honor upon the memory of their master. It is possible, indeed, that Socrates himself might, in some degree, be influenced by superstitious credulity concerning this dæmon; for it is expressly attested by Xenophon that he believed that the Gods sometimes communicate to men the knowledge of future events, and that on this principle he encouraged the practice of divination.

It was one of the maxims of Socrates, "that a wise man will worship the Gods according to the institutions of the state to which he belongs." He taught, however a doctrine concerning religion much more pure and rational than that which was delivered to the people by the priests, and he reprobated the popular fables concerning the Gods. Convinced of the weakness of the human understanding, and perceiving that the pride of philosophy had led his predecessors into futile speculations on the nature and origin of things, he judged it most consistent with true wisdom to speak with caution and reverence concerning the divine nature. Nevertheless, there can be no doubt that, whilst he did not deny the existence of inferior divinities, he acknowledged the being and providence of one Supreme Deity, and paid homage, with a pious mind, to the Sovereign Power.

In fine, Socrates, both on account of his abilities as a moral preceptor, and on account of his personal merit, unquestionably deserves to be ranked in the first order of human beings. "The man," says Xenophon, "whose memoirs I have written, was so pious, that he undertook nothing without asking counsel of the Gods; so just, that he never did the smallest injury to any one, but rendered essential services to many; so temperate, that he never preferred pleasure to virtue; and so wise, that he was able, even in the most difficult cases, without advice, to judge what was expedient and right. He was eminently qualified to assist others by his counsel; to penetrate into men's characters; to reprehend them for their vices; and to excite them to the practice of virtue. Having found all these excellences in Socrates, I have ever esteemed him the most virtuous, and the happiest of men."

The wisdom and the virtues of this great man, whilst they procured him many followers, also created him many enemies. There were at this time in Athens a large body of professional preceptors of eloquence, distinguished by the appellation of Sophists. By the mere pomp of words, these men made a magnificent display of wisdom, upon a slight foundation of real knowledge; and they taught an artificial structure of language, and a false method of reasoning, by means of which they were able, in argument, to make the worse appear the better cause. At the same time that they arrogantly assumed to themselves the merit of every kind of learning, they publicly practiced the art of disputing with plausibility on either side of any question, and professed to teach this art to the Athenian youth. By these imposing pretensions they collected in their schools, a numerous train of young men, who followed them in hope of acquiring those talents which would give them weight and authority in popular assemblies. In such high repute were these Sophists, that they were liberally supported, not only by contributions from their pupils, but by a regular salary from the State, and were in many instances distinguished by public honors, and employed in offices of magistracy.

That such systematical provision should be made for corrupting the principles and taste of the Athenian youth, was much lamented by all honest men, and particularly by Socrates, whose good sense revolted against every idle abuse of language and pernicious perversion of reason, and whose public spirit would not suffer him to remain an inactive spectator of this growing evil. In order to dissipate the fascination which these pretenders to wisdom had spread over the minds of youth, Socrates daily employed himself, after his peculiar manner, in perplexing them with questions, which were ingeniously contrived to expose their ignorance and convince the public of their dishonesty. The result was that the Sophists began to be deserted, and the Athenian youth to return to the love and pursuit of true wisdom. The contest, though salutary to Athens, proved, in the issue, fatal to Socrates.

The Sophists, finding their reputation and emoluments daily declining, became inveterate in their enmity against this bold reformer, and eagerly seized every occasion of exposing him to public ridicule or censure. Whilst Socrates was prosecuting his design of instructing the Athenian youth with increasing reputation and success, his enemies devised an expedient, by means of which they hoped to check the current of his popularity. They engaged Aristophanes, the first buffoon of the age, to write a comedy, in which Socrates should be the principal character. Aristophanes, pleased with so prominent an occasion of displaying his low and malignant wit, undertook the task, and produced the comedy of *The*

Clouds, still extant in his works. In this piece Socrates is introduced hanging in a basket in the air, and thence pouring forth absurdity and profaneness. The philosopher, though he seldom visited the theatre, except when the tragedies of Euripides were performed, attended the representation of this play, at a time when the house was crowded with strangers, who happened to be at Athens, during the celebration of a Bacchanalian festival. When the performer who represented Socrates appeared upon the stage, a general whisper passed among the benches on which the strangers sat, to inquire who the person was whom the poet meant to satirize. Socrates, who had taken his station in one of the most public parts of the theatre, observed this circumstance, and immediately, with great coolness, rose up, to gratify the curiosity of the audience, and continued standing during the remainder of the representation. One of the spectators, astonished at the magnanimity which this action discovered, asked him whether he did not feel himself much chagrined to be thus held up to public derision? "By no means," replied Socrates, "I am only a host at a public festival, where I provide a large company with entertainment." It is related that when Socrates heard Plato recite his Lysis, he said, "How much does this young man make me say which I never conceived."

The Athenians, who had always a strong propensity to jealousy and detraction, foolishly suffered themselves to be amused by this infamous libel upon the first character in their city. But the seasonable confidence which Socrates discovered in his own innocence and merit, and the uniform consistency and dignity of his conduct, screened him for the present from the assaults of envy and malice. When Aristophanes attempted, the year following, to renew the piece with alterations and additions, the representation was so much discouraged that he was obliged to discontinue it. The consequence was, that the Sophists, and other opponents of Socrates, who appear to have made use of the expedient of theatrical representation in order to sound the inclinations of the public, chose to postpone the further prosecution of their malignant intention to a more favorable opportunity.

From this time Socrates continued, for many years, to pursue without interruption, his laudable design of instructing and reforming his fellow-citizens. At length, however, when the inflexible integrity with which he had discharged the duty of a senator, and the firmness with which he had opposed every kind of political corruption and oppression, both under the democracy and the oligarchy, had greatly increased the number of his enemies, the conspiracy which had long been concerted against his life was resumed. After the dissolution of the tyranny, clandestine arts were employed to raise a general prejudice against him. The people were industriously reminded that Critias, who had been one of the most cruel of the Thirty Tyrants, and Alcibiades, who had insulted religion by defacing the public statues of Mercury, and performing a mock representation of the Eleusinian mysteries, had in their youth been disciples of Socrates.

The minds of the people being thus artfully prepared for the sequel, the enemies of Socrates preferred a direct accusation against him before the supreme court of judicature. His accusers were Anytus, a leather-dresser, who had long entertained a personal enmity against Socrates, for reprehending his avarice, in depriving his sons of the benefit of learning, that they might pursue the gains of trade; Melitus, a young rhetorician, who was capable of undertaking anything for the sake of gain, and Lycon, who was glad of any opportunity of displaying his talents.

This charge was delivered upon oath to the senate, and Crito, a friend of Socrates, became surety for his appearance on the day of trial. Anytus soon afterwards sent a private message to Socrates, assuring him, that if he would desist from censuring his conduct he would withdraw his accusation. But Socrates refused to comply with so degrading a condition, and with his usual spirit replied, "Whilst I live I will never disguise the truth, nor speak otherwise than my duty requires." The interval between the accusation and the trial he spent in philosophical conversations with his friends, choosing to discourse upon any other subject rather than his own situation. Hermogenes, one of his friends, was much struck with this circumstance, and asked him why he did not employ his time in preparing his defence? "Because," replied Socrates, "I have never in my life done anything unjust." The eminent orator Lysias composed an apology, in the name of his master, which he requested him to adopt; but Socrates excused himself by saying, "Though it is eloquently written, it will not suit my character."

When the day of trial arrived, his accusers appeared in the senate, and attempted to support their charge in three distinct speeches, which strongly marked their respective characters. Plato, who was a young man, and a zealous follower of Socrates, then rose up to address the judges in defence of his master; but, whilst he was attempting to apologize for his youth, he was abruptly commanded by the court to sit down. Socrates, however, needed no advocate. Ascending the chair with all the serenity of conscious innocence, and with all the dignity of superior merit, he delivered, in a firm and manly tone, an unpremeditated defence of himself, which silenced his opponents, and ought to have convinced his judges. After tracing the progress of the conspiracy which had been raised against him to its true source, the jealousy and resentment of men whose ignorance he had exposed, and whose vices he had ridiculed and reproved, he distinctly replied to the several charges brought against him by Melitus. To prove that he had not been guilty of impiety towards the Gods of his country, he appealed to his frequent practice of attending the public religious festivals. The crime of introducing new divinities, with which he was charged, chiefly, as it seems, on the ground of the admonitions which he professed to have received from an invisible power, he disclaimed, by pleading, that it was no new thing for men to consult the Gods, and receive instructions from them. To refute the charge of his having been a corrupter of youth, he urged the example which he had uniformly exhibited of justice, moderation, and temperance, the moral spirit and tendency of his discourses, and the effect which had actually been produced by his doctrine upon the manners of the young. Then, disdaining to solicit the mercy of his judges, he called upon them for that justice, which their office and their oath obliged them to administer, and professing his faith and confidence in God, resigned himself to their pleasure.

The judges, whose prejudices would not suffer them to pay due attention to this apology, or to examine with impartiality the merits of the cause, immediately declared him guilty of the crimes of which he stood accused. Socrates, in this stage of the trial, had a right to enter his plea against the punishment which the accusers demanded, and instead of the sentence of death, to propose some pecuniary amercement. But he at first peremptorily refused to make any proposal of this kind, imagining that it might be construed into an acknowledgment of guilt, and asserted that his conduct merited from the State reward rather than punishment. At length, however, he was prevailed upon by his friends to offer, upon their credit, a fine of thirty *minæ*. The judges, notwithstanding, still remained inexorable: they proceeded without further delay, to pronounce sentence upon him; and he was condemned to be put to death by the poison of hemlock. Socrates received the sentence with perfect composure, and by a smile testified his contempt both for his accusers and his judges. Then, turning to his friends, he expressed his entire satisfaction in the recollection of his past life, and declared himself firmly persuaded that posterity would do so much justice to his memory as to believe that he had never injured or corrupted any one, but had spent his days in serving his fellow-citizens, by communicating to them, without reward, the precepts of wisdom. Conversing in this manner, he was conducted from the court to the prison, which he entered with a serene countenance and a lofty mind, amidst the lamentations of his friends.

On the day of the condemnation, it happened that the ship, which was employed to carry a customary annual offering to the island of Delos, set sail. It was contrary to the law of Athens, that during this voyage, any capital punishment should be inflicted within the city. This circumstance delayed the execution of the sentence against Socrates for thirty days. So long an interval of painful expectation, however, only served to afford further scope for the display of his constancy. When his friends were with him, he conversed with his usual cheerfulness. In their absence, he amused himself with writing verses. He composed a hymn in honor of Apollo and Diana, and versified a fable of Æsop. His friends, still anxious to save so valuable a life, urged him to attempt his escape, or at least to permit them to convey him away; and Crito went so far as to assure him that, by his interest with the jailer, it might be easily accomplished, and to offer him a retreat in Thessaly; but Socràtes rejected the proposal, as a criminal violation of the laws; and asked them, "Whether there was any place out of Attica which death could not reach."

News being at length brought of the return of the ship from Delos, the officers to whose care he was committed delivered to Socrates, early in the morning, the final order for his execution, and immediately, according to the law, set him at liberty from his bonds. His friends who came early to the prison, that they might have an opportunity of conversing with their master through the day, found his wife sitting by him with a child in her arms. As soon as Xanthippe saw them she burst into tears, and said, "O Socrates, this is the last time your friends will ever speak to you, or you to them." Socrates, that the tranquillity of his last moments might not be disturbed by her unavailing lamentations, requested that she might be conducted home. With the most frantic expressions of grief, she left the prison. An interesting conversation then passed between Socrates and his friends, which chiefly turned upon the immortality of the soul. In the course of this conversation Socrates expressed his disapprobation of the practice of suicide, and assured his friends that his chief support in his present situation, was an expectation, though not unmixed with doubts, of a happy existence after death. "It would be inexcusable in me," said he, "to despise death, if I were not persuaded that it will conduct me into the presence of the Gods, who are the most righteous governors, and into the society of just and good men; but I derive confidence from the hope that something of man remains after death, and that the condition of good men will then be much better than that of the bad." Crito afterwards asking him in what manner he wished to be buried, Socrates replied with a smile, "As you please, provided I do not escape out of your hands." Then, turning to the rest of his friends, he said, "Is it not strange, after all that I have said to convince you that I am going to the society of the happy, that Crito still thinks this body, which will soon be a lifeless corpse, to be Socrates? Let him dispose of my body as he pleases, but let him not, at its interment, mourn over it as if it were Socrates."

Towards the close of the day Socrates retired into an adjoining apartment to bathe, his friends, in the meantime, expressing to one another their grief at the prospect of losing so excellent a father, and being left to pass the rest of their days in the solitary state of orphans. After a short interval, during which he gave some necessary instructions to his domestics, and took his last leave of his children, the attendant of the prison informed him that the time for drinking the poison was come. The executioner, though accustomed to such scenes, shed tears as he presented the fatal cup. Socrates received it without change of countenance, or the least appearance of perturbation; then, offering up a prayer to the Gods, that they would grant him a prosperous passage into the invisible world, with perfect composure he swallowed the poisonous draught. His friends around him burst into tears. Socrates alone remained unmoved. He upbraided their pusillanimity, and entreated them to exercise a manly constancy, worthy of the friends of virtue. He continued walking till the chilling operation of the hemlock obliged him to lie down upon his bed. After remaining for a short time silent, he requested Crito (probably in order to refute a calumny which might prove injurious to his friends after his decease) not to neglect the offering of a cock which he had vowed to Esculapius. Then covering himself with his cloak, he expired. Such was the fate of the virtuous Socrates! "A story," says Cicero, "which I never read without tears."

The friends and disciples of this illustrious teacher of wisdom were deeply affected by his death, and attended his funeral with every expression of grief. Apprehensive, however, for their own safety, they soon afterwards privately withdrew from the city, and took up their residences in distant places. Several of them visited the philosopher Euclid, of Megara, by whom they were kindly received.

No sooner was the unjust condemnation of Socrates known through Greece than a general indignation was kindled in the minds of good men, who universally regretted that so distinguished an advocate for virtue should have fallen a sacrifice to jealousy and envy. The Athenians themselves, so remarkable for their caprice, who never knew the value of their great men till after their death, soon became sensible of the folly, as well as criminality, of putting to death the man who had been the chief ornament of their city, and of the age, and turned their indignation against his accusers. Melitus was condemned to death, and Anytus, to escape a similar fate, went into voluntary exile. To give a further proof of the sincerity of their regret, the Athenians, for awhile, interrupted public business; decreed a general mourning; recalled the exiled friends of Socrates; and erected a statue to his memory in one of the most frequented parts of the city. His death happened in the first year of the ninety-sixth Olympiad, and in the seventieth year of his age.

SOLON.

This eminent philosopher flourished about the year 597 before Christ. Plutarch gives the following account of him: His father having injured his fortune by indulging his great and munificent spirit, though the son might have been supported by his friends, yet as he was of a family that had long been assisting others, he was ashamed to accept of assistance himself; and, therefore, in his younger years, applied himself to merchandise. Some, however, say that he travelled rather to gratify his curiosity, and extend his knowledge, than to raise an estate. For he professed his love of wisdom, and when far advanced in years, made this declaration,—"I grow old in the pursuit of learning." He was not too much attached to wealth, as we may gather from the following verses:—

The man that boasts of golden stores,
Of grain that loads his bending floors,
Of fields with fresh'ning herbage green,
Where bounding steeds and herds are seen,
I call not happier than the swain,
Whose limbs are sound, whose food is plain,
Whose joys a blooming wife endears,
Whose hours a smiling offspring cheers.

Yet, in another place, he says—

The flow of riches, though desir'd,
Life's real goods, if well acquir'd,
Unjustly let me never gain,
Lest vengeance follow in their train.

If Solon was too expensive and luxurious in his way of living, and indulged his poetical vein in his description of pleasure too freely for a philosopher, it is imputed to his mercantile life; for, as he passed through many and great dangers, he might surely compensate them with a little relaxation and enjoyment. But that he placed himself rather in the class of the poor than the rich, is evident from these lines:—

For vice, though Plenty fills her horn,
And virtue sinks in want and scorn;
Yet never, sure, shall Solon change
His truth for wealth's most easy range!
Since virtue lives, and truth shall stand
While wealth eludes the grasping hand.

He seems to have made use of his poetical talent at first, not for any serious purpose, but only for amusement, and to fill up his hours of leisure; but afterwards he inserted moral sentences, and interwove many political transactions in his poems, not for the sake of recording or remembering them, but sometimes by way of apology for his own administration, and sometimes to exhort, to advise, or to censure the citizens of Athens. Some are of opinion, that he attempted to put his laws, too, in verse; and they give us this beginning:—

Supreme of Gods, whose power we first address,
This plan to honor and these laws to bless.

Like most of the sages of those times, he cultivated chiefly that part of moral philosophy, which treats of civil obligations. His physics were of a very simple and ancient cast, as appears from the following lines:—

From cloudy vapors falls the treasur'd snow,
And the fierce hail; from lightning's rapid blaze
Springs the loud thunder—winds disturb the deep,
Than whose unruffled breast no smoother scene
In all the works of nature!—

We have a particular account of a conversation which Solon had with Anacharsis, and of another he had with Thales.

Anacharsis went to Solon's house at Athens, knocked at the door, and said,—"He was a stranger, who desired to enter into engagements of friendship and mutual hospitality with him." Solon answered,—"Friendships are best formed at home." "Then do you," said Anacharsis, "who are at home, make me your friend and receive me into your house." Struck with the quickness of his repartee, Solon gave him a kind welcome, and kept him some time with him, being then employed in public affairs and in modelling his laws. When Anacharsis knew what Solon was about, he laughed at his undertaking, and at the absurdity of imagining he could restrain the avarice and injustice of the citizens by written laws, which in all respects resembled spider's webs, and would, like them, only entangle, and hold the poor and weak, while the rich and powerful easily broke through them. To this Solon replied, "Men keep their agreements, when it is an advantage to both parties not to break them; and he would so frame his laws, as to make it evident to the Athenians, that it would be more for their interest to observe them than to transgress them." The event, however, showed that Anacharsis was nearer the truth in his conjecture, than Solon was in his hope. Anacharsis having seen an assembly of the people at Athens, said—"He was surprised at this, that in Greece wise men pleaded causes, and fools determined them."

When Solon was entertained by Thales at Miletus, he expressed some wonder that "he did not marry and raise a family." To this Thales gave no immediate answer; but some days after he instructed a stranger to say,—"That he came from Athens ten days before." Solon inquiring, "What news there was at Athens?" the man, according to his instructions, said,—"None, except the funeral of a young man, which was attended by the whole city; for he was the son (as they told me) of a person of great honor, and of the highest reputation for virtue, who was then abroad upon his travels." "What a miserable man is he," said Solon; "but what was his name?" "I have heard his name," answered the stranger, "but do not recollect it; all I remember is, that there was much talk of his wisdom and justice." Solon, whose apprehensions increased with every reply, was now much disconcerted, and mentioned his own name, asking,—"Whether it was not Solon's son that was dead?" The stranger answering in the affirmative, he began to beat his head, and to do and say such things as are usual to men in a transport of grief.* Then Thales, taking him by the hand, said, with a smile,—"These things which strike down so firm a man as Solon, kept me from marriage and from having children; but take courage, my good friend, for not a word of what has been told you is true." Hermippus says, he took this story from Patæcus, who used to boast that he had the soul of Æsop.

When the Athenians, tired out with a long and troublesome war against the Megarensians for the isle of Salamis, made a law that no one for the future, under the pain of death, should either by speech or writing propose that the city should assert its claim to that island, Solon was very uneasy at so dishonorable a decree, and seeing great part of the youth desirous to begin the war again, being restrained from it only by fear of the law, he feigned himself insane;† and a report spread from his house into the city, that he was out of his senses. Privately, however, he had composed an elegy, and got it by heart, in order to repeat it in public; thus prepared, he sallied out unexpectedly into the market-place with a cap

* Whether on this occasion, or on the real loss of a son, is uncertain, Solon, being desired not to weep, since weeping would avail nothing; he answered with much humanity and good sense,—"And for this cause I weep."

† When the Athenians were delivered from their fears by the death of Epaminondas, they began to squander away upon shows and plays the money that had been assigned for the pay of the army and navy, and at the same time they made it death for any one to propose a reformation. In that case, Demosthenes did not, like Solon, attack their error under a pretence of insanity, but boldly and resolutely spoke against it, and by the force of his eloquence brought them to correct it.

upon his head.* A great number of people flocking about him there, he got upon the herald's stone, and sung the elegy which begins thus:—

> Hear and attend; from Salamis I came
> To show your error.

This composition is entitled *Salamis*, and consists of a hundred very beautiful lines. When Solon had done, his friends began to express their admiration, and Pisistratus in particular exerted himself in persuading the people to comply with his directions; whereupon they repealed the law, once more undertook the war, and invested Solon with the command. The common account of his proceedings is this:—He sailed with Pisistratus to Colias, and having seized the women, who, according to the custom of the country, were offering sacrifice to Ceres there, he sent a trusty person to Salamis, who was to pretend he was a deserter, and to advise the Megarensians, if they had a mind to seize the principal Athenian matrons, to set sail immediately for Colias. The Megarensians readily embracing the proposal, and sending out a body of men, Solon discovered the ship as it put off from the island; and causing the women directly to withdraw, ordered a number of young men whose faces were yet smooth, to dress themselves in their habits, caps, and shoes. Thus, with weapons concealed under their clothes, they were to dance and play by the sea-side till the enemy was landed, and the vessel near enough to be seized. Matters being thus ordered, the Megarensians were deceived with the appearance, and ran confusedly on shore, striving which should first lay hold on the women. But they met with so warm a reception that they were cut off to a man; and the Athenians embarking immediately for Salamis, took possession of the island.

Others deny that it was recovered in this manner, and tell

* None wore caps but the sick.

us, that Apollo, being first consulted at Delphi, gave this answer:—

> Go, first propitiate the country's chiefs
> Hid in Æsopus' lap; who, when interr'd,
> Fac'd the declining sun.

Upon this Solon crossed the sea by night, and offered sacrifices in Salamis to the heroes Periphemus and Cichreus. Then taking five hundred Athenian volunteers, who had obtained a decree, that if they conquered the island, the government of it should be invested in them, he sailed with a number of fishing-vessels and one galley of thirty oars for Salamis, where he cast anchor at a point which looks towards Eubœa.

The Megarensians that were in the place, having heard a confused report of what had happened, betook themselves in a disorderly manner to arms, and sent a ship to discover the enemy. As the ship approached too near, Solon took it, and securing the crew, put in their place some of the bravest of the Athenians, with orders to make the best of their way to the city as privately as possible. In the meantime, with the rest of his men, he attacked the Megarensians by land, and while these were engaged, those from the ship took the city. A custom which obtained afterwards seems to bear witness to the truth of this account; for an Athenian ship, once a-year, passed silently to Salamis, and the inhabitants coming down upon it with noise and tumult, one man in armor leaped ashore, and ran shouting towards the the promontory of Sciradium, to meet those who were advancing by land. Near that place is a temple of Mars erected by Solon; for there it was that he defeated the Megarensians, and dismissed, upon certain conditions, such as were not slain in battle.

However, the people of Megara persisted in their claim, till both sides had severely felt the calamities of war; and then they referred the affair to the decision of the Lacedæmonians. Many authors relate that Solon availed himself of a passage in Homer's catalogue of ships, which he alleged before the arbitrators, dexterously inserting a line of his own; for to this verse,

Ajax from Salamis twelve ships commands,

he is said to have added,

And ranks his forces with th' Athenian power.

But the Athenians look upon this as an idle story, and tell us, that Solon made it appear to the judges, that Philæus and Eurysaces, sons of Ajax, being admitted by the Athenians to the freedom of their city, gave up the island to them, and removed, the one to Brauron, and the other to Melite in Attica; likewise, that the tribe of the Philaidæ, of which Pisistratus was, had its name from that Philæus. He brought another argument against the Megarensians from the manner of burying in Salamis, which was agreeable to the custom of Athens, and not to that of Megara; for the Megarensians inter the dead with their faces to the east, and the Athenians turn theirs to the west. On the other hand, Hereas of Megara insists that the Megarensians likewise turn the faces of the dead to the west; and what is more, that, like the people of Salamis, they put three or four corpses in one tomb, whereas the Athenians have a separate tomb for each. But Solon's cause was further assisted by certain oracles of Apollo, in which the island was called *Ionian* Salamis. This matter was determined by five Spartans, Critolaïdes, Amompharetus, Hypsechidas, Anaxilas, and Cleomenes.

Solon acquired considerable honor and authority in Athens by this affair; but he was much more celebrated among the Greeks in general for negotiating succors for the temple at Delphi, against the insolent and injurious behavior of the Cirrhæans,* and persuading the Greeks to arm for the honor

* The inhabitants of Cirrha, a town seated in the bay of Corinth, after having by repeated incursions wasted the territory of Delphi, besieged the city itself, from a desire of making themselves masters of the riches contained in the temple of Apollo. Advice of this being sent to the *Amphictyons*, who were the states-general of Greece, Solon advised that this matter should be universally resented.

of the God. At his motion it was that the *Amphictyons* declared war, as Aristotle, among others, testifies, in his book concerning the Pythian games, where he attributes that decree to Solon.

The execrable proceeding against the accomplices of Cylon, had long occasioned great troubles in the Athenian state. The conspirators had taken sanctuary in Minerva's temple; but Megacles, then archon, persuaded them to quit it, and stand trial, under the notion that if they tied a thread to the shrine of the goddess, and kept hold of it, they would still be under her protection. But when they came over against the temple of the Furies, the thread broke of itself; upon which Megacles and his colleagues rushed upon them, and seized them, as if they had lost their privilege. Such as were out of the temple were stoned; those that fled to the altars were cut in pieces there; and they only were spared who made application to the wives of the magistrates. From that time those magistrates were called *execrable*, and became objects of the public hatred. The remains of Cylon's faction afterwards recovered strength, and kept up the quarrel with the descendants of Megacles. The dispute was greater than ever, and the two parties more exasperated, when Solon, whose authority was now very great, and others of the principal Athenians, interposed, and by entreaties and arguments persuaded the persons called *execrable* to submit to justice and a fair trial, before three

Accordingly, Clisthenes, tyrant of Sicyon, was sent commander-in-chief against the Cirrhæans; Alcmæon was general of the Athenian quota; and Solon went as counsellor or assistant to Clisthenes. When the Greek army had besieged Cirrha some time, without any great appearance of success, Apollo was consulted, who answered, that they should not be able to reduce the place till the waves of the Cirrhæan sea washed the territories of Delphi. This answer struck the army with surprise; from which Solon extricated them, by advising Clisthenes to consecrate the whole territories of Cirrha to the Delphic Apollo, whence it would follow that the sea must wash the sacred coast. Pausanias (*in Phocicis*) mentions another stratagem, which was not worthy of the justice of Solon. Cirrha, however, was taken, and became henceforth the arsenal of of Delphi.

hundred judges selected from the nobility. Myron, of the *Phylensian* ward, carried on the impeachment, and they were condemned. As many as were alive, were driven into exile; and the bodies of the dead dug up and cast out beyond the borders of Attica. Amidst these disturbances, the Megarensians renewed the war, took Nisæ from the Athenians, and recovered Salamis once more.

About this time the city was likewise afflicted with superstitious fears and strange appearances; and the soothsayers declared, that there were certain abominable crimes, which wanted expiation, pointed out by the entrails of the victims. Upon this they sent to Crete for Epimenides the *Phæstian*,* who is reckoned the seventh among the wise men, by those that do not admit Periander into the number. He was reputed a man of great piety, and loved by the Gods, and skilled in matters of religion, particularly in what related to inspiration and the sacred mysteries; therefore the men of those days called him the son of nymph Balte, and one of the *Curetes* revived. When he arrived at Athens, he contracted a friendship with Solon, and privately gave him considerable assistance, preparing the way for the reception of his laws. For he taught the Athenians to be more frugal in their religious worship, and more moderate in their mourning, by intermixing certain sacrifices with the funeral solemnities, and abolishing the cruel and barbarous customs that had generally prevailed among

* This Epimenides was a very extraordinary person. Diogenes Laërtius tells us, that he was the inventor of the art of lustrating or purifying houses, fields, and persons; which, if spoken of Greece, may be true; but Moses had long before taught the Hebrews something of this nature.—(*Vide* Levit. xvi.) Epimenides took some sheep that were all black, and others that were all white; these he led into the Areopagus, and turning them loose, directed certain persons to follow them, who should mark where they couched, and there sacrifice them to the local diety. This being done, altars were erected in all these places to perpetuate the memory of this solemn expiation. There were, however, other ceremonies practiced for the purpose of lustration, of which Tizetzes, in his poetical chronicle, gives a particular account, but which are too trifling to be mentioned here.

the women before. What is of still greater consequence, by expiations, lustrations, and the erecting of temples and shrines, he hallowed and purified the city, and made the people more observant of justice, and more inclined to union.

When he had seen Munychia, and considered it some time, he is reported to have said to those about him,* "How blind is man to futurity! If the Athenians could foresee what trouble that place will give them, they would tear it in pieces with their teeth rather than it should stand." Something similar to this is related of Thales; for he ordered the Milesians to bury him in a certain recluse and neglected place, and foretold, at the same time, that their market-place would one day stand there. As for Epimenides, he was held in admiration at Athens; great honors were paid him, and many valuable presents made; yet he would accept of nothing but a branch of the sacred olive, which they gave him at his request; and with that he departed.

When the troubles about Cylon's affairs were over, and the sacrilegious persons removed in the manner we have mentioned, the Athenians relapsed into their old disputes concerning the government; for there were as many parties among them as there were different tracts of land in their country. The inhabitants of the mountainous part were, it seems, for a democracy; those of the plains for an oligarchy; and those of the sea-coasts, contending for a mixed kind of government, hindered the other two from gaining their point. At the same time, the inequality between the poor and the rich occasioned the greatest discord; and the State was in so danger-

* This prediction was fulfilled 270 years after, when Antipater constrained the Athenians to admit his garrison into that place. Besides this prophecy, Epimenides uttered another during his stay at Athens; for hearing that the citizens were alarmed at the progress of the Persian power at sea, he advised them to make themselves easy, for that the Persians would not for many years attempt anything against the Greeks, and when they did, they would receive greater loss themselves than they would be able to bring upon the States they thought to destroy.—*Laërt. in Vitâ et Rimen.*

ous a situation, that there seemed to be no way to quell the seditious, or to save it from ruin, but changing it to a monarchy. So greatly were the poor in debt to the rich, that they were obliged either to pay them a sixth part of the produce of the land (whence they were called *Hectemorii* and *Thetes*), or else to engage their persons to their creditors, who might seize them on failure of payment. Accordingly, some made slaves of them, and others sold them to foreigners. Nay, some parents were forced to sell their own children (for no law forbade it), and to quit the city, to avoid the severe treatment of those usurers. But the greater number, and men of the most spirit, agreed to stand by each other, and to bear such impositions no longer. They determined to choose a trusty person for their leader, to deliver those who had failed in their time of payment, to divide the land, and to give an entire new face to the commonwealth.

Then the most prudent of the Athenians cast their eyes upon Solon, as a man least obnoxious to either party, having neither been engaged in oppressions with the rich, nor entangled in necessities with the poor. Him, therefore, they entreated to assist the public in this exigency, and to compose these differences. Phanias, the Lesbian, asserts, indeed, that Solon, to save the State, dealt artfully with both parties, and privately promised the poor a division of the lands, and the rich a confirmation of their securities. At first he was loth to take the administration upon him, by reason of the avarice of some, and the insolence of others; but was, however, chosen archon next after Philombrotus, and at the same time arbitrator and lawgiver; the rich accepting of him readily as one of *them*, and the poor as a good and worthy man. They tell us, too, that a saying of his, which he had let fall some time before, that—"equality causes no war," was then much repeated, and pleased both the rich and the poor; the latter expecting to come to a balance by their numbers and by the measure of divided lands, and the former to preserve an equality at least by their dignity and power. Thus both parties being in great hopes, the heads of them were urgent with Solon to make himself king, and endeavored to persuade him that he might with better assurance take upon him the direction of a city where he had the supreme authority. Nay, many of the citizens that leaned to neither party, seeing the intended change difficult to be effected by reason and law, were not against the entrusting of the government to the hands of one wise and just man. Some, moreover, acquaint us, that he received this oracle from Apollo:—

Seize, seize the helm, the reeling vessel guide,
With aiding patriots stem the raging tide.

His friends, in particular, told him it would appear that he wanted courage, if he rejected the monarchy for fear of the name of tyrant, as if the sole and supreme power would not soon become a lawful sovereignty through the virtues of him that received it. Thus formerly (said they) the Eubœans set up Tynnondas, and lately the Mitylenæans Pittacus for their prince. None of these things moved Solon from his purpose; and the answer he is said to have given to his friends is this:—"Absolute monarchy is a fair field, but it has no outlet." And in one of his poems he thus addresses himself to his friend Phocus:—

———If I spar'd my country,
If gilded violence and tyrannic sway
Could never charm me, thence no shame accrues;
Still the mild honor of my name I boast,
And find my empire there.

Whence it is evident that his reputation was very great before he appeared in the character of a legislator. As for the ridicule he was exposed to for rejecting kingly power, he has described it in the following verses:—

Nor wisdom's palm, nor deep laid policy
Can Solon boast; for when its noblest blessings
Heaven pour'd into his lap, he spurn'd them from him.
Where was his sense and spirit, when enclos'd

He found the choicest prey, nor deign'd to draw it?
Who, to command fair Athens but one day,
Would not himself, with all his race, have fallen
Contented on the morrow?

Thus he has introduced the multitude and men of low minds as discoursing about him. But though he rejected absolute power, he proceeded with spirit enough in the administration. He did not make any concessions in behalf of the powerful, nor, in the framing of his laws, did he indulge the humor of his constituents. Where the former establishment was tolerable, he neither applied remedies, nor used the incision knife, lest he should put the whole in disorder, and not have power to settle or compose it afterwards in the temperature he could wish. He only made such alterations as he might bring the people to acquiesce in by persuasion, or compel them to by his authority, making (as he says)—"force and right conspire." Hence it was, that having the question afterwards put to him,—"Whether he had provided the best of laws for the Athenians?" he answered,—"The best they were capable of receiving." And as the moderns observe, that the Athenians used to qualify the harshness of things by giving them softer and politer names, calling whores *mistresses*, tributes *contributions*, garrisons *guards*, and prisons *castles*; so Solon seems to be the first that distinguished the cancelling of debts by the name of a *discharge*. For this was the first of his public acts, that debts should be forgiven, and that no man for the future should take the body of his debtor for security. Though Androtion and some others say, that it was not by the cancelling of debts, but by moderating the interest, that the poor were relieved, they thought themselves so happy in it, that they gave the name of *discharge* to this act of humanity, as well as to the enlarging of measures and the value of money, which went along with it. For he ordered the *minæ*, which before went but for seventy-three *drachmas*, to go for a hundred; so that, as they paid the same in value, but much less in weight, those that had great sums to pay were relieved, while such as received them were no losers.

The greater part of writers, however, affirm, that it was the abolition of past securities that was called a *discharge;* and with these the poems of Solon agree; for in them he values himself on—"having taken away the marks of mortgaged land,* which before were almost everywhere set up, and made free those fields which before were bound!" and not only so, but—"of such citizens as were seizable by their creditors for debt, some," he tells us, "he had brought back from other countries where they had wandered so long, that they had forgot the Attic dialect, and others he had set at liberty who had experienced a cruel slavery at home."

This affair, indeed, brought upon him the greatest trouble he met with; for when he undertook the annulling of debts, and was considering of a suitable speech, and a proper method of introducing the business, he told some of his most intimate friends, namely Conon, Clinias, and Hipponicus, that he intended only to abolish the debts, and not to meddle with the lands. These friends of his hastening to make their advantage of the secret before the decree took place, borrowed large sums of the rich, and purchased estates with them. Afterwards, when the decree was published, they kept their possessions, without paying the money they had taken up; which brought great reflections upon Solon, as if he had not been imposed upon with the rest, but rather an accomplice in the fraud. This charge, however, was soon removed, by his being the first to comply with the law, and remitting a debt of five talents, which he had out at interest. Others, among whom is Polyzelus the Rhodian, say it was fifteen talents. But his friends went by the name of *Chreocopidæ*, or *debt-cutters*, ever after.

The method he took satisfied neither the poor nor the rich.

* The Athenians had a custom of fixing up billets, to show that houses or lands were mortgaged.

The latter were displeased by the cancelling of their bonds, and the former at not finding a division of lands. Upon this they had fixed their hopes; and they complained that he had not, like Lycurgus, made all the citizens equal in estate. Lycurgus, however, being the eleventh from Hercules, and having reigned many years in Lacedæmon, had acquired great authority, interest, and friends, of which he knew very well how to avail himself in setting up a new form of government; yet he was obliged to have recourse to force rather than persuasion, and had an eye struck out in the dispute, before he could bring it to a lasting settlement, and establish such an union and equality as left neither rich nor poor in the city. On the other hand, Solon's estate was but moderate, not superior to that of some commoners, and, therefore, he attempted not to erect such a commonwealth as that of Lycurgus, considering it as out of his power; he proceeded as far as he thought he could be supported by the confidence the people had in his probity and wisdom.

That he answered not the expectations of the generality, but offended them by falling short, appears from these verses of his:—

Those eyes, with joy once sparkling when they view'd me,
With cold oblique regard behold me now.

And a little after,—

—— Yet who but Solon
Could have spoke peace to their tumultuous waves,
And not have sunk beneath them?

But being soon sensible of the utility of the decree, they laid aside their complaints, offered a public sacrifice, which they called *seisacthia*, or the sacrifice of the *discharge*, and constituted Solon lawgiver and superintendent of the commonwealth; committing to him the regulation not of a part only, but the whole—magistracies, assemblies, courts of judicature, and senate; and leaving him to determine the qualification, number, and time of meeting for them all, as well as to abro gate or continue the former constitution at his pleasure.

First, then, he repealed the laws of Draco, except those concerning murder, because of the severity of the punishments they appointed: which for almost all offences were capital; even those that were convicted of idleness were to suffer death, and such as stole only a few apples or pot-herbs, were to be punished in the same manner as sacrilegious persons and murderers. Hence a saying of Demades, who lived long after, was much admired,—"That Draco wrote his laws not with ink, but with blood." And he himself being asked, "Why he made death the punishment for most offences?" answered, "Small ones deserve it, and I can find no greater for the most heinous."

In the next place, Solon took an estimate of the estates of the citizens; intending to leave the great offices in the hands of the rich, but to give the rest of the people a share in other departments which they had not before. Such as had a yearly income of five hundred measures of wet and dry goods, he placed in the first rank, and called them *Pentacosiomedimni*.* The second consisted of those that could keep a horse, or whose lands produced three hundred measures; these were of the *equestrian* order, and called *Hippoda telountes*. And those of the third class, who had but two hundred measures, were called *Zeugitæ*. The rest were named *Thetes*, and not admitted to any office; they had only a right to appear and give their vote in the general assembly of the people. This seemed at first but a slight privilege, but afterwards showed itself a mat-

* The *Pentacosiomedimni* paid a talent to the public treasury; the *Hippoda telountes*, as the word signifies, were obliged to find a horse, and to serve as cavalry in the wars; the *Zeugitæ* were so called, as being of a middle rank between the knights and those of the lowest order (for rowers who have the middle bench between the Thalamites and the Thranites, are called *Zeugitæ*); and though the *Thetes* had barely each a vote in the general assemblies, yet that (as Plutarch observes) appeared in time to be a great privilege, most causes being brought by appeal before the people.

ter of great importance; for most causes came at last to be decided by them; and in such matters as were under the cognizance of the magistrates, there lay an appeal to the people. Besides, he is said to have drawn up his laws in an obscure and ambigious manner, on purpose to enlarge the authority of the popular tribunal; for as they could not adjust their difference by the letter of the law, they were obliged to have recourse to living judges; I mean the whole body of citizens, who, therefore, had all controversies brought before them, and were in a manner superior to the laws. Of this equality, he himself takes notice in these words:—

> By me the people held their native rights
> Uninjur'd unoppress'd—The great restrain'd
> From lawless violence, and the poor from rapine,
> By me, their mutual shield.

Desirous yet further to strengthen the common people, he empowered any man whatever to enter an action for one that was injured. If a person was assaulted, or suffered damage or violence, another that was able and willing to do it might prosecute the offender. Thus the lawgiver wisely accustomed the citizens, as members of one body, to feel and to resent one another's injuries. And we are told of a saying of his agreeable to this law; being asked,—"What city was best modelled?" he answered;—"That, where those who are not injured, are no less ready to prosecute and punish offenders, than those who are."

When these points were adjusted, he established the council of the *areopagus*,* which was to consist of such as had borne

* The court of *areopagus*, though settled long before, had lost much of its power by Draco's preferring the ephetæ. In ancient times, and till Solon became legislator, it consisted of such persons as were most conspicuous in the state for their wealth, power, and probity; but Solon made it a rule, that such only should have a seat in it as had borne the office of *archon*. This had the effect he designed; it raised the reputation of the *areopagites* very high, and rendered their decrees so venerable, that none contested or repined at them through a long course of ages.

the office of *archon*,* and himself was one of the number. But observing that the people, now discharged from their debts, grew insolent and imperious, he proceeded to constitute another council or senate, of four hundred, a hundred out of each tribe, by whom all affairs were to be previously considered; and ordered that no matter, without their approbation, should be laid before the general assembly. In the meantime, the high court of the *areopagus* were to be the inspectors and guardians of the laws. Thus he supposed the commonwealth, secured by two councils, as by two anchors, would be less liable to be shaken by tumults, and the people would become more orderly and peaceable. Most writers, as we have observed, affirm, that the council of the *areopagus* was of Solon's appointing; and it seems greatly to confirm their assertion, that Draco has made no mention of the *areopagites*, but in capital causes constantly addressed himself to the *ephetæ*; yet the eighth law of Solon's thirteenth table is set down in these very words:—"Whoever were declared infamous before Solon's archonship, let them be restored in honor, except such as having been condemned in the areopagus, or by the ephetæ, or by the kings in the Prytaneum, for murder or robbery, or attempting to usurp the government, had fled their country before this law was made." This on the contrary shows, that before Solon was chief magistrate, and delivered his laws, the council of the *areopagus* was in being; for who could have been condemned in the *areopagus* before Solon's time, if he was the first that erected it into a court of judicature? Unless, perhaps, there be some obscurity or deficiency in the

* After the extinction of the race of the Medontidæ, the Athenians made the office of *archon* annual; and instead of one, they created nine *archons*. By the latter expedient, they provided against the too great power of a single person, as by the former they took away all apprehension of the *archons* setting up for sovereigns. In one word, they attained now what they had long sought—the making their supreme magistrate dependent on the people. This remarkable era of the completion of the Athenian democracy was, according to the *Marmora*, in the first year of the xvivth Olympiad, before Christ 684.

text, and the meaning be, that such as have been convicted of crimes that are now cognizable before the *areopagus*, the *ephetæ*,* and *prytanes*, shall continue infamous, while others are restored. But this I submit to the judgment of the reader.

The most peculiar and surprising of his other laws, is that which declares the man infamous who stands neuter in time of sedition.† It seems he would not have us be indifferent and unaffected with the fate of the public, when our own concerns are upon a safe bottom; nor when we are in health, be insensible to the distempers and griefs of our country. He would have us espouse the better and juster cause, and hazard everything in defence of it, rather than wait in safety to see which side the victory will incline to. That law, too, seems quite ridiculous and absurd, which permits a rich heiress, whose husband happens to be impotent, to console herself with his nearest relations. Yet some say, this law was very properly levelled against those who, conscious of their own inability, match with heiresses for the sake of the portion, and, under color of law, do violence to nature. For when they know that such heiresses may make choice of others to grant their favors to, they will either let those matches alone, or, if they do marry in that manner, they must suffer the shame

* The *ephetæ* were first appointed in the reign of Demophon, the son of Theseus, for the trying of wilful murders, and cases of manslaughter. They consisted at first of fifty Athenians, and as many Argives; but Draco excluded the Argives, and ordered that it should be composed of fifty-one Athenians, who were all to be turned of fifty years of age. He also fixed their authority above that of the areopagites; but Solon brought them under that court, and limited their jurisdiction.

† Aulus Gellius, who has preserved the very words of this law, adds, that one who has stood neuter, should lose his houses, his country and estate, and be sent out an exile.—*Noct. Attic.*, l. ii. c. 12.

Plutarch, in another place, condemns this law; but Gellius highly commends it, and assigns this reason:—The wise and just, as well as the envious and wicked, being obliged to choose some side, matters were easily accommodated; whereas, if the latter only, as is generally the case with other cities, had the management of factions, they would, for private reasons, be continually kept up, to the great hurt, if not the utter ruin, of the State.

of their avarice and dishonesty. It is right that the heiress should not have liberty to choose at large, but only amongst her husband's relations, that the child which is born may, at least, belong to his kindred and family. Agreeable to this is the direction that the bride and bridegroom should be shut up together, and eat of the same quince.*

In all other marriages, he ordered that no dowries should be given; the bride was to bring with her only three suits of clothes, and some household stuff of small value.† For he did not choose that marriages should be made with mercenary or venal views, but would have that union cemented by the endearment of children, and every other instance of love and friendship. Nay, Dionysius himself, when his mother desired to be married to a young Syracusan, told her,—"He had, indeed, by his tyranny broke through the laws of his country, but he could not break those of nature, by countenancing so disproportionate a match." And, surely, such disorders should not be tolerated in any State, nor such matches, where there is no equality of years, or inducements of love, or probability that the end of marriage will be answered. So that to an old man who marries a young woman, some prudent magistrate or lawgiver might express himself in the words addressed to Philoctetes:—

Poor soul! how fit art thou to marry!

And if he found a young man in the house of a rich old woman, like a partridge, growing fat in his private services, he would remove him to some young virgin who wanted a husband. But enough of this.

That law of Solon's is also justly commended, which forbids

* The eating of the quince, which was not peculiar to an heiress and her husband (for all newly-married people ate it), implied that their discourses ought to be pleasant to each other, that fruit making the breath sweet.

† The bride brought with her an earthen pan, called *phrogeteon*, wherein barley was parched; to signify that she undertook the business of the house, and would do her part towards providing for the family.

men to speak ill of the dead. For piety requires us to consider the deceased as sacred; justice calls upon us to spare those that are not in being; and good policy, to prevent the perpetuating of hatred. He forbade his people also to revile the living, in a temple, in a court of justice, in the great assembly of the people, or at the public games. He that offended in this respect, was to pay three *drachmas* to the person injured, and two to the public. Never to restrain anger is, indeed, a proof of weakness or want of breeding; and always to guard against it, is very difficult, and to some persons impossible. Now what is enjoined by law should be practicable, if the legislator desires to punish a few to some good purpose, and not many to no purpose.

His law concerning wills has likewise its merit. For before his time the Athenians were not allowed to dispose of their estates by will: the houses and other substance of the deceased were to remain among his relations. But he permitted any one, that had not children, to leave his possessions to whom he pleased; thus preferring the tie of friendship to that of kindred, and choice to necessity, he gave every man the full and free disposal of his own. Yet he allowed not all sorts of legacies, but those only that were not extorted by frenzy, the consequence of disease or poisons, by imprisonment or violence, or the persuasions of a wife. For he considered inducements, that operated against reason, as no better than force; to be deceived, was with *him* the same thing as to be compelled; and he looked upon pleasure to be as great a perverter as pain.*

He regulated, moreover, the journeys of women, their mournings and sacrifices, and endeavored to keep them clear of all disorder and excess. They were not to go out of town

* He likewise ordained, that adopted persons should make no will; but as soon as they had children lawfully begotten, they were at liberty to return into the family whence they were adopted: or if they continued in it to their death, the estate reverted to the relations of the persons who adopted them.—*Demos in Orat. in Leptin.*

with more than three habits; the provisions they carried with them were not to exceed the value of an *obulus;* their basket was not to be above a cubit high; and in the night they were not to travel but in a carriage, with a torch before them. At funerals, they were forbid to tear themselves,* and no hired mourner was to utter lamentable notes, or to act anything else that tended to excite sorrow. They were not permitted to sacrifice an ox on those occasions; or to bury more than three garments with the body; or to visit any tombs beside those of their own family, except at the time of interment. Most of these things are likewise forbidden by our laws, with the addition of this circumstance, that those who offend in such a manner, are fined by the censors of the women, as giving way to weak passions and childish sorrow.

As the city was filled with persons, who assembled from all parts, on account of the great security in which people lived in Attica, Solon observing this, and that the country withal was poor and barren, and that merchants who traffic by sea do not use to import their goods where they can have nothing in exchange, turned the attention of the citizens to manufactures. For this purpose he made a law, that no son should be obliged to maintain his father, if he had not taught him a trade.† As for Lycurgus, whose city was clear of strangers, and whose country, according to Euripides, was sufficient for twice the number of inhabitants; where there was, moreover, a multitude of *Helotes*, who were not only to be kept constantly em-

* Demosthenes (*in Timocr.*) recites Solon's directions as to funerals as follows:—"Let the dead bodies be laid out in the house according as the deceased gave order, and the day following, before sun-rise, carried forth. Whilst the body is carrying to the grave, let the men go before, the women follow. It shall not be lawful for any woman to enter upon the goods of the dead, and to follow the body to the grave under threescore years of age, except such as are within the degrees of cousins."

† He that was thrice convicted of idleness was to be declared infamous. Herodotus (l. vii.) and Diodorus Siculus (l. i.) agree that a law of this kind was in use in Egypt. It is probable, therefore, that Solon, who was thoroughly acquainted with the learning of that nation, borrowed it from them.

ployed, but to be humbled and worn out by servitude, it was right for him to set the citizens free from laborious and mechanic arts, and to employ them in arms, as the only art fit for them to learn and exercise. But Solon, rather adapting his laws to the state of his country, than his country to his laws, and perceiving that the soil of Attica, which hardly rewarded the husbandman's labor, was far from being capable of maintaining a lazy multitude, ordered that trades should be accounted honorable; that the council of the *areopagus* should examine into every man's means of subsisting, and chastise the idle.

But that law was more rigid, which (as Heraclides of Pontus informs us) excused bastards from relieving their fathers. Nevertheless, the man that disregards so honorable a state as marriage, does not take a woman for the sake of children, but merely to indulge his appetite. He has therefore his rewards; and there remains no pretence for him to upbraid those children, whose very birth he has made a reproach to them.

In truth, his laws concerning women, in general, appear very absurd; for he permitted any one to kill an adulterer taken in the fact;* but if a man committed a rape upon a free woman, he was only to be fined a hundred drachmas; if he gained his purpose by persuasion, twenty; but prostitutes were excepted, because they have their price. And he would not allow them to sell a daughter or sister, unless she were taken in an act of dishonor before marriage. But to punish the same fault sometimes in a severe and rigorous manner, and sometimes lightly and as it were in sport, with a trivial fine, is not agreeable to reason, unless the scarcity of money in Athens at that time made a pecuniary mulct a heavy one. And, indeed, in the valuation of things for the sacrifice, a sheep and a

* No adulteress was to adorn herself, or to assist at the public sacrifices; and in case she did, he gave liberty to any one to tear her clothes off her back, and beat her into the bargain.

medimnus of corn were reckoned each at a *drachma* only. To the victor in the Isthmian games, he appointed a reward of a hundred *drachmas;* and to the victor in the Olympian, five hundred.* He that caught a he-wolf, was to have five *drachmas;* he that took a she-wolf, one; and the former sum (as Demetrius Phalereus asserts) was the value of an ox, the latter of a sheep.

As Attica was not supplied with water from perennial rivers, lakes, or springs, but chiefly by wells dug for that purpose, he made a law, that where there was a public well, all within the distance of four furlongs should make use of it; but where the distance was greater, they were to provide a well of their own. And if they dug ten fathoms deep in their own ground, and could find no water, they had liberty to fill a vessel of six gallons twice a day at their neighbor's. Thus he thought it proper to assist persons in real necessity, but not to encourage idleness. His regulations with respect to the planting of trees were also very judicious. He that planted any tree in his field, was to place it at least five feet from his neighbor's ground; and if it was a fig-tree or an olive, nine; for these extend their roots further than others, and their neighborhood is prejudicial to some trees, not only as they take away the nourishment, but their effluvia is noxious. He that would dig a pit or a ditch, was to dig it as far from another man's ground as it was deep; and if any one would raise a stock of bees, he was to place them three hundred feet from those already raised by another.

Of all the products of the earth, he allowed none to be sold to strangers but oil; and whoever presumed to export anything else, the *archon* was solemnly to declare him accursed, or to pay himself a hundred *drachmas* into the public treas-

* At the same time he contracted the rewards bestowed upon wrestlers, esteeming such gratuities useless, and even dangerous; as they tended to encourage idleness, by putting men upon wasting that time in exercises, which ought to be spent in providing for their families.

ury. This law is in the first table. And therefore it is not absolutely improbable, what some affirm, that the exportation of figs was formerly forbidden, and that the informer against the delinquent was called a sycophant.

He likewise enacted a law for reparation of damage received from beasts. A dog that had bit a man was to be delivered up bound to a log of four cubits long;* an agreeable contrivance for security against such an animal.

But the wisdom of the law concerning the naturalizing of foreigners is a little dubious; because it forbids the freedom of the city to be granted to any but such as are forever exiled from their own country, or transplant themselves to Athens with their whole family, for the sake of exercising some manual trade. This, we are told, he did, not with a view to keep strangers at a distance, but rather to invite them to Athens, upon the sure hope of being admitted to the privilege of citizens; and he imagined the settlement of those might be entirely depended upon, who had been driven from their native country, or had quitted it by choice.

That law is peculiar to Solon which regulates the going to entertainments made at the public charge, by him called *parasitein.*† For he does not allow the same person to repair to them often; and he lays a penalty upon such as refuse to go when invited; looking upon the former as a mark of epicurism, and the latter of contempt of the public.

* This law and several others of Solon, were taken into the twelve tables. In the consulate of T. Romilius and C. Veturius, in the year of Rome, 293, the Romans sent deputies to Athens, to transcribe his laws, and those of the other lawgivers of Greece, in order to form thereby a body of laws for Rome.

† In the first ages the name of *parasite* was venerable and sacred, for it properly signified one that was a messmate at the table of sacrifices. There were in Greece several persons particularly honored with this title, much like those whom the Romans called *epulones*, a religious order instituted by Numa. Solon ordained that every tribe should offer a sacrifice once a month, and at the end of the sacrifice make a public entertainment, at which all who were of that tribe should be obliged to assist by turns.

All his laws were to continue in force for a hundred years, and were written upon wooden tables, which might be turned round in the oblong cases that contained them. Some small remains of them are preserved in the *Prytanium* to this day. They were called *cyrbes*, as Aristotle tells us; and Cratinus, the comic poet, thus spoke of them:—

> By the great names of Solon and of Draco,
> Whose cyrbes now but serve to boil our pulse.

Some say, those tables were properly called *cyrbes*, on which were written the rules for religious rites and sacrifices, and the other *axones*. The senate, in a body, bound themselves by oath to establish the laws of Solon; and the *thesmothetæ*, or guardians of the laws, severally took an oath in a particular form, by the stone in the market-place, that for every law they broke, each would dedicate a golden statue at Delphi of the same weight with himself.*

Observing the irregularity of the month,† and that the moon neither rose nor set at the same time with the sun, as

* Gold, in Solon's time, was so scarce in Greece, that when the Spartans were ordered by the oracle to gild the face of Apollo's statue, they inquired in vain for gold all over Greece, and were directed by the pythoness to buy some of Crœsus, king of Lydia.

† Solon discovered the falseness of Thales' maxim, that the moon performed her revolution in thirty days, and found that the true time was twenty-nine days and a half. He directed, therefore, that each of the twelve months should be accounted twenty-nine or thirty days alternately. By this means a lunar year was formed of 354 days; and to reconcile it to the solar year, he ordered a month of twenty-two days to be intercalated every two years, and at the end of the second two years, he directed that a month of twenty-three days should be intercalated. He likewise engaged the Athenians to divide their months into three parts, styled the beginning, middle, and ending; each of these consisted of ten days, when the month was thirty days long, and the last of nine, when it was nine-and-twenty days long. In speaking of the two first parts, they reckoned according to the usual order of numbers, *viz.* the first, &c. day of the moon, beginning; the first, second, &c. of the moon, middle; but with respect to the last part of the month, they reckoned backwards, that is, instead of saying, the first, second, &c. day of the moon, ending, they said, the tenth, ninth, &c. of the moon, ending. This is a circumstance which should be carefully attended to

it often happened that in the same day she overtook and passed by him, he ordered that the day be called *hene kai nea* (the old and the new); assigning the part of it before the conjunction to the old month, and the rest to the beginning of the new. He seems, therefore, to have been the first who understood that verse in Homer, which makes mention of a day wherein "the old month ended and the new began."*

The day following he called the new moon. After the twentieth he counted not by adding, but subtracting, to the thirtieth, according to the decreasing phases of the moon.

When his laws took place,† Solon had his visitors every day finding fault with some of them, and commending others, or advising him to make certain additions or retrenchments. But the greater part came to desire a reason for this or that article, or a clear and precise explication of the meaning and design. Sensible that he could not well excuse himself from complying with their desires, and that if he indulged their importunity, the doing it might give offence, he

* Odyss. xiv. 162.

† Plutarch has only mentioned such of Solon's laws as he thought the most singular and remarkable: Diogenes Laërtius and Demosthenes have given us an account of some others that ought not to be forgotten:—"Let not the guardian live in the same house with the mother of his wards. Let not the tuition of minors be committed to him who is next after them in the inheritance. Let not an engraver keep the impression of a seal which he has engraved. Let him that puts out the eye of a man who has but one, lose both his own. If an archon is taken in liquor, let him be put to death. Let him who refuses to maintain his father and mother, be infamous; and so let him that has consumed his patrimony. Let him who refuses to go to war, flees, or behaves cowardly, be debarred the precincts of the *forum*, and places of public worship. If a man surprises his wife in adultery, and lives with her afterwards, let him be deemed infamous. Let him who frequents the houses of lewd women, be debarred from speaking in the assemblies of the people. Let a pander be pursued, and put to death if taken. If any man steal in the day-time, let him be carried to the eleven officers; if in the night, it shall be lawful to kill him in the act, or to wound him in the pursuit, and carry him to the aforesaid officers; if he steals common things, let him pay double, and if the convictor thinks fit, be exposed in chains five days; if he be guilty of sacrilege, let him be put to death."

determined to withdraw from the difficulty, and to get rid at once of their cavils and exceptions; for, as he himself observes,

Not all the greatest enterprise can please.

Under pretence therefore of traffic, he set sail for another country, having obtained leave of the Athenians for ten years' absence. In that time he hoped his laws would become familiar to them.

His first voyage was to Egypt, where he abode some time, as he himself relates,

On the Canopian shore, by Nile's deep mouth.

There he conversed upon points of philosophy, with Psenophis the Heliopolitan, and Senchis the Saïte, the most learned of the Egyptian priests; and having an account from them of the Atlantis Island,* (as Plato informs us,) he attempted to describe it to the Grecians in a poem. From Egypt he sailed to Cyprus, and there was honored with the best regards of Philocyprus, one of the kings of that island, who reigned over a small city built by Demophon, the son of Theseus, near the river Clarius, in a strong situation indeed, but very indifferent soil. As there was an agreeable plain below, Solon persuaded him to build a larger and pleasanter city there, and

* Plato finished this history from Solon's memoirs, as may be seen in his Timæus and Critias. He pretends, that this Atlantis, an island situated in the Atlantic ocean, was bigger than Asia and Africa; and that notwithstanding its vast extent, it was drowned in one day and night. Diodorus Siculus says, the Carthaginians, who discovered it, made it death for any one to settle in it. Amidst a number of conjectures concerning it, one of the most probable is, that in those days the Africans had some knowledge of America. Another opinion worth mentioning is, that the *Atlantides*, or *Fortunate* islands, were what we now call the Canaries. Homer thus describes them:—

Stern winter smiles on that auspicious clime:
The fields are florid with unfading prime.
From the bleak pole no winds inclement blow,
Mould the round hail, or flake the fleecy snow;
But from the breezy deep the blest inhale
The fragrant murmurs of the western gale.

to remove the inhabitants of the other to it. He also assisted in laying out the whole, and building it in the best manner for convenience and defence; so that Philocyprus in a short time had it so well peopled, as to excite the envy of the other princes. And therefore, though the former city was called *Aipeia*, yet, in honor of Solon, he called the new one *Soli*. He himself speaks of the building of this city, in his Elegies, addressing himself to Philocyprus:—

For you be long the Solian throne decreed!
For you a race of prosperous sons succeed
If in those scenes to her so justly dear,
My hand a blooming city help'd to rear,
May the sweet voice of smiling Venus bless,
And speed me home with honors and success!

As for his interview with Crœsus, some pretend to prove from chronology that it is fictitious. But since the story is so famous, and so well attested, nay (what is more) so agreeable to Solon's character, so worthy of his wisdom and magnanimity, I cannot prevail with myself to reject it for the sake of certain chronological tables, which thousands are correcting to this day, without being able to bring them to any certainty. Solon, then, is said to have gone to Sardis, at the request of Crœsus; and when he came there, he was affected much in the same manner as a person born in an inland country, when he first goes to see the ocean; for as he takes every great river he comes to for the sea, so Solon, as he passed through the court, and saw many of the nobility richly dressed, and walking in great pomp amidst a crowd of attendants and guards, took each of them for Crœsus. At last, when he was conducted into the presence, he found the king set off with whatever can be imagined curious and valuable, either in beauty of colors, elegance of golden ornaments, or splendor of jewels; in order that the grandeur and variety of the scene might be as striking as possible. Solon, standing over against the throne, was not at all surprised, nor did he pay those compliments that were expected; on the contrary, it was plain to all persons f discernment, that he despised such vain ostentation and littleness of pride. Crœsus then ordered his treasures to be opened, and his magnificent apartments and furniture to be shown him; but this was quite a needless trouble; for Solon, in one view of the king, was able to read his character. When he had seen all, and was conducted back, Crœsus asked him, "If he had ever beheld a happier man than he?" Solon answered,—"He had; and that the person was one Tellus, a plain but worthy citizen of Athens, who left valuable children behind him; and who having been above the want of necessaries all his life, died gloriously fighting for his country." By this time he appeared to Crœsus to be a strange, uncouth kind of rustic, who did not measure happiness by the quantity of gold and silver, but could prefer the life and death of a private and mean person to *his* high dignity and power. However, he asked him again,—"Whether after Tellus, he knew another happier man in the world?" Solon answered,—"Yes, Cleobis and Biton, famed for their brotherly affection, and dutiful behavior to their mother; for the oxen not being ready, they put themselves in the harness, and drew their mother to Juno's temple, who was extremely happy in having such sons, and moved forward amidst the blessings of the people. After the sacrifice, they drank a cheerful cup with their friends, and then laid down to rest, but rose no more; for they died in the night without sorrow or pain, in the midst of so much glory." "Well!" said Crœsus, now highly displeased, "and do you not then rank us in the number of happy men!" Solon, unwilling either to flatter him, or to exasperate him more, replied,—"King of Lydia, as God has given the Greeks a moderate proportion of other things, so likewise he has favored them with a democratic spirit, and a liberal kind of wisdom, which has no taste for the splendors of royalty. Moreover, the vicissitudes of life suffer us not to be elated by any present good fortune, or to admire that felicity which is liable to change. Futurity carries for every man many various and uncertain events in its bosom. He, therefore, whom heaven blesses with success to the last, is in our estimation the happy man. But the happiness of him who still lives, and has the dangers of life to encounter, appears to us no better than that of a champion before the combat is determined, and while the crown is uncertain." With these words Solon departed, leaving Crœsus chagrined, but not instructed.

At that time Æsop the fabulist was at the court of Crœsus, who had sent for him, and caressed him not a little. He was concerned at the unkind reception Solon met with, and thereupon gave him this advice,—"A man should either not converse with kings at all, or say what is agreeable to them." To which Solon replied,—"Nay, but he should either not do it at all, or say what is useful to them."

Though Crœsus at that time held our lawgiver in contempt, yet when he was defeated in his wars with Cyrus, when his city was taken, himself made prisoner, and laid bound upon the pile, in order to be burnt, in the presence of Cyrus, and all the Persians, he cried out as loud as he possibly could,—"Solon! Solon! Solon!" Cyrus, surprised at this, sent to inquire of him,—"What God or man it was, whom alone he thus invoked under so great a calamity?" Crœsus answered, without the least disguise,—"He is one of the wise men of Greece, whom I sent for, not with a design to hear his wisdom, or to learn what might be of service to me, but that he might see and extend the reputation of that glory, the loss of which I find a much greater misfortune than the possession of it was a blessing. My exalted state was only an exterior advantage, the happiness of opinion; but the reverse plunges me into real sufferings, and ends in misery irremediable. This was foreseen by that great man, who, forming a conjecture of the future from what he then saw, advised me to consider the end of life, and not to rely or grow insolent upon uncertainties." When this was told Cyrus, wh: was a much wiser man than

Crœsus, finding Solon's maxim confirmed by an example before him, he not only set Crœsus at liberty, but honored him with his protection as long as he lived. Thus Solon had the glory of saving the life of one of these kings, and of instructing the other.

During his absence, the Athenians were much divided among themselves; Lycurgus being at the head of the low country, Megacles, the son of Alcmæon, of the people that lived near the sea-coast, and Pisistratus of the mountaineers, among which last was a multitude of laboring people, whose enmity was chiefly levelled at the rich. Hence it was, that though the city did observe Solon's laws, yet all expected some change, and were desirous of another establishment; not in hopes of an equality, but with a view to be gainers by the alteration, and entirely to subdue those that differed from them.

While matters stood thus, Solon arrived at Athens, where he was received with great respect, and still held in veneration by all; but, by reason of his great age, he had neither the strength nor spirit to act or speak in public as he had done. He, therefore, applied in private to the heads of the factions, and endeavored to appease and reconcile them. Pisistratus seemed to give him greater attention than the rest; for Pisistratus had an affable and engaging manner. He was a liberal benefactor to the poor;* and even to his enemies he behaved with great candor. He counterfeited so dexterously the good qualities which nature had denied him, that he gained more credit than the real possessors of them, and stood foremost in the public esteem, in point of moderation and equity, in zeal for the present government, and aversion to all that endeavor-

* By the poor we are not to understand such as asked alms, for there were none such at Athens. "In those days," says Isocrates, "there was no citizen that died of want, or begged in the streets, to the dishonor of the community." This was owing to the laws against idleness and prodigality, and the care which the *areopagus* took that every man should have a visible livelihood.

ed at a change. With these arts he imposed upon the people; but Solon soon discovered his real character, and was the first to discern his insidious designs. Yet he did not absolutely break with him, but endeavored to soften him, and advise him better; declaring both to him and others, that if ambition could but be banished from his soul, and he could be cured of his desire of absolute power, there would not be a man better disposed, or a more worthy citizen in Athens.

About this time, Thespis began to change the form of tragedy, and the novelty of the thing attracted many spectators; for this was before any prize was proposed for those that excelled in this respect. Solon, who was always willing to hear and to learn, and in his old age more inclined to anything that might divert and entertain, particularly to music and good fellowship, went to see Thespis himself exhibit, as the custom of the ancient poets was. When the play was done, he called to Thespis, and asked him,—"If he was not ashamed to tell so many lies before so great an assembly?" Thespis answered,—"It was no great matter, if he spoke or acted so in jest." To which Solon replied, striking the ground violently with his staff,—"If we encourage such jesting as this, we shall quickly find it in our contracts and agreements."

Soon after this, Pisistratus, having wounded himself for the purpose, drove in that condition into the market-place, and endeavored to inflame the minds of the people, by telling them his enemies had laid in wait for him, and treated him in that manner on account of his patriotism. Upon this the multitude loudly expressed their indignation; but Solon came up, and thus accosted him:—"Son of Hippocrates, you act Homer's Ulysses but very indifferently; for he wounded himself to deceive his enemies, but you have done it to impose upon your countrymen." Notwithstanding this, the rabble were ready to take up arms for him; and a general assembly of the people being summoned, Ariston made a motion that a body-guard of fifty clubmen should be assigned him. Solon stood up and opposed it with many arguments, of the same kind with those he has left us in his poems :—

> You hang with rapture on his honey'd tongue.

And again,—

> Your art, to public interest ever blind,
> Your fox-like art still centres in yourself.

But when he saw the poor behave in a riotous manner, and determined to gratify Pisistratus at any rate, while the rich, out of fear, declined the opposition, he retired with this declaration, that he had shown more wisdom than the former, in discerning what method should have been taken ; and more courage than the latter, who did not want understanding, but spirit to oppose the establishment of a tyrant. The people having made the decree, did not curiously inquire into the number of guards which Pisistratus employed, but visibly connived at his keeping as many as he pleased, till he seized the citadel. When this was done, and the city in great confusion, Megacles, with the rest of the Alcmæonidæ, immediately took to flight. But Solon, though he was now very old, and had none to second him, appeared in public, and addressed himself to the citizens, sometimes upbraiding them with their past indiscretion and cowardice, sometimes exhorting and encouraging them to stand up for their liberty. Then it was that he spoke those memorable words,—"It would have been easier for them to repress the advances of tyranny, and prevent its establishment; but now it was established, and grown to some height, it would be more glorious to demolish it." However, finding that their fears prevented their attention to what he said, he returned to his own house, and placed his weapons at the street door, with these words,—"I have done all in my power to defend my country and its laws." This was his last public effort. Though some exhorted him to fly, he took no notice of their advice, but was composed enough to make verses, in which he thus reproaches the Athenians :—

If fear or folly has your rights betray'd,
Let not the fault on righteous heav'n be laid,
You gave them guards, you rais'd your tyrants high,
T' impose the heavy yoke that draws the heaving sigh.

Many of his friends alarmed at this, told him the tyrant would certainly put him to death for it, and asked him what he trusted to, that he went such imprudent lengths? He answered,—"To old age." However, when Pisistratus had fully established himself, he made his court to Solon, and treated him with so much kindness and respect, that Solon became as it were his counsellor, and gave sanction to many of his proceedings. He observed the greatest part of Solon's laws, showing himself the example, and obliging his friends to follow it. Thus, when he was accused of murder before the court of *areopagus*, he appeared in a modest manner to make his defence; but his accuser dropped the impeachment. He likewise added other laws, one of which was, that "persons maimed in the wars should be maintained at the public charge." Yet this, Heraclides tells us, was in pursuance of Solon's plan, who had decreed the same in the case of Thersippus. But, according to Theophrastus, Pisistratus, not Solon, made the law against idleness which produced at once greater industry in the country, and tranquillity in the city.

Solon, moreover, attempted in verse a large description, or rather fabulous account of the Atlantis island,* which he had learned of the wise men of Saïs, and which particularly concerned the Athenians; but by reason of his age, not want of leisure (as Plato would have it), he was apprehensive the work would be too much for him, and therefore did not go through with it. These verses are a proof that business was not the hinderance:—

I grow in learning as I grow in years.

* This fable imported, that the people of Atlantis, having subdued all Lybia and a great part of Europe, threatened Egypt and Greece; but the Athenians making head against their victorious army, overthrew them in several engagements, and confined them to their own island.

And again :—

Wine, wit, and beauty still their charms bestow,
Light all the shades of life, and cheer us as we go.

Plato, ambitious to cultivate and adorn the subject of the Atlantis island, as a delightful spot in some fair field unoccupied, to which also he had some claim, by his being related to Solon, laid out magnificent courts and enclosures, and erected a grand entrance to it, such as no other story, fable or poem, ever had. But as he began it late, he ended his life before the work. Phanias tells us Solon died in the archonship of Hegestratus. The story of his ashes being scattered about the isle of Salamis appears absurd and fabulous; and yet it is related by several authors of credit, and by Aristotle in particular.

Diogenes Laertius says that his bones were burned in Salamis, and his ashes scattered over the ground by his own order. And he has written the following epigram upon him :—

The Cyprian flame devoured great Solon's corse,
  Far in a foreign land; but Salamis
Retains his bones, whose dust is turned to corn.
  The tablets of his laws do bear aloft
His mind to heaven. Such a burden light
  Are these immortal rules to th' happy wood.

SPEUSIPPUS.

Speusippus was the successor of Plato in the Academy, to whose doctrines he always adhered, though he was not of the same disposition as he. For he was a passionate man, and a slave to pleasure. Accordingly, they say that he once in a rage threw a puppy into a well; and that for the sake of amusement, he went all the way to Macedonia to the marriage of Cassander.

The female pupils of Plato, Lasthenea of Mantinea, and Axiothea of Philus, are said to have become disciples of Speusippus also. And Dionysius, writing to him in a petulant manner, says, "And one may learn philosophy too from your female disciple from Arcadia; moreover, Plato used to take his pupils without exacting any fee from them; but you collect tribute from yours, whether willing or unwilling."

He was the first man, as Diodorus relates in the first book of his Commentaries, who investigated in his school what was common to the several sciences; and who endeavored, as far as possible, to maintain their connection with each other. He was also the first who published those things which Isocrates called secrets, as Cæneus tells us. And the first, too, who found out how to make light baskets of bundles of twigs.

But he became afflicted with paralysis, and sent to Xenocrates, inviting him to become his successor in the school. Once when he was being borne in a carriage into the Academy, he met Diogenes, and said "Hail;" and Diogenes replied, "I will not say hail to you who, though in such a state as you are, endure to live." Others relate the story thus: When Diogenes refused to return his salutation, he at the same time said, "Such a feeble wretch ought to be ashamed to live;" to which Speusippus replied that he "lived not in his limbs but in his mind."

Speusippus said to a rich man who was in love with an ugly woman, "What do you want with her? I will find you a much prettier woman for ten talents." In a fit of despondency he committed suicide. Diogenes Laertius wrote the following epigram upon him:—

Had I not known Speusippus thus had died,
No one would have persuaded me that he
Was e'er akin to Plato; who would never
Have died desponding for so slight a grief.

STILPO.

Stilpo, a native of Megara, in Greece, was a pupil of some of Euclides' school. But some say that he was a pupil of Euclides himself.

And he was so much superior to all his fellows in command of words and in acuteness, that it may almost be said that all Greece fixed its eyes upon him, and joined the Megaric school. Concerning him Philippus of Megara speaks thus, word for word:—"For he carried off from Theophrastus, Metrodorus the speculative philosopher, and Timagoras of Gela; and Aristotle the Cyrenaic, he robbed of Clitarchus and Simias; and from the dialecticians' school also he won men over, carrying off Pœoneius from Aristides, and Dippilus of the Bosphorus from Euphantus, and also Myrmex of the Venites, who had both come to him to argue against him, but they became converts and his disciples." Besides these men, he attracted to his school Phrasidemus the Peripatetic, a natural philosopher of great ability, Alcimus the rhetorician, the most eminent orator in all Greece at that time; and Crates, with a great number of others, among whom was Zeno the Phœnician.

He was very fond of the study of politics. Though he was married, he lived also with a courtesan, named Nicarete. And he had a licentious daughter, who was married to a friend of his named Simias, a citizen of Syracuse. And as she would not live in an orderly manner, some one told Stilpo that she was a disgrace to him. But he said, "She is not more a disgrace to me than I am an honor to her."

Ptolemy Soter, it is said, received him with great honor; and when he had made himself master of Megara, he gave him money, and invited him to sail with him to Egypt. But he accepted only a moderate sum of money, and declined the journey proposed to him, but went over to Ægina, until

Ptolemy had sailed. Also when Demetrius, the son of Antigonus, had taken Megara, he ordered Stilpo's house to be saved, and took care that everything that had been plundered from him should be restored to him. But when he wished Stilpo to give him in a list of all that he had lost, he said that he had lost nothing of his own; for that no one had taken from him his learning, and that he still had his eloquence and his knowledge. And he conversed with Demetrius on the subject of doing good to men with such power, that he became a zealous hearer of his.

They say that he once put such a question as this to a man, about the Minerva of Phidias:—"Is Minerva the Goddess the daughter of Jupiter?" And when the other said, "Yes;" "But this," said he, "is not the child of Jupiter, but of Phidias." And when he was brought before the Areopagus for this speech, he did not deny it, but maintained that he had spoken correctly; for that she was not a God (*theos*) but a Goddess (*thea*); for that Gods were of the male sex only.* However, the judges of the Areopagus ordered him to leave the city; and on this occasion, Theodorus, who was nicknamed *Theos*, said in derision, "Whence did Stilpo learn this? and how could he tell whether she was a God or a Goddess?" But Theodorus was in truth a most impudent fellow. But Stilpo was a most witty and elegant-minded man. Accordingly, when Crates asked him if the Gods delighted in adoration and prayer; they say that he answered, "Do not ask these questions, you foolish man, in the road, but in private." And they say, too, that Bion, when he was asked whether there were any Gods, answered in the same spirit:—

> "Will you not first, O! miserable old man,
> Remove the multitude?"

But Stilpo was a man of simple character, and free from all trick and humbug, and universally affable. Accordingly,

* The quibble here is, that θεὸς is properly only masculine, though it is sometimes used as feminine.

when Crates the Cynic once refused to answer a question that he had put to him, and only insulted his questioner—"I knew," said Stilpo, "that he would say anything rather than what he ought." And once he put a question to him, and offered him a fig at the same time; so he took the fig and ate it, on which Crates said, "O Hercules, I have lost my fig." "Not only that," he replied, "but you have lost your question too, of which the fig was the pledge." At another time, he saw Crates shivering in the winter, and said to him, "Crates, you seem to me to want a new dress," meaning, both a new mind and a new garment; and Crates, feeling ashamed, answered him in the following parody:—

> "There* Stilpo too, through the Megarian bounds,
> Pours out deep groans, where Syphon's voice resounds,
> And there he oft doth argue, while a school
> Of eager pupils owns his subtle rule,
> And virtue's name with eager chase pursues."

It is said that at Athens he attracted all the citizens to such a degree, that they used to run from their workshops to look at him; and when some one said to him, "Why, Stilpo, they wonder at you as if you were a wild beast," he replied, "Not so; but as a real genuine man."

He was a very clever arguer; and rejected the theory of species. And he used to say that a person who spoke of man in general, was speaking of nobody; for that he was not speaking of this individual, nor of that one; for speaking in general, how can he speak more of this person than of that person? therefore he is not speaking of this person at all. Another of his illustrations was, "That which is shown to me, is not a vegetable; for a vegetable existed ten thousand years ago, therefore this is not a vegetable." They say that once when he was conversing with Crates, he interrupted the discourse to go off and buy some fish; and as Crates tried to drag him

* The Greek is a parody on the descriptions of Tantalus and Sisyphus. Hom. Od., ii. 581, 592.

back, and said, "You are leaving the argument;" "Not at all," he replied, "I keep the argument, but I am leaving you; for the argument remains, but the fish will be sold to some one else."

There are nine dialogues of his extant, written in a frigid style. Being asked "What is harder than a stone?" he answered "a fool."

Hermippus says that he died at a great age, after drinking some wine, in order to die more rapidly. And we have written this epigram on him:—

> Stranger, old age at first, and then disease,
> A hateful pair, did lay wise Stilpo low,
> The pride of Megara: he found good wine
> The best of drivers for his mournful coach,
> And drinking it, he drove on to the end.

STRATO.

THEOPHRASTUS was succeeded in the presidency of his school by Strato of Lampsacus, the son of Arcesilaus, of whom he had made mention in his will. He was a man of great eminence, surnamed the Natural Philosopher, from his surpassing all men in the diligence with which he applied himself to the investigation of matters of that nature. He was also the preceptor of Ptolemy Philadelphus, and received from him, as it is said, eighty talents.

They say that he became so thin and weak, that he died without its being perceived. And there is an epigram of ours upon him in the following terms:—

> The man was thin, believe me, from the use
> Of frequent unguents; Strato was his name,
> A citizen of Lampsacus; he struggled long
> With fell disease, and died at last unnoticed.

THALES.

THALES was the son of Euxamius and Cleobule; of the family of the Thelidæ, who are Phœnicians by descent, among the most noble of all the descendants of Cadmus and Agenor, as Plato testifies. And he was the first man to whom the name of Wise was given, when Damasius was Archon at Athens, in whose time also the seven wise men had that title given to them. He was enrolled as a citizen at Miletus when he came thither with Neleus, who had been banished from Phœnicia; but a more common statement is that he was a native Milesian, of noble extraction.

After having been immersed in state affairs he applied himself to speculations in natural philosophy; though, as some people state, he left no writings behind him. For the book on Naval Astronomy, which is attributed to him, is said in reality to be the work of Focus the Samian. But Callimachus was aware that he was the discoverer of the Lesser Bear; for in his Iambics he speak of him thus:

> And, he, 'tis said, did first compute the stars
> Which beam in Charles's wain, and guide the bark
> Of the Phœnician sailor o'er the sea.

According to others he wrote two books, and no more, about the solstice and the equinox; thinking that everything else was easily to be comprehended. According to other statements, he is said to have been the first who studied astronomy, and who foretold the eclipses and motions of the sun, on which account Xenophanes and Herodotus praise him greatly; and Heraclitus and Democritus confirm this statement.

Some again (one of whom is Chærilus the poet) say that he was the first person who affirmed that the souls of men were immortal; and he was the first person, too, who discovered the path of the sun from one end of the ecliptic to the other; and who, as one account tells us, defined the magnitude of the sun as being seven hundred and twenty times as great as that of the moon. He was also the first person who called the last day of the month the thirtieth. And likewise the first to converse about natural philosophy, as some say. But Aristotle and Hippias say that he attributed souls also to lifeless things, forming his conjecture from the nature of the magnet, and of amber. And Pamphile relates that he, having learnt geometry from the Egyptians, was the first person to describe a right-angled triangle in a circle, and that he sacrificed an ox in honor of his discovery. But others, among whom is Apollodorus the calculator, say that it was Pythagoras who made this discovery. It was Thales also who carried to their greatest point of advancement the discoveries which Callimachus in his Iambics says were first made by Euphebus the Phrygian, such as those of the scalene angle, and of the triangle, and of other things which relate to investigations about lines. He seems also to have been a man of the greatest wisdom in political matters. For when Crœsus sent to the Milesians to invite them to an alliance, he prevented them from agreeing to it, which step of his, as Cyrus got the victory, proved the salvation of the city. But Clytus relates, as Heraclides assures us, that he was attached to a solitary and recluse life.

Some assert that he was married, and that he had a son named Cibissus; others, on the contrary, say that he never had a wife, but that he adopted the son of his sister; and that once being asked why he did not himself become a father, he answered, that it was because he was fond of children. They say, too, that when his mother exhorted him to marry, he said, "No, by Jove, it is not yet time." And afterwards, when he was past his youth, and she was again pressing him earnestly, he said, "It is no longer time."

Hieronymus, of Rhodes, also tells us, in the second book of his Miscellaneous Memoranda, that when he was desirous to show that it was easy to get rich, he, foreseeing that there would be a great crop of olives, took some large plantations of olive trees, and so made a great deal of money.

He asserted water to be the principle of all things, and that the world had life, and was full of dæmons: they say, too, that he was the original definer of the seasons of the year, and that it was he who divided the year into three hundred and sixty-five days. And he never had any teacher except during the time that he went to Egypt, and associated with the priests. Hieronymus also says that he measured the Pyramids: watching their shadow, and calculating when they were of the same size as that was. He lived with Thrasybulus, the tyrant of Miletus, as we are informed by Minyas.

Now, it is known to every one what happened with respect to the tripod that was found by the fishermen and sent to the wise men by the people of the Milesians. For they say that some Ionian youths bought a cast of their net from some Milesian fishermen. And when the tripod was drawn up in the net there was a dispute about it; until the Milesians sent to Delphi; and the God gave them the following answer:—

> You ask about the tripod, to whom you shall present it;
> 'T is for the wisest, I reply, that fortune surely meant it.

Accordingly they gave it to Thales, and he gave it to some one, who again handed it over to another, till it came to Solon. But he said that it was the God himself who was the first in wisdom; and so he sent it to Delphi. But Callimachus gives a different account of this in his Iambics, taking the tradition which he mentions from Leander the Milesian; for he says that a certain Arcadian of the name of Bathydes, when dying, left a goblet behind him with an injunction that it should be given to the first of the wise men. And it was given to Thales, and went the whole circle till it came back to Thales, on which he sent it to Apollo Didymæus, adding (according to Callimachus) the following distich:—

> Thales, who's twice received me as a prize,
> Gives me to him who rules the race of Neleus.

And the prose inscription ran thus:—

Thales the son of Euxamius, a Milesian, offers this to Apollo Didymæus, having twice received it from the Greeks as the reward for virtue.

And the name of the son of Bathydes who carried the goblet about from one to the other, was Thyrion, as Eleusis tells us in his history of Achilles. And Alexander the Myndian agrees with him in the ninth book of his Traditions. But Eudoxus of Cnidos, and Evanthes of Miletus, say that one of the friends of Crœsus received from the king a golden goblet, for the purpose of giving it to the wisest of the Greeks; and that he gave it to Thales, and that it came round to Chilo, and that he inquired of the God at Delphi who was wiser than himself; and that the God replied, Myson, whom we shall mention hereafter. (He is the man whom Eudoxus places among the seven wise men instead of Cleobolus; but Plato inserts his name instead of Periander.) The God accordingly made this reply concerning him:—

I say that Myson, the Ætœan sage,
The citizen of Chen, is wiser far
In his deep mind than you.

The person who went to the temple to ask the question was Anacharsis; but again Dædacus, the Platonic philosopher, and Clearchus, state that the goblet was sent by Crœsus to Pittacus, and so was carried round to the different men. But Andron, in his book called The Tripod, says that the Argives offered the tripod as a prize for excellence to the wisest of the Greeks; and that Aristodemus, a Spartan, was judged to deserve it, but that he yielded the palm to Chilo; and Alcæus mentions Aristodemus in these lines:—

And so they say that Aristodemus once
Uttered a truthful speech in noble Sparta:
'T is money makes the man; and he who 's none,
Is counted neither good nor honorable.

But some say that a vessel fully loaded was sent by Periander to Thrasybulus, the tyrant of the Milesians; and that, as the ship was wrecked in the sea, near the island of Cos, this tripod was afterwards found by some fishermen. Phanodicus says that it was found in the sea near Athens, and so brought into the city; and then, after an assembly had been held to decide on the disposal, it was sent to Bias—and the reason why has been mentioned in our account of Bias. Others say that this goblet had been made by Vulcan, and presented by the Gods to Pelops, on his marriage; and that subsequently it came into the possession of Menelaus, and was taken away by Paris when he carried off Helen, and was thrown into the sea near Cos by her, as she said that it would become a cause of battle. And after some time, some of the citizens of Lebedos having bought a net, this tripod was brought up in it; and as they quarrelled with the fishermen about it, they went to Cos; and not being able to get the matter settled there, they laid it before the Milesians, as Miletus was their metropolis; and they sent ambassadors, who were treated with neglect, on which account they made war with the Coans; and after each side had met with many revolutions of fortune, an oracle directed that the tripod should be given to the wisest; and then both parties agreed that it belonged to Thales; and he, after it had gone the circuit of all the wise men, presented it to the Didymæan Apollo. Now, the assignation of the oracle was given to the Coans in the following words:—

The war between the brave Ionian race
And the proud Meropes will never cease,
'Till the rich golden tripod which the God,
Its maker, cast beneath the briny waves,
Is from your city sent, and justly given
To that wise being who knows all present things,
And all that 's past, and all that is to come.

And the reply given to the Milesians was—

You ask about the tripod:

and so on, as I have related it before. And now we have said enough on this subject.

But Hermippus, in his Lives, refers to Thales what has been by some people reported of Socrates; for he recites that he used to say that he thanked fortune for three things:—first of all, that he had been born a man and not a beast; secondly, that he was a man and not a woman; and thirdly, that he was a Greek and not a barbarian.

It is said that once he was led out of his house by an old woman for the purpose of observing the stars, and he fell into a ditch, and bewailed himself, on which the old woman said to him—"Do you, O Thales, who cannot see what is under your feet, think that you shall understand what is in heaven?" Timon also knew that he was an astronomer, and in his Silli he praises him, saying:—

Like Thales, wisest of the seven sages,
That great astronomer.

And Lobon, of Argos, says, that which was written by him extends to about two hundred verses; and that the following inscription is engraved upon his statue:—

Miletus, fairest of Ionian cities,
Gave birth to Thales, great astronomer,
Wisest of mortals in all kinds of knowledge.

And these are quoted as some of his lines:—

It is not many words that real wisdom proves;
Breathe rather one wise thought,
Select one worthy object,
So shall you best the endless prate of silly men reprove.

And the following are quoted as sayings of his:—"God is the most ancient of all things, for he had no birth: the world is the most beautiful of things, for it is the work of God: place is the greatest of things, for it contains all things: intellect is the swiftest of things, for it runs through everything: necessity is the strongest of things, for it rules everything: time is the wisest of things, for it finds out everything."

He said also that there was no difference between life and

death. "Why, then," said some one to him, "do not you die?" "Because," said he, "it does make no difference." A man asked him which was made first, night or day, and he replied, "Night was made first by one day." Another man asked him whether a man who did wrong, could escape the notice of the Gods. "No, not even if he thinks wrong," said he. An adulterer inquired of him whether he should swear that he had not committed adultery. "Perjury," said he, "is no worse than adultery." When he was asked what was very difficult, he said, "To know one's self." And what was easy, "To advise another." What was most pleasant? "To be successful." To the question, "What is the divinity?" he replied, "That which has neither beginning nor end." When asked what hard thing he had seen, he said, "An old man a tyrant." When the question was put to him how a man might more easily endure misfortune, he said, "If he saw his enemies more unfortunate still." When asked how men might live most virtuously and most justly, he said, "If we never do ourselves what we blame in others." To the question, "Who was happy?" he made answer, "He who is healthy in his body, easy in his circumstances, and well-instructed as to his mind." He said that men ought to remember those friends who were absent as well as those who were present, and not to care about adorning their faces, but to be beautified by their studies. "Do not," said he, "get rich by evil actions, and let not any one ever be able to reproach you with speaking against those who partake of your friendship. All the assistance that you give to your parents, the same you have a right to expect from your children." He said that the reason of the Nile overflowing was, that its streams were beaten back by the Etesian winds blowing in a contrary direction.

Apollodorus, in his Chronicles, says, that Thales was born in the first year of the thirty-fifth Olympiad; and he died at the age of seventy-eight years, or, according to the statement of Sosicrates, at the age of ninety, for he died in the fifty-eighth

Olympiad, having lived in the time of Crœsus, to whom he promised that he would enable him to pass the Halys without a bridge, by turning the course of the river.

Thales died while present as a spectator at a gymnastic contest, being worn out with heat and thirst and weakness, for he was very old, and the following inscription was placed on his tomb:—

> You see this tomb is small—but recollect,
> The fame of Thales reaches to the skies.

I have also myself composed this epigram on him in the first book of my epigrams, or poems in various metres:—

> O mighty sun, our wisest Thales sat
> Spectator of the games, when you did seize upon him;
> But you were right to take him near yourself,
> Now that his aged sight could scarcely reach to heaven

THEMISTIUS.

Themistius, who was born in an obscure town of Paphlagonia, fixed his residence at Constantinople, and taught eloquence and philosophy with great success. He had many disciples, both Pagan and Christian; among the former was Libanius; among the latter, Gregory Nazianzen. He enjoyed the favor of the emperors, by whom he was admitted to the highest honors. Constantius, in the year three hundred and fifty-five, received him into the senate, and afterwards, in return for an eloquent eulogium, presented him with a brazen statue. Julian received him as a friend, and frequently corresponded with him. In the year three hundred and sixty-two he was appointed by this emperor prefect of Constantinople. He enjoyed equal distinction under the succeeding emperors, from whom he obtained by his eloquence whatever he wished. Theodosius the Great, during his visit to the Western empire, entrusted Themistius with the care and education of his son Arcadius. His eloquence, wisdom, and ability in public affairs, united with uncommon gentleness of temper and urbanity of manners, were the foundation of that long course of civil honors by which his life was distinguished. About the year three hundred and eighty-seven Themistius withdrew, at an advanced age, from public business, and soon after died.

A memorable example of the liberal spirit of Themistius is related by ecclesiastical historians. The emperor Valens, who favored the Arian party, inflicted many hardships and sufferings upon the Trinitarians, and daily threatened them with still greater severities. Themistius, to whom these measures were exceedingly displeasing, addressed the emperor upon the subject in an eloquent speech, in which he represented the diversity of opinions among the Christians as inconsiderable, compared with that of the Pagan philosophers; and pleaded that this diversity could not be displeasing to God, since it did not prevent men from worshipping him with true piety. By these and other arguments Themistius prevailed upon the emperor to treat the Trinitarians with great lenity.

THEOPHRASTUS.

Theophrastus was a native of Eresus, the son of Melantas, a fuller. He was originally a pupil of Leucippus, his fellow citizen, in his own country; and subsequently, after having attended the lectures of Plato, he went over to Aristotle. And when he withdrew to Chalcis, he succeeded him as president of his school, in the hundred and fourteenth Olympiad.

It is also said that a slave of his, by name Pomphylus, was a philosopher.

Theophrastus was a man of great acuteness and industry, and he was the tutor of Menandar, the comic poet. He was also a most benevolent man, and very affable. Accordingly, Cassander received him as a friend; and Ptolemy sent to invite him to his court. And he was thought so very highly of at Athens, that when Agonides ventured to impeach him on a charge of impiety, he was very nearly fined for his hardihood. And there thronged to his school a crowd of disciples to the number of two thousand. In his letter to Phanias, the Peripatetic, among other subjects he speaks of the court of justice in the following terms: "It is not only out of the question to find an assembly, but it is not easy to find even a company, such as one would like; but yet recitations produce corrections of the judgment. And my age does not allow me to put off everything and to feel indifference on such a subject." In this letter he speaks of himself as one who devotes his whole leisure to learning.

And though he was of this disposition, he nevertheless went away for a short time, both he and all the rest of the philosophers, in consequence of Sophocles, the son of Amphiclides, having brought forward and carried a law that no one of the philosophers should preside over a school unless the council and the people had passed a resolution to sanction their doing so; if they did, death was to be the penalty. But they returned again the next year, when Philion had impeached Sophocles for illegal conduct; when the Athenians abrogated his law, and fined Sophocles five talents, and voted that the philosophers should have leave to return, that Theophrastus might return and preside over his school as before.

His name had originally been Tyrtanius, but Aristotle changed it to Theophrastus, from the divine character of his eloquence.*

It is also related that Aristotle used the same expression about him and Callisthenes, which Plato employed about Xenocrates and Aristotle himself. For he is reported to have said, since Theophrastus was a man of extraordinary acute-

* From *theios*, divine, and *phrasis*, diction.

ness, who could both comprehend and explain everything, and as the other was somewhat slow in his natural character, that Theophrastus required a bridle, and Callisthenes a spur.

It is said, too, that he had a garden of his own after the death of Aristotle, by the assistance of Demetrius Phalerius, who was an intimate friend of his.

The following very practical apophthegms of his are quoted. He used to say that it was better to trust to a horse without a bridle than to a discourse without arrangement. And once, when a man preserved a strict silence during the whole of a banquet, he said to him, "If you are an ignorant man, you are acting wisely; but if you have had any education, you are behaving like a fool." And a very favorite expression of his was, that "time was the most valuable thing that a man could spend."

He died when he was of a great age, having lived eighty-five years, when he had only rested from his labors a short time. And we have composed the following epigram on him:—

> The proverb then is not completely false,
> That wisdom's bow unbent is quickly broken;
> While Theophrastus labored, he kept sound,
> When he relaxed, he lost his strength and died.

They say that on one occasion, when dying, he was asked by his disciples whether he had any charge to give them; and he replied, that he had none, but that they should "remember that life holds out many pleasing deceits to us by the vanity of glory; for that when we are beginning to live, then we are dying. There is, therefore, nothing more profitless than ambition. But may you all be fortunate, and either abandon philosophy (for it is a great labor), or else cling to it diligently, for then the credit of it is great; but the vanities of life exceed the advantage of it. However, it is not requisite for me now to advise you what you should do; but do you yourselves consider what line of conduct to adopt." And when he had said this, as report goes, he expired. And the Athenians accompanied him to the grave, on foot, with the whole population of the city, as it is related, honoring the man greatly.

XENOCRATES.

Xenocrates was the son of Agathenor, and a native of Chalcedon. From his early youth he was a pupil of Plato, and also accompanied him in his voyages to Sicily. He was by nature of a lazy disposition, so that they say that Plato said once, when comparing him to Aristotle,—"The one requires the spur, and the other the bridle." And on another occasion, he said, "What a horse and what an ass am I dressing opposite to one another!"

In other respects Xenocrates was always of a solemn and grave character, so that Plato was continually saying to him, —"Xenocrates, sacrifice to the Graces." And he spent the greater part of his time in the Academy, and whenever he was about to go into the city, they say all the turbulent and quarrelsome rabble in the city used to make way for him to pass by. And once, Phryne the courtesan wished to try him, and pretending that she was pursued by some people, she fled and took refuge in his house; and he admitted her indeed, because of what was due to humanity; and as there was but one bed in the room, he, at her entreaty, allowed her to share it with him; but at last, in spite of all her entreaties, she got up and went away, without having been able to succeed in her purpose; and told those who asked her, that she had quitted a statue and not a man. But some say that the real story is, that his pupils put Lais into his bed, and that he was so continent, that he submitted to some severe operations of excision and cautery.

He was so abstemious in the use of food, that his provision was frequently spoiled before it was consumed.

So eminent was his reputation for integrity, that when he was called upon to give evidence in a judicial transaction, in which an oath was usually required, the judges unanimously agreed that his simple asseveration should be taken, as a public testimony to his merit.

He was also a man of the most contented disposition; accordingly they say that when Alexander sent him a large sum of money, he took three thousand Attic drachmas, and sent back the rest, saying, that Alexander wanted most, as he had the greatest number of mouths to feed. And when some was sent him by Antipater, he would not accept any of it, as Myornianus tells us in his Similitudes. And once, when he gained a golden crown, in a contest as to who could drink most, which was offered in the yearly festival of the Choes by Dionysius, he went out and placed the crown at the feet of the statue of Mercury, which was at the gate where he was also accustomed to deposit his garland of flowers. It is said, also, that he was once sent with some colleagues as an ambassador to Philip; and that they were won over by gifts, and went to his banquets and conversed with Philip; but that he would do none of these things, nor could Philip propitiate him by these means; on which account, when the other ambassadors arrived in Athens, they said that Xenocrates had gone with them to no purpose; and the people were ready to punish him; but when they had learnt from him that they had now more need than ever to look to the welfare of their city, for that Philip had already bribed all their counsellors, but that he had been unable to win him over by any means, then they say that the people honored him with redoubled honor. They add also, that Philip said afterwards, that Xenocrates was the only one of those who had come to him who was incorruptible. And when he went as ambassador to Antipater on the subject of the Athenian captives at the time of the Samian war, and was invited by him to a banquet, he addressed him in the following lines:—

> I answer, Goddess human, is thy breast
> By justice sway'd, by tender pity prest?
> Ill fits it me, whose friends are sunk to beasts,
> To quaff thy bowls, or riot in thy feasts:
> Me would'st thou please, for them thy cares employ,
> And them to me restore and me to joy.*

And Antipater, admiring the appropriateness of the quotation, immediately released them.

On one occasion, when a sparrow was pursued by a hawk, and flew into his bosom, he caressed it, and let it go again, saying that "We ought not to betray a suppliant." And being ridiculed by Bion, he said that he would not answer him, for that tragedy, when ridiculed by comedy, did not condescend to make a reply. To one who had never learnt music, or geometry, or astronomy, but who wished to become his disciple, he said, "Be gone, for you have not yet the handles of philosophy." But some say that he said, "Be gone, for I do not card wool here." And when Dionysius said to Plato that some one would cut off his head, he, being present, showed his own, and said, "Not before they have cut of mine." On one occasion, when he did not reply to some detractive insinuations, he was asked why he was silent? He answered, "I have sometimes repented of speaking, but never of holding my peace."

They say, too, that once, when Antipater had come to Athens and saluted him, he would not make him any reply before he had finished quietly the discourse which he was delivering.

Being exceedingly devoid of every kind of pride, he often used to meditate with himself several times a day; and always allotted one hour of each day, it is said, to silence. He used to compare himself to a vessel with a narrow orifice, which receives with difficulty, but firmly retains whatever is put into it.

* Hom. Od. x. 387. Pope's Version, 450.

But the Athenians, though he was such a great man, once sold him because he was unable to pay the tax to which the metics were liable. And Demetrius Phalereus purchased him, and so assisted both parties, Xenocrates by giving him his freedom, and the Athenians in respect of the tax upon metics.

He succeeded Speusippus, and presided over the school for twenty-five years, beginning at the archonship of Lysimachides, in the second year of the hundred and tenth Olympiad.

And he died in consequence of stumbling by night against a dish, and falling into a reservoir of water, being more than eighty-two years of age. And in one of our epigrams we speak thus of him:—

> He struck against a brazen pot,
> And cut his forehead deep,
> And crying cruel is my lot,
> In death he fell asleep.
> So thus Xenocrates did fall,
> The universal friend of all.

XENOPHON.

Xenophon, the son of Gryllus, a citizen of Athens, was of the borough of Erchia; he was a man of great modesty, and as handsome as can be imagined.

They say that Socrates met him in a narrow lane, and put his stick across it, and prevented him from passing, by asking him where all kinds of necessary things were sold. And when he had answered him, he asked him again where men were made good and virtuous. And as he did not know, he said, "Follow me, then, and learn." And from this time forth, Xenophon became a follower of Socrates.

He was the first person who took down conversations as they occurred, and published them among men, calling them memorabilia. He was also the first man who wrote a history of philosophers.

Aristippus, in the fourth book of his treatise on Ancient Luxury, says that he loved Clinias; and that he said to him, "Now I look upon Clinias with more pleasure than upon all the other beautiful things which are to be seen among men; and I would rather be blind as to all the rest of the world, than as to Clinias. And I am annoyed even with night and with sleep, because then I do not see him; but I am very grateful to the sun and to daylight, because they show Clinias to me."

He became a friend of Cyrus in this manner: He had an acquaintance, by name Proxenus, a Bœotian by birth, a pupil of Gorgias of Leontini, and a friend of Cyrus. He being in Sardis, staying at the court of Cyrus, wrote a letter to Athens to Xenophon, inviting him to come and be a friend to Cyrus. And Xenophon showed the letters to Socrates, and asked his advice. And Socrates bade him go to Delphi, and ask counsel of the God. And Xenophon did so, and went to the God; but the question he put was, not whether it was good for him to go to Cyrus or not, but how he should go; for which Socrates blamed him, but still advised him to go. Accordingly he went to Cyrus, and became no less dear to him than Proxenus. And all the circumstances of the expedition and the retreat, he himself has sufficiently related to us.

But he was at enmity with Menon the Pharsalian, who was commander of the foreign troops at the time of the expedition; and amongst other reproaches, he says that he was much addicted to the worst kind of debauchery. And he reproaches a man of the name of Apollonides with having his ears bored.

But after the expedition, and the disasters which took place in Pontus, and the violations of the truce of Seuthes, the king of the Odrysæ, he came into Asia to Agesilaus, the king of Lacedæmon, bringing with him the soldiers of Cyrus, to serve for pay; and he became a very great friend of Agesilaus. About the same time he was condemned to banishment by the Athenians, on the charge of being a favorer of the Lacedæmonians. Being in Ephesus, and having a sum of money in gold, he gave half of it to Megabyzus, the priest of Diana, to keep for him till his return; and if he never returned, then he was to expend it upon a statue, and dedicate that to the Goddess; and with the other half he sent offerings to Delphi. From thence he went with Agesilaus into Greece, as Agesilaus was summoned to take part in the war against the Thebans. The Lacedæmonians made him a friend of their city.

He was a man of great distinction in all points, and very fond of horses and of dogs, and a great tactician, as is manifest from his writings. And he was a pious man, fond of sacrificing to the Gods, and a great authority as to what was due to them, and a very ardent admirer and imitator of Socrates.

He also wrote near forty books; though different critics divide them differently. After the battle, which was fought at Mantinea, they say that Xenophon offered sacrifice, wearing a crown on his head; but when the news of the death of his son arrived, he took off the crown; but after that, hearing that he had fallen gloriously, he put the crown on again. And some say that he did not even shed a tear, but said, "I knew that I was the father of a mortal man." And Aristotle says, that innumerable writers wrote panegyrics and epitaphs upon Gryllus, partly out of a wish to gratify his father.

ZENO.

Zeno was the son of Innaseas, or Demeas, and a native of Citium, in Cyprus, which is a Grecian city, partly occupied by a Phœnician colony.

He had his head naturally bent on one side. And he was

thin, very tall, of a dark complexion; in reference to which some one called him an Egyptian Clematis: he had fat, flabby, weak legs, on which account Persæus, in his Convivial Reminiscenses, says that he used to refuse many invitations to supper; and he was very fond, as it is said, of figs both fresh and dried in the sun.

He was a pupil of Crates. After that, they say that he became a pupil of Stilpon and Xenocrates, for ten years. He is also said to have been a pupil of Polemo. But Hecaton, and Apollonius, of Tyre, in the first book of his essay on Zeno, say that when he consulted the oracle, as to what he ought to do to live in the most excellent manner, the God answered him that he ought to become of the same complexion as the dead, on which he inferred that he ought to apply himself to the reading of the books of the ancients. Accordingly, he attached himself to Crates in the following manner. Having purchased a quantity of purple from Phœnicia, he was shipwrecked close to the Piræus; and when he had made his way from the coast as far as Athens, he sat down by a bookseller's stall, being now about thirty years of age. And as he took up the second book of Xenophon's Memorabilia and began to read it, he was delighted with it, and asked where such men as were described in that book lived; and as Crates happened very seasonably to pass at the moment, the bookseller pointed him out, and said, "Follow that man." From that time forth he became a pupil of Crates; but though he was in other respects very energetic in his application to philosophy, still he was too modest for the shamelessness of the Cynics. On which account, Crates, wishing to cure him of this false shame, gave him a jar of lentil porridge to carry through the Ceramicus; and when he saw that he was ashamed, and that he endeavored to hide it, he struck the jar with his staff, and broke it; and as Zeno fled away, and the lentil porridge ran all down his legs, Crates called after him, "Why do you run away, my little Phœnician, you have done no harm?" For some time then he continued a pupil of Crates, and when he wrote his treatise entitled the Republic, some said, jokingly, that he had written it upon the tail of the dog.

But at last he left Crates, and became the pupil of the philosophers whom I have mentioned before, and continued with them for twenty years. So that it is related that he said, "I now find that I made a prosperous voyage when I was wrecked." But some affirm that he made this speech in reference to Crates. Others say, that while he was staying at Athens he heard of a shipwreck, and said, "Fortune does well in having driven us on philosophy." But as some relate the affair, he wás not wrecked at all, but sold all his cargo at Athens, and then turned to philosophy.

And he used to walk up and down in the beautiful colonnade which is called the Priscanactium, and which is also called *poikile*, (*i. e.* ornamented with variegated painting,) from the paintings of Polygnotus, and there he delivered his discourses, wishing to make that spot tranquil; for in the time of the thirty, nearly fourteen hundred of the citizens had been murdered there by them.

Accordingly, for the future, men came thither to hear him, and from this his pupils were called Stoics, and so were his successors also, who had been at first called Zenonians, as Epicurus tells us in his Epistles. And before this time, the poets who frequented this colonnade (*stoa*) had been called Stoics; but now Zeno's pupils made the name more notorious. Now the Athenians had a great respect for Zeno, so that they gave him the keys of their walls, and they also honored him with a golden crown, and a brazen statue; and this was also done by his own countrymen, who thought the statue of such a man an honor to their city. And the Cittiæans, in the district of Sidon, also claimed him as their countryman.

He was also much respected by Antigonus, who, whenever he came to Athens, used to attend his lectures, and was constantly inviting him to come to him. But he begged off himself, and sent Persæus, one of his intimate friends, who was the son of Demetrius, and a Cittiæan by birth, and who flourished about the hundred and thirtieth Olympiad, when Zeno was an old man. The letter of Antigonus to Zeno was as follows, and it is reported by Apollonius, the Syrian, in his essay on Zeno.

KING ANTIGONUS TO ZENO THE PHILOSOPHER, GREETING.

"I think that in good fortune and glory I have the advantage of you; but in reason and education I am inferior to you, and also in that perfect happiness which you have attained to. On which account I have thought it good to address you, and invite you to come to me, being convinced that you will not refuse what is asked of you. Endeavor, therefore, by all means to come to me, considering this fact, that you will not be the instructor of me alone, but of all the Macedonians together. For he who instructs the ruler of the Macedonians, and who leads him in the path of virtue, evidently marshals all his subjects on the road to happiness. For as the ruler is, so is it natural that his subjects for the most part should be also."

And Zeno wrote him back the following answer:—

ZENO TO KING ANTIGONUS, GREETING.

"I admire your desire for learning, as being a true object for the wishes of mankind, and one too that tends to their advantage. And the man who aims at the study of philosophy has a proper disregard for the popular kind of instruction which tends only to the corruption of the morals. And you, passing by the pleasure which is so much spoken of, which makes the minds of some young men effeminate, show plainly that you are inclined to noble pursuits, not merely by your nature, but also by your own deliberate choice. And a noble nature, when it has received even a slight degree of training, and which also meets with those who will teach it abundantly, proceeds without difficulty to a perfect attainment of virtue. But I now find my bodily health impaired by old age, for I am eighty years old: on which account I am unable to come to you. But I send you some of those who have studied with me, who in that learning which has reference to the soul, are in no respect inferior to me, and in their bodily vigor are greatly my superiors. And if you associate with them you will want nothing that can bear upon perfect happiness."

So he sent him Persæus and Philonides, the Theban, both of whom are mentioned by Epicurus, in his letter to his brother Aristobulus, as being companions of Antigonus.

I have thought it worth while also to set down the decree of the Athenians concerning him; and it is couched in the following language:—

"In the archonship of Arrhenides, in the fifth presidency of the tribe Acamantis, on the twenty-first day of the month Maimacterion, on the twenty-third day of the aforesaid presidency, in a duly convened assembly, Hippo, the son of Cratistoteles, of the borough of Xypetion, being one of the presidents, and the rest of the presidents, his colleagues, put the following decree to the vote. And the decree was proposed by Thrason of Anacæa, the son of Thrason.

"Since Zeno, the son of Innaseas, the Cittiæan, has passed many years in the city, in the study of philosophy, being in all other respects a good man, and also exhorting all the young men who have sought his company to the practice of virtue, and encouraging them in the practice of temperance; making his own life a model to all men of the greatest excellence, since it has in every respect corresponded to the doctrines which he has taught; it has been determined by the people (and may the determination be fortunate) to praise Zeno, the son of Innaseas, the Cittiæan, and to present him with a golden crown in accordance with the law, on account of his virtue and temperance, and to build him a tomb in the

Ceramicus, at the public expense. And the people has appointed by its vote five men from among the citizens of Athens, who shall see to the making of the crown and the building of the tomb. And the scribe of the borough shall enrol the decree and engrave it on two pillars, and he shall be permitted to place one pillar in the Academy, and one in the Lyceum. And he who is appointed to superintend the work shall divide the expense that the pillars amount to, in such a way that every one may understand that the whole people of Athens honors good men both while they are living and after they are dead. And Thrason of Anacæa, Philocles of the Piræus, Phædrus of Anaphlystos, Medon of Acharnæs, Mecythus of Sypalyttas, and Dion of Pænia, are hereby appointed to superintend the building of the tomb."

These then are the terms of the decree.

But Antigonus, of Carystos, says that Zeno himself never denied that he was a native of Cittium. For that when on one occasion, there was a citizen of that town who had contributed to the building of some baths, and was having his name engraved on the pillar, as the countryman of Zeno the philosopher, he bade them add, "Of Cittium."

At another time, when he had had a hollow covering made for some vessel, he carried it about for some money, in order to procure present relief for some difficulties which were distressing Crates his master. And they say that he, when he first arrived in Greece, had more than a thousand talents, which he lent out at nautical usury. And he used to eat little loaves and honey, and to drink a small quantity of sweet smelling wine. He had a very few youthful acquaintances of the male sex, and he did not cultivate them much, lest he should be thought to be a misogynist. And he dwelt in the same house with Persæus; and once, when he brought in a female flute-player to him, he hastened to bring her back to him.

He was, it is said, of a very accommodating temper; so

much so, that Antigonus, the king, often came to dine with him, and often carried him off to dine with him, at the house of Aristocles the harp-player; but when he was there, he would presently steal away.

It is also said that he avoided a crowd with great care, so that he used to sit at the end of a bench, in order at all events to avoid being incommoded on one side. And he never used to walk with more than two or three companions. And he used at times to exact a piece of money from all who came to hear him, with a view of not being distressed by numbers; and this story is told by Cleanthes, in his treatise on Brazen Money. And when he was surrounded by any great crowd, he would point to a balustrade of wood at the end of the colonnade which surrounded an altar, and say, "That was once in the middle of this place, but it was placed apart because it was in people's way; and now, if you will only withdraw from the middle here, you too will incommode me much less."

When Demochares, the son of Laches, embraced him once, and said that he would tell Antigonus, or write to him of everything which he wanted, as he always did everything for him, Zeno, when he had heard him say this, avoided his company for the future. And it is said, that after the death of Zeno, Antigonus said, "What a spectacle have I lost." On which account he employed Thrason, their ambassador, to entreat of the Athenians to allow him to be buried in the Ceramicus. And when he was asked why he had such an admiration for him, he replied, "Because, though I gave him a great many important presents, he was never elated, and never humbled."

He was a man of a very investigating spirit, and one who inquired very minutely into everything; in reference to which, Timon, in his Silli, speaks thus:—

I saw an aged woman of Phœnicia,
Hungry and covetous, in a proud obscurity,

Longing for everything. She had a basket
So full of holes that it retained nothing.
Likewise her mind was less than a simdapsus.*

He used to study very carefully, with Philo, the dialectician, and to argue with him at their mutual leisure; on which account he excited the wonder of the younger Zeno, no less than Diodorus his master.

There were also a lot of dirty beggars always about him, as Timon tells us, where he says:—

Till he collected a vast cloud of beggars,
Who were of all men in the world the poorest,
And the most worthless citizens of Athens.

And he himself was a man of a morose and bitter countenance, with a constantly frowning expression. He was very economical, and descended even to the meanness of the barbarians, under the pretence of economy.

If he reproved any one, he did it with brevity and without exaggeration, and, as it were, at a distance. I allude, for instance, to the way in which he spoke of a man who took exceeding pains in setting himself off; for as he was crossing a gutter with great hesitation, he said, "He is right to look down upon the mud, for he cannot see himself in it." And when some Cynic one day said that he had no oil in his cruse, and asked him for some, he refused to give him any, but bade him go away and consider which of the two was the more impudent. He was very much in love with Chremonides; and once, when he and Cleanthes were both sitting by him, he got up; and as Cleanthes wondered at this, he said, "I hear from skilful physicians that the best thing for some tumors is rest." Once, when two people were sitting above him at table at a banquet, and the one next him kept kicking the other with his foot, he himself kicked him with his knee; and when he turned round upon him for doing so, he said, "Why then do

* A sort of guitar or violin.

you think that your other neighbor is to be treated in this way by you?"

On one occasion he said to a man who was very fond of young boys, that "Schoolmasters who were always associating with boys had no more intellect than the boys themselves." He used also to say that the discourses of those men who were careful to avoid solecisms, and to adhere to the strictest rules of composition, were like Alexandrine money, they were pleasing to the eye and well-formed like the coni, but were nothing the better for that; but those who were not so particular he likened to the Attic tessedrachmas, which were struck at random and without any great nicety, and so he said that their discourses often outweighed the more polished style of the others. And when Ariston, his disciple, had been holding forth a good deal without much wit, but still in some points with a good deal of readiness and confidence, he said to him, "It would be impossible for you to speak thus, if your father had not been drunk when he begat you;" and for the same reason he nicknamed him the chatterer, as he himself was very concise in his speeches. Once, when he was in company with an epicure who usually left nothing for his messmates, and when a large fish was set before him, he took it all as if he could eat the whole of it; and when the others looked at him with astonishment, he said, "What then do you think that your companions feel every day, if you cannot bear with my gluttony for one day?"

On one occasion, when a youth was asking him questions with a pertinacity unsuited to his age, he led him to a looking glass and bade him look at himself, and then asked him whether such questions appeared suitable to the face he saw there. And when a man said before him once, that in most points he did not agree with the doctrines of Antisthenes, he quoted to him an apophthegm of Sophocles, and asked him whether he thought there was much sense in that, and when he said that he did not know, "Are you not then ashamed," said he, "to pick out and recollect anything bad which may have been said by Antisthenes, but not to regard or remember whatever is said that is good?" A man once said, that the sayings of the philosophers appeared to him very trivial; "You say true," replied Zeno, "and their syllables, too, ought to be short, if that is possible." When some one spoke to him of Polemo, and said that he proposed one question for discussion and then argued another, he became angry, and said, "At what value did he estimate the subject that had been proposed?" And he said that a man who was to discuss a question ought to have a loud voice and great energy, like the actors, but not to open his mouth too wide, which those who speak a great deal but only talk nonsense usually do. And he used to say that there was no need for those who argued well to leave their hearers room to look about them, as good workmen do who want to have their work seen; but that, on the contrary, those who are listening to them ought to be so attentive to all that is said as to have no leisure to take notes.

Once when a young man was talking a great deal, he said, "Your ears have run down into your tongue." On one occasion a very handsome man was saying that a wise man did not appear to him likely to fall in love; "Then," said he, "I cannot imagine anything that will be more miserable than you good-looking fellows." He also used often to say that "Most philosophers were wise in great things, but ignorant of petty subjects and chance details;" and he used to cite the saying of Caphesius, who when one of his pupils was laboring hard to be able to blow very powerfully, gave him a slap, and said, that "excellence did not depend upon greatness, but greatness on excellence." Once, when a young man was arguing very confidently, he said, "I should not like to say, O youth, all that occurs to me." And once, when a handsome and wealthy Rhodian, but one who had no other qualification, was pressing him to take him as a pupil, he, as he was not inclined to receive him, first of all made him sit on the dusty seats that he might dirt his cloak, then he put him down in the place of the poor that he might rub against their rags, and at last the young man went away. One of his sayings used to be, that "Vanity was the most unbecoming of all things, and especially so in the young." Another was, that "One ought not to try and recollect the exact words and expressions of a discourse, but to fix all one's attention on the arrangement of the arguments, instead of treating it as if it were a piece of boiled meat, or some delicate eatable." He used also to say, that "Young men ought to maintain the most scrupulous reserve in their walking, their gait, and their dress;" and he was constantly quoting the lines of Euripides on Capaneus, that—

> His wealth was ample,
> But yet no pride did mingle with his state,
> Nor had he haughty thought, or arrogance,
> More than the poorest man.

And one of his sayings used to be that "Nothing was more unfriendly to the comprehension of the accurate sciences than poetry;" and that "There was nothing that we stood in so much need of as time." When he was asked what a friend was, he replied, "Another I." They say that he was once scourging a slave, whom he had detected in theft; and when he said to him, "It was fated that I should steal;" he rejoined, "Yes, and that you should be beaten." He used to call beauty the flower of the voice; but some report this as as if he had said that the voice is the flower of beauty. On one occasion, when he saw a slave belonging to one of his friends severely bruised, he said to his friend, "I see the footsteps of your anger." He once accosted a man who was all over unguents and perfumes, "Who is this who smells like a woman?" When Dionysius Metathemenus asked him why he was the only person whom he did not correct, he replied, "Because I have no confidence in you." A young man was talking a great deal o' nonsense, and he said to him, "This is the reason why we have two ears and only one mouth, that we may hear more and speak less."

Once, when he was at an entertainment and remained wholly silent, he was asked what the reason was; and so he bade the person who found fault with him to tell the king that there was a man in the room who knew how to hold his tongue; now the people who asked him this were ambassadors who had come from Ptolemy, and who wished to know what report they were to make of him to the king. He was once asked how he felt when people abused him, and he said, "As an ambassador feels when he is sent away without an answer." Apollonius of Tyre tells us, that when Crates dragged him by the cloak away from Stilpo, he said, "O Crates, the proper way to take hold of philosophers is by the ears; so now do you convince me and drag me by them; but if you use force towards me, my body may be with you, but my mind with Stilpo."

He used to devote a good deal of time to Diodorus; and he studied dialectics under him. And when he made a good deal of progress he attached himself to Polemo because of his freedom from arrogance, so that it is reported that he said to him, "I am not ignorant, O Zeno, that you slip into the garden-door and steal my doctrines, and then clothe them in a Phœnician dress." When a dialectician once showed him seven species of dialectic argument in the mowing argument,* he asked him how much he charged for them, and when he said "A hundred drachmas," he gave him two hundred, so exceedingly devoted was he to learning.

They say, too, that he was the first who ever employed the word duty (*kathēkon*), and who wrote a treatise on the subject. And that he altered the lines of Hesiod thus:—

* A species of argument so called, because he who used it mowed or knocked down his adversaries.—Aldob.

He is the best of all men who submits
To follow good advice; he too is good,
Who of himself perceives whate'er is fit.*

For he said that that man who had the capacity to give a proper hearing to what was said, and to avail himself of it, was superior to him who comprehended everything by his own intellect; for that the one had only comprehension, but the one who took good advice had action also.

When he was asked why he, who was generally austere, relaxed at a dinner party, he said, "Lupins too are bitter, but when they are soaked they become sweet." And Hecaton, in the second book of his Apophthegms, says, that in the entertainments of that kind, he used to indulge himself freely. And he used to say that "it was better to trip with the feet, than with the tongue." And that "goodness was attained by little and little, but was not itself a small thing." Some authors, however, attribute this saying to Socrates.

He was a person of great powers of abstinence and endurance; and of very simple habits, living on food which required no fire to dress it, and wearing a thin cloak, so that it was said of him:—

The cold of winter, and the ceaseless rain,
Come powerless against him; weak is the part
Of the fierce summer sun, or fell disease,
To bend that iron frame. He stands apart,
In nought resembling the vast common crowd;
But, patient and unwearied, night and day,
Clings to his studies and philosophy.

The comic poets, without intending it, praise him in their

---

* The lines in Hesiod are:—

That man is best, whose unassisted wit
Perceives at once what in each case is fit.
And next to him, he surely is most wise,
Who willingly submits to good advice.

very attempts to turn him into ridicule. Philemon speaks thus of him in his play entitled the Philosophers :—

> This man adopts a new philosophy,
> He teaches to be hungry ; nevertheless,
> He gets disciples. Bread his only food,
> His best desert dried figs ; water his drink.

But some attribute these lines to Posidippus. And they have become almost a proverb. Accordingly, it used to be said of him, "More temperate than Zeno the philosopher." Posidippus also writes thus in his Men Transported :—

> So that for ten whole days he did appear
> More temperate than Zeno's self.

For in reality he did surpass all men in this description of virtue, and in dignity of demeanor, and, by Jove, in happiness. For he lived ninety-eight years, and then died, without any disease, and continuing in good health to the last. But Persæus, in his Ethical School, states that he died at the age of seventy-two, and that he came to Athens when he was twenty-two years old. But Apollonius says that he presided over his school for forty-eight years.

He died in the following manner. When he was going out of his school, he tripped and broke one of his toes; and striking the ground with his hand, he repeated the line out of the Niobe :—

> I come ; why call me so?

And immediately he strangled himself, and so he died. But the Athenians buried him in the Ceramicus, and honored him with the decrees which I have mentioned before, bearing witness to his virtue. Antipater, the Sidonian, wrote an inscription for him, which runs thus :—

> Here Cittium's pride, wise Zeno, lies, who climb'd
> The summits of Olympus ; but unmoved
> By wicked thoughts ne'er strove to rise on Ossa
> The pine-clad Pelion ; nor did he emulate
> The immortal toils of Hercules ; but found
> A new way for himself to the highest heaven,
> By virtue, temperance, and modesty.

And Zenodotus, the Stoic, a disciple of Diogenes, wrote another:—

You made contentment the chief rule of life,
Despising haughty wealth, O God-like Zeno.
With solemn look, and hoary brow serene,
You taught a manly doctrine; and didst found
By your deep wisdom, a great novel school,
Chaste parent of unfearing liberty.
And if your country was Phœnicia,
Why need we grieve? from that land Cadmus came,
Who gave to Greece her written books of wisdom.

Athenæus, the epigrammatic poet, speaks thus of all the Stoics in common:—

O, ye who've learnt the doctrines of the Porch,
And have committed to your books divine
The best of human learning; teaching men
That the mind's virtue is the only good.
And she it is who keeps the lives of men,
And cities, safer than high gates or walls.
But those who place their happiness in pleasure,
Are led by the least worthy of the Muses.

And we also have ourselves spoken of the manner of Zeno's death, in our collection of poems in all metres, in the following terms:—

Some say that Zeno, pride of Cittium,
Died of old age, when weak and quite worn out
Some say that famine's cruel tooth did slay him;
Some that he fell, and striking hard the ground,
Said, "See, I come, why call me thus impatiently?"

For some say that this was the way in which he died. this is enough to say concerning his death.

But Demetrius, the Magnesian, says, in his essay on People of the Same Name, that his father Innaseas often came to Athens, as he was a merchant, and that he used to bring back many of the books of the Socratic Philosophers, to Zeno, while he was still only a boy; and that, from this circumstance, Zeno had already become talked of in his own country; and that in consequence of this he went to Athens, where he attauhed himself to Crates. And it seems, he adds, that it was he who first recommended a clear enunciation of principles, as the best remedy for error. He is said, too, to have been in the habit of swearing "By Capers," as Socrates swore "By the Dog."

Some, indeed, among whom is Cassius the Sceptic, attack Zeno on many accounts, saying first of all that he denounced the general system of education in vogue at the time, as useless, which he did in the beginning of his Republic. And in the second place, that he used to call all who were not virtuous, adversaries, and enemies, and slaves, and unfriendly to one another, parents to their children, brethren to brethren, and kinsmen to kinsmen; and again, that in his Republic, he speaks of the virtuous as the only citizens, and friends, and relations, and free men, so that in the doctrine of the Stoic, even parents and their children are enemies; for they are not wise. Also, that he lays down the principle of the community of woman both in his Republic and in a poem of two hundred verses, and teaches that neither temples nor courts of law, nor gymnasia, ought to be erected in a city; moreover, that he writes thus about money: "That he does not think that men ought to coin money either for purposes of traffic, or travelling." Besides all this, he enjoins men and women to wear the same dress, and to leave no part of their person uncovered.

And that this treatise on the Republic is his work we are assured by Chrysippus, in his Republic. He also discussed amatory subjects in the beginning of that book of his which is entitled the Art of Love. And in his Conversations he writes in a similar manner.

Such are the charges made against him by Cassius, and also by Isidorus, of Pergamus, the orator, who says that all the unbecoming doctrines and assertions of the Stoics were cut out of their books by Athenodorus, the Stoic, who was the curator of the library at Pergamus. And that subsequently they were replaced, as Athenodorus was detected, and placed in a situation of great danger; and this is sufficient to say about those doctrines of his which were impugned.

The disciples of Zeno were very numerous. The most eminent were, first of all, Perseus, of Cittium, the son of Demetrius, whom some call a friend of his, but others describe him as a servant and one of the amanuenses who were sent to him by Antigonus, to whose son, Halcymeus, he also acted as tutor. And Antigonus once, wishing to make trial of him, caused some false news to be brought to him that his estate had been ravaged by the enemy; and as he began to look gloomy at this news, he said to him, "You see that wealth is not a matter of indifference."

ZENO, THE ELEATIC.

Zeno was a native of Velia. Apollodorus, in his Chronicles, says that he was by nature the son of Telentagoras, but by adoption the son of Parmenides.

Timon speaks thus of him and Melissus:—

> Great is the strength, invincible the might
> Of Zeno, skilled to argue on both sides
> Of any question, the universal critic;
> And of Melissus too. They rose superior
> To prejudice in general; only yielding
> To very few.

And Zeno had been a pupil of Parmenides, and had been on other accounts greatly attached to him.

He was a tall man. Aristotle, in his Sophist, says that he was the inventor of dialectics, as Empedocles was of rhetoric. And he was a man of the greatest nobleness of spirit, both in philosophy and in politics. There are also many books extant, which are attributed to him, full of great learning and wisdom.

He, wishing to put an end to the power of Nearches, the tyrant (some, however, call the tyrant Diomedon), was arrested, as we are informed by Heraclides, in his abridgment of Satyrus. And when he was examined as to his accomplices, and as to the arms which he was taking to Lipara, he named all the friends of the tyrant as his accomplices, wishing to make him feel himself alone. And then, after he had mentioned some names, he said that he wished to whisper something privately to the tyrant; and when he came near him he bit him, and would not leave his hold till he was stabbed. And the same thing happened to Aristogiton, the tyrant slayer. But Demetrius, in his treatise on People of the Same Name, says that it was his nose that he bit off.

Moreover, Antisthenes, in his Successions, says that after he had given him information against his friends, he was asked by the tyrant if there was any one else. And he replied, "Yes, you, the destruction of the city." And that he also said to the bystanders, "I marvel at your cowardice, if you submit to be slaves to the tyrant out of fear of such pains as I am now enduring." And at last he bit off his tongue and spit it at him; and the citizens immediately rushed forward, and slew the tyrant with stones. And this is the account that is given by almost every one.

But Hermippus says that he was put into a mortar and pounded to death. And we ourselves have written the following epigram on him :—

Your noble wish, O Zeno, was to slay
A cruel tyrant, freeing Elea
From the harsh bonds of shameful slavery,
But you were disappointed ; for the tyrant
Pounded you in a mortar. I say wrong,
He only crushed your body, and not you.

Zeno was an excellent man in other respects; and he was also a despiser of great men in an equal degree with Heraclitus; for he, too, preferred the town which was formerly called Hyele, and afterwards Elea, being a colony of the Phocæans, and his own native place, a poor city possessed of no other importance than the knowledge of how to raise virtuous citizens to the pride of the Athenians; so that he did not often visit them, but spent his life at home.

They say that when he was reproached, he was indignant; and that when some one blamed him, he replied, "If when I am reproached, I am not angered, then I shall not be pleased when I am praised."

This Zeno flourished about the seventy-ninth Olympiad.

THE END.

www.ingramcontent.com/pod-product-compliance
Lightning Source LLC
LaVergne TN
LVHW020111110826
845151LV00001B/129

* 9 7 8 1 4 2 5 5 4 4 4 4 7 *